the Happy Hooker

Stitch 'n Bitch Crochet

The Happy Hooker

Debbie Stoller

Illustrations by Adrienne Yan
Fashion photography by John Dolan

WORKMAN PUBLISHING • NEW YORK

 Published simultaneously in Canada by Thomas Allen & Son Limited.

Library of Congress Cataloging-in-Publication Data

Stoller, Debbie.
Stitch 'n bitch crochet: The happy hooker / by Debbie Stoller.
p. cm.
Includes index.
ISBN-13: 978-0-7611-3985-0 (alk. paper); ISBN-10: 0-7611-3985-0 (alk. paper)
ISBN-13: 978-0-7611-3986-7; ISBN-10: 0-7611-3986-9
1. Crocheting. 2. Crocheting—Patterns. I. Title.
TT820.S857 2005
746.43'4—dc22 2005043518

Book design: Janet Vicario with Munira Al-Khalili

Workman Publishing Company, Inc.
225 Varick Street
New York, NY 10014-4381
workman.com

Printed in the United States

First printing February 2006
16 15 14 13 12 11

for my mother,

johanna c. stoller,

who gave me a love of all things crafty

Acknowledgments

First and foremost, I owe my greatest thanks to the talented and tireless designers whose work appears in this book. I feel truly honored that these 40 women were willing to share their impressive and fun designs with me, and I am grateful.

I am so very indebted to my brand-new agent, Flip Brophy, who not only served as a skilled business advisor and negotiator on this book, but also as a sort of Fairy Godmother who helped me find ways to make my workload more manageable. Now I can go to the ball!

I want to thank my assistant on this book, Christina Roest, who did so much work in the beginning stages of production, and I am so appreciative of the work that Katy Moore did on a number of the patterns in this book, most notably Strut, Yeehaw Lady, and Bikini in a Bag.

At Workman, I am thankful to Peter Workman for agreeing that the subject of crochet deserved its own book, and I am ever-indebted to my fearless editor and champion of the Stitch 'n Bitch cause, Ruth Sullivan, whose thorough and careful efforts always improve and clarify my work immeasurably. I owe special thanks to my technical editor, Karen Manthey, who did such a wonderful job of painstakingly combing through each pattern, stitch by stitch, as well as creating the diagrams and schematics, and to copyeditor and crocheter extraordinaire Judit Bodnar. I'd like to thank designer Janet Vicario, who is so much fun to work with, for once again bringing her creative eye and patient mind to this Stitch 'n Bitch project and design assistant Munira Al-Khalili for helping get everything to look just right. And I really appreciate the organizational efforts of production editor Irene Demchyshyn and editorial assistant Beth Hatem for keeping everything running as smoothly as possible.

I'm so glad that my favorite illustrator, Adrienne Yan, was available to make such sweet, careful drawings to go with the text, and I owe my deepest thanks to photographer John Dolan for taking the beautiful photos and for allowing us all to hang out at his gorgeous house. Thanks also to the fabulous stylist, Jenni Lee, for pulling together an endless assortment of clever outfits, to hair and makeup artist Bryan Lynde, and to photo editor Leora Kahn for pulling the entire photo shoot together. And thank you to the models, who not only posed wearing heavy woolen sweaters in the middle of a heat wave, but somehow managed to look cool while doing so, and a special shout-out to the good people of Be Green Cafe in Asbury Park, New Jersey, where much of this book was written.

Once again I am thankful to the women of *BUST* magazine, and especially to my co-publisher, Laurie Henzel, for being a great friend and for making it possible for me to take some time off to write this book. I also want to thank my parents, Johanna and Bernard Stoller, for letting me know how proud they are of me.

And to Michael Uman, my longtime partner and best friend, who for ten years has been my rock. I am so grateful for your constant encouragement, and your loving support.

contents

part one
Hooking up
LEARNING TO CROCHET

5. the shape of things to come

6. hooked on a feeling

7. picture this

8. off the hook

part two

crochet away

THE PATTERNS

part one

Hooking up

LEARNING TO CROCHET

1

voulez-vous crochet avec moi?

When folks who were familiar with my previous Stitch 'n Bitch books, which are both about knitting, first heard that I was planning to write a book about crocheting, some of them were a little shocked. "Do you even crochet?" they'd ask, rather accusingly. How could it be that I, a *knitter,* was qualified to write a book about crocheting? How was it possible that *any* knitter could have anything of value to say to crocheters? Didn't I know that knitters and crocheters are like Sharks and Jets—they don't get along, they keep off each other's turf, they break into fights on the playground?

Yes, I know, I know. But have Tony and Maria taught us *nothing*? Can't we see that we're all sisters (and brothers) under the stitch? Sure, I'm a knitter. But I also crochet. In fact, I learned to crochet—and enjoyed it—long before knitting ever felt good in my hands. In the tradition I come from, if you enjoy doing needlework, you enjoy doing needlework in whatever form it takes. My Dutch mother and all the women on her side of the family were needle wielders of wide and varied skills: sewing, embroidering, knitting, and crocheting—they did it all. I grew up enjoying each of these crafts as well, and I've always wanted to learn more. After watching my Great Aunt Jo diligently tatting elaborate thread edgings onto her handkerchiefs year after year, I finally borrowed a book from the library and tried to learn it, too.

I particularly revel in the way that doing needlework inextricably binds me to my female relatives. With each stitch, I follow in the footsteps (handsteps?) of my ancestors, carrying on centuries-old traditions and paying respect to their wide and varied crafting skills. My connection is more than theoretical. Some of my fondest memories are of summer vacations visiting my mother's relatives in Holland, where, in the evenings, we'd sit together and work on our various needlework projects—my mother perhaps crocheting a lacy curtain, my Aunt Hetty stitching one of her gorgeous appliqué wall hangings, my grandmother most likely knitting socks, while I might be working away on a small counted cross-stitch project. Looking back on it, I suppose these idyllic get-togethers were, in a way, my first Stitch 'n Bitch sessions.

I don't remember exactly when I learned how to crochet. All I know is that my very first crochet project was a panda bear that I had found a pattern for in one of my mother's magazines. I must have been about eleven years old. I worked on that thing day after day, but unfortunately, my stitches were way too loose, and the panda turned out almost as big as I was, with a giant encephalitic head that flopped over and rested on his distended belly. Still, for years he sat, pathetically floppy, on top of my bed. To me he was beautiful; after all, I had created him. I was his mother.

While I was growing up in Brooklyn, New York, I enjoyed doing needlework the way some kids liked playing stickball. I never wanted to go out and play; I preferred staying in and making clothes for my Barbie dolls on my miniature sewing machine. I savored the wonderful feeling that came over me whenever I was engaged in a needlework project. And even today, it is the sense of calm satisfaction I get from needlework that has kept me drawn to it. Blissfully immersed in stitching, I feel peaceful and centered, my mind both fully relaxed and entirely focused, as I make satisfying progress stitch by stitch, row by row. The feeling is, in a word, delicious.

Yet, for many years, I forsook the ways of the stitch. Throughout the eighties and most of the nineties, while I was in college, then in grad school, and then starting my own business, I didn't make much time for needlework. That all changed when we decided a number of years ago to begin running craft projects in *BUST*, the women's magazine that I cofounded and still edit. We introduced the idea with a simple pattern for a crocheted kerchief. I hadn't crocheted in years, but, to test out the directions for that pattern, I bought myself some pretty cotton yarn and a nice crochet hook. I then needed to reteach myself how to crochet, and stat. So I dragged one of my favorite needlework encyclopedias to the beach one weekend, along with the yarn and hook, and set to work. The first few stitches went smoothly—I made a chain of loops, following the book's directions, wrapping the yarn around my hook and pulling loops through loops as if I was born to do it. Even the next row came quite naturally, as I followed the illustrations to reinsert my hook into each of those initial loops and pull up yet more loops of yarn, building a row of what's known as single crochet stitches into the original base chain of loops.

Then, on the next row, my book abandoned me. Now that I needed to make single crochet stitches into other single crochet stitches, instead of chain loops, I was on my own. Where was the hook supposed to be inserted into those stitches? I wasn't sure, so I just shoved my hook under a strand of yarn that looked to be about right and carried on my merry way—all the way until that kerchief was done. It looked okay, it fit my head, and we sent the article off to print. And I was excited about having become reacquainted with this simple, pleasurable craft. All the joys I had known as a child—the serenity, the satisfaction, and the centeredness—had come flooding back to me as I held the yarn and hook in my hands, and I vowed to keep at it.

It wasn't until a few months later that I realized that although the pattern was correct, I had made the entire kerchief incorrectly. While leafing through a tiny crochet pamphlet in a thrift store, I came across an illustration that clearly showed that I was supposed to insert my hook under *two* strands of yarn on every row after the first one. I had created a variation of the single crochet stitch known as single crochet ribbing, which was fine, but it's not how the thing was supposed to be made. Why didn't the book I was using bother to tell me something so important? Were beginners expected to learn this craft using such incomplete directions, or were these books merely intended as a refresher course for folks who already knew how to crochet? As I continued to relearn the craft of crochet, I felt, at times, like some sort of Sherlock Holmes, sniffing through book after book until I found the clue I needed to really understand how to make certain stitches or execute particular techniques. And time after time I'd run into conflicting information or outright misinformation. There was no single source that really showed me, clearly and unambiguously, everything I needed to know.

Shortly after my interest in needlecrafts was rekindled by crochet, I retaught myself how to knit, and that craft quickly developed into an all-encompassing obsession that threatened to obliterate everything else in my life. Still, I never turned my back on my hooks. Throughout my knitting career, crocheting remained

my warm-weather fiber craft of choice. I would knit my way through fall, winter, and spring, then put the fuzzy wooly yarns and long bamboo sticks away in exchange for cool balls of cotton yarn and compact aluminum hooks. Summer would find me sitting on the beach, crocheting baby blankets, stuffed animals, bags, and afghans. The sand would easily shake out of my cotton work, and having a smaller area to deal with—just a stubby hook and a single loop—was much more manageable than working a large wooly item that would sit on my lap as I worked long rows of knitting off of lengthy needles. Besides, my preferred knitting method involves having one needle tucked under my armpit. Just think how well that would work on a hot, sweaty day. Yuck.

During those years, the knitting boom was becoming a worldwide phenomenon—more young people were taking up the craft than had done so in decades, and they were gathering to knit together in Stitch 'n Bitch groups, inspired by the one I had started at a café in New York City. Soon these groups were popping up everywhere, from Anchorage to Amsterdam, Cleveland to Canberra, Los Angeles to Liverpool. While some crocheters attended these Stitch 'n Bitch groups, they were in the minority. But as knitters advanced further and further in their craft, having gotten comfortable with the basics, then increasing their knowledge with every passing year, some knitters—who had once feared any project involving crochet the way a vampire fears garlic—were beginning to look past the points of their needles and toward crocheting as another way to expand their skills. At the same time crocheters themselves, unhappy with the lack of attention paid to their craft, were beginning to make a stand, and their numbers at Stitch 'n Bitch groups were on the rise.

Contemporary fashions added further fuel to the desire among crafters and noncrafters alike to hook up with a new hobby, as cute crocheted tops and bags began appearing in both chic boutiques and chain stores, and on fashion runways from Manhattan to Milan. Yet where were the patterns for items as appealing as these? As much as I enjoyed crocheting, I had a hard time finding ways to put my skills into action. Most of the available crochet patterns were for things that, while I could appreciate their beauty and the skill required to create them, I had no interest in making. While delicate lacy doilies looked like they'd be fun to do, I didn't really have a need for them, and bulky, patriotic-themed afghans weren't really my style, either. Patterns for sweaters and summer tops seemed to be few and far between, and of the ones I was able to find, most looked boxy and odd.

I was not alone in my frustration. Happy hookers—who, it turns out, outnumber knitters by three to one—were starting to come up with their own patterns, based both on items they'd seen in various shops and what they saw in their mind's eye. Some of these folks were selling their patterns on their own Web sites, others were sharing them with friends and family, and still others were keeping them to themselves, sometimes displaying images of their completed creations on various crafting and crocheting Web sites. It was exactly like what had happened among knitters a mere four or five years ago. I wanted to help get these patterns out into the hands of the many crocheters who, like me, were hungry for more up-to-date projects. And for those who were inspired to take up the hook after seeing what it was capable of making, I wanted to write up some clear and complete instructions, so that even absolute beginners could learn the craft from a book. The idea for *Stitch 'n Bitch: The Happy Hooker* was born.

A Brief History of Hooking

Compared to other fiber arts, crocheting is the new kid on the block. While weaving was already being done 20,000 years ago and knitting's been around for a millennium, crocheting is a mere 200 years young. Yet the history of crochet is, like a crocheted piece itself, complex and nonlinear, taking many twists and turns and branching off in a variety of directions at the same time.

There isn't terribly much agreement about when or how crocheting developed, but it is known that the first printed crochet pattern appeared in a Dutch magazine (my peeps!) early in the nineteenth century. Over the next few decades, crochet became well established in Europe as a way to re-create the look of fine laces that were available only to the extremely wealthy, making them affordable to a much larger portion of the population. Rich folks didn't like having just anyone walking around sporting fancy lace, however, so they put down crochet work as being something only commoners would wear, and claimed that crocheting wasn't as respectable as knitting or other needlework. It was a stigma that, 160 years later, crochet still hasn't quite managed to shake.

Eventually, though, the wealthy themselves found reason to take up the hook. As the appalling working conditions of lace makers became known to American women, they started to get interested in creating the work themselves rather than supporting the abusive practices of the lace-making industry. There was also another reason behind their rejection of foreign-made lace. In a book published at the time, a lace manufacturer admitted that he expected his workers to turn a few tricks on the side to make up for his not paying them a living wage. Soon lace, including crocheted lace, began to be seen as morally tainted—it's made by prostitutes! As Donna Kooler suggests in *The Encyclopedia of Crochet,* this may even explain how the word "hooker" came to have such wayward connotations. Women who wanted to be sure their lace was as pure as the white thread it was made of decided they'd better learn to hook it up for themselves.

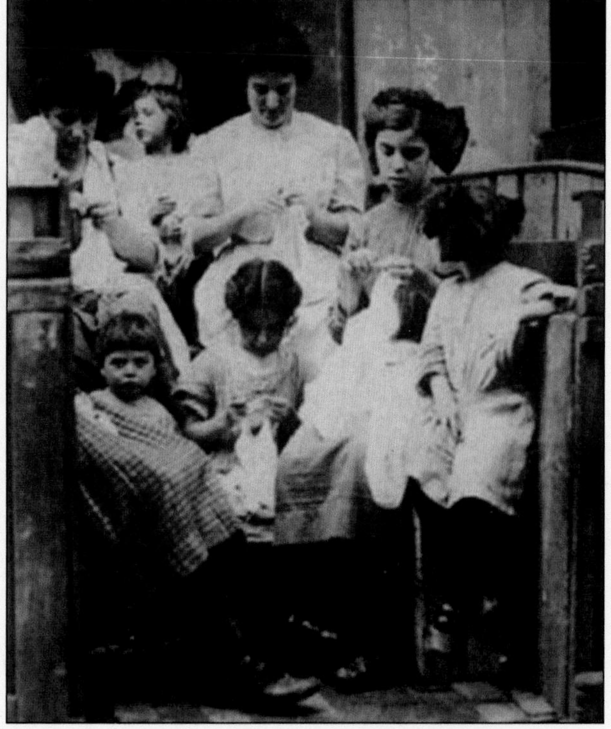

The family that crochets together, stays together: women and children crocheting, 1912

Yet no sooner had crocheters taken up their hooks than they put them down again and opened up their wallets to help those less fortunate. During the Irish potato famine of 1846 to 1850, an economic disaster for the island nation, a group of Ursuline nuns taught local women and children the technique of thread crochet. This work, which was known as "Irish Crochet," was clearly sin-free, and it became incredibly popular. Shipped off and sold across Europe and in

America, it was purchased not only for its beauty but also as a way for the middle class to make a charitable donation to the troubled Irish population.

Later on in the century, fueled by both the many good patterns and well-written directions that were being published in women's magazines and Victorian ladies' increasing amounts of leisure time, crocheting became a passionate pastime among them, as well as a beloved craft of American pioneer women. These crocheters worked up lightweight baby caps and lacy collar pieces, along with necessities such as capes and gloves. And as men's and women's fashionable hairstyles required the use of oily pomades, they began to make something else, too: little lacy pieces that could decorate the tops of expensive furniture while protecting them from the stains of pomaded heads. Thus, crochet became a pretty way to perform a dirty job, and from these humble roots the doily was born.

Head honcho supports poncho: Martha Stewart shows that crocheting is a good thing, 2005

By the late 1920s, women were chopping off their oily locks, loosening their corsets, and crocheting scandalous lacy underwear, as well as modern cloches to wear atop their It-Girl bobs. It was a boom time for crochet, which would wax and wane in popularity over the rest of the century, often tied to the economics of the time. Since crochet work uses up so much thread, when times were hard and supplies were dear, such as during the Depression and the second World War, crocheting was kept to a minimum. Afterward, it would find its way back into women's hands, as both a relief and a luxury.

But perhaps at no time in the past century was crocheting more popular in this country than it was in the late 1960s and early 1970s, when it became associated with hippies. Simple open-work vests that could be worked up in no time became part of the uniform of the counterculture set, and minidresses worked in a riot of bright colors reflected the anything-goes attitude of the times. Crochet made for the perfect craft for hippies filled with a desire to live off the land and do it themselves. It was easy to learn, and the projects were so simple to execute, they could even be done under the influence of mind-expanding substances. Looking back at creations from that era, it appears that many of them were.

In the years following that wacky time, crochet kind of burned out, becoming irrelevant to all but those interested in wearing purple-and-green-striped woolen pants. Yet slowly but surely, it's been making a comeback, appearing on runways in the form of high-fashion frocks and in the mall in the form of mass-market ponchos. And when Martha Stewart was released from prison wearing a poncho a fellow inmate had crocheted for her, the craft came to be seen as even more of a good thing. Today's crocheted fashion incorporates every style of the craft that has come before it—from intricate Irish-crochet-inspired lacy tops to the simple tanks and wraps of crochet's hippie heyday. And it has found its way back into the hands of both women and men who are looking for a way to create something that is both beautiful and useful; something that can reward them with a feeling of satisfaction when it's completed, as well as a peacefulness while it's being made. Putting a modern-day spin on a centuries-old hobby, they are taking the craft in directions it has never seen before, creating clothing and household items and gifts and sculptures and mathematical models and wearing the name "hooker" with pride.

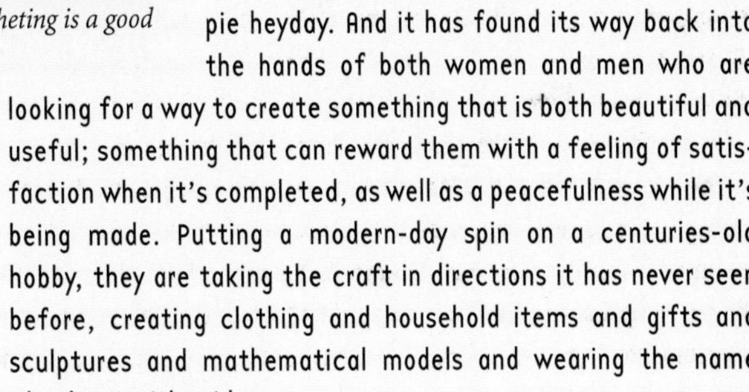

Wrapper's Delight

The Joys of Crochet

If you've picked up this book to hook yourself up with a brand-new skill, you've come to the right place. Crocheting is a great, rewarding craft, because you really only need to learn and get comfortable with a single technique—that of wrapping your hook around a strand of yarn, then pulling that strand through one or two other loops—and you're off and running. Just about every stitch in crochet is about repeating that movement over and over. Crocheting doesn't require many tools—just a hook and some yarn, pretty much—and it's super-portable. Tuck your project into a bag and you can easily work on it in the park, in a café, on the bus—hell, crocheting is so manageable you can even do it standing up, *waiting* for the bus.

Not only can you learn the basics of crochet with relative ease, but you can also finish your first projects in a short amount of time. Because crocheting incorporates so much air into its fabric, your work progresses at a surprisingly quick clip. Choose the right type of project and you can probably wrap it up in an evening. Other items can be done in a weekend. And if you're looking to sink your teeth into a meatier project, just look for something with more intricate lace textures or one that's done with a finer yarn or a smaller hook. There's enough here to keep you busy, and challenged, for a long, long time.

Crocheting is an impressively versatile craft that allows you to churn out chunky hats and scarves as last-minute gifts even as it tempts you to devote many pleasurable hours to creating heirloom-quality lace. It is equally terrific for creating sturdy, cold-weather woolen garments and frothy, even titillating cotton confections to strut your stuff in during the hottest days of summer. And it has been able to bring pleasure and satisfaction to the surprisingly diverse hands of dainty Victorian ladies pursuing a leisure-time activity in their fancy parlors; the dirt-under-their fingernails, freak-flag-flying, hippie-dippy chicks of the seventies expressing themselves with yarns of many colors; skater boyz hooking up hipster caps to wear, shirtless, on the beach; and skillful contemporary grandmothers lovingly stitching elaborate afghans and cozy caps for their grandchildren. But perhaps best of all, the craft of crochet promises to deliver to all who engage in it the same reward that I discovered as a child: the fun and satisfaction of creating something beautiful with our own two hands, and a delicious, soothing, Zen-like sense of calm.

Secrets of the Yarn-Yarn Sisterhood

Crocheting vs. Knitting

Any fiber crafter worth his or her yarn stash can tell the difference between knit and crocheted items. And oh, how we delight in our superiority when we see one mistaken for the other. Fashion magazines often display "knitted lace tunics" that are actually crocheted; catalogs show us "crocheted sweaters" that are, in fact, knit; and we gleefully point out these mistakes to whomever will listen. People who participate in neither craft are woefully unable to distinguish between the construction of these fabrics, but we stitch mavens find it practically blasphemous to refer to a crocheted item as having been knit or vice versa.

Yet there is one mistake that I've frequently witnessed both crocheters and knitters make, and that is to think that crocheting and knitting are interchangeable. I've even seen books that promise to help crocheters translate knitting patterns into the language of hookers. But knitting and crocheting are not two different methods of achieving the same outcome. Knitting, with its regular rows of V-shaped stitches that can expand like an accordion and then contract again, gained popularity hundreds of years ago as a way to create stretchy, tubular fabric that was much better at covering tubular body parts (feet, arms, torsos) than woven fabric was. (Can you imagine wearing pieces of burlap, tied together, as socks? Before knitting was invented, that's pretty much what folks did). Crocheting, on the other hand, originated much more recently as a way to create beautiful, fanciful laces. The long chains of looped stitches and wrapped threads that are so simple to create with a hook allow crochet work to enclose air between delicate lengths of thread, producing elaborately lacy stitch patterns that knitters can only dream of. When the stitches are shorter and more compact, crocheting results in fabric that is denser and less stretchy than knitting, making it better for structured or more sculptured items that can use that type of solidity, such as bags and certain kinds of hats. In fact, when knitters want to make a bag that doesn't threaten to let their change fall through, their only option is to line it with fabric or felt it so that the fibers matt together. Finally, while knit fabric is constructed like so many lines of text on a page, restricted to being made one row of stitches at a time, crocheted fabric is built a single stitch at a time, which means it can grow in any direction—up, down, back, forth, and in a circle. This makes crochet an ideal method for creating complex shapes such as flowers and lacy squares as well as solid, sculptural items such as fabulous stuffed animals (my lame panda notwithstanding).

For all of crocheting's other advantages over knitting, there is none better than this: Crocheting is *easier* than knitting. While the most basic element of crocheting and knitting is similar—you are pulling a loop of yarn through another loop of yarn—when you crochet, you get to pull that loop with a hook. In knitting, you have to do the same with a pointed stick. Just think about it: If someone were rescuing you from a raging body of water, would you rather they lowered a large hook for you to grab onto or a pointed stick? For the same reason, pulling a loop of yarn through another loop with a hook is simpler than doing it with a stick; it's easier to keep your original loop on there, and the new one is less likely to slip off. Not only that, but in crocheting you hold your yarn in one hand and your hook in the other—a situation that works out great for most humans: two items, two hands. When you knit, you have two knitting needles *and* some yarn—thus, one more thing to manipulate than you have hands. And that makes knitting more awkward to get used to, as well. Best of all, when you crochet you are dealing with only one stitch at a time. So if a loop falls off your hook, you can just pick it up with your hook and carry on. At most, one stitch will unravel, which is certainly no cause for panic. For knitters, on the other hand, a dropped stitch can unravel many rows down and wreak all kinds of havoc. Finally, when you're working lacy stitch patterns in crochet, you are less likely to create mistakes because the construction of the fabric is so obvious and logical. On the other hand, it's very easy to make errors while creating lace in knitting, and spending hours undoing rows of intricate lace work has led many a knitter into the arms of crochet.

Nothing's perfect, and crocheting has its disadvantages, as well. For one thing, it uses about a third more yarn than knitting does to make the same amount of fabric—which means that things can get pricey if you aren't careful. Of course, crocheting fabric that incorporates a lot of open space can help offset this cost. And let's face it, crocheted fabric is just never going to be as good at creating stretchy tubes as knitting is. It's been said that you shouldn't make sweaters using crochet and that simply isn't true—this book includes a number of great crocheted sweaters. But if you're looking to make a traditional ski sweater or a shapely sock, look elsewhere. Crocheted socks are not going to be as sock-like as knit socks are, nor will a crocheted sweater ever be as curve-hugging as a knit sweater. Of course, the converse is also true: Sure, you can take a hank of cotton yarn and a pair of needles and, with some clever stitch trickery, knit up a presentable lacy cardigan, but you won't be able to do it with as much ease and grace as you can with crochet.

But why should we try and force different techniques into doing something they were never intended to? Instead, let's just learn and love each of these two clever crafts for what they really are, deep down inside, and then let them do what they do best. Let's be free to be you and me, free to crochet and to knit, free to twirl hooks and click needles. Because the fact of the matter is that knitters and crocheters have much more in common with one another than they have differences. And as needleworkers, who have a hard enough time garnering respect from a world that seems to believe that the only valuable pastimes are those that involve making money, spending money, or losing weight, we should stand side by side with our sister (and brother) stitchers, hooks holding needles and needles holding hooks, a unified force of fiber enthusiasts, learning one another's crafts, sharing our skills, and helping to eradicate any misunderstandings between us. Then we should, like, go have a sock hop in the gym. It's a lot better than the alternative—remember how *West Side Story* ended?

RAP SHEET

A Guide to Crochet Lingo

Just as gangsters have their own code words for various shady locations and criminal activities, so, too, do fiber enthusiasts. Peruse any crochet blog or bulletin board and you'll immediately be lost in a swamp of abbreviations, acronyms, and weirdo terms. Here's a guide to some of the most common:

LYS Local Yarn Store. The small, independent shop in your area that carries an overwhelming number of yarns of different types of fibers, as well as crocheting and knitting supplies. Not to be confused with your local craft megamart.

SEX Stash Enrichment Expedition. It's what you do at your LYS. SEX is particularly fun if you engage in it with a close friend, or even a large group of friends!

UFO Unfinished Object. Many crocheters have a good number of these, hanging in tote bags in the back corners of their closets or stuffed into baskets and shoved under the bed. Though they are a constant source of shame and anxiety, they are also a sign that you've crossed over the line from casual crocheter to truly obsessed.

WIP Work in Progress. Similar to a UFO, in that it's unfinished, a WIP is a project that you're actively making progress on. While you might want to include your UFOs with your WIPs, anything that your hands haven't touched in more than six months can't fairly be considered to be "in progress." If you have to take it out of the bag because you can't remember what's in there, it doesn't count.

Crochet-along Similar to a sing-along but without the music, words, or bouncing ball, a crochet-along occurs when a number of crocheters agree to tackle the same project, independently, then compare their notes and progress in person, at a Stitch 'n Bitch group, or online through a Web site or bulletin board set up for the purpose. It's like the *Amazing Race* but done from home, sitting in a chair, and holding yarn.

Frogging There will come a day when you'll arrive at the terrifying realization that the hat you're making for your father will barely fit your Chihuahua. Nevertheless, you'll continue working on it for a few hours or days more, until you finally admit to God, yourself, and another human being that the project is unsalvageable. Then, and only then, will you be willing to "frog," or rip it out, wind up the yarn, and get ready to start all over again. Why is this called "frogging"? Because "rip it" sounds like "ribbit," the sound a frog makes. Hey, I couldn't make this stuff up.

2

Hook, Line, and Sinker

THE TOOLS OF CROCHET

Unlike with some other crafts, you don't need much gear to get started crocheting—some yarn, a single crochet hook, and a pair of scissors will do the trick. That's not to say you won't eventually need an extra room just to house your crochet supplies, however, because when it comes to yarn, the possibilities are endless. Crochet is especially fantastic when done in cotton, and there is always plenty of good-quality, inexpensive cotton yarn available at your local craft megamart. Of course, crochet is not limited to being worked in cotton; it can be done in wool, linen, hemp, alpaca, wool blends, and good old durable acrylic. As I mentioned in the previous chapter, crochet can use up to a third more yarn than knitting does, which is perhaps why many crocheters limit their yarn choices to what can be found for a reasonable price at craft shops.

In this book, I've made a point of including projects that are made from a wide variety of materials, including affordable acrylic, moderately priced mohair, and splurge-worthy silky cotton. If you're a crocheter who's never ventured outside the confines of the craft store, it may be time to make an excursion to a Local Yarn Shop (LYS), where better-quality yarns and unusual fibers are to be had, and treat yourself to working with some of the fantastic yarns described in this chapter. The pure, sensuous pleasure you'll derive from working with high-quality yarns (especially those made of natural fibers) and the repeated joy of wearing them close to your skin once your project is done are well worth the added cost. In other words, try to work with the best materials you can afford. That said, if you're just learning to crochet, you might want to begin your hooking adventures with something less pricey so that the mistakes you're guaranteed to make as a beginner will cost you time rather than money. And if you're a fiber snob, perhaps coming to crochet from knitting, reaquaint yourself with some of the lovely cotton and wool-blend yarns available at the craft store. Not everything you make to cover your arms and legs has to cost you an arm and a leg.

Hookers at the point

Getting to Know Crochet Hooks

All hooking begins with—you guessed it—a hook. Crochet hooks are clever little buggers that are usually made of plastic, aluminum, or steel, although they are also available (for more moolah) in wood and bamboo. Crochet hooks have a number of parts that are worth getting to know. Let's take a look at each one:

The point or head is the tip of the "hook" part of the crochet hook. It's what you'd use to poke someone who was annoying you. It needs to be small and pointy enough to slip through loops, yet not so pointy that it snags or splits your stitches on entry. Most crochet hooks sport nice rounded points.

The throat is the slender part of the hook. Larger hooks have larger throats and are used with thicker yarns; smaller hooks have thinner throats and are used

ANATOMY of A crochet Hook

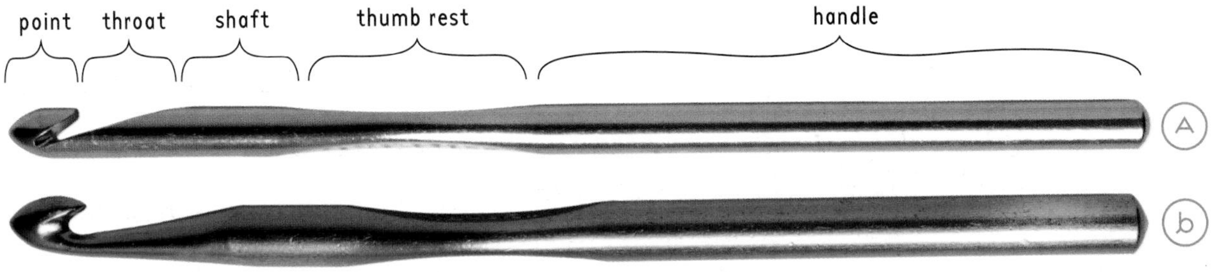

with finer yarns. A crochet hook's throat (see page 13) can be like a straight slice into the metal that makes the hook look a bit like a mid-century modern piece of art (A) or more shapely, leading up to a bulbous point with a rounded, doglike snout (B). I far prefer the slice-style throat, because it's much quicker to work with. It does a great job of holding the yarn where you need it, yet doesn't get caught on the loop when you're pulling the yarn back through a stitch. I have a couple of snout-like hooks in my collection, and I always end up flinging them across the room in frustration. For me, using them is like trying to cut fabric with dull scissors. Not fun!

I'M JUST TALKIN' 'BOUT SHAFT

The size of your hook is determined by the diameter of its shaft. Thicker hooks are usually used with thicker yarns, and they produce larger loops. Thinner hooks produce smaller loops. That's why it's important, while you're crocheting, to be careful to keep your loop on the shaft of the hook. If you leave it on the narrower part of the hook—the throat—your stitches will come out too small and tight and you won't get the right gauge (see page 34).

The shaft (stop laughing, Beavis) is the part of the hook just below the throat—and it's where you carry the yarn loop. Since this is where your loop hangs out, it pretty much determines the size of your crochet stitches. A thicker shaft means a larger, looser crochet stitch; a thinner shaft will yield smaller, tighter stitches.

The thumb rest or grip is my favorite part of the crochet hook, if it isn't too weird to *have* a favorite part of a crochet hook. It's a nice flat spot where you put your thumb and middle finger to hold and turn your hook through a variety of graceful ballet steps. Some of the thinnest, finest hooks don't have a thumb rest for you to grab onto, but you can buy a little spongy tube to slip over a hook to create a friendly spot to grip the otherwise smooth handle.

The handle is basically the remaining part of the hook, which is usually about four inches long, including the thumb rest. It tucks nicely against the palm of your hand as you work.

The many moods of standard hooks

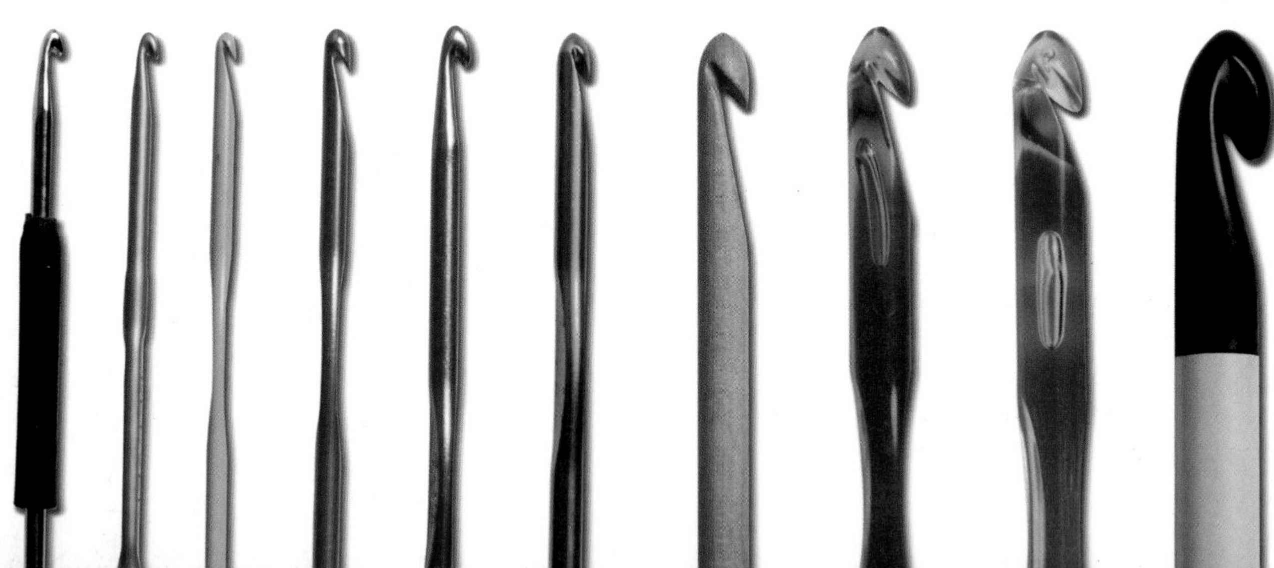

Size Matters

Hooks are sized according to the thickness of the shaft, in a complicated numbering and lettering scheme that was clearly thought up by some madman who was out to exact revenge on poor, innocent crocheters. "Standard hooks" (sometimes called yarn hooks) are sized using letters, randomly beginning with the letter B for the smallest one and going all the way up to the letter S for one so big you could probably pull someone off a stage with it. These hooks are also sometimes referred to by number (B is 1, C is 2, etc.), or by the diameter of the shaft in millimeters (a B hook shaft is 2.25 millimeters in diameter, a C is 2.75 millimeters, and so on). Most of the smaller of these standard-size hooks are made of aluminum or plastic; the truly large ones are made of plastic or lightweight wood. Try wielding a giant hook made of solid aluminum and you'll quickly understand why lighter materials are used for the biggies.

Crochet Hook Sizes

Millimeter Range	U.S. Size Range*
2.25 mm	B-1
2.75 mm	C-2
3.25 mm	D-3
3.5 mm	E-4
3.75 mm	F-5
4 mm	G-6
4.5 mm	7
5 mm	H-8
5.5 mm	I-9
6 mm	J-10
6.5 mm	K-10½
8 mm	L-11
9 mm	M/N-13
10 mm	N/P-15
15 mm	P/Q
16 mm	Q
19 mm	S

*Letter or number may vary. Rely on the millimeter (mm) sizing.

The thinnest hooks are made of steel, probably because a point that small made of a weaker material would simply snap off. These tiny steel hooks are usually used with thread to make lace, and they have their own numbering system, which goes from size 00 (the largest!) to size 14 (the smallest!). They are also referenced by their diameter in millimeters, with size 00 measuring 3.50 millimeters in diameter and size 14 being only a measly 0.75 millimeter thick. You could probably almost get your head around the idea that yarn hooks get larger as their numbers get larger while thread hooks get smaller as their numbers get larger. But there's another maddening fact: The largest steel hooks (00, 0, 1, and 2) overlap in size with the smallest "standard" hooks (B, C, D, and E). And there's yet more fun to be had: Hooks from the U.K. have a numbering system that is the reverse of the U.S. system—there, the larger the number, the smaller the hook. When in doubt, just look for the size in millimeters (which I've included for every pattern in this book). At least there's one thing you can depend on in this crazy, mixed-up world.

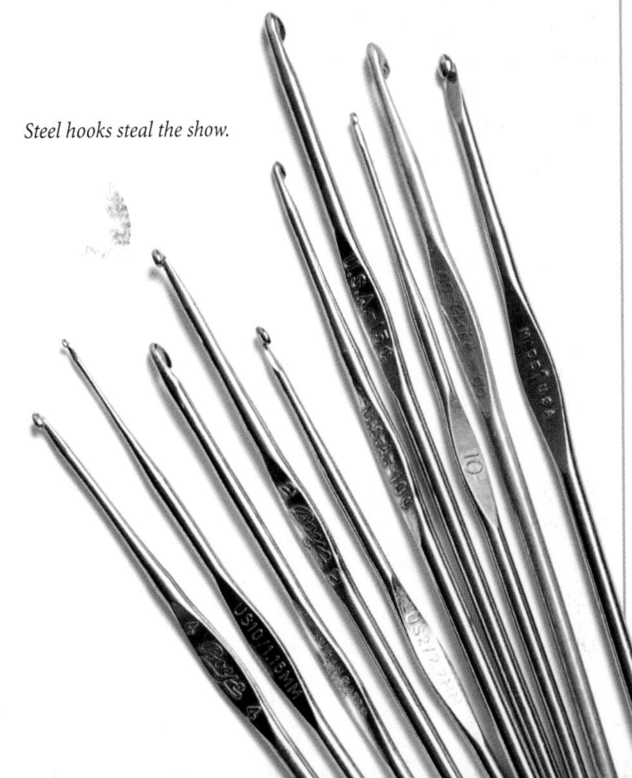

Steel hooks steal the show.

fiber supplementation

Choosing Your Yarn

Step into any yarn store and you'll see bumpy yarns and smooth yarns, puffy yarns and sleek yarns, brightly colored yarns and yarns in natural tones, yarn that is a single shade and variegated yarns of many colors, yarns with metallic glitz, yarns that look like ribbons, and yarns with a variety of flotsam and jetsam woven in. But the variations in yarn are more than just what meets the eye. What a yarn is made of—its fiber content, in yarn-speak—is also a very important quality and will determine whether your project will be warming or cooling to wear, will be silky or scratchy against your skin, will absorb moisture or will repel it, and can be thrown in the washer or will, like a diva, demand to be hand-washed.

Just like in the game 20 Questions, fibers can be divided into one of three categories: animal, vegetable, or mineral. These different sources of fibers give yarn (and the items you make from them) distinctive qualities. Yarn spun from plant-derived fibers (cotton, hemp, and linen from flax) are especially absorbent—which makes them great to use on garments you'll wear in hot weather, when you might get a little moist. Like the perfect paper towel, a top made of cotton or linen will just wick that moisture away from you. They're also hypoallergenic, so they're great for anyone who's allergic to wool, and, since they're plucked from plants, they're okay by vegans, too.

Yarn made from animal-produced fibers (such as sheep's wool, angora, or silk) is also very absorbent. A sweater made from wool can absorb up to one-third its weight in water before it—and you—feel wet. Animal fibers are Mother Nature's favorite way of keeping creatures warm and dry, and once you've crocheted something using an animal-based fiber, you'll see she wasn't kidding around. If you've never worn a sweater or a hat made of 100% wool before, doing so can be a real revelation. It will keep you so warm and comfortable that you'll swear there was a little electric heater hidden inside somewhere.

Man-made fibers, such as acrylic, are petroleum-based—meaning they're essentially plastic. While that may sound unappealing, don't let it scare you off. Acrylic yarn has a number of valuable advantages over natural-fiber yarns: It's cheaper, and it's far easier to wash (fabrics made of animal and plant fibers usually require all kinds of *tsuris* to clean). Yet, while clothes made of acrylic yarn have the benefit of being machine-washable and -dryable, they won't be nearly as warm as those made of animal fibers, or as absorbent as those made of plant-based fibers. And, truth be told, some acrylic yarn is made so cheaply that it downright squeaks. If you can afford it and don't have any practical (you're making something that needs to be washed a lot—like a baby's bib) or physical (you're allergic) reasons to avoid it, give animal- or plant-based yarns a try.

Here are some of the most popular yarn fibers available today, and what makes 'em so special:

Plant Based

Cotton

Crochet and cotton go together like peanut butter and chocolate—each is great on its own, but they're even better together. In fact, crochet pretty much owes its life to this humble plant. It was only when cotton became widely and cheaply available—due largely to the invention of the cotton gin at the end of the eighteenth century—that the thought of futzing with large amounts of this fiber for largely frivolous purposes became conceivable. Before that time, cotton was as dear as silk.

Lovely and soft, cotton is a dream to crochet with. It's light and crisp and can show off lacy stitches to their best advantage. In its natural state, however, cotton has a matte, dull finish. That can work well for many items, but if you want something with a bit of sheen, look for cotton that has been mercerized. I don't know who Mercer was, but he figured out a dandy way to dip cotton into a bath of lye and make it emerge happy and shiny (I wouldn't, but then again, I'm not cotton). Mercerized cotton is strong and slippery smooth; it can even resemble silk in its sleekness. The thinnest strands of cotton, with names like "bedspread weight," are usually mercerized, while sturdy "kitchen cotton" is most frequently left in its natural, earthy, duller state. Use whichever type is most suitable for your project and your personal taste—sometimes you feel like a matte, sometimes you don't.

Different types of cotton plants produce different types of cotton. Egyptian cotton has longer fibers than most other cotton and is grown—where else?—in Egypt. When this long-haired cotton is spun, it produces thread or yarn that is smoother and therefore softer than its shorter-haired cousins. Pima cotton comes from a plant that is a cross between Egyptian cotton and the common American (Uplands) cotton. Like its Egyptian father, it has long hair and thus yields silky, strong, and lustrous cotton, and like its American mother, it can grow right here in the U.S.A. Cotton is also known for its willingness to take on dye, which means you'll find this fiber available in every color of the rainbow (and perhaps even a few that aren't). Cotton isn't very stretchy, though, so if you're looking for something with at least a little elasticity, look for a blend of cotton and wool or cotton and acrylic (see page 18).

Linen

Making clothing from linen goes back—and I'm talking way back—to around 8000 B.C. Linen yarn is spun from the long fibers of the flax plant, and it's super-strong and cool. Stuff crocheted with linen yarn will be nice and crisp, but will wrinkle easily. I like working with this fiber just because it is so ancient. Use it and get in touch with your inner hunter-gatherer.

Rayon

Rayon is often considered a synthetic fiber, but it's actually plant based. It's definitely man-made, but man makes it out of wood pulp using some strange alchemical process that I'd best not go into here (because I couldn't if I tried). Rayon yarn is as soft and shiny as silk but not nearly as expensive. And like other plant-based fibers, it's highly absorbent (more so than cotton), so it's great for summer items.

Animal Based

Wool

Of course you know that wool comes from sheep. What you might not know is that different breeds of sheep yield different kinds of wool. Wool from Icelandic sheep, for instance, which grow long, shaggy coats, is rough and can be scratchy, but it can be as strong as steel wool. Merino wool is at the other extreme; it's made from the superfine fleece of Merino sheep and it's even softer than cotton, but it has a tendency to "pill" (grow little balls of fuzz). Merino is one of my favorite fibers to work with—it's not terribly expensive, and it feels great against your skin.

Mohair
This fuzzy, glamorous wool comes from the fleece of a goat—the angora goat. The fiber is gorgeous and terrifically tempting, but beware: Mohair can be scratchy when it's worn right next to the skin, so a pure mohair scarf might not be the best idea. On the other hand, a mohair capelet or cardigan would be right on.

Cashmere
Cashmere is the most luxuriously soft and fluffy yarn of all, and it's combed from the bellies of cashmere goats (now, there's a job I'd like to try). Cashmere is expensive, so to make a sexy sweater that won't break your bank, try a cashmere yarn blend that is less pricey.

Alpaca
Alpaca wool comes from an animal that's a species of llama, and it is exceedingly—some might say excessively—warm. That's great for hats and scarves and mittens, but it could be overkill in a sweater, where you might be better off using an alpaca and wool blend.

Angora
Sweater girls of the fifties based their reputations on this stuff, which comes from bunnies, not angora goats, and practically screams "touch me." Wonderfully fine and fluffy, angora feels like it's made out of a baby's hair. Unfortunately, angora yarn can also shed like a rabbit, so save it for accents—collars and cuffs, for instance—or try making one of those figure-flaunting sweaters using an angora and wool blend.

Silk
Silk is spun from the long fibers of unraveled silkworm cocoons. It's an extremely strong fiber—those silkworms are pretty clever—and yarn made from it is beautifully lustrous and shiny. Silk is also expensive, but its lightness makes it a great choice for a special summer tank top or a shawl.

Synthetics

Acrylic
Because it washes so well, acrylic yarn is the perfect choice for projects intended for babies and pets, since such items need to be laundered frequently. And being inexpensive makes it a good choice for beginners or anyone on a tight crocheting budget. But, unless you're allergic, try to buy a brand that has at least some wool or cotton blended in—it will be much nicer to work with and wear. Most of the coolest and weirdest new yarns—such as fuzzy, fake-fur types of yarn or yarn

with a glittery finish—are made using acrylic yarns. So put away your fiber snobbery and dive right in to working with petroleum-based acrylic yarns. The water's fine.

Nylon

Nylon is such a super-strong fiber that if Spider-Man were into crocheting, it's probably what he'd use. It's stretchy, shiny, and easy to wash. That said, it's also, you know, *nylon*—good for raincoats and rugs but not so appealing for a handmade garment that's supposed to be cozy and comfy. However, spin a little nylon together with another fiber—wool or cotton, say—and you've got a little bit of superhero power in an otherwise mortal yarn. Nylon blends are more resistant to wear and tear than straight naturals are, and nylon is often used as the base thread on eyelash yarns (to hold the eyelashes in place), ribbon yarns, and other fantasy yarns that sport wild and interesting textures.

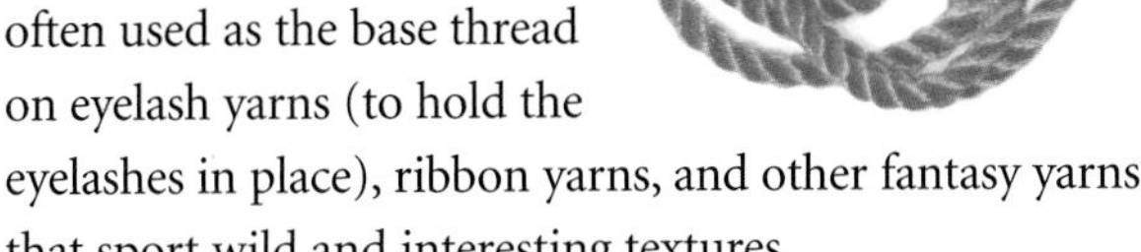

in the thick of it

Yarn Weights

Yarn comes in a variety of thicknesses, called "weights" (it has nothing directly to do with their actual weight). There are American and British names for each of these weights, and grouping yarns by weight is somewhat less than exact—there can be a lot of variety within one category. The Crochet Yarn Council of America has come up with a yarn categorization system (see page 24) that is a bit more specific. It is helpful when you want to replace the yarn called for in a pattern with a different yarn, because it's a good idea to find another in the same weight category. Nevertheless, the following names are what most folks still use when discussing various weights of yarn. Here are five of the most common yarn weights (alternative names are given in parentheses).

Fingering (baby, 4-ply) weight

This very thin yarn is good for making light, fine garments such as sweaters or wraps for babies and lacy shawls.

Sport (double-knitting, or DK) weight

Now here's a very curiously named yarn weight. I mean, just what kind of sports item would you make out of this stuff? A crocheted jock strap? Sport-weight yarn is roughly twice as thick as fingering yarn, so at least that "double knitting" name makes sense. It is a good weight for children's items and summer garments.

Worsted (Aran) weight

Despite its name, worsted might be the "bestest" yarn out there. It's certainly the most common weight, and there are more kinds of worsted-weight yarns on the market than anything else. Worsted is about twice as thick as sport yarn (Aran is just a tad heavier), and it's great for bags, scarves, hats, sweaters, afghans, and just about anything else you can think of. Get to know worsted-weight yarn: It is your new best friend.

Chunky (bulky) weight

The plot thickens. Chunky and bulky yarns are around twice as thick as worsted, and they're good for making items that could use some additional loft (aka thickness) and warmth, such as hats and scarves or extra-cozy sweaters.

Extra-bulky (super-bulky) weight

When it's time to bring in the big guns, use extra-bulky yarn. This fat, almost ropey stuff is even thicker than chunky and works up quickly on an extra-large hook, making it great for last-minute gifts such as hats, bags, and scarves.

string theory
Crochet Thread

When most people think of crochet, they think of doilies. And when they think of doilies, they think of delicate, white, lacy circles that are too fine to be created by any of the yarn weights I've just told you about. And they are correct. That's because the real, true crocheted lace we associate with our grandmothers and other crocheters with mad skillz—and even a good number of the lacy crocheted clothing items that are available in stores—are made with cotton or cotton blend yarn that is even thinner than fingering weight. This extra-fine cotton yarn is called "crochet thread," and it's sold according to an entirely different set of weight standards. Thread weights are identified by numbers, and larger numbers signify thinner thread. Size 50, for instance, is as thin as sewing thread, while size 10 and heavier are what you'd use to make doilies or fine old school–style bedspreads. In fact, some crochet cotton is even referred to as being "bedspread weight." These very thin threads are worked using those tiny little hooks made of steel, and you'll need nerves of steel to work with them, too, as they create items that grow very, very slowly. There aren't any projects in this book that call for crochet thread, but if you find that you are a big fan of lace, you might try taking on a doily or a filet crochet piece or even a tiny flower. In fact, this kind of work is simply called "thread crochet," and it is understood by crocheters of every stripe to be a practice reserved for those with advanced skills, prison inmates with loads of time on their hands, or folks with a masochistic streak.

see me, feel me, touch me
Yarn Textures and Crochet

If you've set foot in a yarn store for even a second, you've probably noticed that yarn comes in a butt-load of textures—from smooth to nubby, sleek to puffy, and compactly braided to loosely twisted. You can use any of these for crochet, although some will be more pleasant to work with than others. Yarns that are terribly nubby or slubby (meaning they're uneven, with thicker and thinner areas) can be a pain to crochet with because your hook can have a hard time hanging onto the nubby bits. And yarns that are strandy or not very tightly twisted can really drive you nuts: Your hook can grab some but not all of the strands, or split the stitches (the hook might go through the middle of the strand of yarn instead of clean underneath it). If you aren't sure whether a yarn you like will be fun or infuriating to work with, ask the store owner if you may make a small swatch of it with the hook size you intend to use. She just might let you do that. Alternatively, she might help you figure out if it's a good choice for your type of crochet work, and if it isn't, she might be able to direct you to something similar that would be more pleasant to work with.

crocheting takes balls

. . . and Skeins, and Hanks

Usually, yarn comes in balls (relatively round) or skeins (oblong), and if you're lucky, you will have what's called a center-pull ball or skein: The yarn will feed out from the center, and the ball won't bounce and roll around so much when you're working. Finding the beginning of the yarn, however, can be tricky; often it's hidden under the yarn label. You might need to go poking around inside the ball to find it. If all else fails, just start with whichever loose end you can find.

If the yarn comes in a hank, which is essentially a big coil of yarn wrapped up in a twist, you can ask the friendly folks at your yarn store to wind it into a ball for you—they usually have a little contraption in their shop for doing just that. Alternatively, you can wind it yourself. The easiest way to do this is to pop the untwisted hank over a friend's outstretched hands, then wind away (you've seen this done in cartoons hundreds of times). In the absence of a pair of helping hands, just place your feet about a foot apart (hah!) and hang the hank over them to keep your yarn from getting all tangled up as you wind your ball.

HOW TO MAKE A CENTER-PULL BALL

Open your hand so that it faces you, then lay the end of the yarn across your palm, leaving about a 6-inch-long tail hanging free. Wind the yarn in a figure eight around your thumb and pointer about fifteen to twenty times.

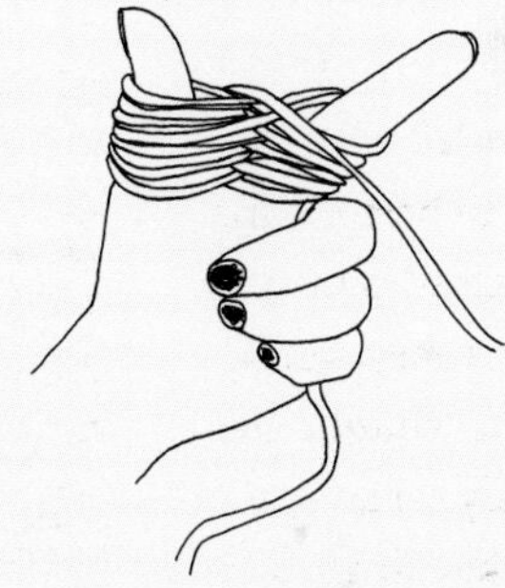

Remove the wrapped yarn from your fingers and fold it in half. Place your thumb over the part where the long tail enters the yarn wad and begin winding the yarn into a ball. Keep winding this way and that until all your yarn is wound, always holding your thumb over the spot where the yarn tail enters the ball.

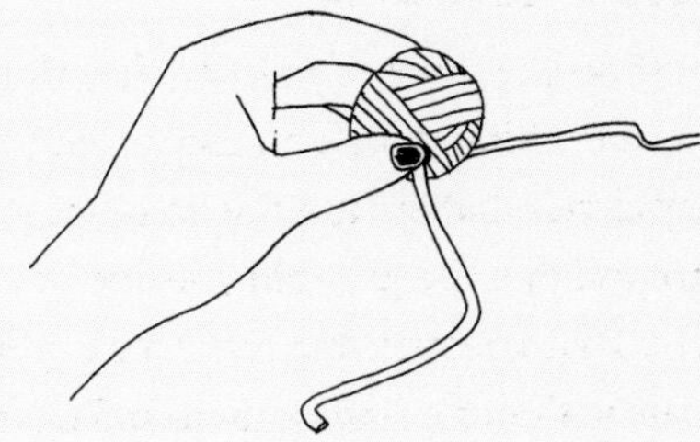

HOW TO READ A YARN LABEL

A. Yarn Brand and Name: In this case, we've got us a ball of Joseph's Cotton.

B. Fiber Content: What is this stuff made of, anyway? Human hair? Spun dryer lint? Fiber content is one of the first things to check out on the label, and it will always give you the percentages of each.

C. Weight and Length: The weight here is the actual weight of the ball of yarn, and the length tells how many yards (or meters) of yarn there are to be found in it.

D. Color and Dye lot: Sometimes yarns are given creative color names; other times different shades are simply identified by a sequence of numbers or letters. The dye lot refers to the batch of dye that was used to color this ball of yarn. It's usually a nonsensical jumble of letters and numbers. The important thing is to purchase all your yarn from the same dye lot, because even a slight variation in color can show up in a crocheted piece. All the yarn from the same dye lot is certain to be the exact same shade.

E. Suggested Hook or Needle Size: If you're lucky, the yarn label will even tell you what hook size is recommended for that yarn. That's not to say you can't use a larger or smaller hook. It's just a suggestion, after all. Unfortunately, more often than not, only the suggested knitting needle size is given. But here's the amazing part: If you can find the millimeter size of the suggested knitting needle, you can use a crochet hook of the corresponding diameter with the yarn. So, if the label says to use Size 6, 4.0 mm knitting needles, you just go ahead and use a size G, 4.0 mm crochet hook on that bad boy!

F. Care Instructions: These kooky hieroglyphics are important to know when you've finished making your piece and want to wash it. The images here tell you that the yarn should be hand washed in water no warmer than 104° F, that it should not be machine dried, and that it should not be bleached. For more symbols, check out the guide at Lion Brand Yarn's site (www.lionbrand.com/yarns/yarnCare.html), where all of them are listed.

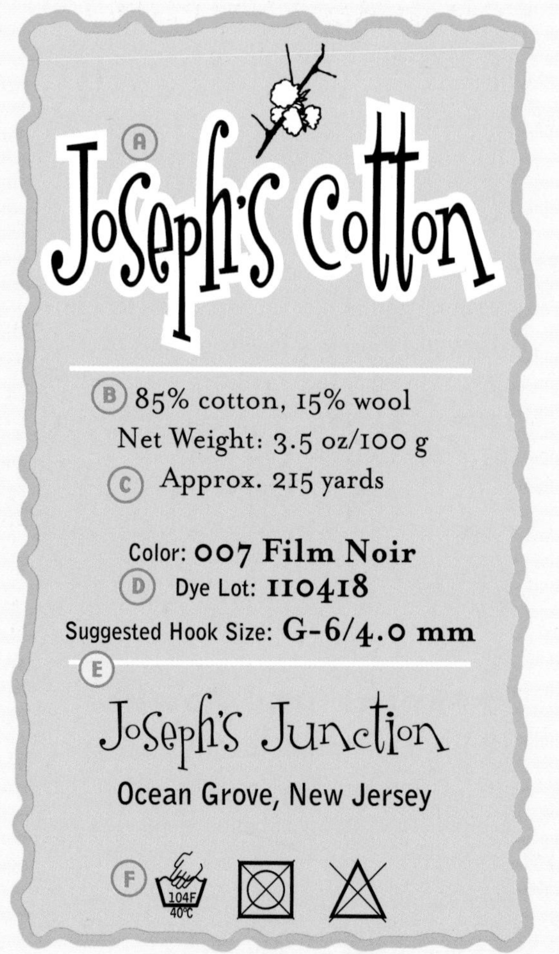

tool time

Other Crocheting Supplies

While you'll always have a hook, your working yarn, and an extra ball or skein (of each color if you're using more than one) in your crocheting bag, for some projects you may find these other supplies useful, as well:

Metal gauge This rectangular object, with a little peephole cut out of the side, is just the thing to measure your gauge (see page 34 for the definition of "gauge"). It usually has some holes in it to check the size of your crochet hook, in case somehow the number or letter has worn off (although, the way these are stamped into both metal and plastic hooks, this won't happen often). The smallest hole you can fit the handle through is the size of your hook.

Measuring tape Working on a project without having a measuring tape is kind of like being a cop without his gun: You may look impressive, but you don't have anything to back you up. Is the sleeve done or do you still need to keep going? Is it time to start the decreases on your hat? Little retractable tape measures are my favorite because they are so compact, but any kind will do the trick.

Tapestry needles You'll need these blunt-ended needles at the end of a project when it's time to weave away the ends and sew the pieces together. You can buy a set of them in their own little holder almost anywhere that carries sewing notions, which is pleasant, and anything you can use to make the finishing process more pleasant is a plus.

Scissors While you'll often keep working till you run out of yarn, sometimes something will need to be snipped. When that time comes, you'll be happy to have a little pair of scissors on you instead of being reduced to gnawing through the yarn with your teeth. Embroidery scissors are nice and small, and there are also scissors that fold up. In a pinch or on a plane, you can always use nail clippers or children's blunt-tipped scissors.

Split stitch markers Especially if you're working in a circle, you'll want to use a marker to identify the beginning of each round. You can also place markers to remind you where you made an increase, or where a sleeve should be sewn in. Make sure you don't buy the kind of stitch markers that knitters use, which are closed, or you'll have to cut them out of your work. Split markers can be inserted and lifted right out of your fabric. Laying a piece of contrasting-color yarn between stitches (it's best if it's cotton so it won't shed fibers) can do the same job as stitch markers, and just as well.

Safety pins These also work as stitch markers. Just don't use the kind with coils, because they can get snagged on your stitches and you may end up in a nasty fight when you try to remove them from your work. The coilless kind is better. I always use safety pins to hold my crochet pieces together before sewing them up, to keep everything lined up and even. And I suggest you do, too.

STANDARD YARN WEIGHT SYSTEM

Crochet hooks kind of match up with various yarn thicknesses, as follows:

Yarn Weight Symbol & Category Names	1 Super Fine	2 Fine	3 Light	4 Medium	5 Bulky	6 Super Bulky
Type of Yarns in Category	Sock, Fingering, Baby	Sport, Baby	DK, Light Worsted	Worsted, Afghan, Aran	Chunky, Craft, Rug	Bulky, Roving
Crochet Gauge* Ranges in Single Crochet to 4 Inches	21–32 sts	16–20 sts	12–17 sts	11–14 sts	8–11 sts	5–9 sts
Recommended Hook in Metric Size Range	2.25–3.5 mm	3.5–4.5 mm	4.5–5.5 mm	5.5–6.5 mm	6.5–9 mm	9 mm & larger
Recommended Hook U.S. Size Range	B-1 to E-4	E-4 to 7	7 to I-9	I-9 to K-10½	K-10½ to M-13	M-13 & larger

*GUIDELINES ONLY: The above reflect the most commonly used gauges and hook sizes for specific yarn categories.

3

get shorty

MAKING THE CHAIN STITCH, SINGLE CROCHET, AND SLIP STITCH

When you crochet, you're simply taking a hook, grabbing a strand of yarn, and pulling that strand through something—it could be a loop of yarn, it could be a space between two stitches. Stick your hand through a fence and pull out a flower from the yard behind it, and you're basically doing the motion of crochet. But while the action itself is easy enough, you'll need to repeat it hundreds if not thousands of times to make a crocheted item (and if you're working on something big, probably about a million kabillion), which means you'll want to learn how to do it in a way that is both comfortable and quick. In crocheting, finding a good way to hold your hook and yarn can make the difference between spending time on a relaxing hobby using only a crochet hook and some yarn, and engaging in a losing battle with a crooked piece of metal and a wad of tangled string.

The most basic crochet stitch is called "single crochet." It's a squat little stitch that makes me think of a Lego block. Stack a bunch of these bricklike stitches on top of each other and you can make a wall of fabric. And it won't be unlike a wall, either: Fabric made of single crochet stitches can be quite rigid, which makes it great for things that are sculptural (stuffed animals) or need to retain their shape (a handbag), but not so good for something that needs to drape and cling to curves. Make a sweater out of solid single crochet and you risk looking like you're wearing a full-body cast.

But single crochet is a great place to start learning the craft, as most other stitches are merely the taller, more willowy sisters of this stitch. They can help you make the more supple fabric that you'd desire for items of clothing, but they owe everything they know to that old battle ax, single crochet.

In this chapter, you'll learn how to hold the yarn and hook comfortably. Then I'll teach you how to make a chain of stitches and how to make a single crochet stitch into each of those chains. Finally, you'll learn how to make slip stitches so you can get your hook to a different location on your piece without adding any height. Are ya ready, boots? Start hooking!

knot really
Making a Slipknot

Before you can do much of anything in crochet, you need to introduce your yarn to your hook. You'll do that by creating a slip knot and slipping the resulting loop onto your crochet hook. Making a slip knot is one of those things that's way easier to do than it is to explain, but here goes:

1. Wrap your yarn, clockwise, around the pointer and middle finger of your left hand, with about a 6-inch "tail" end lying across your palm. Leave the ball end hanging a bit behind where the yarn crosses at the top of the loop.

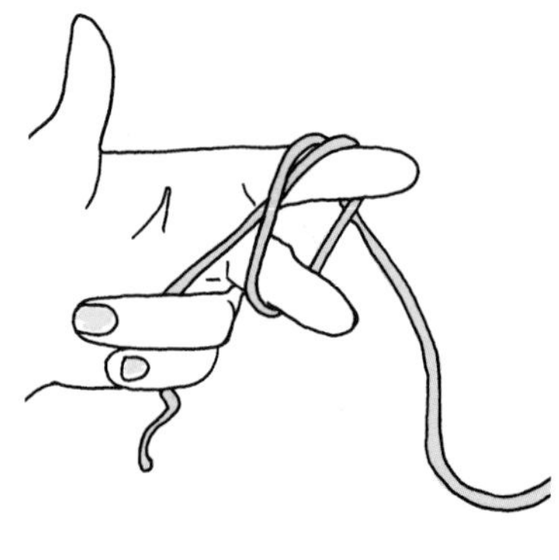

2. Stick the thumb and pointer finger of your right hand through that loop, grab the strand of yarn that's attached to the ball, and pull a loop through.

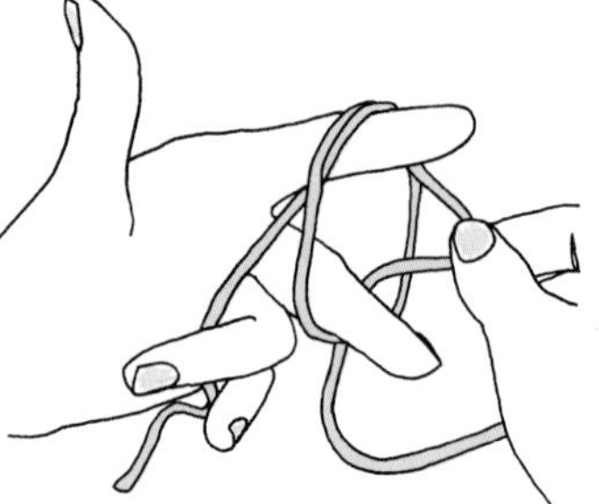

3. Drop the loop off of your left hand and gently tug on the tail end. You'll have a rather large loop with a knot holding it shut.

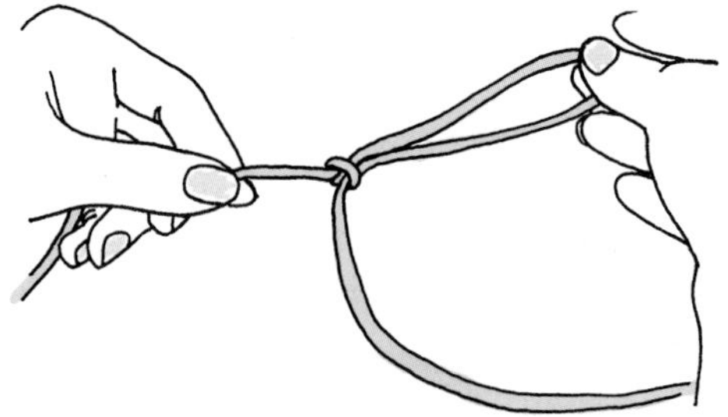

4. Slip that loop over your crochet hook, and pull on the ball end of yarn until the loop is closed around the hook—but not too tight. Leave some breathing room—like a loosened necktie at the end of a wild night.

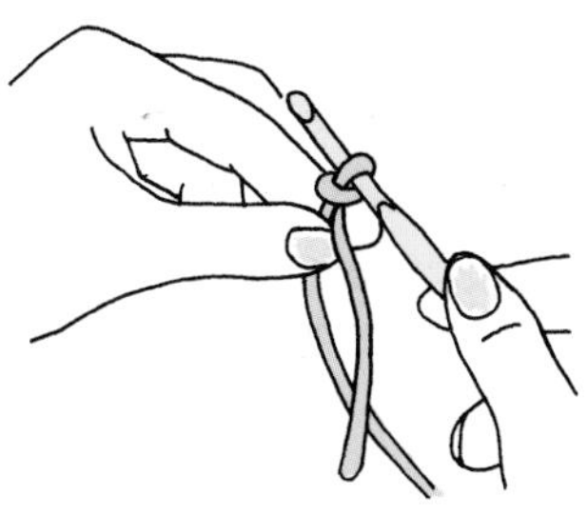

Hold everything

Holding Your Yarn and Hook

Finding a nice, comfortable way to hold the yarn and hook is key in crocheting, although it may feel awkward at first. The goal here is to have the yarn come feeding off the ball and over the top of your finger, with just the right amount of tension, so that your hook can just go to town this way and that. You'll be holding your hook in your right hand, if you're a righty, and your yarn in your left. For lefties, you can either try and learn to crochet this way, or reverse everything—and I mean **everything**—in this book.

CONTINENTAL DRIFT

Yarn Holds from Knitting

If you're a Continental knitter, meaning you hold your working yarn in your left hand while you knit and "pick" stitches from it with the needle in your right hand, you're already a couple of steps ahead of the game when it comes to crochet. You can hold the yarn in your left hand in exactly the same way you do for knitting, and you can hold your crochet hook in your right hand in almost exactly the same way you hold a needle. In fact, you'll find that "picking" stitches from the yarn is pretty much the same as the way that a crochet hook slides up and grabs loops to make crochet stitches.

1. Start by picking up the hook, with the slipknot on it, in your right hand. Hold it the way you would hold a knife if you were trying to cut a tough steak (or a key if you were trying to unlock a door). The mouth of the hook should be facing you. Place your thumb and middle finger on either side of the thumb rest (the flat part of the hook), and let your pointer finger rest on top of the loop you have on the hook, keeping it on the shaft of the hook. Close your last two fingers around the handle (you can hold the tail out of the way with these fingers, too).

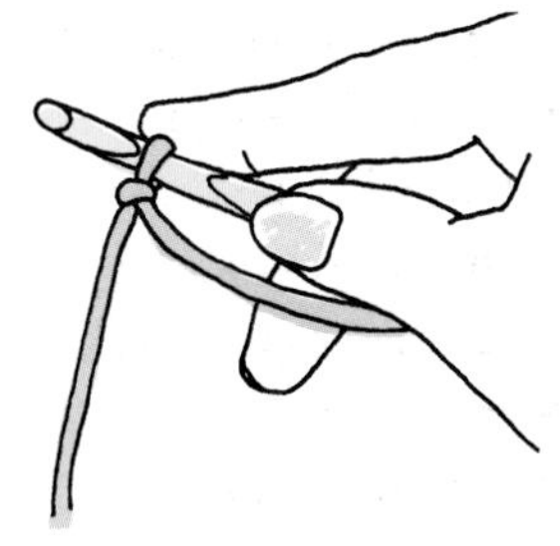

2. Now let's get your left hand comfortable feeding the yarn. With the ball end of the yarn hanging down from the hook, wrap the yarn, clockwise, around the pinky finger of your left hand.

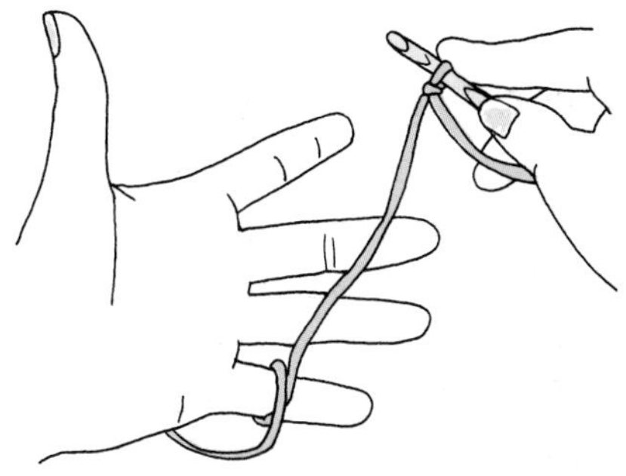

3. Close your lower three fingers loosely around the yarn.

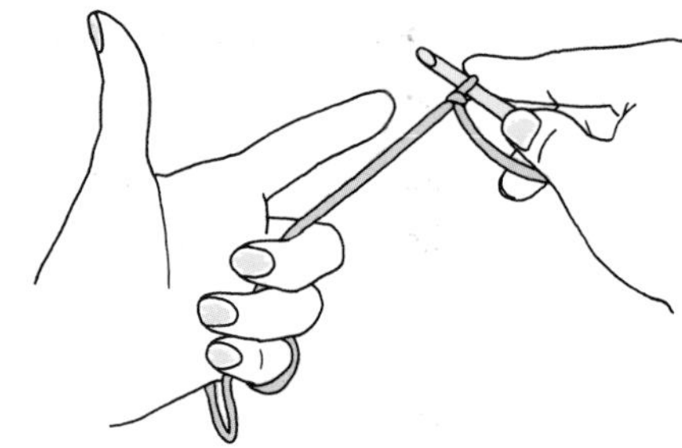

4. Dip your pointer finger under the strand of yarn, so that it runs over the top of the second knuckle.

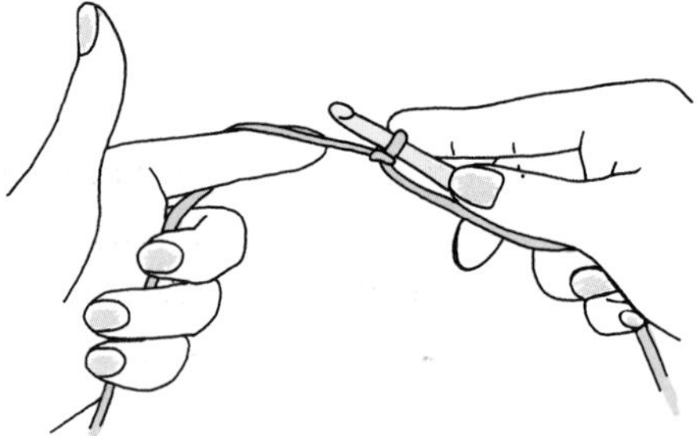

5. With your left thumb and middle finger, hold on to the base of the slipknot. You're now in the right position for crocheting. Look at what you've got: a nice, stable little triangle made with your hands, hook, and yarn. Your yarn strand is strung across from your left finger to the hook in your right hand, taut but not tight, and your hook is ready to start going to town on it.

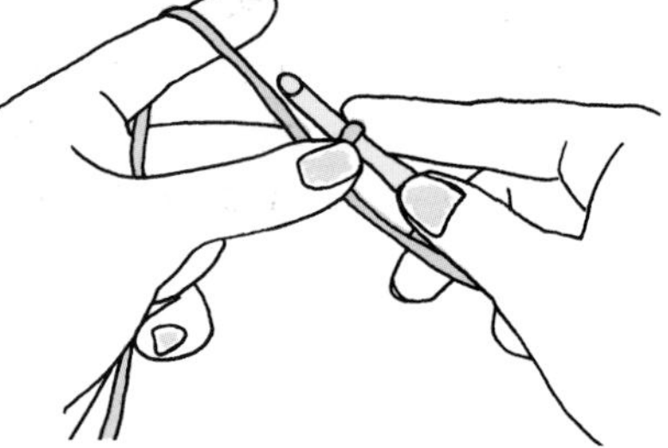

HATE THE PINKY WRAP?

Here Are Some Other Ways to Hold the Yarn

1. Don't wrap the yarn around your pinky, and just close your lower three fingers over it.

2. Weave the yarn under your pinky, over your ring finger, under your middle finger, and over your pointer, then close the lower three fingers over it.

3. BYOH (bring your own hold): Any other method that works for you—for instance, if there is some way you are used to holding the yarn in your left hand when knitting Continental style (see page 27)—is fine, as long as you have a strand of yarn that feeds up and over a finger (could be pointer, could be middle finger, whatever works) and also allows you to hold the base of that slipknot with your thumb and someone else (middle finger, ring finger, no matter). Having those fingers available to stabilize the work in progress is crucial to being able to crochet comfortably and quickly.

CHAIN OF FOOLS

Making the Chain Stitch (ch)

A piece of crochet fabric has to start with a base, and making a bunch of chain stitches is the way most pieces start out—consider it the foundation of your building, before you start laying on little bricks of single crochet. But first, take a moment to look at your crochet hook. Do you see how wide it is? When you are making these chain stitches, remember that your hook is going to have to fit through the links in the chain when it comes back down the foundation to lay those bricks. So it's very important when making a chain to work loosely and leave enough room for your hook to come back through these stitches without too much struggle later on.

To get the chain started, most instructions will tell you to wrap your yarn around your crochet hook counterclockwise. However, that's not quite what you'll be doing. In crocheting, you do often have a strand of yarn wrapped around your hook. But rather than wrapping the yarn with a finger around an inert, stable hook, you will actually be swirling the hook counterclockwise around the yarn instead. The yarn won't be moving much, but the crochet hook, as Maggie Righetti so nicely describes it in her book *Crocheting in Plain English,* will be "dancing in air."

So let it dance already. To make a chain, follow these steps:

1. Push the crochet hook up so that the slipknot loop is resting on the grip of the hook, then swirl the hook from left to right, counterclockwise, so that the strand of working yarn lies across its throat. This is called yarning over.

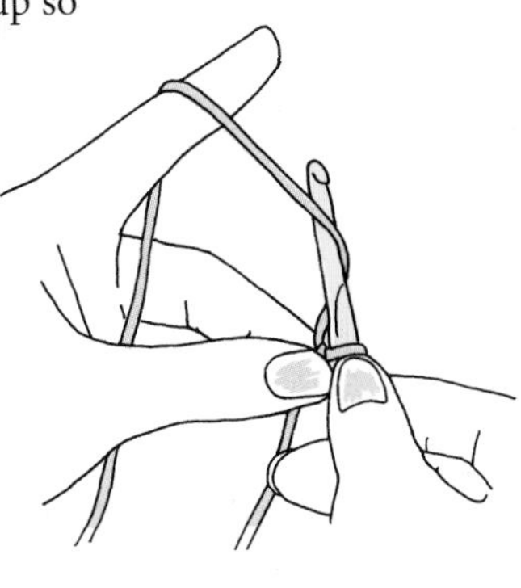

2. Turn the hook toward you and down so that it grabs this strand in its "mouth" and its "nose" is pointing into the crotch (really—that's what it is) of the loop already on the hook. Pull it through. Your left thumb and middle finger, which are holding the base of the slipknot, can help stretch the loop by pulling it a bit away from the hook, making it easier to pull the new loop through.

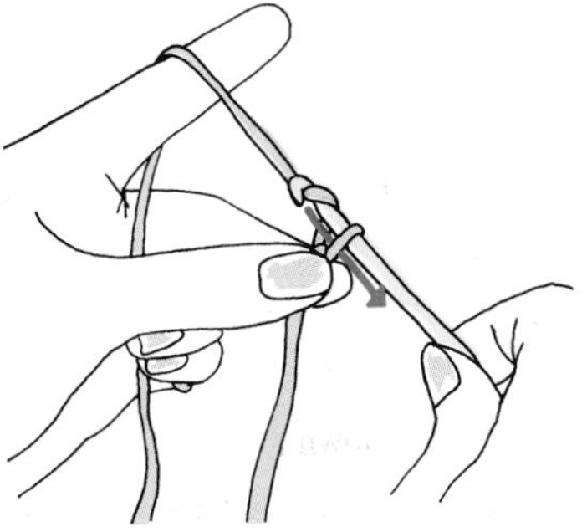

3. Okay, now slide the hook back up so that the loop you've just made is on the shaft. If you leave it near the throat, the stitch will be too small. Adjust your left thumb and middle finger so that instead of holding that slipknot, they are holding the loop that you just let off the hook, so to speak. You don't have to readjust your fingers after every single stitch. Usually after about 3 or 4 chains, however, you'll want them to grab hold of a stitch that's closer to the hook so that you can maintain the right tension.

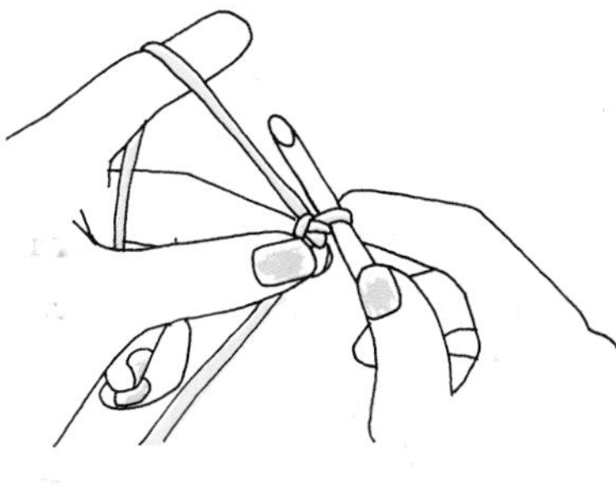

Keep on chainin'. You always want to keep a bit of tension between the hook in your right hand and the work you're holding in your left hand, to keep those chains stretched out. You want them just loose enough to slip your hook into easily when you build on this foundation chain.

Continue to make chains until you've got, let's say, 21 of them. That will give you a swatch that's big enough to measure and work with easily. You can keep count as you make them, but it's easy to lose track on a longer chain, so be sure to count the stitches of your finished chain, too.

ANATOMY OF A CROCHET CHAIN

To count the links in your made chain, let your chain dangle from the hook. On one side (the front), you'll see a series of Vs. It is these Vs that you count to see how many chains you have. But there are two rules:

1. DON'T count the loop that's sitting on the hook.

2. DON'T count the slipknot itself. (But do count the loop that comes out of it.) While you are making a chain, you can try counting "1" every time you pull the hook through a loop.

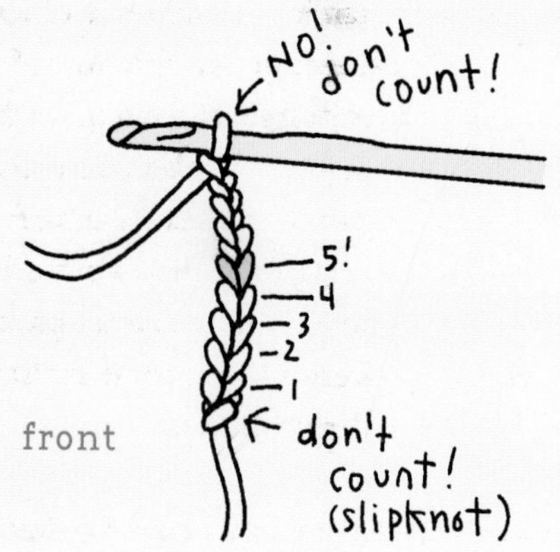

Now turn the chain over and look at what's on the other side (the back). You'll see that each V has a little bump on the back, which I like to think of as the chain's "butt." It's important to familiarize yourself with these three strands that make up each chain—the two arms of the V and the butt—'cause you'll need to know them when you go on to the next part: making a row of single crochet stitches into this base chain.

butt!

back

by Hook or by crook

Making Single Crochet ("sc") Stitches into the Chain

Crochet can be a cruel taskmistress, and she'll let you know who's boss from the start. The very first row of crocheting—when you are working into the base chain—can be a real challenge. Consider it a test of sorts. Once the gods of crochet see that you have the perseverance to make it through this first difficult row, they'll see to it that every row you do afterward is much easier. Because it's true: Even seasoned crocheters find working into the base chain pretty dang unpleasant.

Now that you have a "base chain," you can crochet any type of basic stitches into it—but we'll begin by crocheting a row of **single crochet** stitches. The trickiest part here is inserting the hook into the chain—there are a number of ways to do it, as you'll see later, but the method I give below seems to be the one that is most technically correct. Try it first, then give the other methods a whirl. The good news is that once you've got that hook in the right spot, completing the single crochet is a breeze.

1. Begin by inserting your hook *under both strands of the V* in the *second stitch from the hook.* (You never count the stitch that's *on* the hook). Here's where you'll be really glad you made those chains nice and loose. But even with loose chains, it can be tough to get the hook in

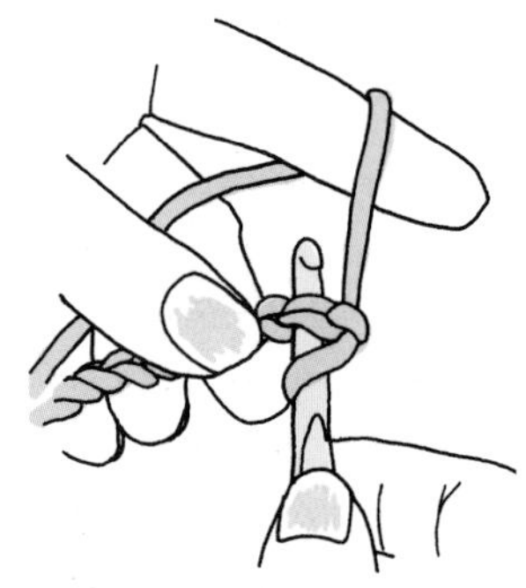

there correctly. I usually turn my hook so the nose is pointing to the left and use the thumb and middle finger of my left hand to help ease the hook into the right location. I even use those fingers to lift the strands of the V so the hook can get in there.

2. Once the hook is through, the rest is pretty simple: Twirl the hook from left to right (counterclockwise) around the working yarn so that the strand lies across its throat, turn the nose of the hook so that it grabs the yarn and faces left, and pull the loop through. Now you've got two loops on the hook. Hurray!

3. Push the hook up through those two loops about an inch and twirl it around the working strand again, same way as before. Pull the strand through *both* loops on the hook. Single crochet done! *C'est fini!*

Continue on down the line, inserting your hook under the V of the next chain, pulling through the working strand so you have two loops on your hook, then pulling the strand through both loops. Make one single crochet at a time into each chain, until you've made one in the last chain but not the slipknot (heck, it's a knot—you probably couldn't get your hook in there if you tried).

And Now for Something Completely Different

Other Ways to Crochet into the Chain

In the first chapter, I explained that crocheting is one of the youngest of the needle arts. One advantage of being so youthful is that there doesn't seem to be a "set" method of how a number of things should be done. And nowhere is that more evident than in the multitude of ways that people choose to crochet into that first row of chain stitches. The directions just given seem to be the most "correct," but pick up any two crochet instruction books and see if they don't give contradictory information. Better yet, ask any two crocheters. Below are a few more ways to try. Use the one you like the best; I promise, there aren't any crochet police around to come arrest you for doing it differently. At least, not yet.

Middle Man: Crocheting into the Center of the V

I came across this method of crocheting into the chain rather recently, and it has since become my favorite. It's a heck of a lot easier to accomplish than inserting your hook under the two strands of the V, and yet the results are quite similar. For this method, begin by turning the chain so that the Vs are facing you. Then insert your hook smack into the center of the V—between the "arms"—and at the same time *under* the butt strand behind the V. Feel free to use

your left thumb and forefinger to help lift that butt strand over your hook. Again, remember to skip the first chain from the hook and begin with the second when you start the row.

Backdoor Betty: Crocheting into the "Butt" of the Chain

Here's a method that leaves a nice edge at the bottom of your work. Flip the chain over so that the bottom strand, or "butt," is facing up. Skip the first chain from the hook and insert your hook under the butt of the second chain from the hook. It is definitely easier to insert the hook under the butt than it is to get it nicely under the Vs. Plus, this method leaves the Vs free if, later on, you want to go back and crochet a fancy edging onto the bottom of your piece. However, crocheting into the butt should only be used here, in the very first row. If you need to crochet into chain stitches later on in your work, you should use one of the two methods given above, both of which have you inserting your hook under two strands of the yarn.

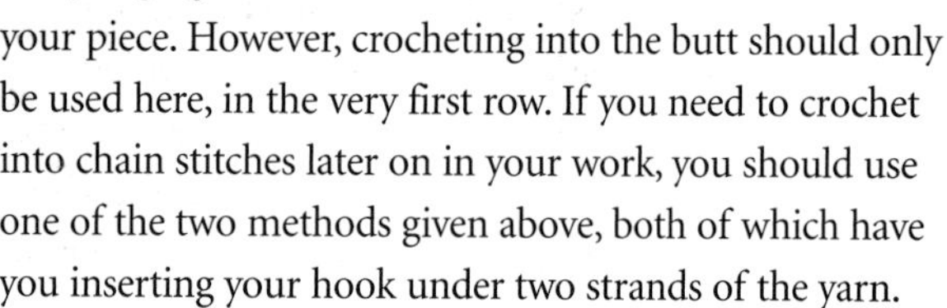

Naughty by Nature: Cheating Your Way Under Only One Strand of the Chain

Now here's a not-so-technically-correct way to crochet into the chain. There are a good number of books that show it this way, and there are plenty of crocheters who do it this way, too—many of whom have taught themselves to crochet using these books. To crochet into the chain using the cheater's method, simply insert your hook under only *one* strand of the V. It's certainly easier to do than the other methods I've described, but the results are also less aesthetically pleasing, as it can leave large loose loops at the bottom of your work. But you can certainly get away with doing it this way, and it may very well be the most popular method going. Hell—if you can live with those unsightly holes, good on ya.

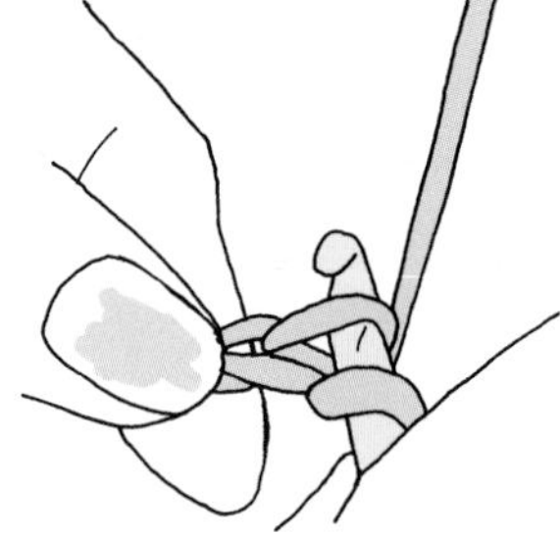

Okay, so you've made your first row of single crochet, and you survived getting your hook into each and every last chain stitch, using whatever means necessary. You've passed the test of will, and the crochet gods are now smiling upon you. They'll see to it that this second row of single crochet (and every row hereafter) is *way* easier to complete than that first row was.

the turning chain **(t-ch)**

In crocheting, you are often called on to do a very special thing at the end of a row, before starting the next row. It's called making a *turning chain.* Crochet stitches can range from short to very, very tall, and you need to get your hook up to the height of the stitches you are about to make in the new row. The turning chain is like the ladder that gets you there. For single crochet it is only 1 chain stitch high—just a little step stool—so before starting the next row of single crochets, you will make one chain stitch. Now, keeping your hook in that loop, turn your work away from you, counterclockwise, so that all the completed stitches are sitting off to the left, and you're at the start of a row. (The turning chain could just as easily be made *after* turning your work, but I like to do it before.) By the way, when you skipped the first chain from the hook when crocheting into the foundation chain, that skipped chain was actually the turning chain for row 1. Surprise!

single crochet, row 2
Electric Boogaloo

On the second row of single crochet, and every row thereafter, you're going to insert your hook under both strands of the V at the top of the stitch (and there are no sneaky ways around it). Not to worry, though. You'll find that it's much easier to crochet into a stitch than into the chain. Crochet stitches are kind of three-dimensional, and the Vs are all lying neatly across the top of the last row of Lego-like stitches you made.

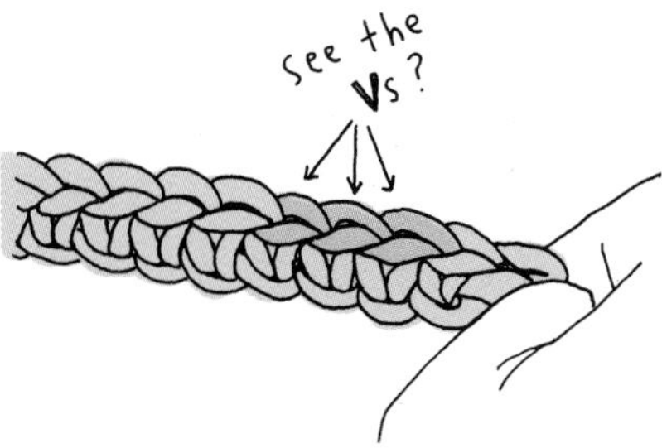

To start your second row of crochet, skip the first chain (the turning chain) after the loop on the hook, and insert your hook under the top two strands of the V of the first single crochet stitch of your work.

The rest is the same: Grab the strand of yarn with your hook and pull it through (you'll have two loops on the hook). Grab the strand and pull it through both loops on the hook. You have one loop left on the hook—

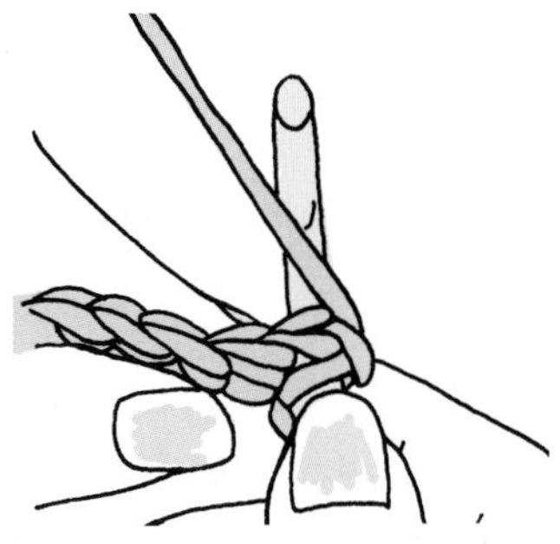

and you've made 1 single crochet stitch. Now make a single crochet through every V, or single crochet stitch, in the row, including the last one, which may be a little bit tighter than the others. Then, when you're done, make a chain stitch (your turning chain), turn the work, and go back again.

When you're making single crochet stitches, you'll stack a stitch on top of every stitch in the row below except the previous row's turning chain. You probably couldn't find that turning chain if you tried—it's squashed up alongside the first stitch in the row. I'm just mentioning it because, in the next chapter, you'll learn to make some taller stitches that will require you to make a stitch into the turning chain. But we'll get to that later.

swinging singles
The Structure of Crochet

Try making a few more rows of single crochet, then stop. Let's take a closer look at what you've got.

For one thing, you should have 20 stitches in each row. Do you? Count the Vs across the top of your last row and see if there are 20 of 'em. If you have less, you've got a problem. Maybe you aren't making a single crochet in the last stitch of your row. Pay careful attention to how you are working the ending and beginning of your rows. Try getting at least 4 rows of work that remains the same width (even if it's less than 20 stitches). Then we can talk.

Now, take a close look at your single crochet work. With all that yarning over and pulling loops through loops, the structure of an individual crochet stitch can be less than obvious. Figuring out where one stitch ends and another begins can be especially challenging. If you examine the last row of stitches you made, you'll see that a single crochet stitch is three-dimensional and, seen from the front, looks like a V with another V lying across the top of it, sort of like a lid. In fact, you can think of your crochet stitches as being a bit like a to-go cup of latte from your favorite java hut. A single crochet stitch is a short shot, while later on you'll learn to make taller stitches—more like those grande and venti cups. They'll always have that lid on top, though, just like all good coffee does. Also, observe that the "cup" Vs are not stacked directly on top of each other, but are a bit offset, which is probably just how you'd stack 'em, too, if you had to make a wall of coffee cups.

There's one more thing to notice about your rows of crochet stitches: They don't look exactly the same. In one row, you have a series of dashes above each stitch, which makes them very easy to count. On the next row, however, you don't see that little dash. Instead, the tops of all the stitches make a long furrow or dent across the fabric. Why does each row look different? Because you're working back and forth in rows, so you see one row of stitches from the front, and the next row of stitches from *behind.* Stick your fingernail in a dent and look at it from the other side, and you'll see that it's a dash. Seeing the dashes and dents in a piece of single crochet work makes it easy to count the rows. Dashes signify the top of one row; a long dent is the top of the next row.

Your work itself has a front and a back, too. How can you tell which is which? There's really only one way, and it's super easy: Check out the tail of the slipknot. If it's on the left side of your work, you are looking at the front. If it's on the right side of your work, you are looking at the back. (For lefties it's the opposite, of course.) The piece of fabric itself, however, doesn't look very different on either side. Knowing front from back doesn't make a hell of a lot of difference, except for sometimes, when you're working on a fancier, shaped piece of crochet (the front of a sweater, for instance). Then it's important to know which side is which.

Did you notice that your fabric is just a little curly? Don't let it bother you: It's the nature of the beast. Single crochet makes a tight, solid fabric that tends to curl around itself a little at first. As you continue, that curl will become a little looser. And when you're done, you can "block" the fabric and get rid of the curl altogether.

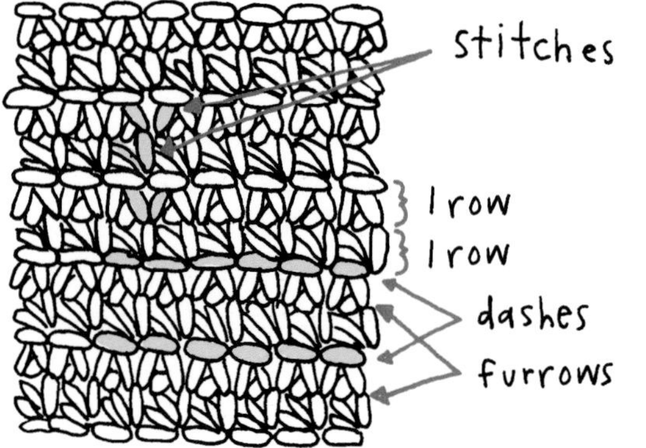

gauge before beauty

Understanding Gauge

Gauge is a very important concept in crocheting (as it is in knitting). It's the number of stitches and rows made by your particular hands using your particular yarn and your particular hook in a specific amount of space (say, two inches across). Hookers who crochet more tightly than you do will make more stitches in the same amount of space, even if they use the same yarn and hook. And someone who crochets more loosely than you will make fewer stitches to fill that space. And if you use a different hook (even if both hooks are labeled "G"), you might also make more or fewer stitches in the same space—maybe there's just something about that hook that makes you crochet a bit looser or a bit tighter.

Let's figure out what your gauge is for the swatch you just made. First, you'll need to have about 4 inches worth of fabric to get an accurate measurement, so if you don't have that yet, keep on making rows of single crochet till you get there. Now lay your swatch flat on a table and hold a measuring tape against it. What you want to do is count the number of stitches in a 2-inch-wide section of fabric—so measure in the center because stitches near the edge aren't as even. Remember, it's easiest to do this by counting the dashes. If you have a half-dash left at the end, count that, too (don't round it off; count it as ½ stitch). Now double that number to get your gauge for 4 inches (the way gauge is often given in a pattern), or halve it to figure out your gauge of stitches per inch. In the gauge swatch shown here, there are exactly 9 stitches per 2 inches, or 18 stitches per 4 inches and 4½ stitches per inch.

Next, turn your measuring tape so you can count the number of rows you get in 2 inches. Put the "0" point of your tape measure into a dent or furrow row. Then count the rows—the next dash is at the top of row 1, the next furrow is at the top of row 2, etc. Count only the tops of rows. If you end up with half a row left, count it as ½. Again, double your number to figure the number of rows in 4 inches and halve for the number of rows in 1 inch. In our swatch, the gauge is 10 rows per 2 inches or 20 rows per 4 inches, and 5 rows per inch.

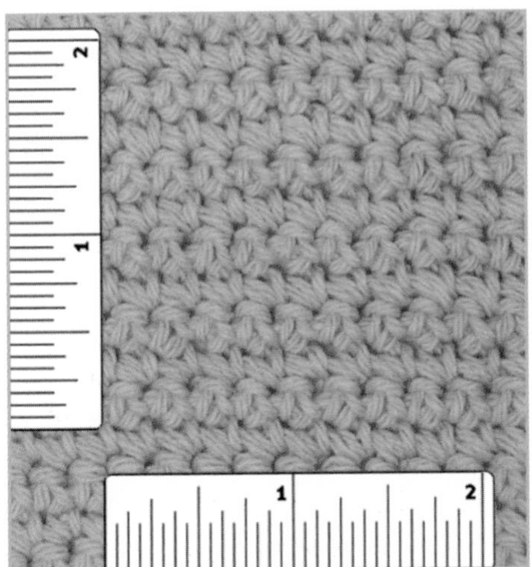

Gauge is super important when you are trying to follow a pattern, because a pattern is completely based on making a certain number of stitches to achieve a specific width of fabric. If your gauge is not the same as the one in the pattern—even if it's off by just a little bit—you may end up with a tank top that is a couple of inches narrower than the pattern intends. And that can make all the difference between a top that you're happy to wear and one that crushes your ribs when you put it on.

A pattern might say, for instance, that the gauge needed is 16 stitches and 16 rows per 4-inch square. Now let's say you go out and buy the exact yarn and hook size the pattern calls for, but when you work up a test swatch, you find that you're getting 18 stitches and 18 rows in a 4-inch square. You're fitting *more* stitches into the same space—meaning your stitches are smaller than the pattern calls for. Do you down a couple of stiff shots so you can loosen up and start making larger stitches? No, sirree. All you do is get yourself a hook one size larger and make a new swatch. If that one measures up, you're good to go. If not, go up a hook size and try again.

On the other hand, if your first swatch turned out to have fewer stitches than called for—say, only 14 of the buggers instead of 16—you'd swatch again with a hook one size smaller, until you get the gauge you are looking for. Got it? Good!

Slip Sliding Away

The Slip Stitch (sl)

There's still room to slip in one last stitch in this chapter. The slip stitch in crochet is one that has no height, and so, if you are going to do a row of it, you don't need to make a turning chain at the end of the row.

Because it adds no height to a piece, the slip stitch is sometimes used to get your hook from one location to another without having to cut your yarn and then reattach it someplace else. It's kind of like when you move your cursor along an already drawn line on an Etch-A-Sketch to get to another spot without adding an extra line. To make it, slip your crochet hook under the top two strands of the V in the first single crochet of the row, twirl your hook to grab a strand of yarn, as usual, but then pull that strand through both the V and the loop on the hook. Aha! Slip stitch made.

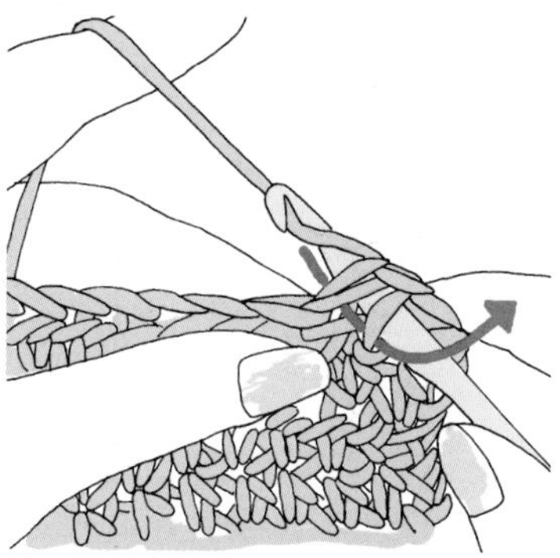

The slip stitch is so nice and flat and sneaky that it's also used to join one piece of crocheting to another almost invisibly. Practice making slip stitches across the top of all 20 single crochet stitches in your row, so you get nice and good at making 'em.

Say Goodnight, Gracie

Finishing Off Your Work

Okay, your work here is done; it's time to sign off. Finishing a piece of crochet work couldn't be easier. Simply cut the yarn about 6 inches from your last stitch, hook the strand, pull it all the way through (including the cut end) the loop that's on your hook, and tighten the strand.

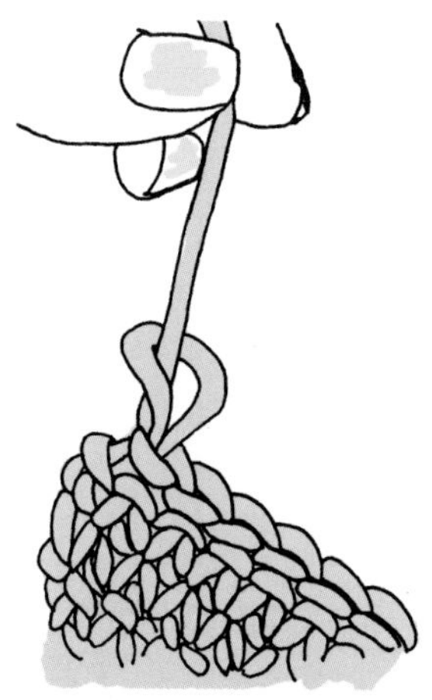

Now sit back and look at your friend, the swatch. You've learned so much from him: how to make the chain stitch, single crochet, and slip stitch; how to make a turning chain, how to count stitches and rows, and how to measure gauge. He's an oddly shaped little thing, but he's yours. Weave away his ends with a darning needle (see page 89) and put him in your bag: He'll come in handy someday to clean your sunglass lenses or wipe off your computer screen. And he'll always be there to remind you of your very first baby steps in crochet.

4

walking tall

MAKING HALF-DOUBLE CROCHET, DOUBLE CROCHET, AND TRIPLE CROCHET.

In the last chapter, you learned how to make the mother of all crochet stitches: the single crochet. In this chapter, you'll learn how to make her sisters, all of whom are simply taller variations on the single crochet stitch. Once you've learned the stitches in this chapter, you'll pretty much know all there is to making stitches in crochet. Everything else—from granny squares to fancy lace stitches to ripply patterns—are all done using combinations of these stitches. And here's the best part: They are easy to do. Try each one out and I'm pretty sure you'll be sighing with relief to discover just how straightforward crochet really is. Crochet pulls no punches, there is no trickery—it's just pulling loops through loops with that twirling hook of yours. So let's get going.

Ain't No Half-Steppin'

The Half-Double Crochet (hdc) Stitch

The half-double crochet stitch seems to be a little confused. It starts out like a double crochet stitch, which you'll meet next, but then refuses to reach its full height and finishes off like a single crochet stitch. It's taller than the single crochet stitch, to be sure, but not nearly as confident.

1. To begin a row of half-double crochet stitches, you'll need a **turning chain of 2 stitches.** To make the stitch, start by whipping your hook counterclockwise around your yarn, as you always do, so that you have a strand lying across its throat. Then, if you're working into a base chain, insert your hook into the **3rd chain from the hook.** If you're working into a row of stitches, insert your hook under both strands of the V of the first stitch of the row—it will be the 3rd V after the loop on the hook.

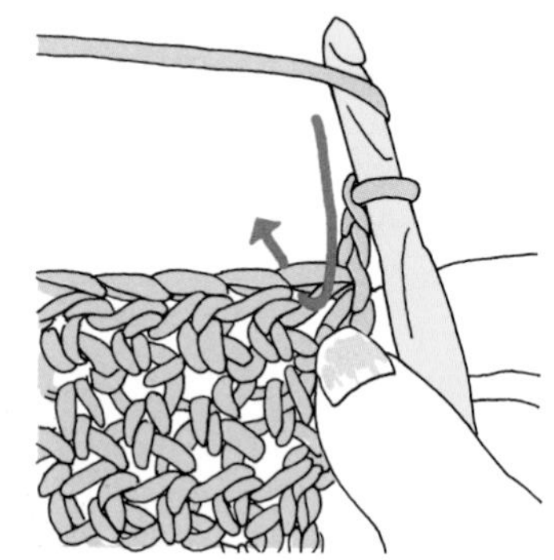

2. Wind your hook around the yarn again and pull a strand through.

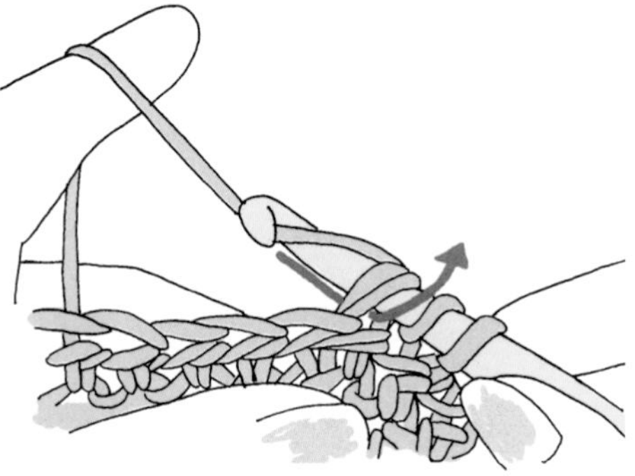

3. You should have 3 loops of yarn on your hook. Wind your hook again, grabbing the working strand of yarn, and pull it through all 3 of those loops. That's it, you're done. Continue on to the next stitch and the next one, all the way to the end of the row. Don't forget to keep inserting your hook under the top V of each stitch if you're working into a row of stitches, and do *not* make a stitch into the turning chain of the previous row.

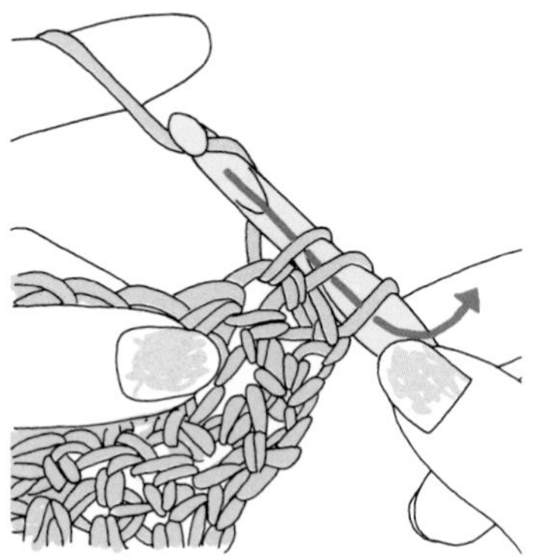

Try making a few rows of half-double crochet and see what you think about it. With all that yarning over, it's slower going than making single crochet stitches, but because each stitch is taller than single crochet, your fabric will grow faster—you don't have to make as many rows of stitches to achieve the same length. It also makes a looser, more flexible fabric than single crochet does, which makes it more appropriate for articles of clothing. The stitches are shaped differently from single crochet, and you won't have such obvious dashes to help you count your stitches, but because of their height, the individual stitches are pretty easy to count when you're trying to measure your gauge.

double your pleasure

The Double Crochet (dc) Stitch

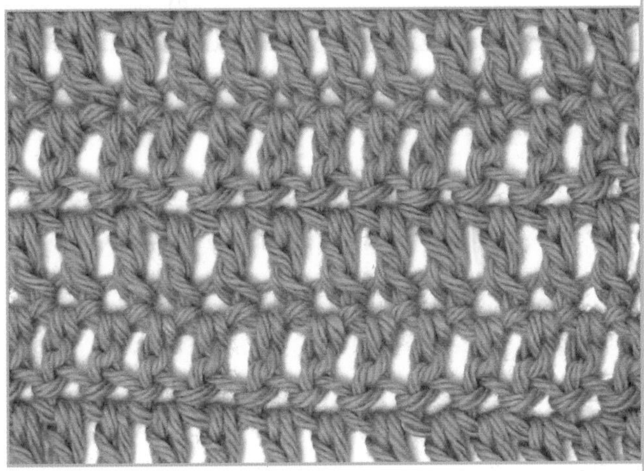

Double crochet is a fun stitch, and it's one of the most common stitches you are likely to encounter in your crocheting career. It's simple, speedy, and tall, so your work will grow quickly.

1. For double crochet, you'll want to make a **turning chain of 3 stitches** before starting each new row. To make the stitch, start by whipping your hook around your yarn so you have a strand lying across its throat.

Next, insert your hook into a stitch. If you are crocheting into a base chain, you'll want to start by inserting your hook into the **4th chain from the hook**—remember, your last 3 chains form the turning chain here. If you're working into a row of stitches, **skip the stitch at the base of the turning chain.** Instead, insert your hook under the two strands of the V on the top of the **2nd stitch.**

2. Once your hook is inserted, twirl your hook around the yarn again, and pull up a loop.

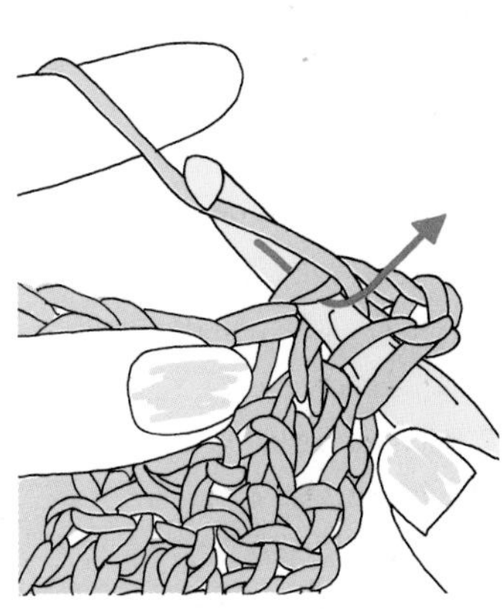

3. You now have 3 loops of yarn on your hook. Hook the strand of yarn again and pull it through only 2 of those loops.

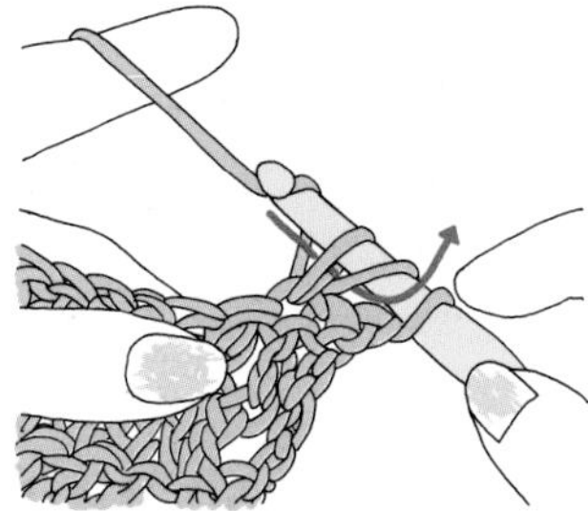

4. Now there are 2 loops left on your hook. Twirl your hook and grab the strand, then pull it through both of those loops.

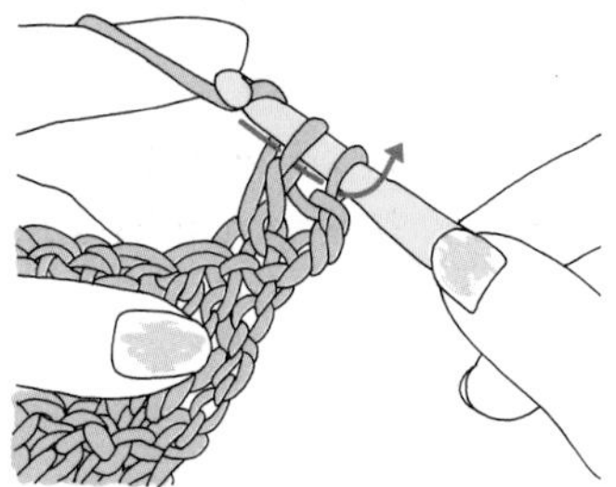

Now you're back to where you started—with only 1 loop on the hook—and your double crochet stitch is done. Continue across the row of stitches.

stalking the top of the wild turning chain (tch)

You just learned that when you make rows of double crochet, you skip the stitch that is at the base of the turning chain. Why do you skip that first stitch? Because for double crochet stitches and any taller stitches, the turning chain counts as the first stitch of the row. We don't want to add any extra stitches here, so, since the turning chain is our first stitch, we'll make our first double crochet into the top of the 2nd stitch in the row below. If you're wondering how you can skip that stitch and still maintain the same number of stitches in each row, you are thinking like a very clever person indeed. Because you can't. In fact, stitches as tall as double crochet and taller require one more thing of you, which shorter stitches do not: At the end of each row, you have to make one stitch into the top of the turning chain of the row below it. It makes sense, since after all, that turning chain now counts as a stitch, as good as any other.

Trying to find the top of that turning chain can be a bit tricky, but look for the V that follows the V in the top of the last stitch—that's where you put this last wily stitch of each row. Just when you thought you'd never have to deal with inserting your hook into another yucky chain stitch, you discover that in double crochet and taller stitches, you have to do it at the end of each and every row. Where do you insert the hook? Well, you can use my favorite method of crocheting into the chain, which means inserting your hook into the center of the V, and under the butt loop, so that you have two strands on top of the hook. You could also use the more challenging method of inserting your hook so that it is under the top two strands of the V. Either way, don't just

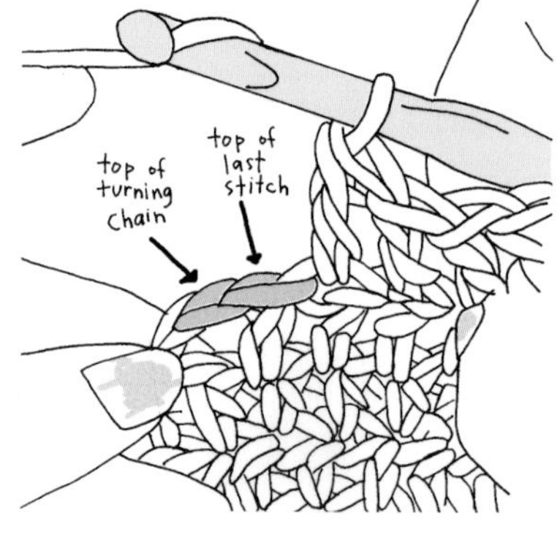

DOUBLE-EDGED SWORD

THE EDGES OF DOUBLE CROCHET

If you take a close look at your double crochet swatch, you might notice that you have gaps at the beginning of each row, where you skip the stitch at the base of the turning chain. That's also just as it's supposed to be, and if your piece is going to get sewn up the sides when you're done, no one will ever see those holes. Even in a piece where the edges are visible, most folks leave them as is. But if you just can't live with them, here's something to try: Instead of making 3 turning chains, turn your work and make a single crochet in the first stitch (the one you'd usually skip), then chain 2. That single crochet plus the 2 chain stitches become your turning chain (you have to put a stitch in the top of this turning chain at the end of each row). This leaves smaller gaps at the beginning of each row, but it's not very commonly done.

Mind the gap?

go under one loop or you'll leave big ugly holes in your work. Blech.

Now that you know you have to get your hook in there, try to remember to make the chains of your turning chain nice and loose, and don't be afraid to use your fingers to lift the strands over your hook. Try making a number of practice rows of double crochet, so you can get used to skipping the first stitch of the row and crocheting into the turning chain at the end of the row.

three's company

The Triple Crochet (tr) Stitch

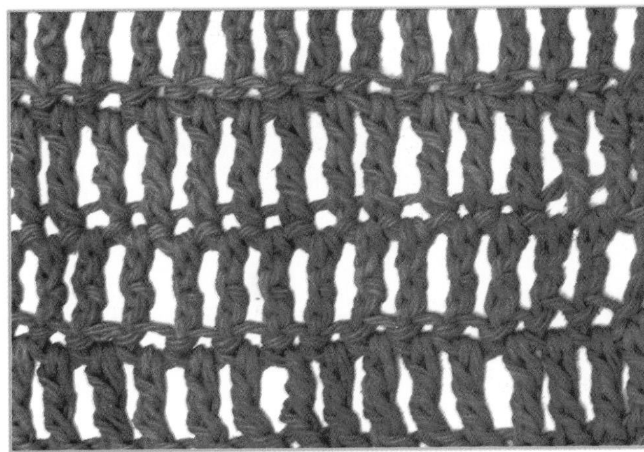

Ready to go to even greater lengths with your crochet? Try the triple crochet stitch. It has one more step than double crochet.

1. To make this stitch, start with a **turning chain of 4 stitches.** Then swing your hook so that you wrap your yarn around it *twice.* If you're crocheting into the base chain, insert your hook into **the 5th chain from the hook.** If you're crocheting into a row of stitches, skip the stitch at the base of the turning chain and insert your hook under both strands of the V at the top of the next stitch.

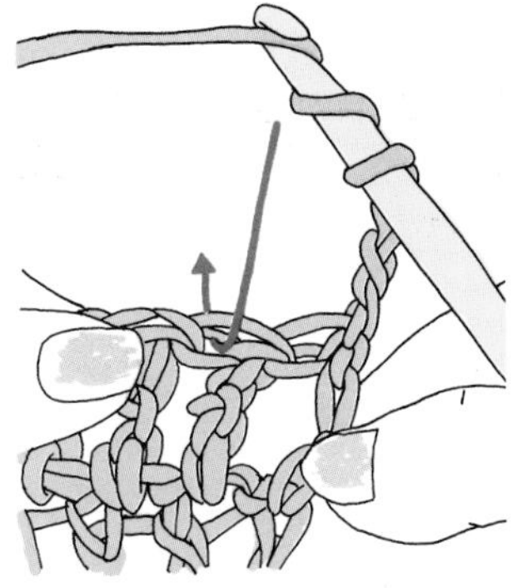

2. Now swing your hook around the yarn again and pull a strand through.

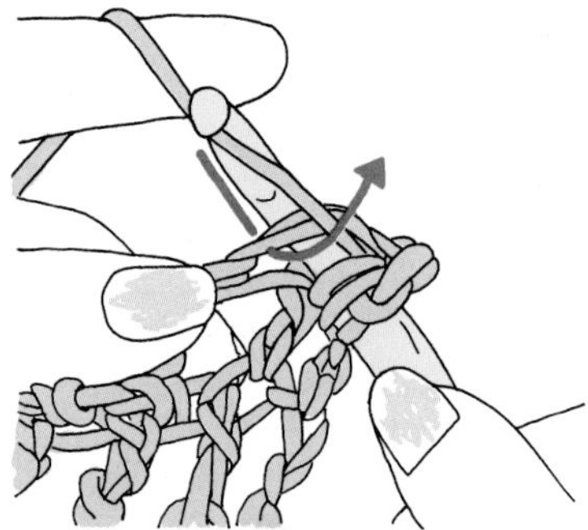

3. You should have 4 loops on your hook. Hook a strand and pull it through 2 of these loops.

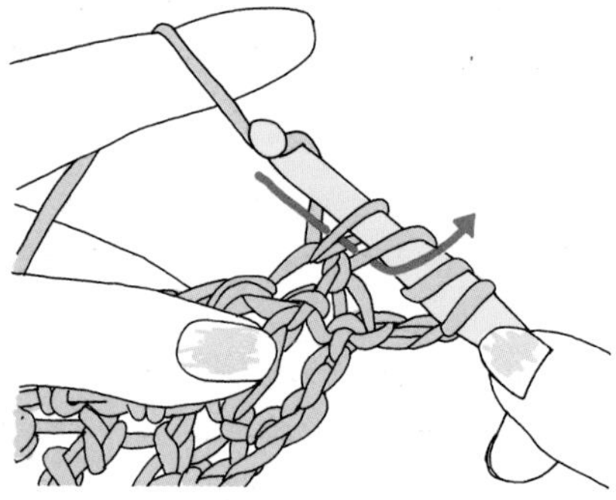

4. You have 3 loops left on your hook. Hook the strand again and pull it through 2 of these loops.

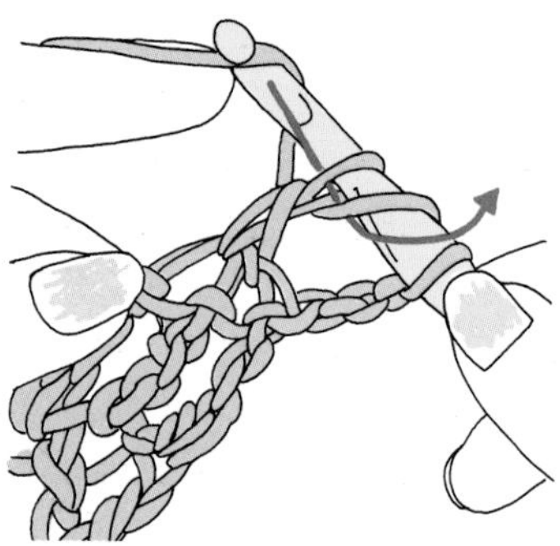

5. You have 2 loops left. Hook the yarn one more time and pull it through the last 2 loops.

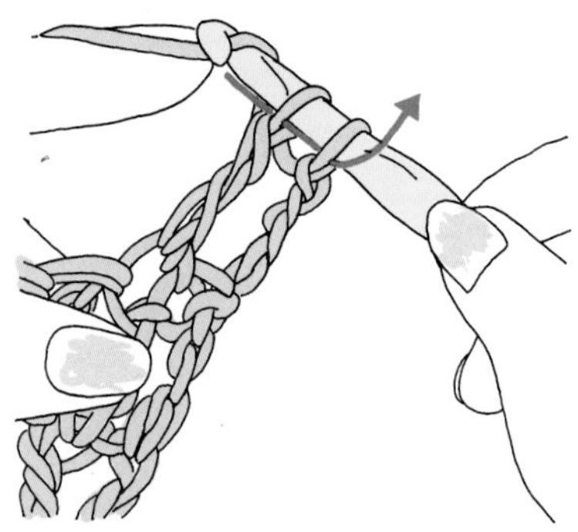

You have only one loop left, and your triple crochet is done. Just look at how dang tall it is! Repeat steps 1 through 5 all the way across your row. Just like double crochet, the triple crochet stitch (and all taller stitches) requires you to make your final stitch into the top of the previous row's turning chain. But by now you're a pro at that and have no fear of it, of course. To continue on, chain 4, turn your work, wind yarn over twice and insert your hook under the V of the second stitch of the row and so forth and so on.

Up to the Highest Heights

Double Triple (dtr) and Triple Triple (ttr) Crochet

Right about now you might be thinking: Hey, if I can make a tall stitch by wrapping the yarn once and dropping off loops two at a time, and I can make an even taller one by wrapping the yarn twice and dropping the loops off two at a time, what happens if I wrap the

WHO WHAT WHERE?

Stitch name	# of Stitches for turning chain	Where first stitch of each row is made	Where last stitch of each row is made
Single Crochet (sc)	1	Stitch at base of turning chain	Last stitch of previous row
Half-Double Crochet* (hdc)	2	Stitch at base of turning chain	Last stitch of previous row
Double Crochet (dc)	3	Skip stitch at base of turning chain; crochet into next stitch	Top of previous row's turning chain
Triple Crochet (tr)	4	Skip stitch at base of turning chain; crochet into next stitch	Top of previous row's turning chain

*Some books say that even for half-double crochet, you should skip the stitch at the base of the turning chain and crochet into the next stitch, and at the end of the row, you should crochet into the turning chain of the previous row. But I find that stumpy little turning chain next to impossible to crochet into, so I prefer the method I give here, which is also taught by the National NeedleArts Association—so there!

yarn three or even four times? Will the stitches get taller and taller and taller?

The answer is yes, and, in fact, someone else already thought of this. That's how she or he invented the double triple and triple triple crochet stitches, which are kind of ridiculously tall and not all that frequently used, but worth knowing anyway.

For the **double triple** crochet stitch, you start with a **turning chain of 5 stitches.** Put 3 wraps of yarn on your hook. If you're working into a base chain, insert your hook into the 6th chain from the hook; if you're working into a row of stitches, skip the stitch at the base of the chain and insert the hook into the next stitch. Now, grab a strand of yarn with your hook and pull it through. You have 5 loops on the hook. Hook the yarn and pull it through two of those loops. Then keep on winding yarn around your hook and pulling it through two loops at a time until you have only 1 loop left on the hook. Double triple crochet stitch made.

For the **triple triple stitch,** you start with—can you guess?—**a turning chain of 6 stitches.** Yarn over four times. If you're working into a base chain, insert your hook into the 7th chain from the hook; if you are working into a row of stitches, skip the stitch at the base of the turning chain and insert the hook into the stitch after that. When you pull your strand through, you'll have 6 loops on the hook. Work off 2 loops at a time in the same way you do for shorter stitches, until you have only 1 loop left on the hook. Triple triple crochet stitch made.

This could go on forever and, in fact, it does, with stitches such as double triple triple and quadruple triple triple. But we're not gonna get into those here, 'cause they're just too crazy!

YOU SAY TOMATO

STITCH NAMES IN THE U.K.

It's been said that Americans and Brits are two people separated by a common language, and that's doubly true for American and British crocheters. Perhaps it's a leftover from the days of the American Revolution, when folks on this side of the pond wanted to do anything they could to distinguish themselves from those on the other side. But whatever the reason, British crochet stitches, though made exactly the same as American ones, have confusingly similar names that mean very different things. Keep this in mind if you find yourself in possession of a British crochet pattern or book.

And just so you know, some American crochet books call triple crochet "Treble" crochet and double triple "Double Treble." Go figure.

AMERICAN NAME	BRITISH NAME
Slip Stitch (sl st)	Single Crochet (sc)
Single Crochet (sc)	Double Crochet (dc)
Half-Double Crochet (hdc)	Half Treble (htr)
Double Crochet (dc)	Treble (tr)
Triple Crochet (tr)	Double Treble (dtr)
Double Triple Crochet (dtr)	Treble Treble (trtr)

coming to the end of your rope

How to Add Yarn

Now that you're a crocheting demon, one day you're going to come to the end of your yarn. And when you do, you're gonna want to know how to continue crocheting with a new ball of yarn, so you can keep on keepin' on. That's not the only reason you'd want to add new yarn, however: If you ever want to use more than one color (and who wouldn't?) in a crochet project, you'll need to know how to stop working with one ball of yarn and start working with another.

The good news is that you can start working with a new ball of yarn anywhere in your work (although, if you're making stripes, you'll want to do it at the end of a row). To add a new ball of yarn, work a stitch until you have only 2 loops left on your hook. Now, grab the old yarn and about a 6-inch tail of the new yarn in the bottom three fingers of your right hand (the hand that is holding the hook). Wrap the new yarn over your left-hand fingers as usual, grab the strand with your crochet hook, and pull it through those two loops you have on your hook, thereby completing the stitch (see figure). Make a few more stitches, then stop for a moment and pull on the tail of the old yarn to tighten the last loop around the new yarn. Make a square knot with the tails of the old and new yarn, and carry on. Later, you can go back and weave those tail ends into your work. And remember, if you're doing stripes, you'll want to add the new yarn while you're making the last stitch in the previous row, so that the turning chain of the new row will be made with the new color.

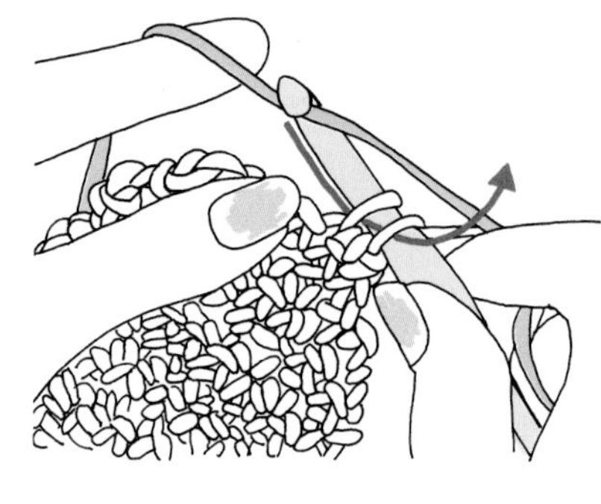

Sometimes you have to add new yarn after you've already bound off the old yarn. That's easy, too. Just start with a slipknot on your hook, leaving about a 6-inch tail, insert the hook into your work where the crocheting is supposed to start, and get a move on. You can hold the tail in the bottom 3 fingers of your right hand to keep it out of your way when you're starting, and hold the rest of the yarn in your left hand as usual.

Abbreviation Nation

Understanding Crochet Directions

In the last two chapters, you've learned all the basic stitches you'll ever need to know in crochet. You may have noticed that, as each stitch was introduced, a few letters followed, and you may have wondered what the heck they were doing there. Well, I'm here to tell you. Those were simply the abbreviations for these most commonly used crochet stitches. They're used to save space in crochet patterns and keep them from taking up as many pages as the *American Heritage Dictionary.* Thus, encountering a "dc" in your pattern has nothing to do with our nation's great capital, but instead directs you to make a double crochet stitch. Likewise, the seemingly mysterious "ch-1 sp" means "chain-1 space." To the uninformed, a crochet pattern may look like a confusing bowl of alphabet soup, but to those in the know, it is as clear as the n on your f. Each time a new stitch is introduced in this book, it will be followed by its abbreviation. For a list of abbrevs, see page 95.

5

the shape of things to come

INCREASING, DECREASING, AND WORKING IN A CIRCLE

Making rectangular pieces of fabric using those lovely, long crochet stitches can be a breeze, but eventually you'll need to depart from the straight and narrow. You'll have to make things that grow narrower at the top than they are at the bottom—a hat that fits the shape of your head, for instance. You'll want to make things that grow wider at the top, such as a sleeve for an awesome sweater. And you'll want to crochet things into other shapes, too, such as flowers, circles, squares, or scoop out a hole for a neck or take a bite out of the side of a sweater so that a sleeve can get sewn in there.

Luckily, crochet is a very kindly craft (except for that first dang row), and the methods for increasing or decreasing stitches are logical and straightforward.

And once you experience the magic of crocheting a beautiful flat circle (and learning the math behind it), you will be even more impressed with crochet's amazing versatility. In fact, it is crochet's ability to sculpt shapes with stitches that is, I think, one of its most impressive qualities.

increase the piece

Adding Stitches

Adding new stitches in a row is so nice, you'll wanna do it twice. **To add an extra stitch anywhere along the length of your piece,** just make two stitches into the same stitch. If you need to increase only one stitch in a row, you'll definitely want to make it in the center of your work. Often, though, you'll want to increase one stitch at each edge of your work (beginning and end), so that the piece grows evenly wider on both sides like an upside-down triangle. For single crochet and half-double crochet, just make two stitches into the first and last stitches of the row.

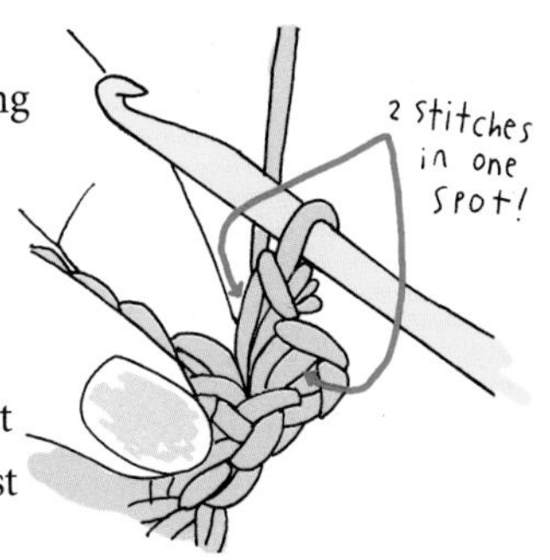

For double crochet and all taller stitches, remember you have that stitch at the base of the turning chain that you always skip? How handy! Just crochet into that stitch instead of skipping it and voilà! You'll get an extra stitch at the beginning of the row. Of course, at the end of the row you'll still need to make two stitches into the turning chain of the previous row, instead of only one. No pain—yet gain!

When you need **to increase more than one stitch at the beginning of a row,** you can add extra chains on to your turning chain, then crochet into those chains. Remember that if you're adding to a double crochet or taller, you'll already be making a stitch into that first stitch (instead of skipping it). So if you want to add 5 stitches at the end of a piece of double crochet, crochet 7 chains before turning around (4 extra chains plus 3 turning chains), stitch into the 4th, 5th, 6th, and 7th stitches from the hook (adds 4 new stitches plus the 3 chains that form the turning chain).

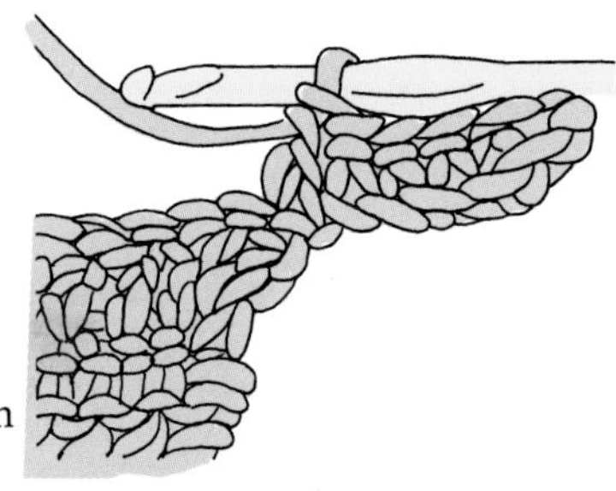

Now make a stitch in the first stitch. You've got 5 more stitches than you started out with.

To increase more than one stitch at the end of a row, things are a bit trickier, but still manageable. Just make each extra stitch into the outermost, lowermost loop of the last stitch of the row.

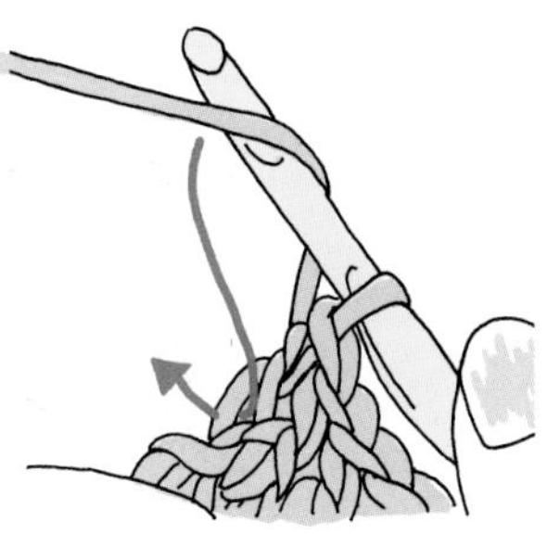

Do the same into this new stitch—make a stitch into its outermost, lowermost loop. These stitches won't be quite as tall as the other stitches in the row, but after you've completed your piece and blocked it, it should all even out.

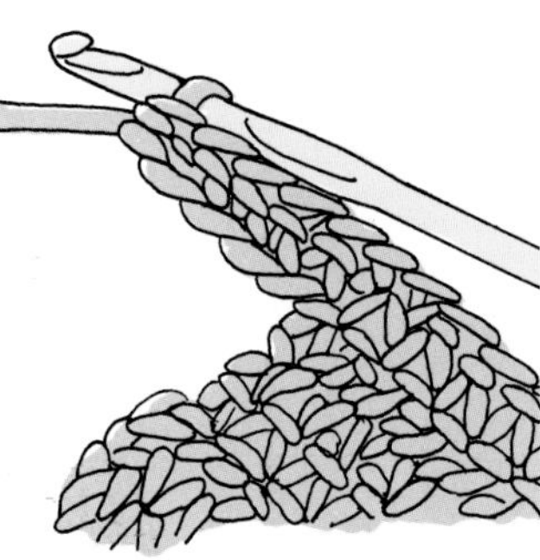

When Less is More

Decreasing Stitches

Decreasing in crochet is just as simple as increasing, if a bit tougher to explain. The idea is the same, however: To decrease a stitch, you'll make 1 stitch in the space where 2 would usually be. To do that, you'll start by making a stitch but leaving out the very last step (where you end up with only 1 loop on your hook). In other words, you'll start the next stitch with 2 loops on your shaft. When you get to the last step of the decrease stitch, you'll pull the yarn through *all* the loops (or more) on the hook, making 1 stitch out of 2.

To help you see this decrease in action, here are the directions for the most common stitches: single, half-double, double, and triple. Try them out for size. I bet you'll soon realize that you'll never need to look back at these directions again—decreasing is a breeze.

Single Crochet Decrease

1. Insert your hook into the next stitch, pull the strand through (2 loops on hook). Now *don't* hook the yarn and pull it through these 2 loops (which would be your last step). Instead, insert your hook into the next stitch and pull the strand through. You've got 3 loops on your hook.

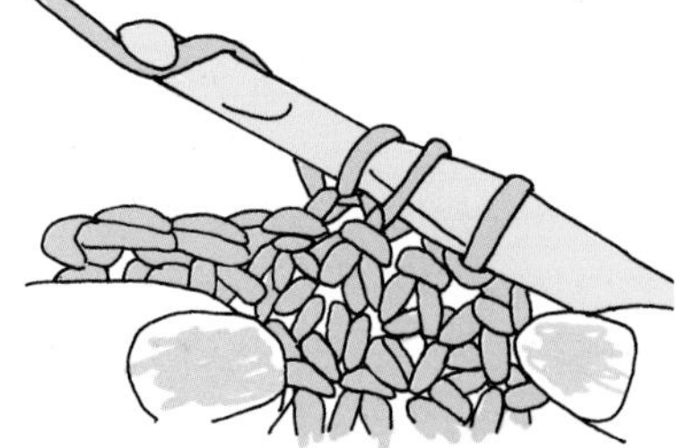

2. Next, pull the strand through all 3 loops. Hallelujah! Decrease done!

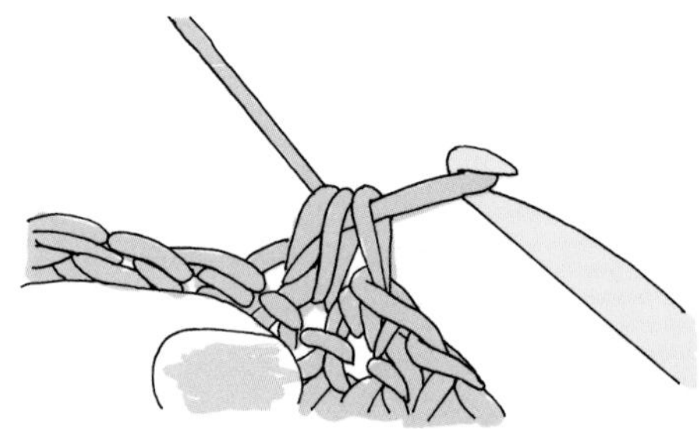

Half-Double Crochet Decrease

This one gets a bit bulky, but it can be done.

1. Wind your yarn over your hook as usual, insert your hook into the next stitch, and pull through a loop (half-double made but not finished, 3 loops on hook). Don't wrap the yarn and pull through these loops; instead, hook the yarn, insert your hook into the next stitch, then pull the strand through. Now you've got 5 loops on your hook. Yipes!

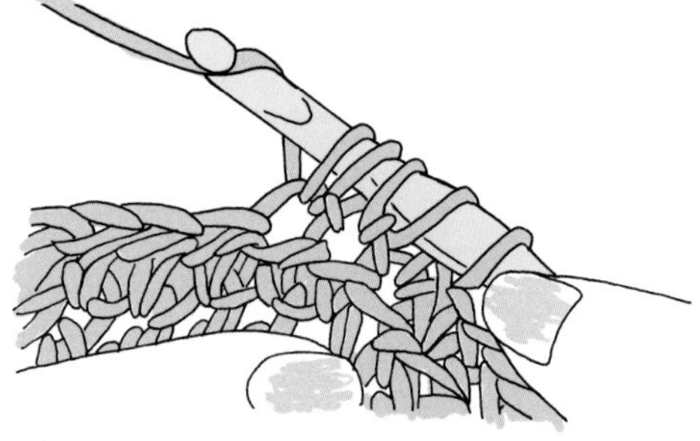

2. To finish, just hook your yarn and pull it through all the loops. You've decreased!

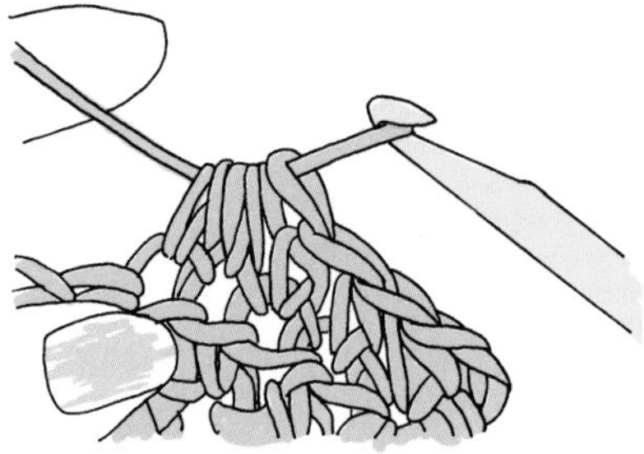

Double Crochet Decrease

1. Start by hooking your yarn as usual, inserting your hook through the next stitch, and pulling up a loop (3 loops on hook). Wind your yarn again and pull it through 2 of the loops, the way you normally would. Now, begin another double crochet stitch instead of finishing the first one: Hook your yarn, insert the hook into the next stitch, and grab the strand and pull it through (4 loops on hook). Yarn over and pull the strand through 2 of those loops (3 loops on hook). You've done all but the last step of that second double crochet stitch.

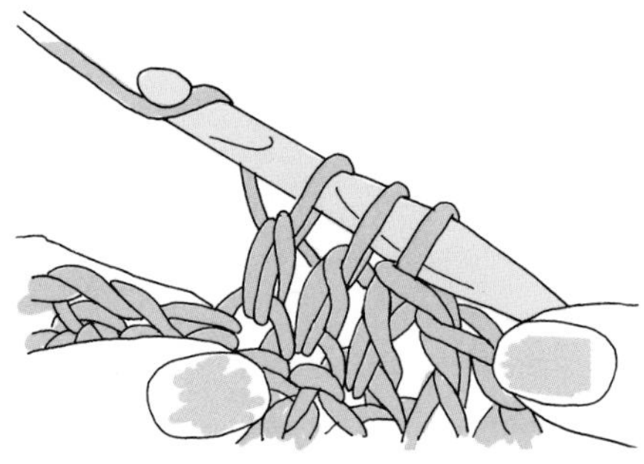

2. For your last step, hook your yarn and pull it through all 3 loops on the hook. You see? You just combined the last step for 2 stitches, thereby turning them into 1. It's a beautiful thing.

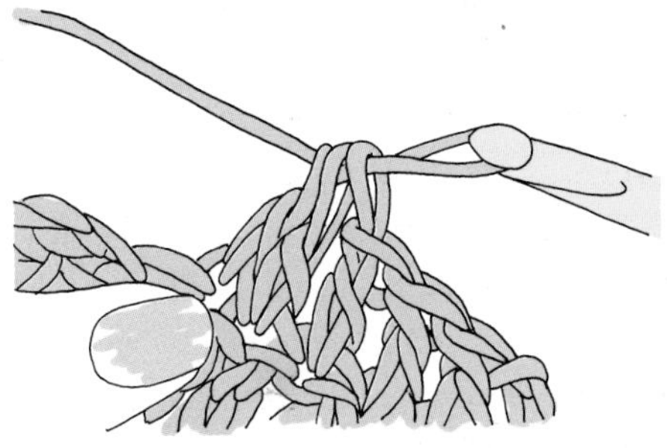

Triple Crochet Decrease

Same old story. Work a triple crochet until you have 2 loops on the hook, then start your next triple crochet. Twirl your hook around the yarn twice, insert the hook into the next stitch, and pull up a loop (5 loops on hook). Continue with your triple crochet, drawing yarn through 2 loops at a time until you have 3 loops on the hook. Now pull the yarn through all 3 loops. Decreasing deed done.

Ménage à trois

Decreasing More than One Stitch at a Time

Now that you see how the decrease is done, you can also imagine how you might decrease more than 1 stitch at a time: Simply complete each of 3 (or more) stitches up to the step just before the last, then knock them all off at once in a single clever pull-the-yarn-through-all-the-loops maneuver.

Decreasing at the Edges

Just as with increases, sometimes you want to abruptly decrease stitches on either side of your work to create a 90-degree angle. You'll be happy to know that, in crochet, this couldn't be easier.

To decrease stitches at the beginning of a row, just make a slip stitch over each stitch to be decreased. This will get your hook over to the left a few stitches without adding any height to your work. Of course, when you start crocheting again, you'll need to make the necessary turning chain.

To decrease stitches at the end of the row, just don't crochet them! If you want to make 3 fewer stitches at the end of the row, stop making stitches when you're 3 stitches from the end. That's all! Ain't crocheting grand?

What Goes Around Comes Around

Crocheting a Circle

Now that you can increase, you're ready to try one of the coolest things that crochet can do: work in a circle. Since crocheting is worked one stitch at a time, you aren't limited to making rows of stitches—you can crochet up, down, back, forth, and you can go around and around. Of course, if you just keep crocheting in a circle, stacking rows on top of rows, you'll end up with a tube of stitches. But if you increase stitches on each round, you can make something even more exciting: a flat circle. Here's how to make a nice flat circle using double crochet stitches.

1. Start by making a chain of 6 stitches. Then form a ring with the chain by making a slip stitch into the first chain.

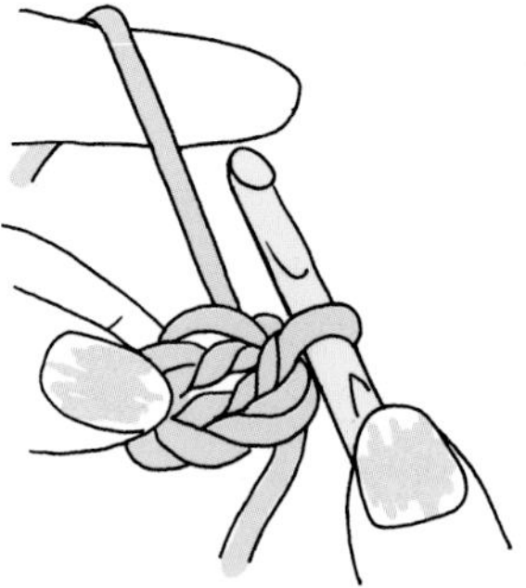

2. Next, make a chain of 3 stitches (your turning chain), and make 11 double crochet stitches into the center hole of the ring (instead of into the chain stitches themselves). Crocheting directly into the ring is fun—and you don't have to insert your hook into those dastardly chains. Push the stitches back on the ring a bit if they start getting crowded. Your double crochet stitches should pretty much cover up the chain ring.

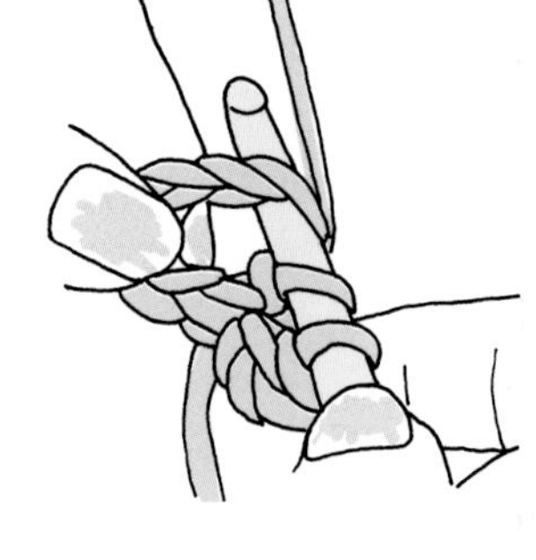

3. After your 11 double crochet stitches, make a slip stitch into the top (3rd chain stitch) of the turning chain that you already made. Voilà, a 12-stitch circle (remember, the 3-chain turning chain forms the first stitch of the new round).

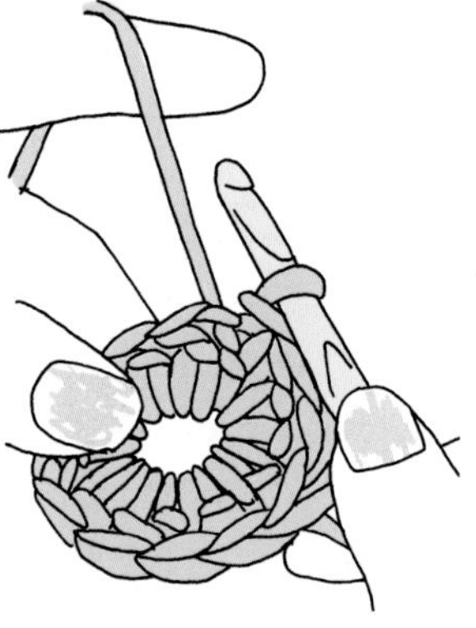

Now you're ready to make a second round of stitches. Of course, if this next row is going to lie flat (and thus make a wider circle) you will have to increase stitches. And guess what—you already know how 'cause you just did it. The rule of thumb for increasing stitches in a circle, to make it lie nice and flat, is that each row should increase by the number of stitches you made into the ring. For us, that means that each round should increase by 12 stitches.

So for row 2, we are going to go from making 12 stitches around to making 24 stitches around. How to do it? Just crochet 2 new stitches into each existing stitch. Start by making your turning chain of 3 stitches (this becomes stitch #1), and make a double crochet into the stitch at the base of your turning chain (this is stitch #2). Now, into the top of each of the remaining 11 double crochet stitches around the circle, you will double crochet twice. When you get back to the turning chain, make a slip stitch into the top of it.

On the third round, you'll want to add another 12 stitches again, increasing 24 stitches to 36. The way to do that is to increase by one stitch in every *second* stitch, instead of in every stitch as you did on the second row. This means you'll make your turning chain of 3 stitches, then make 2 double crochet stitches into the next stitch. Make 1 double crochet in the stitch after that, and 2 double crochet stitches in the one after that. You should end by making 2 double crochet stitches in the last stitch before the turning chain. Slip stitch into the turning chain to complete the round.

Ready for another round? Here you're going from 36 stitches to 48 stitches—increasing your stitches by 12 again. To do it, you'll increase once every 3 stitches. So, make your turning chain, crochet a stitch into the stitch after that, then make 2 double crochets into the stitch after that.

As you do this, you should be creating a circle that lies quite flat. To make it bigger and bigger, just follow the same pattern: For each circle, add 1 to the number of stitches between your increases. So, on the next round, you'd increase once every 4 stitches by crocheting a single stitch into each of 3 stitches, then 2 stitches into the 4th stitch. And so on.

What happens if your circle won't lie flat? What do you do if it starts to curl in and look like a yarmulke, meaning that the circle isn't quite wide enough on each round. Or what if the circle begins getting a bit ruffly around the edges, meaning that there are too many stitches to the round? Well, here's what you do: You simply adjust your circle as you go, making a few more stitches (to fix the yarmulke situation), or a few less stitches (to correct the ruffle). Once again, remind yourself that there are no crochet police around. Your goal is not to obey the rules of crocheting a flat circle given here; your goal is to make a flat circle.

Hole Lotta Nothing

Making a Circle with a Smaller Hole

If you take a look at the flat circle you've been making, you might be able to imagine that, if you were indeed looking for a yarmulke effect or even a full-fledged hat, you'd create it by crocheting around and around and simply increasing only enough stitches each row to make the cup- or caplike shape that you were trying to achieve. But there's one small problem: There is a hole in the center of this circle, where you crocheted all those stitches into the ring. In most instances (unless you want to pull a ponytail through the top), you would want to decrease the effect and make the hole as small as possible.

There are two ways to do this, and each involves beginning your circle in a slightly different manner.

For the easier method, you don't make a chain ring at all. Instead, you start making all of the stitches into your very first chain stitch—the one coming out of the slipknot. So, for instance, to start a circle of double crochet stitches, chain 4 stitches (3 for the turning chain and one for the center of the circle). Double crochet into the fourth chain from the hook, and then continue to make double crochet stitches into that same chain until you have a nice circle of double crochet stitches. This will make for a very small hole in the center of your circle.

The second method, also called the "adjustable" or magic ring method, is a bit harder, but it yields almost no hole at all. It's a little awkward at first, but the results are so cool that you'll be more than willing to deal with it. Instead of crocheting into a ring of stitches or even into a single stitch, as you just learned, you'll be crocheting into a loop of yarn—not *even* a real stitch—which, when you're done, can be made to—poof!—disappear.

1. Start by making a circle with about 6 inches of the tail of yarn. Make the circle so that the tail crosses behind and to the right of the ball end of your yarn, and hold onto this circle at the point where it crosses with your right hand. Now lace the yarn over your left hand the way you normally would for crocheting (the weirdness starts here already, since usually that tail is attached by a slipknot to your hook, instead of just being held in a loop by your right hand).

2. Transfer the tail loop from your right hand to the left hand, making sure that the tail stays behind the working yarn. Hold it closed at the point where it crosses, using the thumb and middle (or ring) fingers of your left hand. Essentially, the most awkward part of this procedure is done, and you are ready to go on to the cool part.

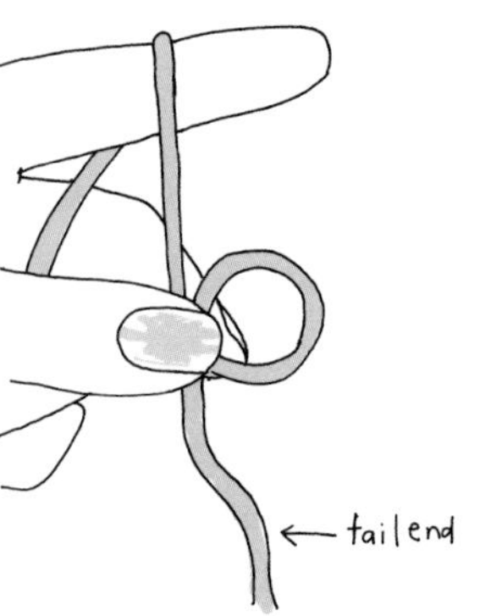

3. Take your hook in your right hand as usual, insert it into the center of the loop, grab the working strand of yarn, and pull it through to the front.

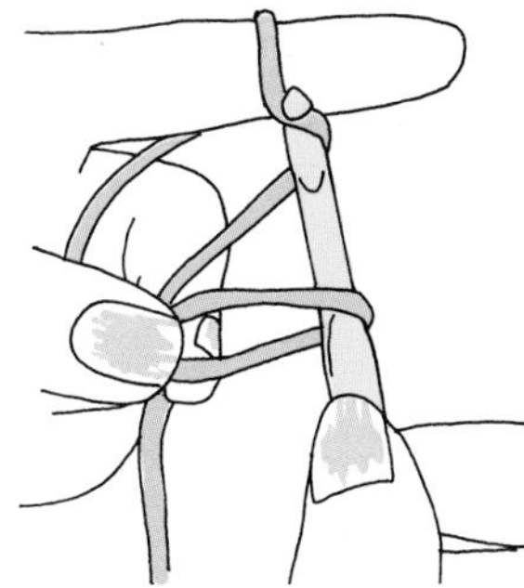

4. Now you are going to make the correct number of turning chains for whatever stitch you want in that first ring—here, lets try a ring of single crochet stitches, so go ahead and chain 1. After that, start making single crochet stitches into the ring, working right over the tail. If your work becomes unwieldly, you can close up the ring a bit by transferring the loop back to your right hand, pulling on the tail to close it a bit, then transferring it back and continuing on.

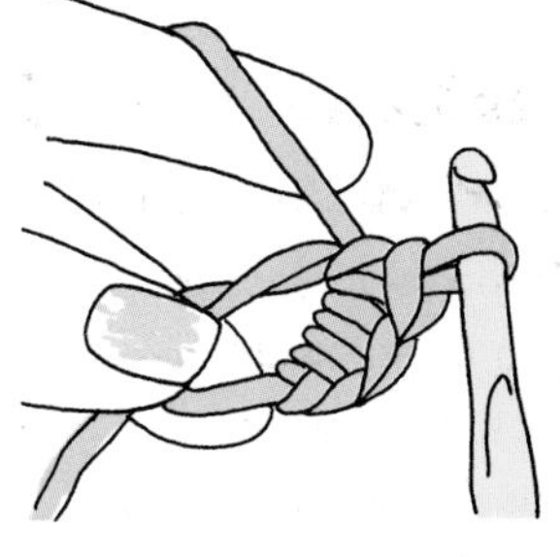

Continue making the number of single crochet stitches you need in the ring—for this example, 8 stitches are enough—and then, before closing the single crochets with a slip stitch, hold onto the ring while pulling on the tail so that the center hole closes up. Say "abracadabra" and watch as that hole just disappears. Love it!

6

Hooked on a feeling

MAKING FANCY STITCHES

Now that you know the basic crochet stitches and how to increase and decrease them across a row, it's time to pull out all the stops and see what crochet can *really* do. It's through the combination of these simple skills that you can whip out gorgeous, airy lace patterns. I realize that admitting this might make the other stitches in this book jealous, but I ain't gonna lie: It's these lacy crochet stitches that had me at "hello." And after you see how easy it is to knock them out yourself, you'll be smitten, too. But making open lacy fabric isn't the only impressive, fancy-pants stuff that crochet can do: In this chapter, you'll also learn how to create interesting, textured fabric with your hook. And as if that weren't enough, we'll even take these open stitches around in a circle so that you can make that most famous (or infamous, depending on your perspective) of crochet creations: the Granny Square.

chart toppers

How to Read a Crochet Chart

In this chapter, the stitches you've learned so far—chain stitch, single crochet, slip stitch, half-double, double, double triple, and even triple triple—are combined to create interesting laces and texures. In most pattern directions, these stitches will be abbreviated in rather clear ways: Chain becomes simply "ch" and single crochet becomes "sc." But there is another way to communicate the directions for how to crochet a piece of fabric or a certain stitch, and that is to use crochet symbols. Each stitch has its own symbol, and, personally, I often find it way clearer to understand what I'm doing by following the symbol charts than by reading the abbreviated directions—symbols let you really visualize what you're doing in a way that having written-out instructions simply won't. Plus, they're international—so you can read patterns no matter what language they're written in (even British English!).

At right is a diagram for a swatch that starts out with 11 chain stitches and is followed by a row of single crochet, 1 row of half-double crochet, 1 row of double crochet, 1 row of triple crochet, and another row of single crochet. You can see that each chain stitch is represented by a small oval; each single crochet is a small "X" sign; each half-double crochet is a "T"; each double is a "T" with a line through it; and each triple is a "T" with two lines through it (the lines sort of represent the number of times you wind the yarn over the hook before making the stitch). The chart is read from bottom to top, and from right to left for the first row (after the base chain), from left to right for the second row, and then from right to left again. Even the turning chains are clearly represented in the chart. Isn't it nice? For a chart of all of the symbols used in this book, turn to page 95.

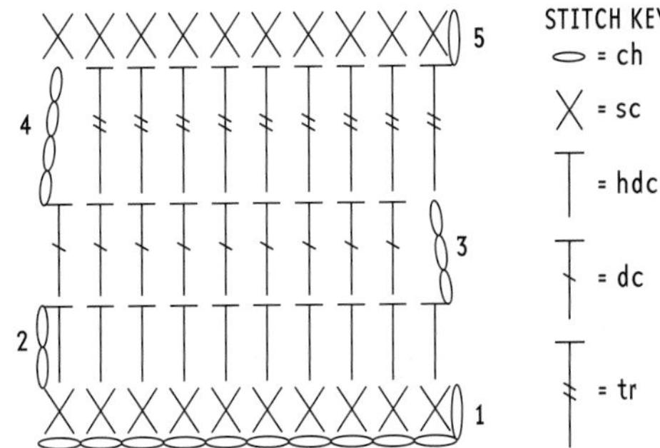

WHICH STITCH IS WHICH?

When working complicated stitch patterns, especially those made with taller stitches, figuring out which stitch you are supposed to work next can get a little confusing. Which V goes with which stitch? Or, to bring up an earlier analogy, which lid goes to which cup? The best thing to do, in such instances, is not to look at the posts, or "cups," of the stitches at all. Instead, look at the Vs lying across the top of the row and count these to figure out where you are supposed to insert your hook. They'll prove to be more reliable landmarks than the stitches themselves, which can get stretched out and distorted when they're part of an intricate stitch pattern. In the shell pattern that follows, for instance, when making your single crochet, you might want to insert your hook into the 3rd V from where you made your group of 5 double crochets. That will give you accurate results, even if you aren't quite sure about where the top of the third double crochet is.

V is for Victory

The V Stitch

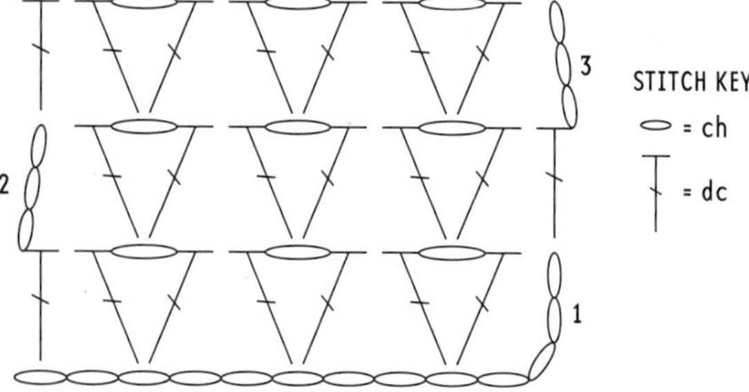

If you remember, crochet began life as a way to re-create fancy (and expensive) lace. So it should come as no surprise that it is an ideal way to make open lacy textures. The V stitch is one of the simplest ways to accomplish this, and it's a great introduction to how lace is constructed in crochet.

To begin, make a chain that is a multiple of 3, plus an additional 4 chains for the edge. For a nice-size test swatch, let's start with 34 (30 + 4) chains. Make a double crochet in the 5th chain from the hook. Chain 1, and make a second double crochet into the *same stitch.* You've made 3 stitches—2 double crochets and a chain—in 1 stitch. Now skip the next two chains and make another V into the following chain the same way: 1 double crochet, 1 chain, and another double crochet stitch, all in the same chain. Skip the next two chains, and continue making these double crochet–chain–double crochet Vs until you have only 2 chain stitches left. Here you will skip the next chain and work only one double crochet into the last chain.

The next row is where the fun really picks up—here, you can not only say good-bye to inserting your hook into those annoying chain stitches, but you also won't have to worry about counting anymore. Start by making a 3-chain turning chain, then turn your work around. Now, you'll be making your next V into the chain-1 space that's in the center of the last V of the previous row. That's right—you won't be inserting your hook into the chain stitch itself, or into any other stitch, for that matter—but rather the friendly space that the chain stitch created between the two double crochet arms of your V stitch. So let's do it: Double crochet into the chain space (see figure below). Chain 1, then double crochet once more into the same space. Ah! Wasn't that just wonderful? And quick? Now you see why I love to crochet lace! Make a V into every chain space all the way across the row, and when you get to the end, make a double crochet into the top of the turning chain of the previous row. You're a V-stitch virtuoso!

Double-crocheting into the chain-1 space

Shell Game

Making Shell Stitches

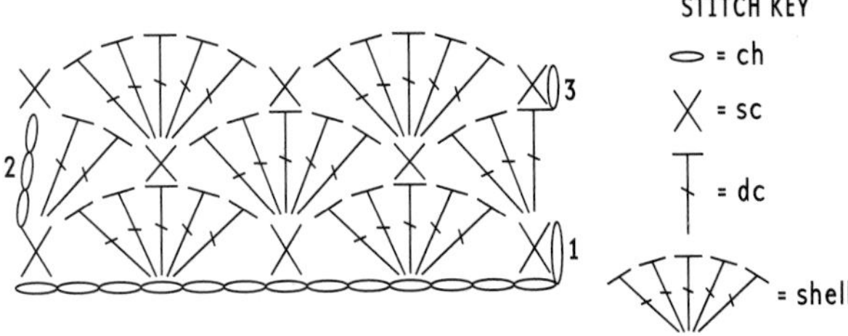

The V stitch is fun, but with shell stitches (also called "fan stitches"), crochet has the chance to really spread its wings. There are a number of shell stitch variations, but most involve making double crochet (or taller) stitches into a single space, then fanning those stitches out by tacking them down with a single crochet stitch on either side.

For the following basic shell stitch pattern, you'll start with a chain that's a multiple of 6 stitches plus 2. For this test swatch, chain (ch) 38 (36 + 2) stitches. Single crochet (sc) into the 2nd chain (ch) from the hook, then skip the next 2 chains (ch) and double crochet (dc) 5 times into the next chain (ch). Skip the next 2 chains (ch) and make a single crochet (sc) into the next chain (ch). Continue in this way—skip 2 chains, 5 double crochets into following chain, skip 2 chains, single crochet into following chain (sk 2 ch, 5 dc into foll ch, sk 2 ch, sc into foll ch)—all the way across the row. You should end with a single crochet (sc) into the last chain (ch).

For row 2, make a 3-ch turning chain, then dc twice into the last sc of the previous row. That turning chain (tch) and those two dc make a nice half-shell at the edge of your work. Make a sc into the top of the third dc of the next shell (it's the dc that's in the center of the shell), and then make 5 dc into the next sc. Continue this way (making a sc into the top of the center dc of the shell, then 5 dc into the next sc) all the way across the row until you get to the last sc. Make 3 dc into the last sc for another half-shell on this end.

For row 3, ch 1, then sc into the first dc of the previous row. Skip (sk) the next 2 dc and make 5 dc into the next sc; sk the next 2 dc and sc into the top of the next dc (the center dc of the shell). Repeat this across the row (sk the next 2 dc, 5 dc into the next sc, sk the next dc, sc into the top of the next dc), until you get to the end of the row, where you'll make a sc into the top of the turning ch of the previous row.

Repeat the last 2 rows to make as much fabric as you want with the shell stitch.

As pretty as this stitch is with just a single color, you can get really exquisite results doing rows in two or three alternating colors. There are also beautiful variations of shell stitches that incorporate V-like stitches, chain spaces, and stacking the fans on top of each other, resulting in a more open fabric, as well as other nifty tricks that can make the fan effect even more elaborate. I ain't gonna front: I love this stitch.

ALL togetHer Now
Making Bobble, Puff, and Popcorn Stitches

The stitch patterns you've tried so far used increasing stitches into a single stitch to create an open fabric. The following stitches use a similar technique, paired with decreases, to result not in lacy or spread-out stitches but in a variety of textured, three-dimensional stitches that are just begging to be used in projects that could benefit from such touchy-feely interest, such as hats or bags. Let's meet them.

bobbLe HeAds
Making the Bobble Stitch

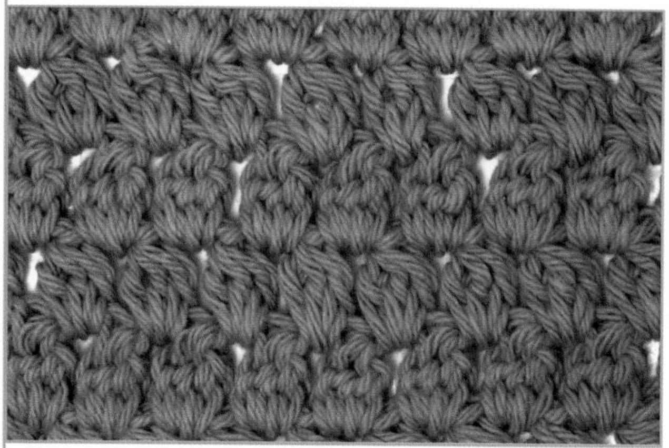

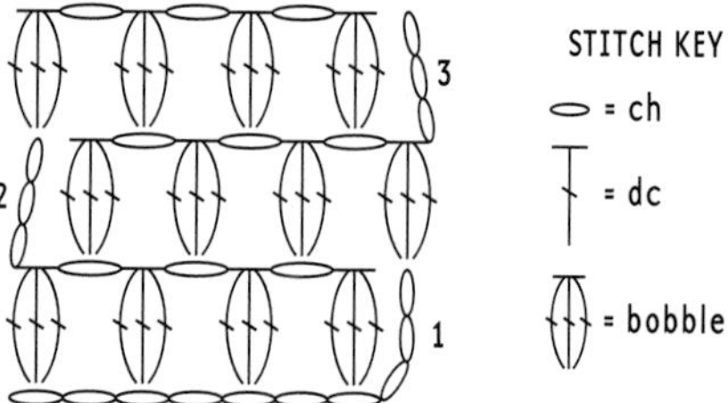

To make this stitch, you'll make 3 double crochet stitches into the same stitch, completing all but the last step of each. Then, to pull them all together and make your bobble, you'll complete them together in a single step—similar to the way you decrease stitches.

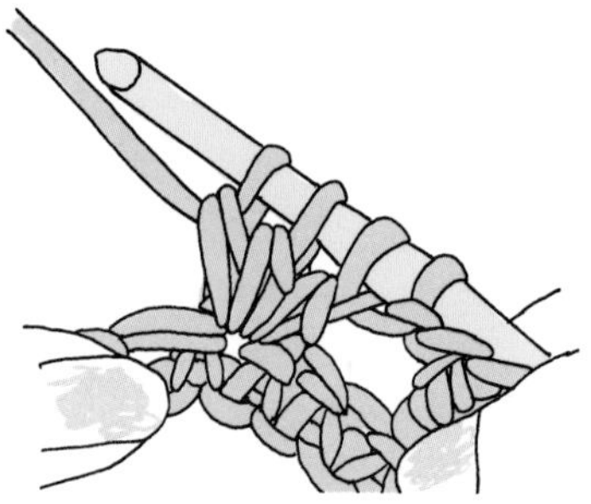

1. Start by making a double crochet stitch into your foundation chain or row and stopping before the last step, when you have 2 loops on your hook. Now, start making a second double crochet *into the same stitch*: Yarn over, insert your hook into the same stitch as before, yarn over and pull the strand through, yarn over and pull through 2 loops, and STOP. You have 3 loops on your hook. Make a third double crochet *into the same stitch,* without finishing it off, just as before, until you have 4 loops on your hook.

2. It's time to bring that bobble together: Simply yarn over and pull the strand through all 4 loops on your hook. Bobble stitch made.

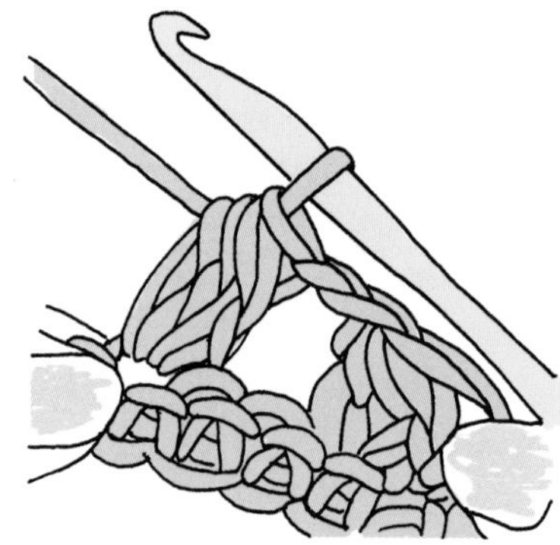

puff daddy

Making the Puff Stitch

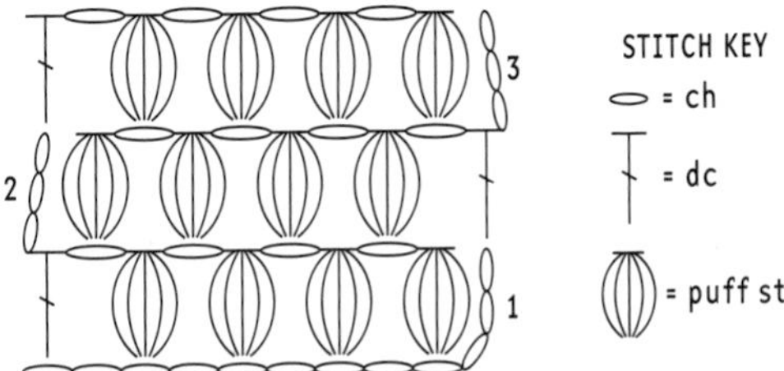

The puff stitch is similar to the bobble stitch, only it's, well, puffier. Here, you won't even make a series of true double crochet stitches; you're just gonna pull up a bunch of big ole loops that you'll pull together at the end. Since puff stitches are fat and bulky, they're often separated by a chain stitch or two, as shown here. To make a nice and puffy puff stitch, lets try it with 5 loops of this kind.

1. Yarn over and insert the hook into the next stitch, pull the strand through, and pull up a loop that's as tall as the stitches you crocheted before the puff stitch (about the height of a double crochet, most likely). You have 3 loops on your hook. Yarn over, insert the hook *into the same stitch,* pull the strand through, and pull up another large loop. You have 5 loops on the hook. Repeat the last step 3 more times (5 times altogether), and you should have 11 loops on your hook.

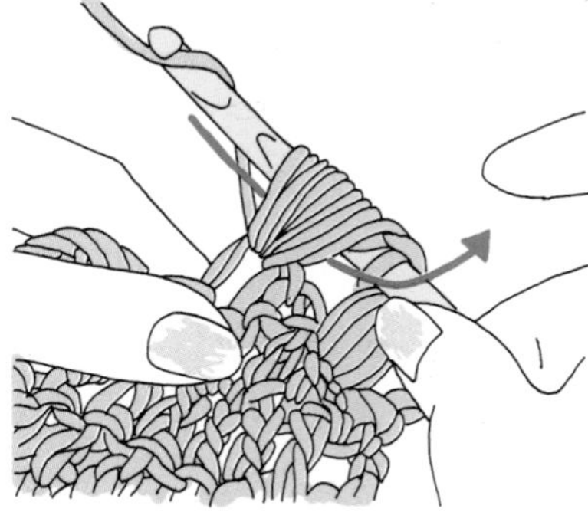

2. It's time to pull off this puff: Yarn over and draw the strand through all the loops on the hook, then close up the puff with a final chain stitch by yarning over and pulling the strand through the loop on your hook.

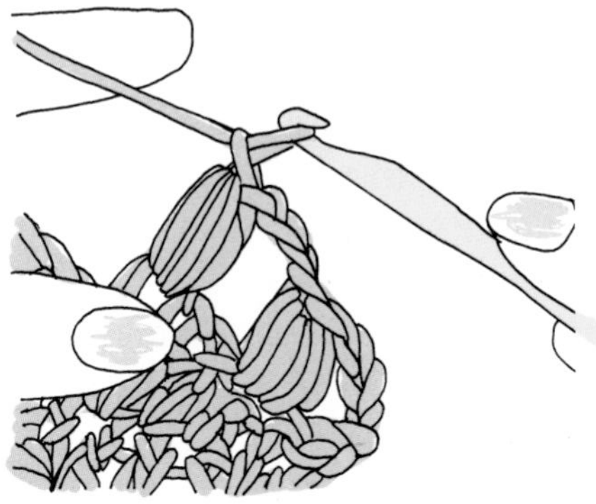

jiffy pop

Making the Popcorn Stitch

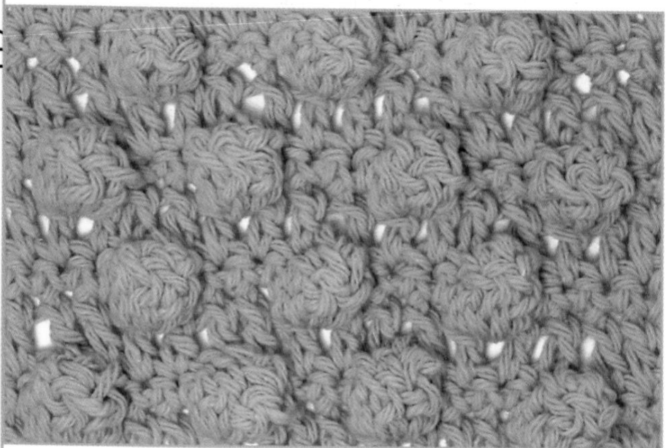

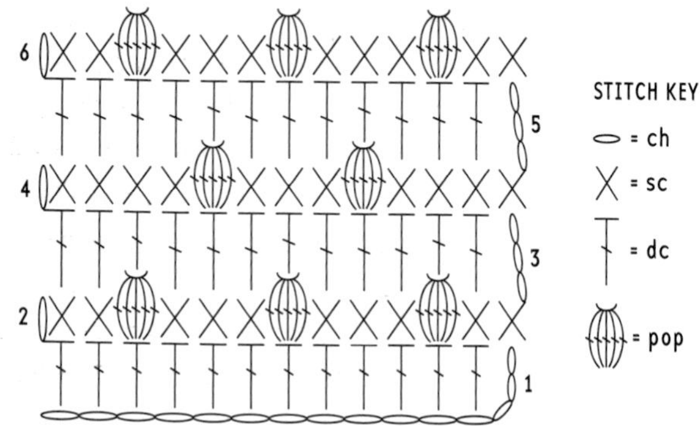

The popcorn stitch is another nice bumpy stitch. It starts out truly simple: Make a number of double crochet (or taller) stitches into the same stitch. It's in closing it off that things really start to pop. Popcorn stitches are so big and assertive that they're usually used sparingly, on a ground of single or double crochets (as in the swatch shown here). So c'mon, let's try one already.

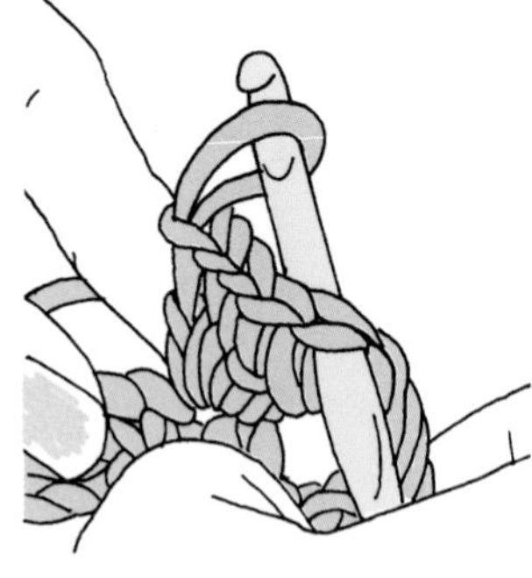

Make 5 complete double crochet stitches *into the next stitch*. Now, pull the loop you have on your hook up a bit so that it is longer than usual, and *remove your hook from the loop*. Don't be scared—it's only for a moment. Insert your hook into the top of the first of the double crochet stitches (the way you would if you were going to make a stitch in there) and grab that loose loop with the hook. Now just pull that loop through, gathering all 5 of the double crochet stitches into a nice little bump. Make a chain stitch to hold your popcorn together, and hold the butter.

LET ME COUNT THE WAYS

Making the Right Number of Chain Stitches

When it comes to making lacy stitches and just about any other crocheting project, it's crucial to start out with the right number of chain stitches. But counting chains as you're making them can be a pain, especially if you have to do a lot of them, and it's easy to lose track. One solution is to place split-stitches markers (see page 23) every 20 chains or so. But you also have another option: When you are making a long foundation chain for a piece, and you think you may have lost count, just make a few extra. That way you'll be certain to have the required number of chains to work your first row into, and you can simply pick loose and unravel any extra ones.

Mesh for Fantasy

Making the Mesh Stitch

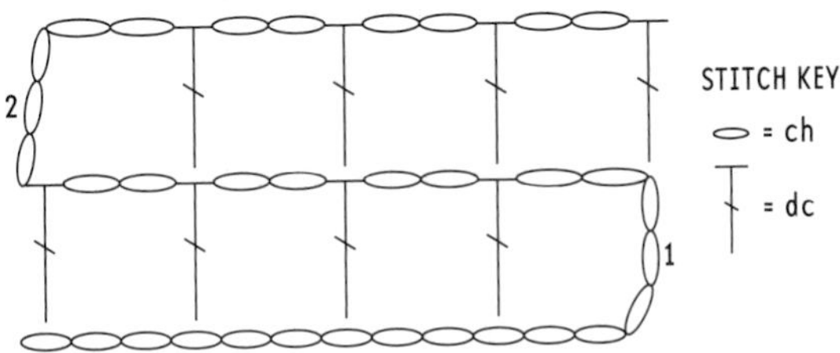

Here's the perfect stitch for crocheters with ADD. That's because the mesh stitch is just a little stitching and a whole lot of air, and with all that air, mesh fabric seems like it grows a mile a minute. To make it, you'll start with a multiple of 3 stitches plus 2. First, double crochet into the 8th stitch from the hook. Chain 2, skip 2 stitches, and double crochet into the next stitch. Carry on this way all the way across the row—chain 2, skip 2 chain stitches, double crochet into next chain (ch 2, sk 2 ch, dc in next ch)—until you get to the end of the row. You should end with a double crochet into the first chain of the foundation chain. Chain 5, turn, and double crochet into the top of the next dc stitch, followed by another ch 2 and a dc into the top of the next dc. This row and the rows that follow end with a double crochet into the top stitch of the turning chain of the previous row—it may be a bit tricky to find, so be sure to skip 2 chains, then make your dc.

What you get with the mesh stitch are large, open boxes, which can be taller, if you use a taller stitch, or wider, if you make more chain stitches and skip more stitches between stitches. Later on, you'll learn how to fill in certain squares in this open mesh to create images—a technique that's known as "filet crochet." For now, though, just revel in the speed and magnificence of the thing. Mesh stitch makes for a nice glam scarf when done in a bulky metallic yarn, or something far more goth when done in a fuzzy, wooly black. To make a scarf, just chain as many stitches as you want your scarf to be wide (in a multiple of 3), chain 5 more (3 for the turning chain and 2 for the top of the first box), and get to work. You'll have an impressive neck warmer completed before you know it.

Net Worth

Making the Fishnet Stitch

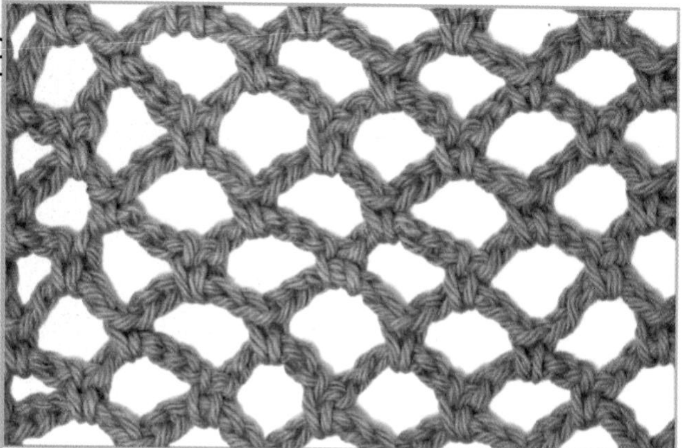

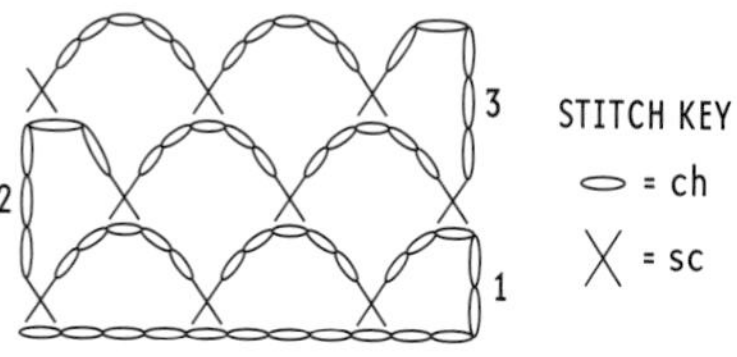

Here's another nice, fast-moving stitch that lets air do half the work of making your piece grow. To do it, chain up a multiple of 4 stitches. Make a single crochet into the 8th chain from the hook, make 5 more chains, skip 3 chains, and make a single crochet into the next chain. Continue this way across the row—chain 5, skip 3 stitches, single crochet into the next stitch—until you get to the end. You should finish the row with a single crochet. Chain 5 stitches and turn.

On the next row, make a single crochet stitch into that first big old chain space, chain 5 stitches, make a single crochet into the next chain space, and carry on till the last chain space, where you'll make a single crochet. Chain 5, turn your work, and head on back again the same way. Really, once you start this one, you'll find it difficult to stop.

Picot Suave

Making the Picot Stitch

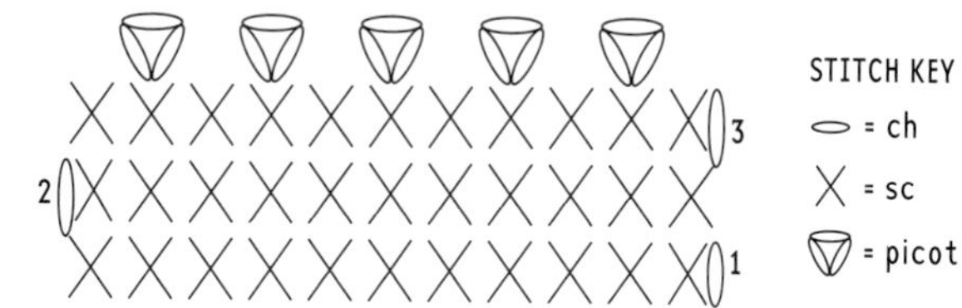

Here's a stitch that can make a pretty bumpy edging along a piece. But remember, it is an edging, done only at the very end of the piece, or sometimes even added on to a completed piece: You won't crochet any more stitches on top of a picot row. There are many ways to make it, but this is the way I like best:

Make a single crochet stitch, then chain 3 (or more) stitches, then double back and insert the hook smack into the middle of the top of the initial single crochet stitch, as well as through the middle of the "legs" of that stitch, and make a slip stitch to fix your picot in place. This is easier done than said, so take a look at the illustration to see what I mean.

Continue making single crochet stitches on down the line, making a picot every 2 or 3 stitches. Now stand back and admire your ba-dump-ba-dump-bump.

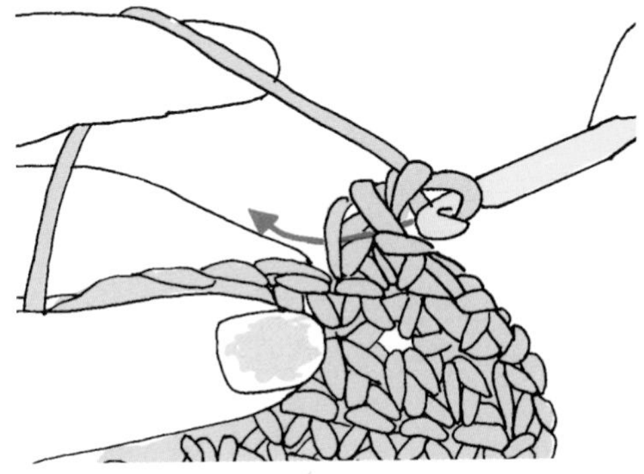

playing hooky

Inserting Your Hook in Other Locations

So far, when crocheting into a row, you've always either inserted your hook under the top two strands of the V, into a space between stitches, or under chains. You can create interesting textures in crochet by putting your hook into still other places, as you'll see in the examples below.

back stabber

Making Ribbing with Crochet

Single crochet, as you know, makes a very flat, smooth, and nonstretchy fabric. You can make a more textured, looser, and stretchier fabric, with raised ridges across it, by inserting your hook under only the back strand of the

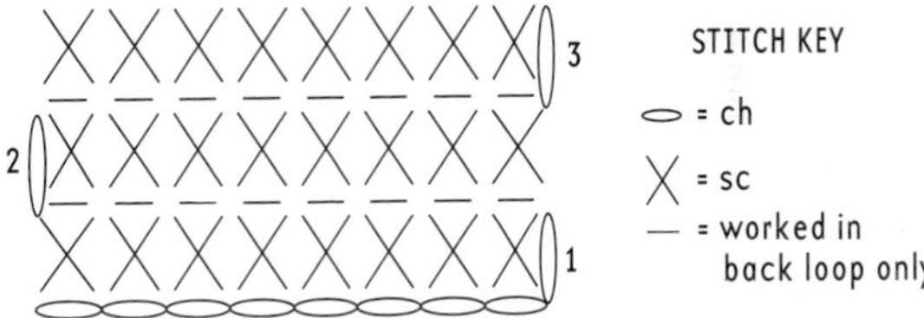

V at the top of each stitch—the strand farthest away from you. (You'd get a similar result by crocheting only into the front strand of each V.) This stitch is called a rib, and it is sometimes used, sideways, for the cuffs at the bottoms of sleeves and sweaters. It also makes fabric that's somewhat stretchier than regular single crochet. Crocheting through the back loop leaves a nice little ridge on the front of your work, while crocheting through the front loop leaves a ridge on the back.

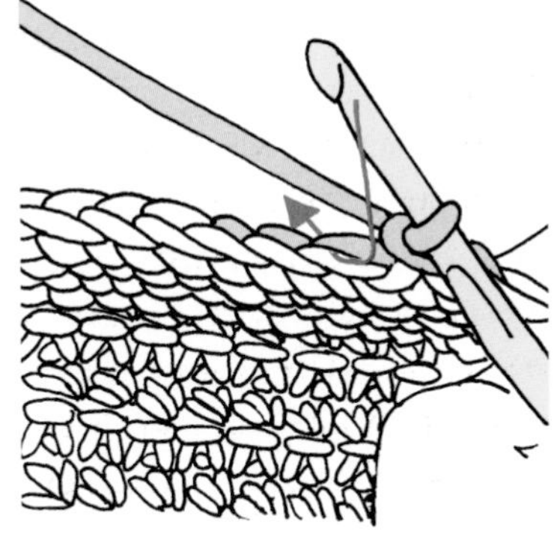

post modern

Crocheting Around the Post

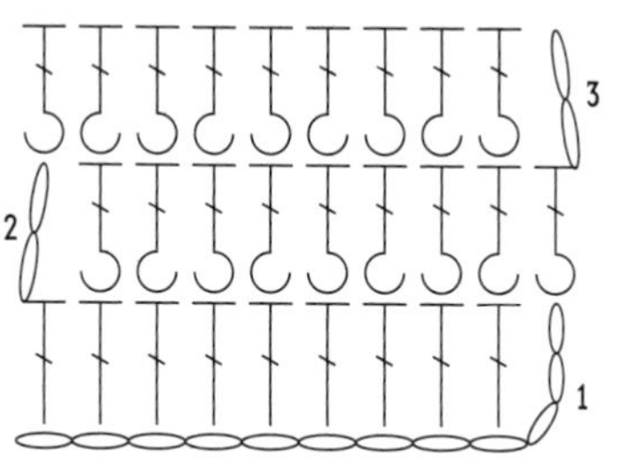

Here's another nice way to create a raised texture on crocheted fabric. It's usually done with double crochet, but it can also be done with taller stitches. There are two ways to make this stitch: around the front or around the back of the post (the section below the V of a double or taller stitch).

Going around the front creates a raised stitch on the side of the work that is facing you (the front); going around the back creates the raised stitch on the side of the work that is facing away from you (the back). If you're working back and forth in rows and you want to have all your raised stitches on the same side of your fabric, as in the swatch shown here, you'll need to know how to do both.

When you're working around the post, you aren't really making your stitch any differently—you just aren't making it into the top of the next stitch, as you usually do. Instead, you are making it around the body of the stitch, which, on a tall stitch, is long and thin, like a stick—or a post. To try it out, begin with a row of double crochet stitches, made in the usual way.

To work around the front of the post

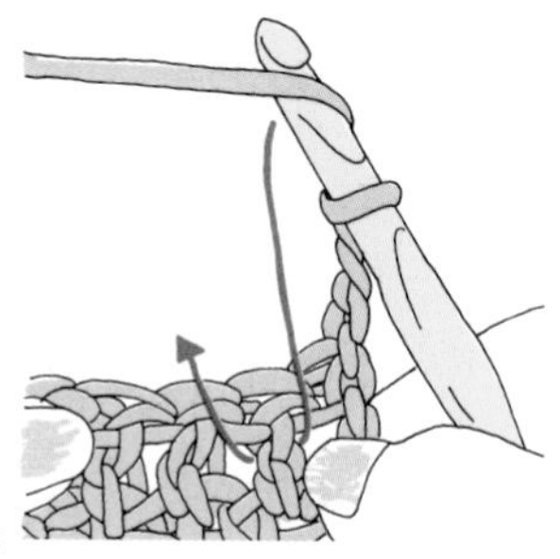

Twirl your hook around the working yarn as usual, then stick your hook into the space to the right of the double crochet in the row below instead of into its V. Then return to the front through the space to the left of that stitch. You've kind of woven your hook around the back of the double crochet stitch, and the post is **in front** of your hook. Grab the strand of working yarn and pull it all the way through with your hook, guiding the yarn behind the post of the double crochet.

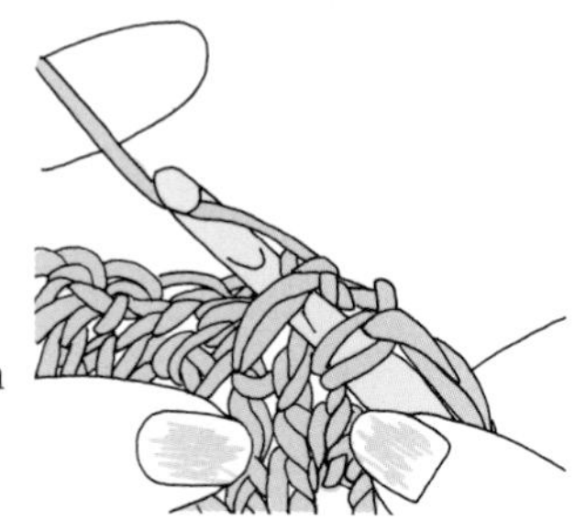

Complete your current stitch the regular way (yarn over, pull strand through 2 loops on hook, yarn over, pull strand through last 2 loops on hook). This is called a front post double crochet (FPdc).

To work around the back of the post

Hook your yarn in the usual way and move the hook to the backside of your work. Push it to the front through the space to the right of the double crochet post in the row below, guide it around the double crochet, and push it to the back through the space to the left of that stitch. You've kind of woven your hook around the front of the stitch, and the stitch is **behind** your hook. Grab the strand of yarn and pull it all the way through with your hook (the strand will lie across the front of the double crochet's post), and complete the stitch the regular way (yarn over, pull strand through 2 loops on hook, yarn over, pull strand through last 2 loops on hook).This is known as a back post double crochet (BPdc).

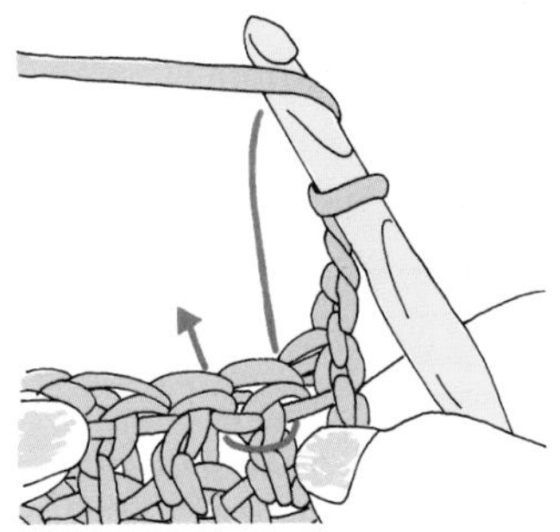

X Marks the Spot

Making the Crossed Stitch

Usually when you crochet, you work in only one direction: from right to left. You work a stitch, and then the stitch to the left of it, all the way across your row (or around your round). But you can make really nice-looking X stitches in your work by going back a stitch or three instead of forward. These X stitches need a pair of legs—if only to have something to cross—and so they are made only with double crochet or taller stitches. To make one, try this: Skip 3 stitches, and double crochet in the next stitch. Chain 1, then double crochet *into the second skipped stitch.* To do this, whip your hook around the yarn as usual, then insert your hook from front to back into the second of the three

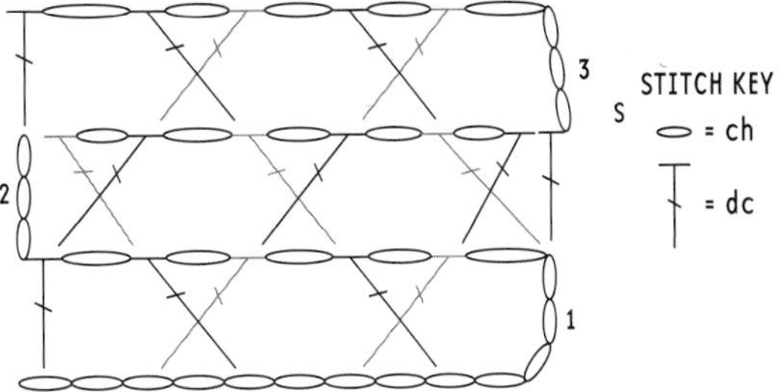

stitches you skipped. When you grab the strand of yarn to continue your double crochet stitch, the working yarn will wrap around the outside of the first double crochet you made, but don't worry about it—that is what is going to help create the crossedness of this crossed stitch. Just grab the yarn, pull it on through, and complete the stitch as usual. The chart given here shows a good way to make a nice swatch of crossed stitches, separated by chain stitches, and staggered between each other on alternating rows. Kinda nice, ain't it?

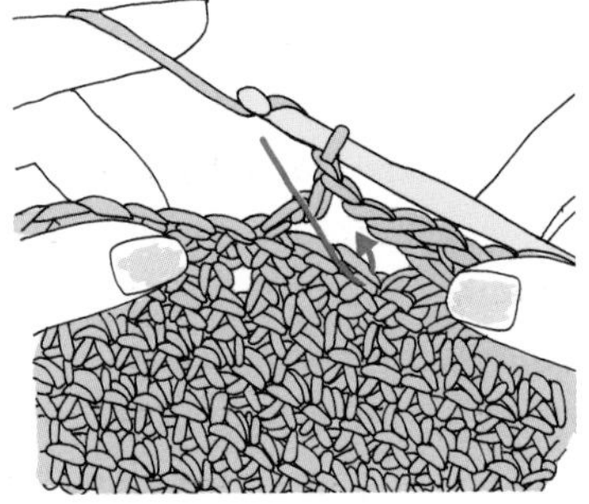

i Like Spike

How to Make a Spike Stitch

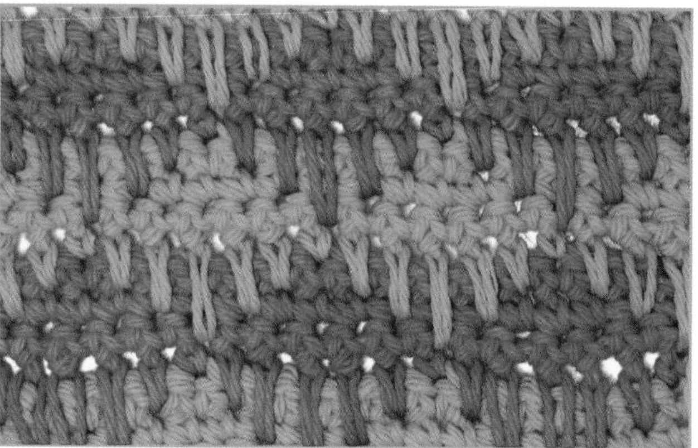

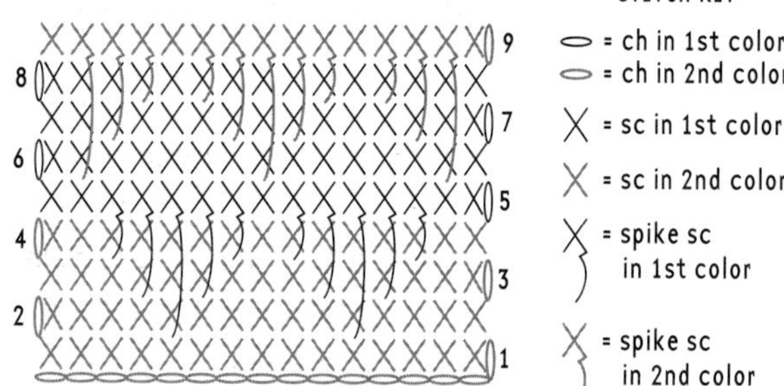

I've got one last trick to show you that is made simply by inserting your hook someplace other than where it usually goes. It's called the spike stitch. This stitch creates long strands of yarn across both the front and back of your fabric, and it's particularly nice when made with 2 or more colors, so that yarn of the second color looks like it's dipping down into the previous row—almost like one of those 1970s sand terrarium designs. It can be made using stitches of any length. To do a spike, make your stitch in the usual way, but first insert your hook into a stitch from the row below—there's usually something of a hole there for you to stick your hook into. And remember, crochet stitches are staggered, so this hole may not be *directly* below the next stitch but off to the side a bit. Now when you draw up your yarn, you need to draw up a much longer loop than usual, so that you can get the stitch up to the row where it's supposed to be in the first place (naughty row-dipping stitch!). Complete the stitch as usual. Enjoy!

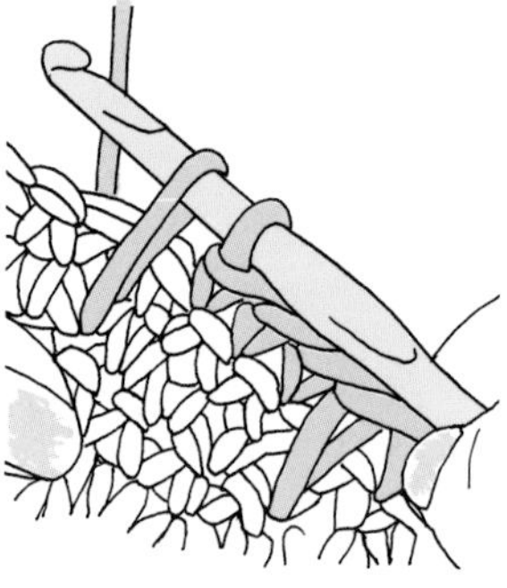

just Like granny used to make

Crocheting the Granny Square

If you grew up in the seventies, as I did, you might fear the granny square—if only because, for a while, clothing was made of nothing else. Granny square vests, granny square shorts, granny square hats. Heck, I bet there was some kid out there who was forced to go to school wearing granny square underwear.

But it's time to give old granny another chance. Not only can these squares be quite beautiful to look at (when they aren't being made in a black-turquoise-red-yellow-green-orange colorway, as was the norm when I was a kid), but they can also be loads of fun to make.

The basis of any granny square is pretty much to make any of the lacy stitches you learned here (and others) for row after row, worked in the round from a foundation ring. To square the shape off, you'll usually increase stitches in the corners. After that, the sky's the limit:

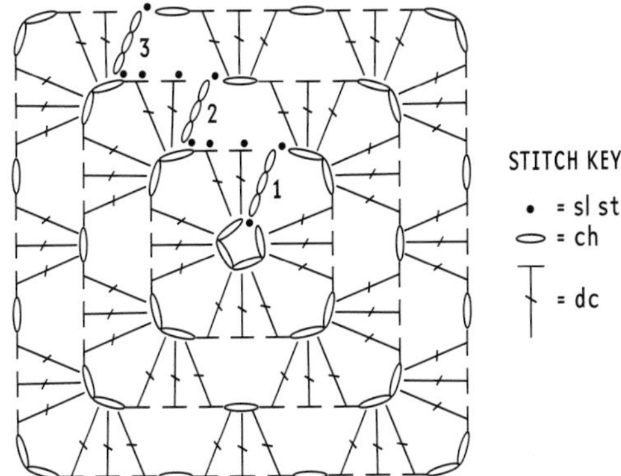

Squares can be as elaborate or as simple as the designer (or you) decides to make them.

To start one of the most basic versions, chain (ch) 4, then join first and last chain to form a ring with a slip stitch (sl st).

Round 1: Ch 3 (turning chain, counts as first stitch), 2 dc into ring, chain 2 (this is the first corner), 3 dc into ring, ch 2 (second corner), 3 dc into ring, ch 2 (third corner), 3 dc into ring, ch 2 (fourth corner). Close off first round with a sl st into the top of the turning chain.

In the next and all following rows, you'll be making your double crochet stitches into chain spaces—Whee! You're crocheting in air!

Round 2: Sl st across the next two dc until you reach the first corner ch-2 space. Ch 3 (turning chain, counts as first stitch). Make 2 dc into the space, ch 2, make 3 dc, and ch 1. In the next ch-2 space (the second corner), make 3 dc, 2 ch, 3 more dc, and a single ch. Repeat this in the next two corners. Sl st into the top of the turning chain to join.

Round 3 ad nauseum infinitum: Sl st your way to the next corner space, 3 dc, 2 ch, 3 dc into each corner, and 3 dc into each ch-1 space, with a ch 1 before and after each dc group (see diagram).

You can go on and on, around and around, and make the hugest granny square ever created, or you could just make one big enough for a baby blanket (but don't forget: It will be a square, not a rectangle). Alternately, you could make many granny squares and sew them together to make an afghan. You could also do each round of your square in a different color, which you would do by finishing off your yarn as you close each round, then starting your new yarn right smack in the chain-2 corner chain space. You'll still always need to start your round with a turning chain of 3 stitches.

That is it, my friend. And here you thought yer old granny was slaving away at something difficult all these years, when it was the ease and simplicity of this stitch that attracted her in the first place. But if you promise not to tell, I won't either. There's no reason to let any of the noncrocheters out there know that granny may well have been taking the easy way out. Let them go on thinking that making a granny square is second in complexity only to cloning stem cells in a petri dish. Then you and granny can go share a good laugh at their expense.

7

picture this

MAKING IMAGES IN CROCHET

You've already seen that crochet can make nice stiff fabric; that it can make open, airy fabric; that it can make amazing three-dimensional textures and beautiful laces; and that it can go around in a perfect circle or an angular square. But what about images? Can you make a blanket featuring a cat under the moonlight, or a set of curtains with bats or butterflies flitting about?

The answer is, of course, yes. In this chapter, I'll show you how to incorporate colorful pictures in your pieces using tapestry crochet, how to use filet crochet to make images emerge from an openwork mesh, and how to make the afghan stitch—which makes the perfect background for cross-stitching images.

covering your tracks

Color Work Using Tapestry Crochet

Tapestry crochet, which is also sometimes called "jacquard crochet" (don't ask me why), is the method used when you want to incorporate more than one color of yarn in a row. It's a bit of a hairball and may take you a while to get the swing of, but it's worth learning. Tapestry crochet is usually done over a field of single crochet stitch, which is good because single crochet stitches are nice and square, meaning you can use regular old graph paper to chart an image you'd like to create. With tapestry crochet, you are basically crocheting some stitches in color A, then some in color B, then others in color A. What happens with that strand of color A while you are working with color B, however, is where the fun (or torment) begins. Some folks just let loose loops of yarn hang on the back side of their work whether they are working rows with the front of the work facing them or with the back facing them.

But how yucky is that! When you're done you'll have a piece with messy yarn loops hanging down, and even if it's on the side that will never be seen (the inside of a pillow, for instance), the idea just bugs me, especially because there is a neater way to do this. You can just crochet right over the yarn that isn't being used, hiding it inside your stitches like a piece of tuna in a sushi roll. This method takes a bit more practice, but it makes your work look good from both sides and avoids creating an unsightly, varicose-vein-like network of yarn strands at the back of your work.

There's only one rule when working a piece of tapestry crochet: Always use the new strand of yarn to complete the last stitch you make in the old color. Usually, that means using the new color when you have the last two loops on your hook and you're about to finish your stitch.

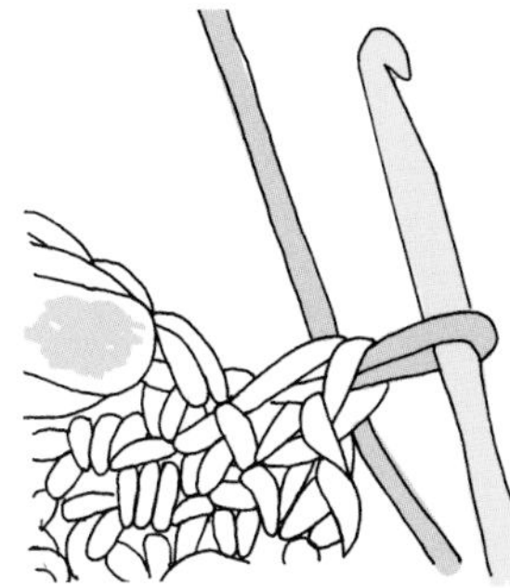

Finishing the last stitch with the new color

For the rest, just crochet as usual, laying your unused color along the top of the previous row's stitches and crocheting right over it. It's like you're making a yarn Twinkie—the last row is the spongy bottom, the unused color is the creamy filling, and the working yarn is the moist cake surrounding it. (Mmm, Twinkies!)

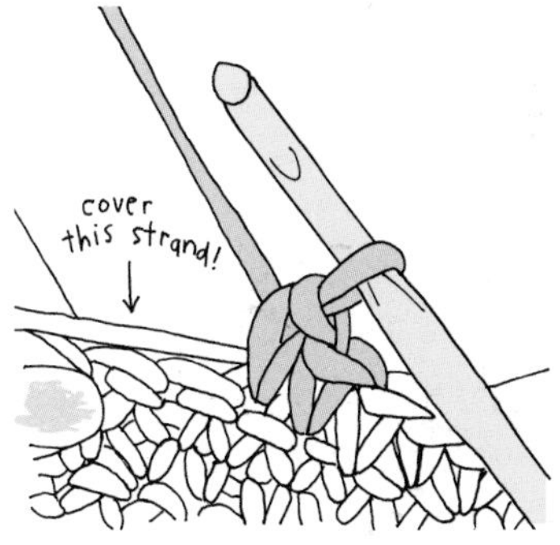

When you need to use the other color yarn again, be sure not to pull the hidden strand tightly. If you do, your work will begin to pucker (eew).

Let's try making the heart image shown here. Notice that the image has been charted on regular old graph paper and every box is a perfect square. That's because we're going to make this test swatch in single crochet, where each stitch is as wide as it is tall—it's a square.

Start by crocheting a base chain of 22 stitches—21 foundation stitches plus one for the turning chain. Single crochet into the second chain from the hook and each chain across—21 stitches. Chain 1, turn, and single crochet across for another 3 rows. On row 5 comes the fun part. Chain 1, turn, and make 9 single crochets in the usual way. On the 10th single crochet, insert the hook, yarn over, pull up a loop, and stop. You have two loops on your hook, and it's time to get out your second color yarn and use it to finish off the stitch, so hang the second color over your hook and pull it through those 2 loops. Now lay the first color yarn to the left, across the Vs of the previous row's stitches (the Twinkie filling on the spongy cake bottom), and make a single crochet stitch around it, with the second color yarn, by inserting your hook under the V as usual and hooking the new yarn (you have 2 loops left). Now bring the second color yarn toward you and let it hang down. Then pick up the first color, hook it, and complete the stitch with it. Continue with your first color across the row (10 stitches).

Since you don't need to make any more stitches in the second color on this row, you can just let it hang where it is; you don't need to carry it along and crochet over it. I've told you to let the yarn hang toward you because, when you come back on the next row, it will be in a nicer position for you to pick it up and continue using than if you left it hanging to the back (though this is probably what your hands instinctively would prefer to do).

Continue reading the chart and crocheting in this manner, working the odd-numbered rows from right to left, and the even-numbered rows from left to right. As you do this, you will notice a few things. For one, sometimes just picking up the new yarn can leave a weensy bit of a strand hanging, especially if you are picking it up a few stitches away from where you last used it. I just like to add that strand, like so much American cheese, to the yarn sandwich. That is to say, be sure to leave it loose

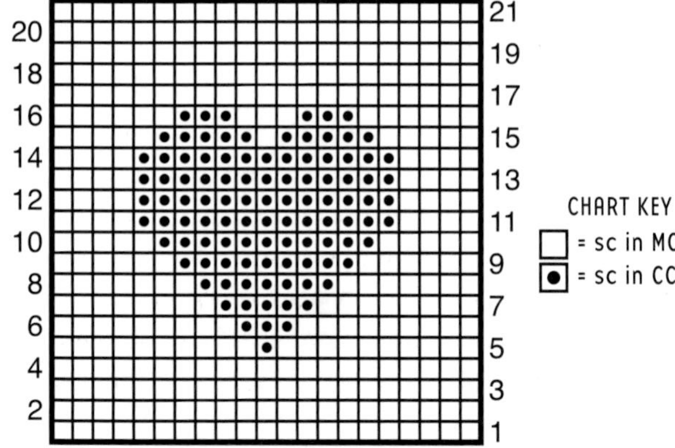

enough, and then crochet over it along with the other color yarn for however many stitches you need to hide it away inside your work.

The other thing you might notice is that your color changes look much nicer and neater when you are looking at them from the front than they do when you look at them from the back. In addition, the color changes don't look perfect. There's often a bit of the other color that gets tangled up at the beginning and the end of your rows, and when you are looking at a row from the back, you can often see the carried-along strand peeping through your stitches. For this reason, some expert tapestry crocheters crochet back and forth without ever turning their work: They actually learn to alternate their left and right hands so that they can keep the front of their work facing them at all times, which means that the carried strand will be visible only from the back of the work, and the back, being the back, will not often be seen. If you should feel so motivated, you can teach yourself that as well. But for most folks, working back and forth in rows will do just fine, even if the results aren't 100 percent flawless. As long as you keep your image nice and simple, you'll get the effect you're after by using the method I've described here.

Finally, you might notice that your yarn balls tend to get a bit tangled up while you're working tapestry crochet. Just untangle them every row or so, or put a rubber band around the unused balls to keep them from unwinding. If you only have a small bit of a second color to work, cut off a long enough strand—about 18 inches or so—to work those stitches. A long strand can easily be flicked out of the way of your main color's ball of yarn. Alternately, if you're working with lots of different colors, you can wind small bits of each yarn onto little bobbins that are sold for this express purpose.

Now You See It, Now You Don't

Working Filet Crochet

In my little Brooklyn apartment, I have a short, lacy curtain that hangs over the window on my front door. During the day, the light shines through the open holes in the work and reveals that the solid areas form the shapes of delicate vines, leaves, and flowers scattered across the fabric. At night, the darkness from outside fills in the empty spaces and the flowers and vines are revealed again. My mother made this piece in very fine crochet cotton over twenty years ago, using a technique called "filet crochet." I have shorter strips of lace curtain hanging in windows; these were worked by my Great-aunt Jo and had belonged to my grandmother until she died a few years ago. As soon as I inherited these pieces of filet crochet work, I promptly hung them in my windows. I love feeling surrounded by the handiwork of my female relatives—it makes me feel safe and warm, especially because I know just how much work went into making these decorative items.

Hanging lace in windows is a practice that dates back centuries and, as far as I can tell, was probably a way to let light in while keeping bugs out—consider them to be the precursors of today's screens. When crochet came along, folks soon realized—especially in the northern countries of Scandinavia and the Netherlands—that it would be a great technique for quickly working up large pieces of mesh to use for lace curtains (you saw how quickly a mesh can be crocheted up in the last chapter). Better yet, they also recognized that if some of the open areas of the lace mesh were closed up, an image would be formed, which would make the curtain a bit less of a bore to live with as well as to create. And thus filet crochet was born. Filet is also used to make tablecloths, bedspreads, and various other items. Its possibilities are just about endless, and the technique is both simple and fun to execute—although it does require following a chart for every row.

Think of filet crochet as the windows of a modern office building, where some shades are drawn (a "closed mesh") and others are open (an "open mesh"). The open mesh (or window) is usually made with two double crochet stitches separated by two chains. A closed mesh is simply four double crochet stitches in a row—the outer two stitches make up the window frame; the inner two are the drawn shade. All in all, it's pretty dang straightforward, but the results can be quite impressive.

Working back and forth making filet crochet windows can yield a mighty purty rectangle, but there's one more thing you need to know if you want to get truly exquisite results, and that's how to increase and decrease meshes at the beginning or end of a row. And because those buggers can have their shades drawn or open, you'll need to know how to increase and decrease both open and closed meshes.

To decrease either an open or closed mesh at the beginning of a row, simply slip stitch across the top of as many stitches as you intend to get rid of. **And to decrease a mesh at the end of a row,** just stop before you get to the end!

To increase either kind of mesh at the beginning of a row, crochet enough additional chain stitches to add the requisite number of boxes, then make your turning chain and get going.

To increase an open mesh at the end of a row, you'll need to use a slightly more complicated method. Start by chaining 2 (for the top of the next window). Then make a triple triple crochet into the outermost, bottommost loop at the base of the last double crochet you made. This means you'll need to yarn over 4 times, then insert your hook into the lowermost, outermost loop at the bottom of the last double crochet you made (see figure below). Next, just yarn over and pull through 2 loops at a time, until you have only 1 loop left on the hook. So why did you just make this ridiculously long triple triple stitch? Well, it is as long as the "windowsill" of your mesh (the 2 chains you skip) plus the side of your "window" (a double crochet). To add another open mesh, chain 2 and

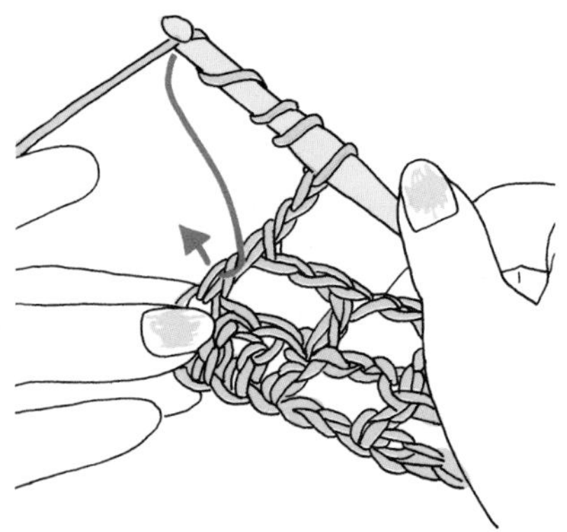

make another ginormous triple triple crochet, inserting your hook into the center of the long post of the previous stitch.

To increase a closed mesh at the end of a row, make a triple crochet for each stitch you need, but insert your hook into the outermost, lowermost loop at the base of the previous stitch. (Remember, a triple crochet is made by yarning over twice.) That means making 3 of these triple crochets—two for the closed shade, and one for the outer edge of your window.

To read a filet chart, such as the bat chart shown here, you read the odd-numbered rows from right to left, and the even-numbered rows from left to right. To start, count the number of boxes (or windows) you have to make for your design—in this case, 12—and multiply that by 3. Then add 3 more, for the turning chain, to get the number of base, or foundation, chain stitches you need. For the bat chart, that means you'll make 12 × 3 = 36, plus another 3 = 39.

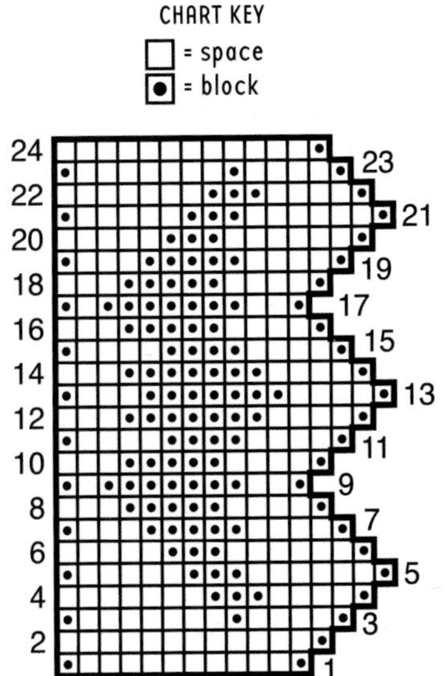

After crocheting the base chain, read the first row of the chart, from right to left. Notice that this chart begins with a closed mesh. So, make a double crochet in the 4th chain from the hook, and another 2 double crochets after that. Next, you have 10 open meshes to make, so just chain 2, skip 2 chains, and double crochet into the next chain; do this 10 times. Your last mesh is closed, so make three final double crochets.

Row 2 is all open meshes, so begin with a 3-chain turning chain, then work your way across the row by chaining 2, skipping 2 chains, and making a double crochet in the next double crochet, to the end. You'll see that your double crochet stitches are always being made into the tops of double crochet stitches in the row below. Now you need to increase a closed mesh at the end of this row. To do that, make a triple crochet into the outermost, lowermost loop at the base of the previous stitch. Make two more stitches like that. Whew! You've increased a closed mesh.

Continue following the chart this way, increasing or decreasing meshes at the beginning or end of rows as called for, and eventually you'll have a lovely bat curtain to hang. You can make this curtain fit the exact width of your window by repeating the entire pattern, starting with row 1, after you've completed row 24, the final row in the chart, as many times as necessary.

Filet crochet is traditionally done using very thin white cotton thread, but there isn't any reason not to do it with, say, purple worsted-weight cotton or anything else. As long as you're working to a nice gauge that gives you clear, open spaces in your mesh and nicely closed spaces with your double crochet solid blocks, no one's going to stop you from giving this age-old technique a modern spin. Just remember to try your yarn and hook on a small test swatch to be sure your image is visible. If you can't see the "open windows" clearly enough, try a larger hook. If the "drawn shades" are letting in too much light, try a smaller hook. Enjoy, and use it to make bags, patches for your jeans, or a giant bedspread featuring an underwater scene—a filet o' fish!

Not without my Afghan

Learning the Afghan Stitch

The Afghan stitch has a bit of an identity problem: Is it knitting or crocheting? It uses an extra-long hook that looks like a cross between a knitting needle and a crochet hook, and it makes a wide, flat fabric that involves first working a lot of loops onto the hook (kind of like a knitting needle) and then working them off two at a time till you have a single loop on the hook again (just like crochet). Not only is it sort of like a bastard child of knitting and crocheting, but the name Afghan stitch is also misleading, since it's not exclusively used for making afghans. Finally, the dang thing goes under a number of aliases, including Tunisian stitch, Scottish knitting, railway stitch, and idiot stitch. I like that last one best, and it's true: The Afghan stitch is so pathetically simple that you're likely to have a lot of "Duh!" moments while you're learning it. In fact, this stitch kind of bugs me with its simplicity (sorry).

The version of the Afghan stitch you'll learn here is the one that became insanely popular among Victorian ladies who were interested in making fabric that could serve as a nice background for their cross-stitch work. That's why I put this straightforward stitch with complex identity issues here in the color section, because, combined with cross-stitching, it can produce a very colorful, beautiful project indeed.

To make it, you'll work with an Afghan hook (below), which is like a crochet hook except that it has no grip (aka thumb rest), it's much, much longer (usually 10 or 14 inches), and it has a little knob at one end. It's long because it needs to hold the loops for the entire width of your fabric; the knob is there to keep those loops from falling off the end and tumbling to their deaths. This also means that an Afghan hook can only work a piece of fabric that is the length of the hook, or just slightly longer. There are some hooks that have a long piece of flexible plastic "cord" at one end, which allows for more stitches to be squeezed on to create a wider swath of fabric. But as wide as the Afghan hook can get, it will never be as wide as an actual afghan-type blanket; if you're interested in using an Afghan hook to make a bed-size blanket, you'll need to work a series of long, wide strips of fabric, or "panels," then stitch them together.

Fabric made with Afghan stitch starts out just like any other crochet piece, with a length of chain stitches. Things start to get a little weird on the very next row, though: Insert your hook into the second chain from the hook (the first chain from the hook is always ignored), hook your yarn, and pull up a loop. You now have two loops on your hook. Next, insert your hook into the next chain, hook your yarn, and pull another loop through. Check it out: 3 loops. Repeat that step—inserting your hook in the next chain and pulling up a loop—for every stitch in the chain. When you're done, you'll have a hook that's just chock full o' loops (figure 1).

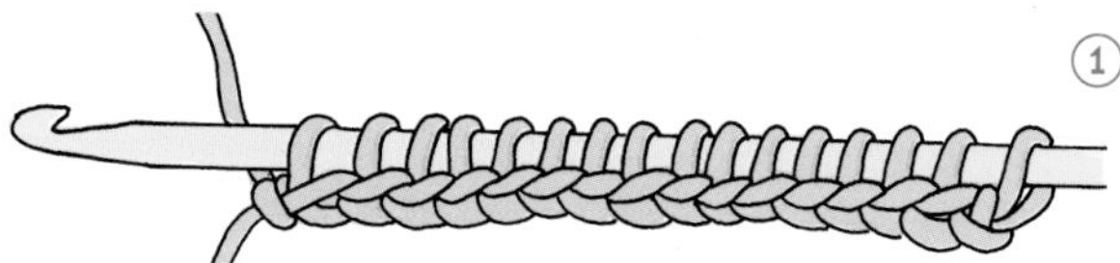

Afghan hook, actual size

The next row in Afghan is called a "return row." That's because you're going to work your way back along this row of loops—without turning your work—until you return to where you started, at the beginning, with only one loop on your hook. Start by hooking your yarn and pulling it through one loop on the hook. This is the equivalent of a turning chain, and it gets your hook up to the correct height for working the next row. Now hook your yarn again and pull it through two loops (figure 2).

②

Hook your yarn again and pull it through the next two loops. If you're a knitter, this may feel a bit like "binding off" stitches, and it kind of is: You keep ending up with fewer and fewer loops on your hook as you work your way along. Now you see how excessively easy the Afghan stitch is. Are you saying "duh" yet?

Just look at what you've got there: a thin little slip of fabric, with vertical strands of thread that look almost like prison bars enclosing a series of sideways-looking stitches (figure 3). It's the prison bars, and not their inmates, that we'll be concerning ourselves with on this

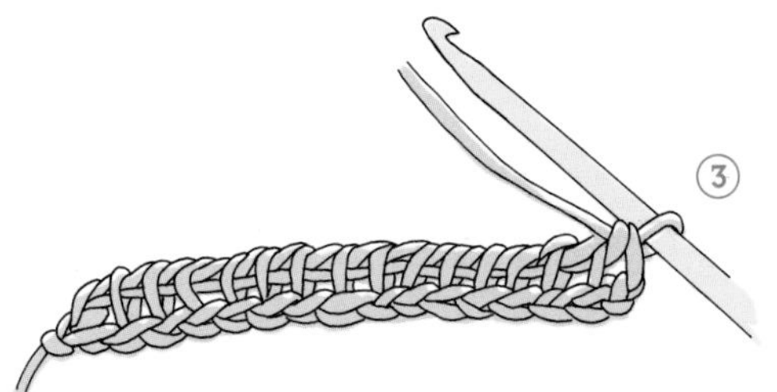

next row, called a "forward row." To make it, insert your hook, from right to left, through the *second* little prison bar you see. Wrap your yarn and pull up a loop (figure 4).

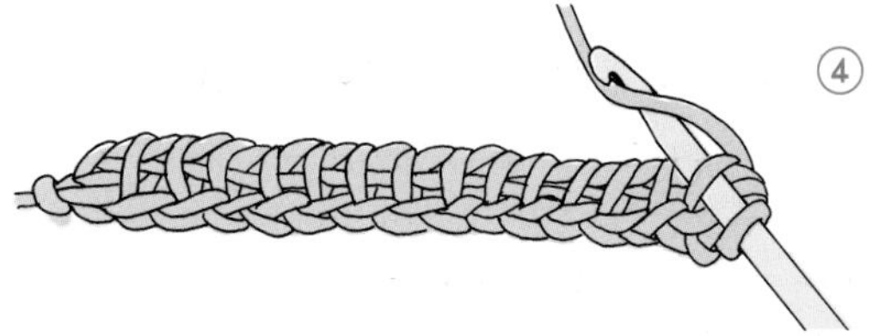

Continue all the way across the row, pulling up a loop by working through each prison bar, but when you get to the next-to-last stitch, insert your hook through the last *two* vertical strands that are there before pulling up a loop (figure 5).

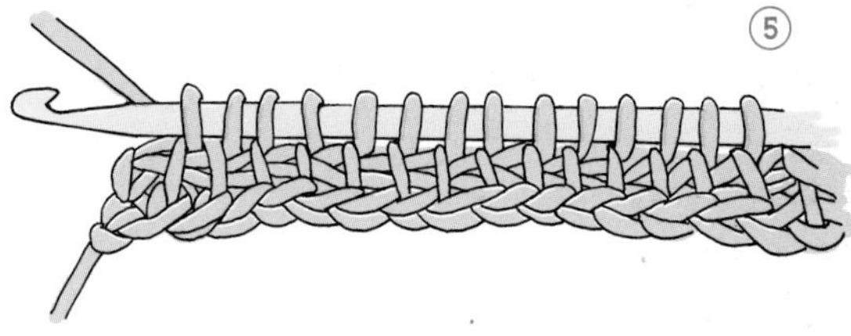

Go back by working a return row, which always begins by pulling a strand through a single loop, then working off the loops two at a time till you end up with just a single loop on the hook.

Work a piece of fabric this way, back and forth, with the front of your work always facing you, until you have a piece of fabric that's a couple of inches long. When you're ready to bind off, end with a return row, then work a slip stitch through each prison bar, all the way across your row. Then cut your yarn and pull it through the loop on the hook. And don't be offended that it's curling up; Afghan stitch is notorious for that, and it can be blocked later on. Now try holding that thing up to the light. Sure, you see the series of prison bars that are on the front of the fabric, but do you also see the four little points of light that surround each of those bars? Those little holes make fabric made with Afghan stitch very easy to be cross-stitched upon. So let's do it.

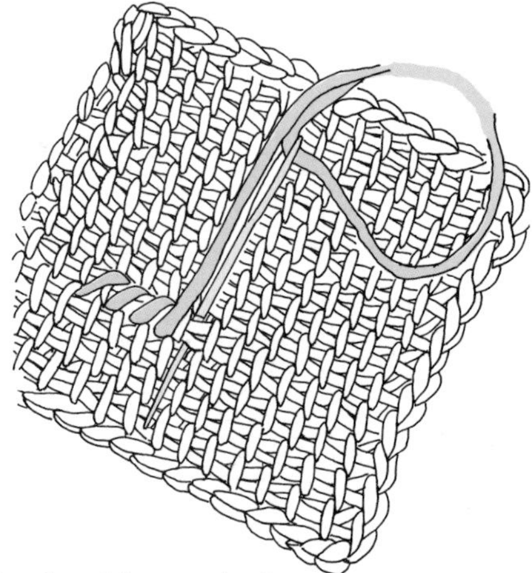

Grab a longish strand of a contrasting color yarn, thread it through a tapestry needle, and bring that needle up through a hole that's on the bottom left side of one of your prison bars. Then push your needle through the hole that's on the top right of that bar, and come back up through the hole that's to the bottom right of that bar.

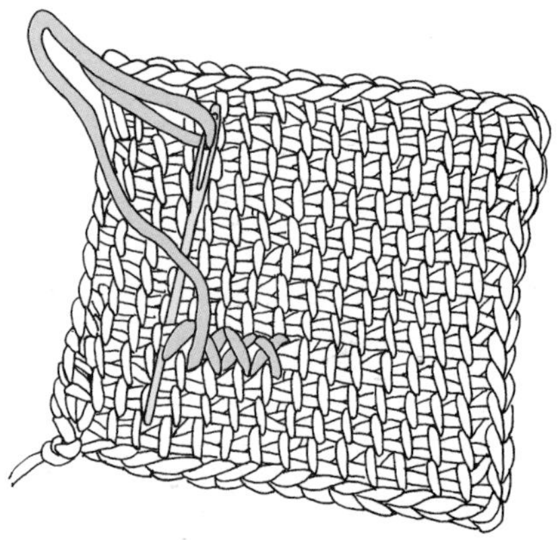

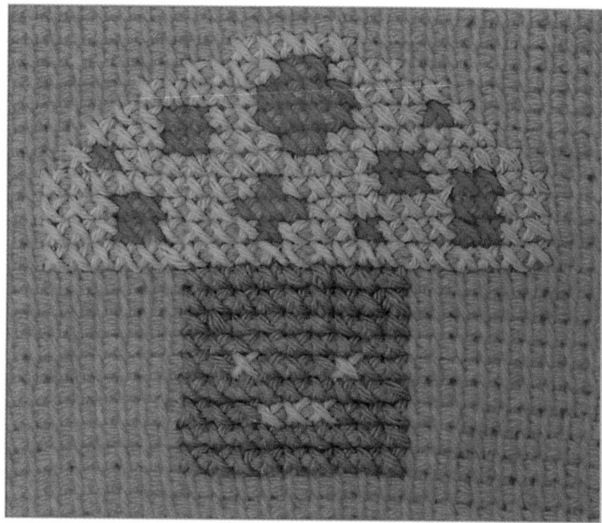

Continue this way across a row, making slanted bars all the way across in one direction. Now it's time to turn those slashes into bonafide Xs: Insert your needle into the hole at the top left of the last prison bar you crossed, pull it through to the back, and come back up through the hole at the bottom left of that bar. First X made. Work all the way across the row like this, turning each slash into an X.

Cross-stitch work allows for truly beautiful images to be created, with wide variations in color and shading. So if you ever feel inspired to make a blanket with an image as detailed as tapestry, the Afghan stitch with cross-stitching worked on top is your man.

Note: There is another way to cross stitch on Afghan work. It doesn't leave so many ugly strands at the back of your work, but it is much harder to do neatly. Instead of inserting your needle all the way through the holes in your fabric, simply slide it under the two horizontal strands that sit between each "prison bar."

8

off the Hook

SEWING YOUR PIECES TOGETHER, BLOCKING, AND ADDING DECORATION

It's no secret: Most crocheters hate the finishing process. Your hook has been flying in the air, whipping around yarn and dancing for days, and now you have to put it away and get out that nasty little sewing needle.

As I admitted in my first book, I secretly like the finishing process. That's because it can be just as challenging and requires just as much skill as the rest of your work, and it gives you a chance to show off your needlework prowess. Stitching a seam perfectly creates an almost invisible join; adding pom-poms and tassels can be as much fun as hanging holiday decorations; and stitching on embroidered embellishments can transform your project from Plain Jane to RuPaul. Sewing on buttons is the one part of the process that even I despise, but at least with crochet you can make your own.

Finally, there's the wonderful process of blocking, which can take your piece from looking drab to looking fab. So there's no need to let the finishing process finish you off. Learn the techniques in this chapter, and you'll be armed and ready to get this part of the job done. Best of all, once it's done, that's it: You're done!

Not Sew Hard as it Seams

Sewing Seams

Crochet, with its lovely, architectural building-block ways, will often let you connect your pieces together *in flagrante*—as you're working on them. A loop of yarn from one piece of fabric can easily be grabbed along and crocheted to another piece of fabric as the second piece is being created, thus eliminating seam sewing altogether.

But most often you'll find yourself with a number of crocheted pieces that need to be connected after they're done. How you choose to attach them will depend on what kind of seam you want (invisible or visible, strong and tight or loose and stretchy) and where you're making the connection (joining the sides of two pieces or the tops of two pieces, or connecting the side of one piece to the top of another). Most seams are made with a tapestry needle. You can also use your crochet hook, although it often leaves a noticeable, scarlike join. We'll begin with the many ways to sew seams, and then I'll show you some ways to hook pieces together.

Blindsided

Weaving the Sides of Two Crocheted Pieces Together

When you are connecting the sides of two crochet pieces, such as the front and back of a sweater, you can very neatly and almost invisibly join them, row to row, by using a sewing technique known as "weaving" (this is very similar to the "mattress" stitch in knitting). To "weave," lay the two crochet pieces side by side, with their right sides facing up. (I like to put them on a table in front of me or on my lap.) Pin the pieces together with safety pins: Begin by pinning the top and bottom, then insert a pin through the middle, and then through the middles of the upper and lower sections. That way, your seam will come out evenly and you won't have leftover fabric at the top of the seam because one piece is a bit longer than the other. By pinning, you can absorb any difference in size evenly along the length of the seam.

Next, thread a tapestry needle with an 18-inch length of yarn (for most seams, you'll use the same yarn you used to crochet the piece). Bring the needle up through the bottommost stitch on the left-hand piece of fabric and pull it through, leaving a 6-inch tail behind (figure 1).

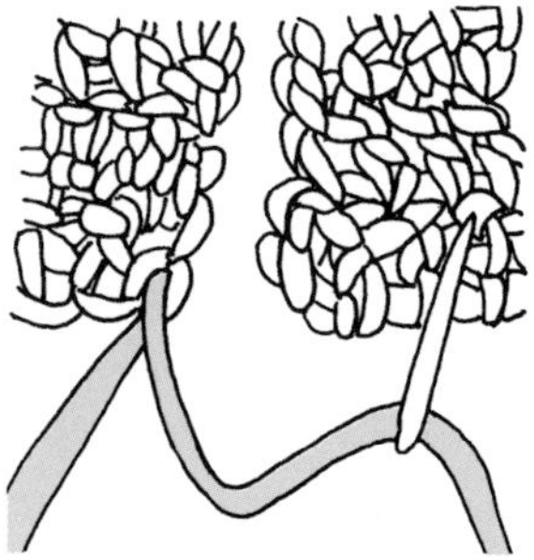

1

Next, bring the needle up through the bottommost stitch on the right-hand piece (figure 2). Repeat these last two steps, bringing the yarn up through the bottommost stitch of the left-hand piece again and then through the right-hand piece. You've made a cute little figure 8 with

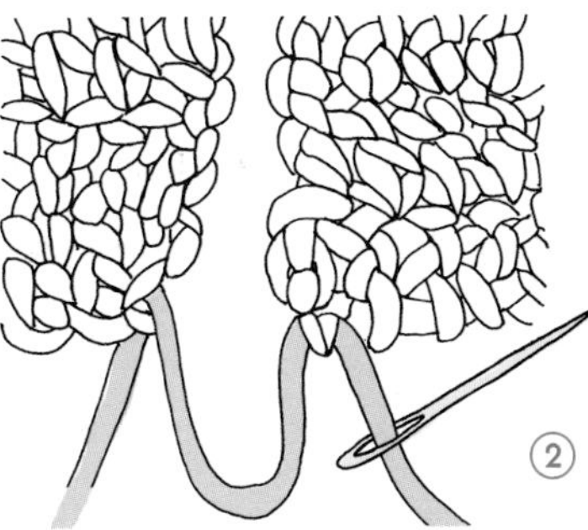

your yarn, which has "tacked" the pieces in place (figure 3). Now pull the yarn through so the two corners are nicely connected, and it's full seam ahead.

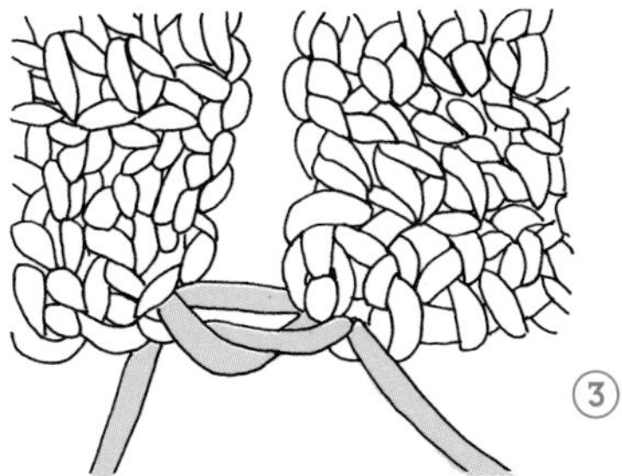

Insert the needle through the same bottommost stitch of your left-hand piece of fabric, and bring the needle up a short way above that. In the case of a single crochet, this is at the top of the stitch; for a double crochet, it's in the middle. (You'll bring the needle right up through the post of the edge stitch). Now do the exact same thing on the other piece: Poke your needle down through the bottommost stitch and come back up a short way above that, still at the edge.

Reinsert your needle in your left-hand piece of fabric *in the same spot* where the needle last came out and bring it back up further along the edge, making the same size stitch as before. (In single crochet, this is the *next* stitch; for double crochet, it's through the top of the stitch.) Repeat on the right-hand piece of fabric.

Keep doing the above—going in where you last came out, and bringing your needle out at the next level. After you've done two or three of them, pull your yarn taut and see how cozily the two pieces sidle up to each other and your yarn disappears into the nice, flat seam (see figure below).

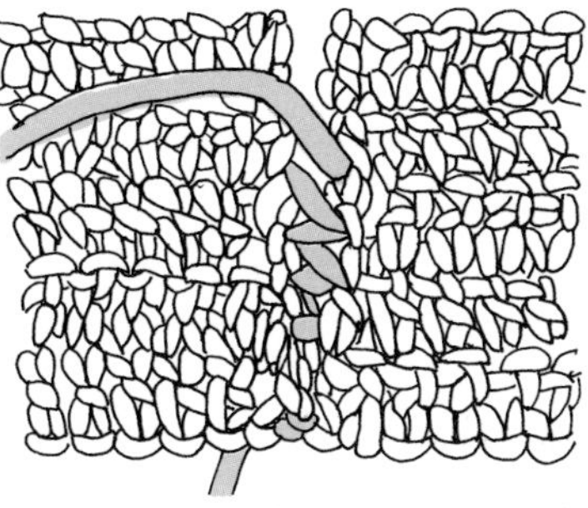

Continue in this manner all the way to the top of your pieces. Note that joining is not an exact science: You are *kinda* coming up in the middle of the post, and you're *sorta* coming out through the top of the post. Also, sometimes you'll be dealing with the posts created by stitches and sometimes with turning chains. The exact spot where your needle comes out doesn't matter, as long as you keep your stitches running along the outermost edge of your work, keeping them the same length, and inserting your needle between the strands of the stitches. (Try not to split the yarn; that will make it difficult to reinsert the needle into exactly the same spot.) And remember, if you are easing a bit of extra fabric into one side or the other, adjust for that as you sew. Maybe you need to bite off a whole double crochet post on one side but only half of one on the other, or maybe you're better off making two tight little stitches into a single crochet stitch to adjust for having an extra row of them on the other side of the seam.

top this

Weaving the Tops of Two Pieces Together

Sewing the tops of two crocheted pieces for shoulder seams, for example, is quite similar to the method above. You begin the same way: by laying the two pieces side by side on a flat surface, with their tops facing each other and their right sides up. But now, instead of having posts and turning chains to deal with, you'll have the tops of stitches—those nice sweet little Vs—to sew together. Pin the pieces together, and tack them using the figure 8 method described on page 78. Next, insert your needle into the bottommost loop of the left-hand piece, then come up in the center of the first V. This means you are coming up between the front and back strands of the top of that stitch—in the crotch of the V. Bring your yarn across the gap to your right-hand piece, insert your needle back into the bottommost loop from top to bottom, and come back up in the center of the first stitch on that side—between the front and back strands of the V.

Now go back to the left-hand piece, insert your needle where you came out last time, and bring the needle up through the center of the next V. Do the same on your right-hand piece. Pull your yarn taut (not tight!) and watch the tops of your two pieces draw up and kiss each other. I swear, it's almost obscene.

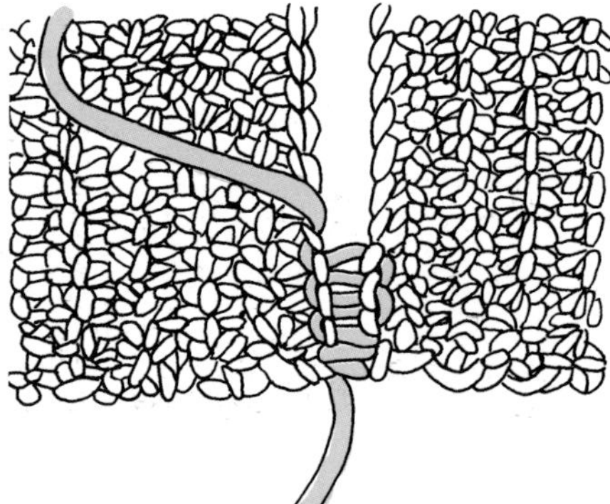

Keep going this way to the end of your seam. If you have to finagle by skipping a V on one side to ease in a bit of extra fabric there, go ahead and do that.

You can also use this method of sewing if you're joining a number of granny squares or other motifs, as each edge of these pieces has the V part of the stitch facing out all around the outside edge. Be careful to align the corners as you do this and to join the corresponding stitches of each motif to each other.

head and shoulders

Weaving the Top of One Piece to the Side of Another

If you haven't guessed by now, making this kind of connection—which you'll do if you're sewing a sleeve into a sleeve hole, for instance—is a combo of the above two methods. Begin in the familiar way—by laying the pieces faceup in front of you, and pinning them to keep things neat. Tack your corners and connect the lowest ones with a fun figure 8 (see page 78). Then, you'll be taking little stitches on one side and little stitches on the other side just as in the methods above, except that on one piece you'll be working with posts and turning chains, and on the other, the top of the piece, you'll have Vs to deal with. Still, this seam is worked the same way as the others; just keep inserting your yarn in the same spot where it came out, and bringing it back up about one stitch width farther up the piece. You want to be careful that your stitches

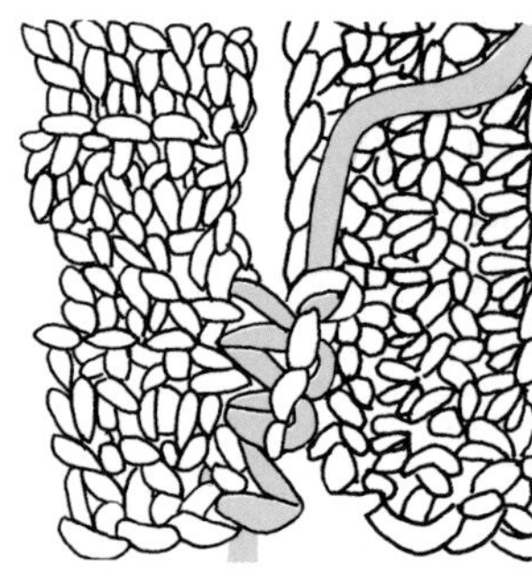

are about the same length on each side so that the pieces will meet nicely and not bunch up on either side. If they're lying flat in front of you and you've pinned them together, you'll be able to see whether you are making the seam evenly. If it isn't even, just take out a few joining stitches, adjust the fabric, and try it again.

whip it good

Making Joins Using the Whipstitch

If you can't be bothered to weave your items stitch by stitch, or if you're joining pieces of fabric that are too bumpy or fuzzy to even see your stitches, there's always the less pleasing but much simpler whipstitch. Whipstitch can be worked from the right side (the outside) or the wrong side (the inside) of your work, but if it's worked from the right side, it will not be invisible. You might like to use a contrasting yarn along the edges to connect granny squares for an afghan; in that case you can work this stitch from the right side. But for a sweater, you'll probably want to work it from the wrong side (which will become the inside, natch) to keep it hidden.

Begin by pinning your pieces together, with their right sides facing up or down, depending on whether you want the whipstitches on the outside or the inside. Connect their lower edges to each other and tack the yarn in place using your old pal, the figure 8 method (see page 78). Then, insert your needle, from the front toward the back, into an edge stitch on the right-hand piece, and bring it back up from back to front through an edge stitch on the left-hand piece. Repeat that motion about a ¼-inch farther along your fabric. You're kind of whipping your yarn through those edges, around and around—almost like making a little spiral-bound book out of them. Try to keep your stitches as close to the edge as possible, and keep them approximately the same distance apart, for neatness' sake.

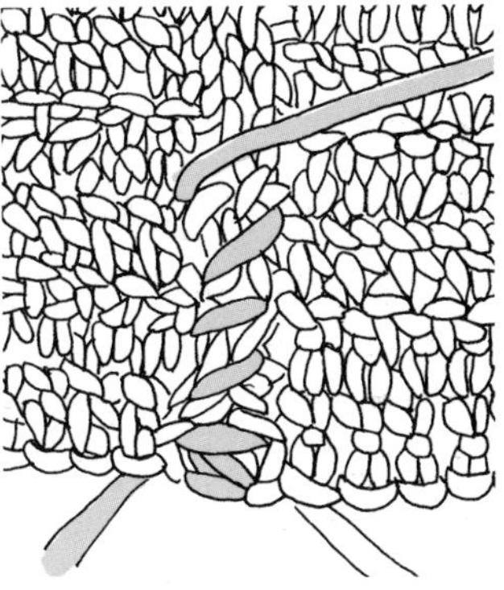

one step forward, two steps back

Seaming with the Backstitch

Sometimes you don't care about a beautiful, neat, or invisible seam. Sometimes—if you're connecting pieces for a sturdy bag, for instance—you just want a strong, nonstretchy seam to keep those dang pieces of fabric together. That's when it's time to get out the backstitch. Unlike the other joining methods, you always do backstitching on the inside of your work. To join two pieces this way, begin by pinning your pieces together with their edges aligned and their right sides facing each other. Tack your yarn in place at the bottom of the seam by making 2 or 3 small stitches on top of each other, through both layers of fabric. Then insert your needle into the fabric

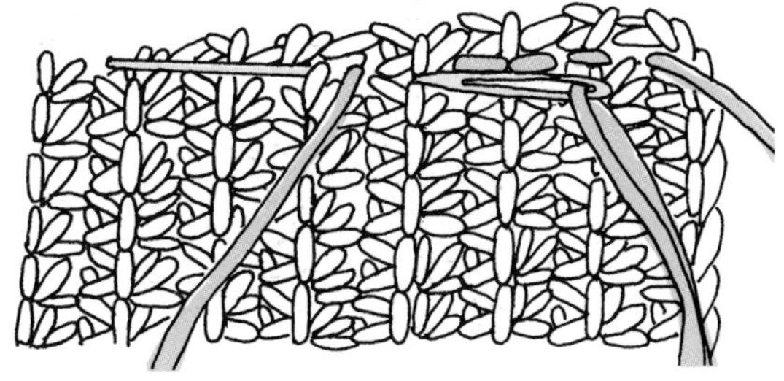

and bring it up about ¼ to ½ inch along your seam, and pull your yarn through. Now backtrack—insert your needle from the front into the original spot where it came up into the fabric, and bring it up about ¼ to ½ inch farther up. Repeat that gesture over and over and you'll soon see why this is called the backstitch: Before you can go forward, you must go back! Try to make this stitch as close to the edge of your work as possible, because the farther away it is, the bulkier your seam will be—and mama don't like no bulky seams.

Hook Your Way to Happiness

Crocheted Seams

I know, I know—the thought of being able to crochet your pieces together sounds so heavenly. "Oh please, Debbie," I can hear you saying, "can't I just crochet my seams? I really hate to sew!" Well, my dears, of course you can. You can crochet all your seams together, using either of the methods I'm about to show you. But remember, I warned you: Crocheted seams are *always* visible if you make them from the outside, and they're pretty bulky when made from the inside. So if you really want to crochet your seams, give it a go. If you don't like the way it's coming out, just unravel it (this can be done quickly), take out your dang sewing needle, and sew that seam. At least you can say you tried.

To connect your pieces using *single crochet or slip stitch,* first pin the pieces together (right sides together if you want an inside seam; wrong sides together for an outside seam). Place a slip loop on your hook and, beginning at the rightmost point, insert your hook under a V if you're working through the top of a piece, through a turning chain or post if you're working on a side, or a single loop if you're working along a foundation row. Hook your yarn and, for the slip stitch method, pull it back through the fabric and the loop on your hook. For the single crochet method, hook the strand and pull it through the fabric, yarn over again, and pull that strand through both loops on the hook. Keep on doing this—working slip stitches or single crochet stitches—all the way along your seam. If you are working through single or double crochet posts, remember that you will want to put more than one slip or single crochet stitch through each post. A double crochet post will probably take 2 stitches, a triple crochet would take 3, and so on. Just try to keep the seam from puckering or ruffling out.

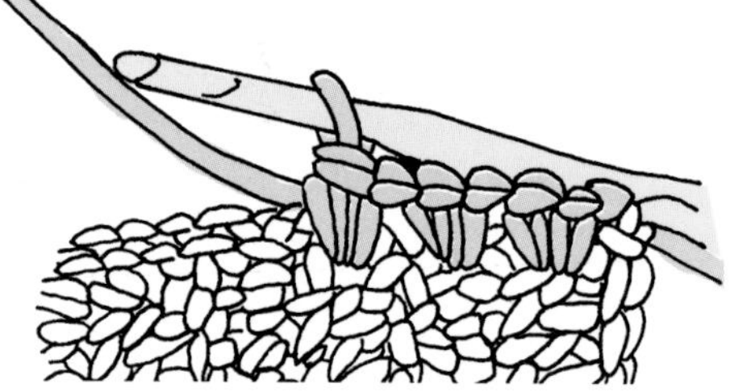

If you're working with the wrong sides of the pieces facing each other, both the slip stitch and the single crochet will create a ridgelike, visible seam on the outside of your work. Of the two, the single crochet creates a prettier edge, with a nice chainlike row of stitches that runs along the top of the ridge. If you have the right sides together, so the seam is on the inside, the single crochet method seems to make a slightly less bulky join as well.

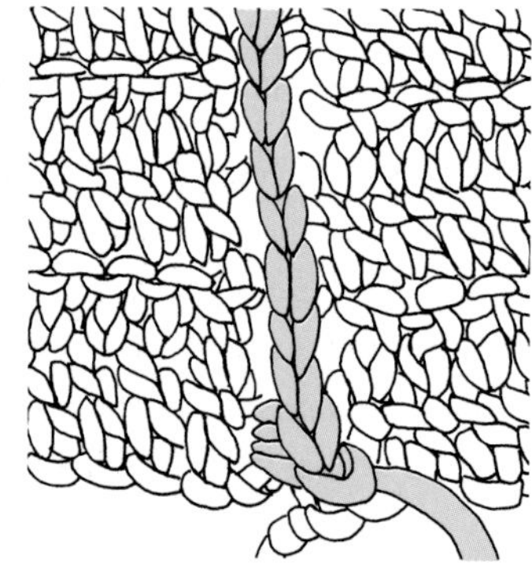

The slip stitch method can do one extra trick, however, which will work if you are connecting only the tops of pieces (as you would with granny squares or other motifs where all the edges are "top" edges). If you lay these pieces down with their right sides up and their edges together, you can create a nice, flat (and still visible) seam using the slip stitch method by picking up only the top (or outermost) strands of the V from a stitch on each side when making your join. This can be really pretty, especially when worked in a contrasting yarn; it's also a great way to make sure that you are connecting motifs in such a way that a stitch on one side is joined to the corresponding stitch on the other. I suggest you try it out sometime.

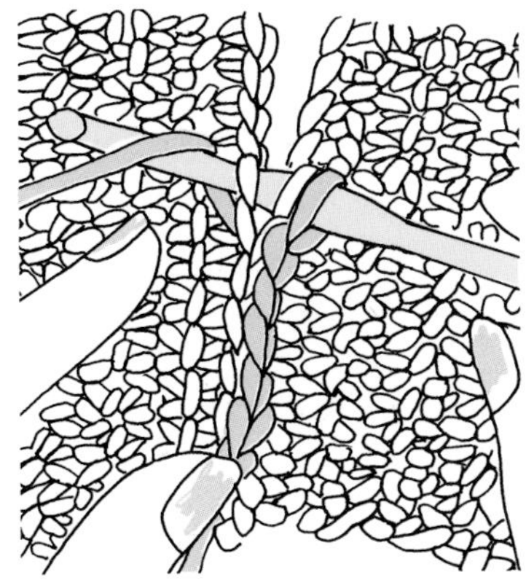

ALL buttoned up

Making Buttonholes

In crocheting, making buttonholes can be really simple—or it can be a real pain in the buttonhole. I like the horizontal ones; the vertical ones not so much.

Horizontal buttonholes are as easy as pie: Crochet to the point where you want your buttonhole to be and, instead of making stitches, chain the number of stitches you want your buttonhole width to be, skip the same number of stitches, then continue crocheting the row. On the next row, when you get to the chain, just crochet into it. For example, let's say you're doing a piece of single crochet and you want a 3-stitch-wide buttonhole. You'd crochet to the point where you want the buttonhole to start, chain 3, skip three stitches, and continue sc with the next stitch. On the way back, you'd crochet till you get to the chain, make 3 sc into the chain, and then carry on, my wayward son.

horizontal buttonhole

Vertical buttonholes are straightforward but annoying. Let's say you want a buttonhole that's 3 single crochet stitches tall and 2 single crochet stitches in from the edge. You'll start by crocheting to the edge, then when you turn, you'll crochet only 2 stitches and turn again (row 1). For rows 2 and 3, you'll crochet only over those two stitches. Finish off your yarn by cutting it about 6 inches from your work and pulling the tail through the last loop. You've created a narrow column of stitches on the outside of your work, and the rest of your piece has been left behind.

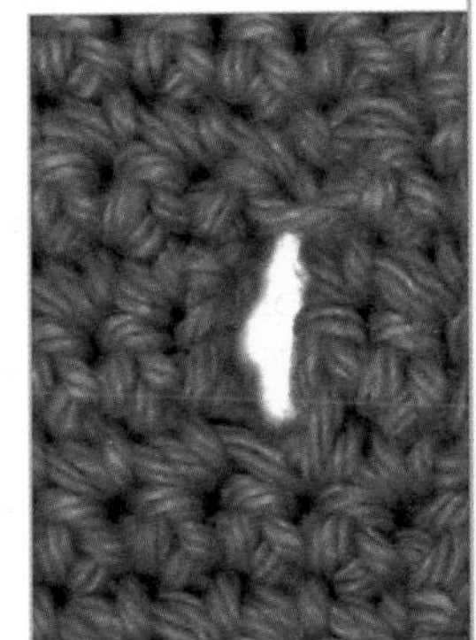

vertical buttonhole

Now you have to go back and make the rest catch up to the column bit: Reattach your yarn in the next stitch after your buttonhole and crochet all the way down the rest of that row (row 1). For the next two rows, crochet back and forth on those stitches, ending, of course, right when you get to the buttonhole. Okay, you know what's coming next, don't you? On the very next row, you'll crochet to the edge, then crochet right across the top of your little extra column. You've reconnected everyone, you've left a neat little buttonhole, and you're on your merry way again. This method leaves 2 hanging yarn strands for each buttonhole, which will not be any fun to work away later, so try and work right over them with your other stitches now.

Those vertical buttonholes can be a bummer, but here's some good news: If you're using double crochet or taller stitches for your piece, you might not even need to make buttonholes. These stitches leave spaces between their posts that are just the right size for slipping a button through, and can be used as their own built-in buttonholes whenever necessary. Just be sure the Three Bears would like your buttons—they should neither slip out of the hole (too small) nor stretch it (too big). You want them to be "just right."

fringe benefits

Adding Fringe to Your Work

Fringe is one of the easiest fancy things to add to your crochet work once it's done. To make it, start by wrapping a length of yarn around a sturdy rectangular thing that's about two inches longer than you want your fringe to be. You can use a book, a DVD, a cigarette pack, or whatever. To make lots of fringe, wrap the yarn a whole bunch of times, then cut it along one edge of the rectangle.

You now have a stack of strands for your fringe. Grab a few strands and fold them in half. This is how thick your fringe will be. Add or take away a few strands till it feels like what you want. Don't worry about the ends not lining up exactly; you'll trim them later. Stick a rather large crochet hook *from front to back* through the space in your crochet work where you want to add fringe. Hook the yarn at the fold and pull it through to the front of the fabric. Then hook the whole batch of fringe and pull it all the way through the loop on the hook. (You may need to use your fingers to help out here, if the bunch of fringe is really thick.) Pull on the ends to tighten and *voilà—le fringe, c'est chic!*

Keep on hanging fringe until your piece is all fringed up. Then trim the bottoms so they're even.

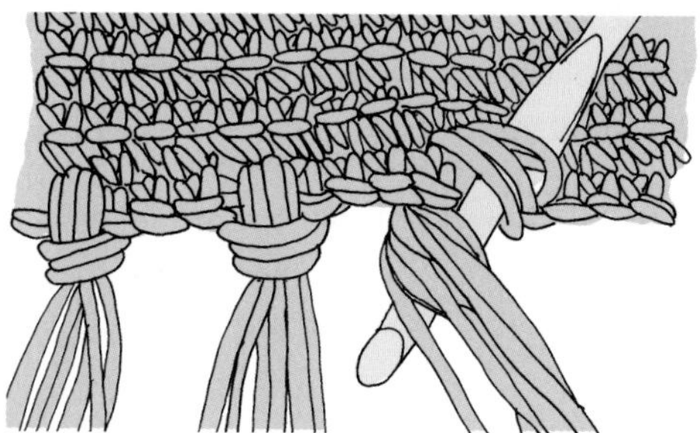

the no-hassle tassel

Hanging Tassels from Your Work

Tassels are a more mature, slightly fancier version of fringe. Jaunty whether hung from the top of a hat or the corner of an afghan, tassels are also easy to make.

1. Get a piece of heavy cardboard that's an inch or two longer than the tassel you want to make. In a pinch, a pack of cards or anything else that's rectangular and sturdy will do. Then take your yarn and wrap your little heart out.

2. Stop when your wrapped yarn is about ¼ inch thick all around. Take another piece of yarn about 8 inches

long, thread it through a tapestry needle, and pass it along the edge of your rectangular item, underneath the wrapped yarn.

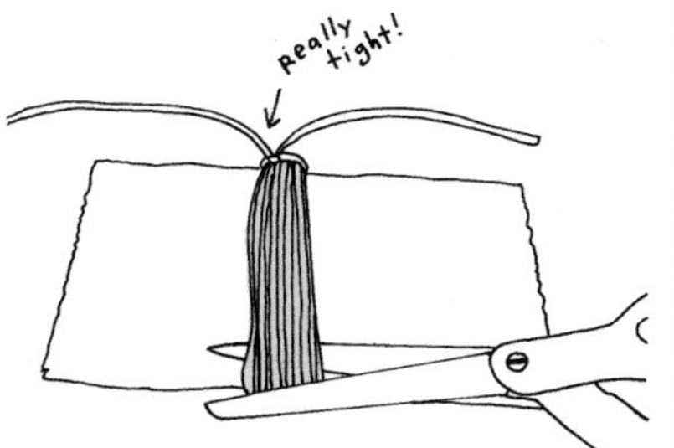

Take out the needle and make a square knot—a very, very tight square knot—leaving a long tail on one end of the yarn. This has to hold all the yarn together, so don't be afraid to pull it really tight and choke the life out of that thing. Then cut through the loops of yarn that are on the opposite side of the rectangle.

3. Tuck the short tail inside the tassel. Take the long tail and wrap it around the folded top of the tassel ¼ to ½ inch from the fold. Again, nice and tight. Thread the yarn through a needle and stick it up through the "head" of the tassel, right up the center. This is the bit of yarn you'll use to attach the tassel to your piece. Tack it on and twirl that thang!

Shake Your Pom-Pom

Adding Pom-Poms to Your Work

Pom-poms are fluffy and fun, and swing deliciously from whatever they are hung on. To make them, pom-poms require that you first create a little pom-pom maker, which is nothing more than two doughnut-shape pieces of cardboard or plastic. (They are also sold at many LYSs, ready-made, expressly for this purpose.) The hole in the center should be about half the size of the circle itself, to give you a nice full pom-pom. And to make it possible to wrap your yarn directly from a ball of yarn rather than working with shorter lengths of yarn, snip a small bite out of the edge of both layers of your pom-pom maker, Pacman-style.

Grab your yarn and start wrapping it around and around and around and around, covering all parts of your pom-pom maker and going for layer after layer of yarn, until that little hole in the center is completely filled with yarn.

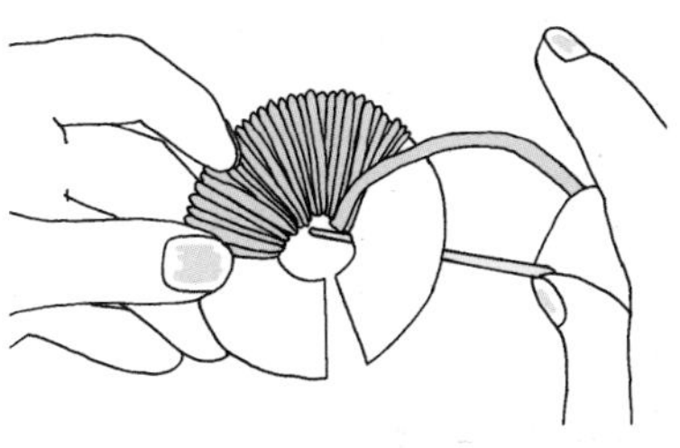

Next, cut through the loops all the way around the outside of the doughnut. Cut an 8-inch-long piece of yarn, pull it up between the two halves of the pom-pom maker, and knot it tightly around the core of the pom-pom. This knot needs to be really really tight, so be sure to eat your spinach the night before. Then pull or cut out the cardboard rings, fluff up your pom-pom, and give it a nice little haircut to even up the ends. Attach the pom-pom to your work with the same yarn you used to tie it together.

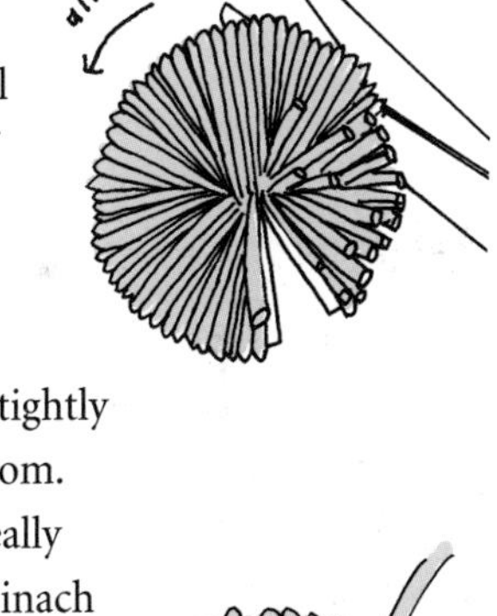

cutting the cord

Making Decorative Cords

In your crocheting life, you will sometimes encounter situations where you'll need to make a cord of some sort: to lace through eyelets to tie something closed, to wrap around your outfit like a belt, to hang from the ends of a hat so you can tie a sweet little bow under your chin, or hell, to connect two mittens so you don't lose them. Luckily, there are a number of simple ways to create such functional and decorative cords, some involving a crochet hook, some not.

crochet cords

The first, and simplest kind of cord is a length of **chain stitch.** Finish it off at the end and, dude, you've got a cord. Two slightly sturdier, thicker variations on this theme are the slip stitch cord and the single crochet cord. For the **slip stitch cord,** just crochet a length of chain a bit longer than you want your cord to be, and then slip stitch all the way back along the length of it. For this cord, it is nicest to crochet through that bottom butt strand of your chain. A **single crochet cord** would be made in a similar way, working single crochet stitches instead of slip stitches along the length of the chain, as you might have guessed. But beware: Such a cord will twist up like a curly fry, and there ain't nothin' you or anyone else on God's green earth can do about it.

twisted cord

This is an entirely different kind of cord, one that can work as a belt and is lovely to behold. (It's sometimes called a "monk's cord.") For this, you'll need a length of yarn at least 6 times as long as the cord you want to make. You can do this with one long strand of yarn or with a few strands held together. Double the strand (or strands) and knot the cut end. Then put the knotted end over a hook or a friend's finger, stick a pencil through the other end, and begin twisting like crazy. Twist and twist and twist until it's tight (oops, beware of your pal's finger). Now for the beauty part: Double that yarn on itself and stand back. Like lovers who have been separated for far too long, those two halves will just twist around each other and become one. Smooth out the yarn and you're done. If you want some fringy stuff hanging off the ends (monk style), just tie a knot in each end an inch or two in from the edge, snip the ends, and comb through them with your fingers.

i Like big buttons and i cannot Lie

Making Your Own Crocheted Buttons

Finding just-right buttons for a project is often the most fun part of the much-dreaded finishing process. Will you get something natural in wood or bone, or something playful like ladybugs or cars, or something glamorous and glittery in rhinestone or mother-of-pearl? Crochet offers yet another option: making your own. Crochet buttons can be entirely DIY, made with nothing but yarn and a crochet hook, or they can be made over a ring or plain button, and needless to say, they'll match perfectly. Here are some ways to make a few.

ball buttons

Make a ball button out of your crocheting yarn as follows:

1. Start by making a slip loop about 18 inches into a length of yarn, and hang it over a crochet hook. Use a smaller hook than is recommended for the yarn; you want to make a nice, tight, solid button here.

2. Working with the ball end of your yarn, chain 3 and join with a slip stitch to make a ring, then make 8 single crochet stitches into the ring; join with a slip stitch to the first single crochet stitch.

3. Next round: Chain 1 and single crochet into the same stitch that you just slipped into. Make 2 single crochet stitches into each of the remaining 7 stitches, and connect with a slip stitch to the first stitch and chain 1.

4. For the next round, make a single crochet into each stitch, connect the ring with a slip stitch, and chain 1.

5. On this row, you will decrease your stitches: Insert your hook into the next stitch, yarn over, and pull up a loop (2 loops on hook), then insert your hook into the following stitch, yarn over, and pull up a loop (3 loops on hook), yarn over, and pull the strand through all three loops on your hook. Repeat this process to the end of your row, decreasing (turning 2 stitches into 1 stitch) each time.

6. Cut an 18-inch tail and pull it through your last loop. Stuff the original 18-inch piece into the ball, as much as you can get in there. Then thread a needle with the remaining tail and sew the bottom of the ball button closed. Use that same yarn to sew your button onto your crocheted piece.

ring buttons

You can crochet over a ring to make a flatter button out of your yarn. Rings of various sizes are sold expressly for this purpose. Starting with a slip loop on your hook, insert your hook through the ring, draw up a loop of yarn, then yarn over and pull it through both loops on the hook. You've made a single crochet over the ring. Keep making single crochets like this until the ring is completely covered, and join the last stitch to the first one with a slip stitch.

If you are using thickish yarn or a smallish ring, once you've covered the entire outside of the ring, the center of the ring will also be chock-full-o-yarn, and you'll have only one step left: Cut your yarn about 12 inches long, thread a needle, and run it through the back loop of the V of each single crochet. Then turn your stitches topsy-turvy by pulling their tops toward the center of the ring and tightening your yarn. For a sturdy finish, take a couple of stitches diagonally across the underside of your button. Connect the button to your work with the same yarn. If you're using finer yarn or a larger ring, you may need to complete another round of single crochet stitches into each of your stitches before you run the strand through them and execute that last little trick.

covered buttons

Finally, you can make what's called a "covered button" by creating a little tea-cozy-like covering for any kind of flat round button. These buttons begin just like the ball button, but rather than beginning your decreases on the fifth row, continue expanding the circle in row four by making 1 single crochet in the first stitch and 2 single crochets in the following stitch, and repeating that all the way around the row. You'll do the same thing again, adding one more stitch between the increases on each round, until the circle is just a bit bigger than your button. Then put your bought button in place and work the decrease round (make 2 single crochets into 1 stitch; see directions for rows of ball button, page 87). Make a slip stitch to close your round, then cut your yarn, leaving a tail about 12 inches long. Thread a tapestry needle, run the yarn through the back loop of the V at the top of each stitch, and tighten it around the button. Use the tail to sew the button onto your item.

you gotta keep 'em decorated

Stitching onto Crochet

Sometimes a piece of crochet work needs just a bit of extra oomph when it's done. This can be especially true of large pieces of single or half-double crochet. Fortunately, that kind of material is perfect for adding colorful embroidered or crocheted designs.

You can add a nice, colorful, snakelike design of **slip stitch chains** across your work in a contrasting color yarn with a technique known as "surface crochet." Simply insert your hook into your crochet work from the front, hang the yarn over your hook (leave a 6-inch tail), and pull that loop out to the front. With the working yarn still in back of your fabric, insert the hook about ¼ inch away, and pull a loop up through the fabric *and* through the loop on your hook. You've made a slip stitch! Using this technique, you can make a nice slip stitch border around a colored section to clean up the edges or to create the outlines of flower petals, vines, leaves, or whatever other kind of design you'd like. Slip stitching is a fun way to add a simple decorative element to your work once it's done.

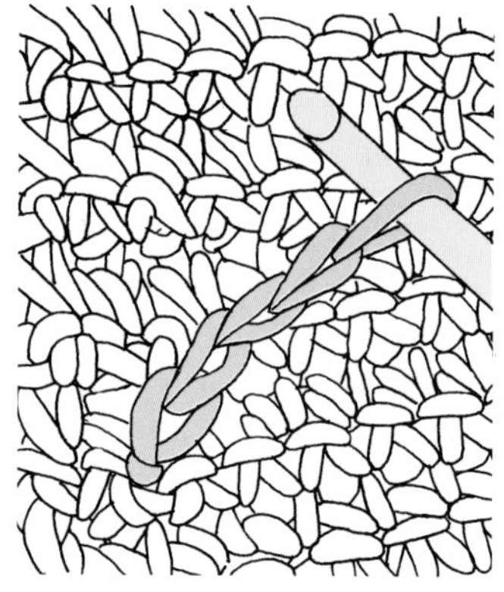

You can also **embroider** your work, making french knots, daisy chain stitches, satin stitches, or cross-stitches, just as you would on any other type of fabric. This works best on the most closed type of crochet work, such as single crochet.

Fabric made using the afghan stitch is a perfect background for cross-stitching, and the method for doing this is covered in chapter 7, pages 74–76.

All's Well That Ends Well

Working Away Yarn Ends

The last thing you'll want to do when finishing up a piece is to make your ends disappear. (Well, it may not be the last thing you'll *want* to do, but it's the last thing you *have* to do.) I don't mind sewing my crocheted pieces together and I have to confess to loving the magic of the blocking process, but sewing away ends is tedious to me. So before we get into doing it, let me tell you a secret: With a bit of forethought and practice, you can pretty much avoid this task. The way to get this finishing task out of your life is to simply crochet over your ends as you create them—work them into your stitches the same way you would work over a second color when you aren't using it in tapestry crochet. This means laying the cut ends over the tops of the stitches you're crocheting into, and then working right over them, enclosing them in your stitch like jelly in a jelly roll. After you've worked over about 2 inches' worth of yarn end, simply snip it off and forget about it forever.

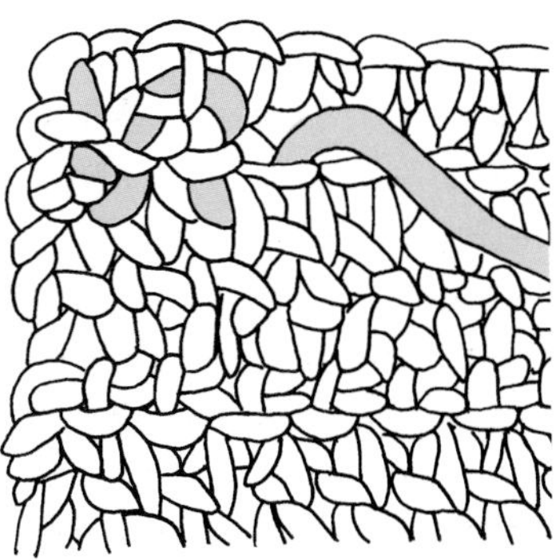

But say you didn't do this while you were working and you're left with lots of ends. The way to make them go away is simply to thread the end through a tapestry needle, then weave your needle in and out of the back of your crochet work, following along the path of the stitches. It's good to weave in both directions when working away ends: following a stitch from its base to its top, then following the next stitch from top to base, and so on. It's also important to hide your yarn inside these stitches without splitting the yarn. When you've done two inches, snip off the excess and call it a day.

Extreme Makeover

Blocking Your Work

Blocking is the almost alchemical process of taking your completed project, which is beautiful but will most likely have a couple of lumps and bumps, and turning it into a professional-looking piece of perfection. Blocking, you should know, works only on natural fibers such as cotton or wool, so don't bother with items made of acrylic (although running them through a simple wash once you're finished can improve their looks, too). Many patterns tell you to block your crocheted pieces to size before you sew them together, but pay them no mind. I don't know a single person who does it that way. Sew everything together, then get down to blocking.

Blocking can be done with steam or with heat from an iron, but I'm too afraid to bring anything that hot near my work. Here's my preferred low-risk method. All you need is a couple of clean towels and a flat surface where you can lay your garment down for a beauty rest.

Begin by filling a sink with lukewarm water. Never use hot water, because hot water can really make wool and some blends go nutso. Add a bit of mild shampoo or special wool wash to the water, mix it up a bit, then dunk your piece in there. Gently swirl it around in the water just a bit. Squeeze the piece to get the suds through it, then let it soak for about ten minutes.

Empty the sink and refill it with clean, cool (not cold) water and rinse your piece. Squeeze all the suds out and drain the sink. Refill the sink and rinse once more. Your piece is now ready to be blocked.

First, squeeze your piece, gently and carefully to get a lot of the water out. Then, get out a big, thick towel. Lay your piece flat, in the shape you want it to be. Roll up the towel, with your piece inside, and squeeze hard to get even more water out. Remember, squeeze, *don't wring.* Toss that soaked towel in the laundry and get out another towel. Lay the towel flat somewhere (on your floor, for instance), and lay your piece out on top. Pull the piece lightly at opposite corners (in other words, on the diagonal) to help the stitches "set." Then stretch it and scrunch it and work it like so much pizza dough into the exact size and shape it is supposed to have. If you've made something very lacy, you might even want to pin the piece to the towel to keep the motifs nice and open as they dry. Then leave the piece alone. It will dry—and it will take a *loooong* time to dry, maybe days, so if you've just finished something that needs to be worn or given as a gift tomorrow, you might need to skip this part. If you have a flat mesh drying rack, put it under the towel—it will speed up the drying process a *lot.* For small items, you can even use a baker's cooling rack. When it does dry, though, it will be just the shape that you've molded it into. There is a limit to the miracle of blocking—pull too much and your yarn will rip or split or fray—but for most jobs, there's just enough give that the blocking process can take it from a really handmade-looking item to something you could find on the racks of a fancy boutique. I told you—block is beautiful!

part two

crochet away

THE PATTERNS

pattern recognition

How to Read a Crochet Pattern

I've met people who tell me they don't like to follow patterns. They're scared, they say, of the nonsensical jumble of letters and numbers that confront them on each page. But there's no reason to be fearful. Crochet patterns are no more frightening than a cooking recipe. There, you know that 1 c means "1 cup" and 2 tsp means "2 teaspoons," and you know that if you follow the directions, line by line, you'll end up with something delicious. The same holds true for crochet patterns: Learn the abbreviations and you'll soon realize that ch 1 means "chain 1" and 2 dc means "2 double crochets." Best of all, follow the directions, line by line, and you'll end up with something fabulous. Everything you need to know to make the wonderful projects that follow are spelled out for you in the patterns—from the supplies you need to every last stitch you need to make. What's not to love?

Each pattern in this book begins by giving you the **finished size** of the project. That's not *your* size—it's the size of what you're making. So if your bust is 36 inches, you won't want to make a top that has a finished size of 36 inches, 'cause that's, like, the size of your skin, and a sweater that size will leave you a bit squashed. One or 2 inches' breathing room in the finished size will let you flaunt your curves but not suffocate you, 2 to 4 inches extra will fit comfortably while not being too snug, and 4 to 6 inches will make for a nice roomy top. Most of the projects in this book are sized for Small, Medium, Large, Extra Large, and Extra Extra Large, and the finished sizes are given in that order. But of course, you probably know, from shopping, that in some brands you're a medium and in others you're a large (or whatever). So when in doubt, go for the first size that is *larger* than your bust measurement—or measure a favorite sweater across the chest and make the size closest to that.

The **materials** section will let you know the type and amount of yarn you need, the hook size to get, and any other notions (buttons, ribbons, etc.) the project requires.

Next up is **gauge,** which is, without exaggeration, the single most important part of any pattern. That's because it's what the entire pattern is based on. If the gauge is 10 stitches per 4 inches, let's say, and you want to make a sweater with a finished measurement of 40 inches, you can be sure that you'll be making 100 stitches around to get to that 40 inches (you do the math). And if your gauge is off—even by only 1 or 2 stitches—you will end up with a sweater that is squishy or one that is baggy.

So, before you start any project, take the yarn you are going to use and the hook size recommended and, for heaven's sake, make yourself a test swatch. Cast on enough stitches for at least a 4-inch width of fabric in the required gauge, work up a nice sizable swatch in whatever stitch the gauge is given for, and measure, measure, measure (see page 35 for how to measure gauge). If you end up with fewer stitches than the pattern calls for (say, 8 stitches per 4 inches instead of 10), then get a crochet hook one size *smaller* and try, try again. Conversely, if you end up with *too many* stitches (say, 12 stitches per 4 inches instead of 10), then try the next *larger* hook size. Unless you have the exactly correct gauge, do not—I repeat, do not—pass Go, do not collect $200. I know, it's a pain in the butt, but it's a bigger pain to spend hours or even weeks working on something that you can never wear because it came out the wrong size.

Gauge is also the key if you want to substitute yarn. If you don't want to use the yarn suggested in the pattern, you can swap it out with something else, *as long as you get the same gauge* as the pattern calls for. For the most predictable results, try to use another yarn that is the same weight (sport, worsted, or whatever the pattern calls for), and has a similar fiber content to that used in the pattern. But basically, if you've got gauge, you've got it all.

Following the gauge are definitions of any **special stitches** used in the pattern. All the rest of the stitches are ones that should be familiar to you from the first part of this book—your friends the chain stitch, single and double crochet, and the rest of the gang—and they will show up in these patterns as well.

Finally, there are **the directions.** Crochet patterns use a number of conventions you should know about. For one thing, there's the issue of size. As I mentioned, many of the patterns here are given for several sizes. But instead of writing out the entire pattern for each size over and over again, it will be written like this: The first number given refers to the smallest size, and the remaining sizes are presented from smallest to largest, in parentheses, and separated by commas. Say you have a pattern for a hat that's made for three sizes: baby bear, mama bear, and papa bear. The pattern tells you

Size for Baby (Mama, Papa) Bear

and the first line of the pattern says

Chain 24 (30, 38) sts.

That simply means that for baby bear's hat, you should chain 24 stitches; for mama bear's hat, make 30 chains; and for papa bear, hook up 38 stitches. It's a good idea, once you've chosen your size for a pattern, to go through it and circle or highlight the numbers that pertain to your size.

To follow a pattern, you'll need to understand **the abbreviations.** On the following page you'll find a list of all the abbreviations used in the patterns in this book.

You'll also need to be able to decode the shorthand that crochet patterns use. First there are the parentheses. Think of whatever directions appear inside the parentheses as a "chunk" of stitches. You might have to make all those stitches into the same stitch, or you might have to repeat that chunk a number of times. Whatever it says after the parentheses will make what you are supposed to do crystal clear. Putting a chunk of stitches together inside parentheses helps you to understand what you're doing and makes the pattern easier to read. So instead of saying

Dc in first stitch, ch 1, dc in same stitch, ch 1, dc in same stitch

the pattern can just say

(dc, ch 1, dc, ch 1, dc) in first stitch

which is so much nicer, so much clearer, and so much purtier!

Next there are the brackets, which are used to set off a chunk of stitches inside parentheses. So, for example, you might come across a little something like this:

(tr, [ch 2, tr] 2 times) in last st

The "2 times" here means to repeat what's inside the brackets two times; the parentheses mean you should do the whole shebang in the same stitch. So you'd make a

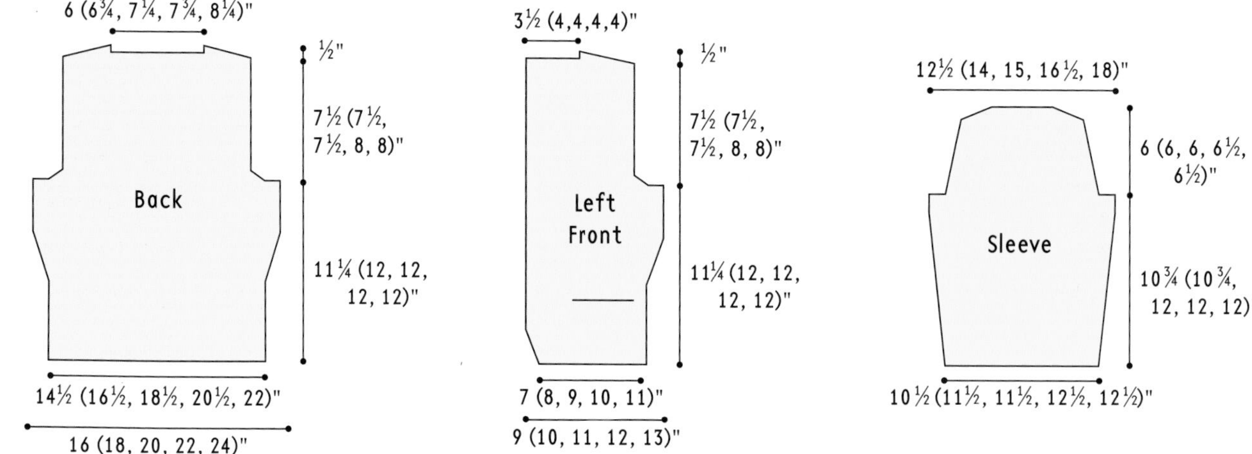

triple crochet, chain 2, triple crochet, chain 2, triple crochet, all in the last stitch.

Finally, there are times when a little snippet of instructions needs to be repeated. That's marked with an asterisk (*) to signify the beginning of what's going to be repeated, and a semicolon (;) to tell you where those directions end. Like this:

> ***dc in next dc, 2 dc in next dc; rep from * across to end of row**

Here, you make a double crochet in the next double crochet stitch, 2 double crochet stitches into the double crochet stitch after that, and then repeat the sequence of stitches—a double crochet into the next double crochet stitch, 2 double crochet stitches into the double crochet stitch after that—until you get to the end of the row. And just in case it all makes you a bit dizzy, the directions frequently tell you, throughout the pattern, how many stitches you should expect to have at the end of each row, so you can make sure you're on the right track.

Many of the patterns in the book also include something called a **schematic,** or drawing of the shape of the piece you are making, along with the measurements each part of the piece should have, following the same baby bear (mama bear, papa bear) conventions (see above). That helps you visualize what it is you're trying to accomplish and lets you check that you are getting it as you go along. If you've checked your gauge and you aren't getting the measurements the schematic says you should have, something is wrong. Maybe you were totally stressed out and

EXPERIENCING TECHNICAL DIFFICULTIES

Each of the patterns in this book was carefully checked and rechecked, not only by the designers themselves, but also by our superb technical editor. Nevertheless, mistakes are sometimes printed. If a pattern just doesn't seem to be working out as expected, check the errata page on my Web site, www.knithappens.com. Similarly, if you locate a mistake, please e-mail me at stitchnbitch@bust.com so I can post the correction right away.

crocheting tightly when you did your gauge swatch, and now that you're really into the groove you're suddenly crocheting much more loosely. Remeasure your gauge on the work in progress. Chances are, it isn't what the pattern calls for. Either frog the thing and start over with a different size hook or decide then and there to give it to someone it will fit.

One last note: I have not rated the patterns here according to their difficulty, as many other books do. That's because I don't believe in it. One hooker's "difficult" is another's easy breezy, and honestly, I think there's no better motivation to learn a new skill than to want to make a project that you just really, truly *have* to have. That said, if you're getting ready to make your *very* first crochet project, avoid the patterns that have complicated lace stitches or a lot of fancy color work going on. But once you've completed that first project made in mostly straightforward single or double crochet, all bets are off. A more advanced crocheter may be able to complete a complex project in a shorter time than a less seasoned crocheter will, but that's no reason not to try and tackle something you want to make. Throw yourself in the water and figure out how to swim—it's the best way to learn.

ABBREVIATIONS

beg	begin(s), beginning
bet	between
BPdc	back post double crochet
CC	contrasting color
ch	chain
cm	centimeter(s)
dc	double crochet
dec	decrease
dtr	double triple crochet
FPdc	front post double crochet
g	gram(s)
hdc	half-double crochet
inc	increase
m	meters
MC	main color
mm	millimeter(s)
oz	ounce(s)
rem	remaining
rep	repeat
rnd(s)	round(s)
RS	right side
sc	single crochet
sk	skip
sl st(s)	slip stitch(es)
st(s)	stitch(es)
tog	together
tr	triple crochet
WS	wrong side
yd	yard(s)
yo	yarn over hook

STITCH KEY

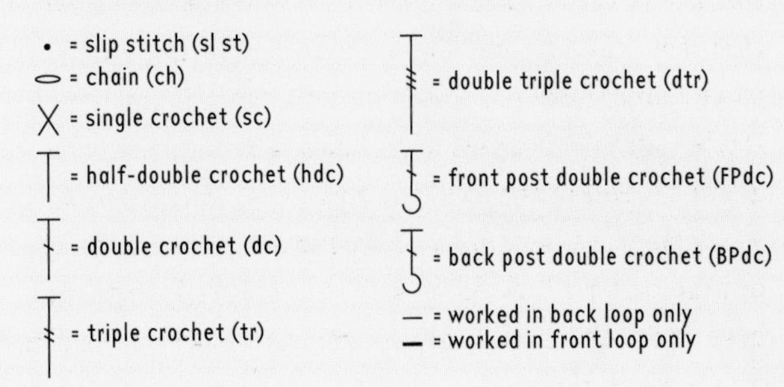

Michelle Ameron

Garden Scarf

I initially learned to crochet for one purpose—to make crocheted flowers. I loved the speed of crochet and the nearly instant gratification and couldn't stop making them. When I'd finish one I'd just put it in a drawer, until I realized I needed to get my act together and make something out of them. So along came Garden Scarf. It's a fun, easy project that moves quickly because the flowers are joined together as they are made. And while it is a scarf, it's bright, summery, and soft enough to wear all year around—perfect for those who, like me, are real wimps around air conditioning in the summer.

SCARF

Flower A

With A, ch 10 and join into a ring with sl st in first ch.

Rnd 1 (RS): Ch 1, work 24 sc in ring, sl st in first sc to join—24 sc.

Rnd 2: Ch 1, *sc in sc, ch 4, sk next 2 sc; rep from * around, sl st in first sc to join—8 ch-4 loops.

Rnd 3: Ch 1, (sc, hdc, 2 dc, hdc, sc) in each ch-4 loop around, sl st in first sc to join. Fasten off.

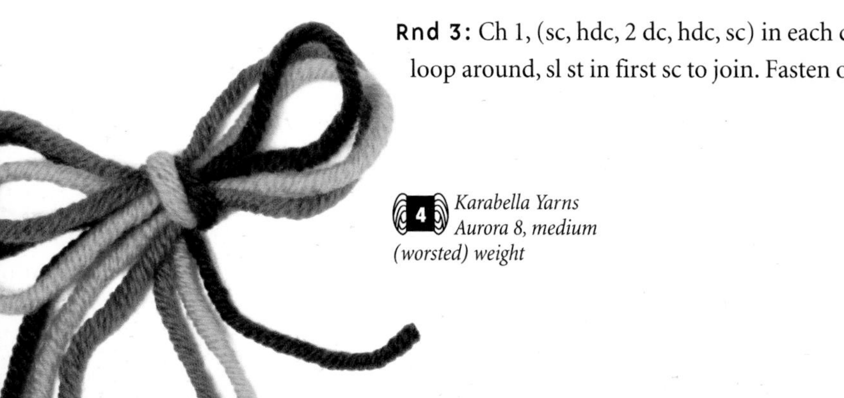

4 *Karabella Yarns Aurora 8, medium (worsted) weight*

Finished Size

4½" wide × 63" long

Materials

Yarn

Karabella Yarns Aurora 8
(100% Extra Fine Merino Wool;
1.75 oz [50 g]/98yd [90 m]):
1 ball each of #10 Dark Olive (A),
#11 Light Olive (B), and #25 Pink (C)

Hook

Size I/9 (5.5 mm) crochet hook
or size needed to obtain gauge

Notions

Yarn needle

Gauge

Each flower = 4½" in diameter

Special Stitches

Joining tr: Insert hook from front to back through post of designated st on previous flower, yo (twice), insert hook in same loop on current flower already holding first part of petal, yo, draw yarn through loop, (yo, draw yarn through 2 loops on hook) 3 times

Joining dc: Insert hook from front to back through post of designated st on previous flower, yo, insert hook in same loop on current flower already holding first part of petal, yo, draw yarn through loop, (yo, draw yarn through 2 loops on hook) twice

Flower B

With A, ch 2.

Rnd 1 (RS): Work 8 sc in second ch from hook, sl st in first sc to join—8 sc.

Rnd 2: Ch 1, work 2 sc in each sc around, sl st in first sc to join—16 sc. Fasten off A.

Rnd 3: With RS facing, join C in first sc, ch 6 (counts as dc, ch 3), sk next sc, *dc in next sc, ch 3, sk next sc; rep from * around, sl st in second ch of turning ch to join—8 ch-3 loops.

Rnd 4 (joining rnd): Ch 1, (sc, hdc, dc, tr, dc, hdc, sc) in each of first 6 ch-3 loops, (sc, hdc, dc) in next ch-3 loop, insert hook from front to back in first dc of any petal in rnd 3 of last flower, yo twice, complete joining tr in same ch-3 loop on current flower, insert hook in next dc on last flower, yo, complete joining dc in same ch-3 loop on current flower, (hdc, sc) in same ch-3 loop on current flower, (sc, hdc) in next ch-3 loop, insert hook in first dc of next petal on last flower, yo, complete joining dc in same ch-3 loop on current flower, insert hook in next dc on last flower, yo twice, complete joining tr in same ch-3 loop on current flower, (dc, hdc, sc) in same ch-3 loop on current flower, sl st in first sc to join—8 petals; 2 petals joined to previous flower. Fasten off.

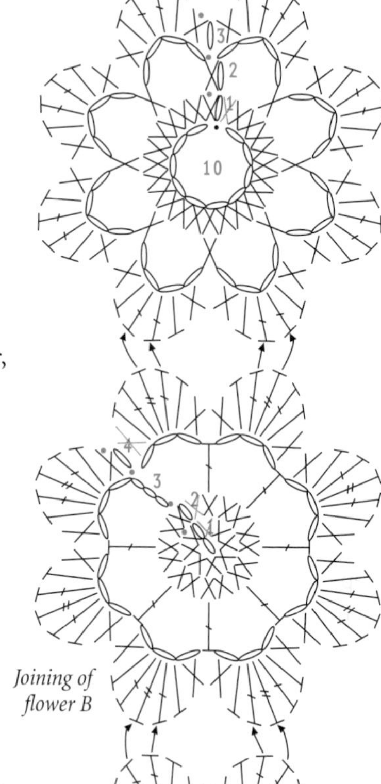

Flower C

With B, work same as flower A through rnd 2.

Rnd 3 (joining rnd): Ch 1, (sc, hdc, 2 dc, hdc, sc) in each of first 6 ch-4 loops, sk 2 petals in rnd 4 of last flower, insert hook from front to back in center tr of next petal on last flower, yo, complete joining dc in same ch-4 loop on current flower, insert hook in next dc on last flower, yo, complete joining dc in same ch-4 loop on current flower, (hdc, sc) in same ch-4 loop on current flower, insert hook from front to back in first dc of next petal on last flower, yo, complete joining dc in same ch-4 loop on current flower, insert hook in next tr on last flower, yo, complete joining dc in same ch-4 loop on current flower, (hdc, sc) in same ch-4 loop on current flower, sl st in first sc to join—8 petals; 2 petals joined to previous flower. Fasten off.

Skipping 2 petals on each side between joined petals, work a total of 14 flowers as follows:

About Michelle After some very generous teaching attempts by women from my Stitch 'n Bitch group, I eventually learned how to crochet on my own. Or rather, Martha Stewart taught me, via her Web site. I've been crocheting for about a year, and in addition to the flower madness, I've been teaching myself to design patterns for small accessories—jewelry and handbags and such. Besides crocheting, I knit, sew, embroider, needle felt, and collect way too many fiber-related supplies. I live in Toronto, where I work as a graphic designer.

Flower D

Rep flower B working rnds 1–2 with B and rnds 3–4 with A.

Flower E

With C, rep flower C.

Flower F

Rep flower B working rnds 1–2 with C and rnds 3–4 with B.

Flower G

With A, rep flower C.

Rep flowers B–G once, then make one more flower B, so that 14 flowers total are completed.

Weave in ends. Lightly block.

Stripes (and Stripes) Forever

SCARF/BELT/GUITAR STRAP

Finished Size

Scarf: 3" × 66"

Directions for Belt are given for size S. Changes for M, L, XL, and XXL are in parentheses.

Belt: $2^1/_2$" or desired width

To fit waist: 23 (27, 31, 35, 39)"

Finished length: 28 (32, 36, 40, 44)" before hemming

Guitar strap: Desired width and length

Materials

Yarn

Brown Sheep Cotton Fleece (80% Cotton/20% Merino Wool; 3.5 oz [100 g]/215 yd [197 m]): 1 skein each of #CW222 Pink Diamond (A), #CW810 Cherry Moon (B), #CW100 Cotton Ball (C), and #CW840 Lime Light (D). (**Note:** 1 skein of each color will be enough to make two scarves if you use A, B, or C for the wider stripe instead of D, on the second scarf.)

Hooks

Sizes F/5 (3.75 mm) and G/6 (4 mm) crochet hooks or sizes needed to obtain gauge

Notions

For belt or guitar strap: Yarn needle, and embroidery thread (or sewing thread doubled twice, 4 strands); "B" or "D" style belt buckle (available from www.mjtrim.com)

Gauge

18 sts and 24 rows sc = 4"

Get your stripe on! This pattern is perfect for beginning hookers because you use only two stitches: single crochet and slip stitch. The more experienced will enjoy how quickly this project works up: You can create a new scarf and belt with each season's must-have colors! The combination of a mostly cotton yarn and the single crochet stitch makes for a very strong fabric. If you follow the simple conversion instructions, you can turn the scarf into a sturdy belt or guitar strap.

SCARF

Note: This is a self-fringing scarf. Join a separate strand of yarn at beginning of each row, leaving an 8" tail. Fasten off at the end of each row, leaving an 8" tail. To eliminate fringe, skip the ch 1 at the beginning and end of each row. Also, there is no need to join a separate strand of yarn for each row unless you are changing color or to leave an 8" tail when joining or fastening off.

With smaller hook and A, leaving an 8" tail, ch 300. Fasten off, leaving an 8" tail, turn.

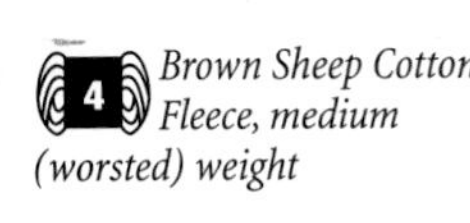

Brown Sheep Cotton Fleece, medium (worsted) weight

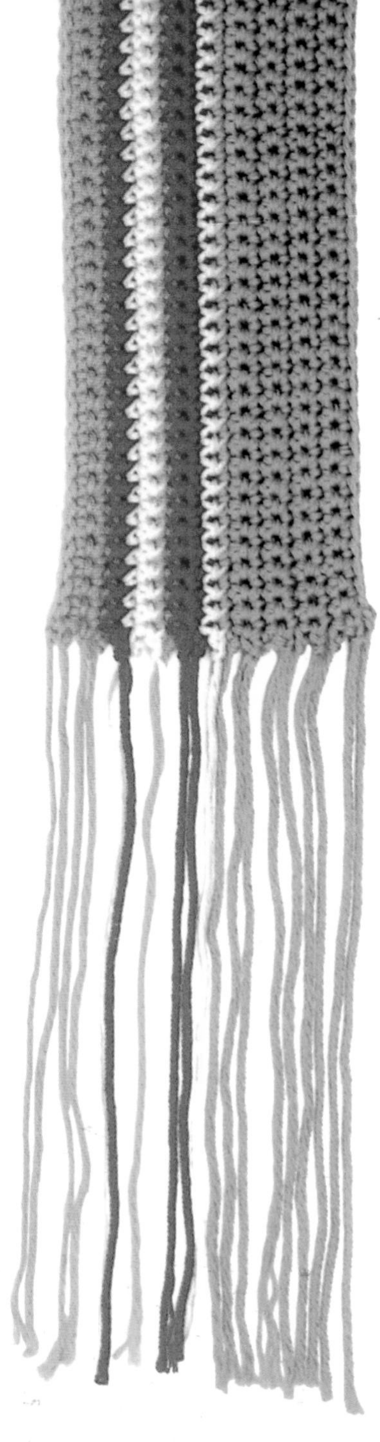

Row 1 (RS): Leaving an 8" tail, with smaller hook and A, ch 1, then sc in second ch of foundation ch, sc in each ch across to second to last ch, ch 1, leaving last ch unworked—298 sc. Fasten off, leaving an 8" tail.

Row 2: Leaving an 8" tail, using smaller hook and A, ch 1, sk first ch of last row, sc in first sc, sc in each sc across to last sc, ch 1, turn, leaving last ch unworked—298 sc. Fasten off, leaving an 8" tail.

Rows 3–18: Rep row 2, working in the following color sequence: 1 more row A; 1 row B; 2 rows C; 1 row A; 2 rows B; 1 row C; 8 rows D

Edging

Row 1: With RS facing, working across opposite side of foundation ch, leaving an 8" tail, with larger hook, join A in first ch, sl st in each ch across. Fasten off, leaving an 8" tail.

BELT

The belt can be made with or without a belt buckle. Use sizes given or adjust length by working foundation ch to desired length to begin.

With smaller hook and A, leaving an 8" tail, ch 128 (146, 164, 182, 200) or desired length. Fasten off, leaving an 8" tail, turn.

Work same as scarf for desired width, in desired stripe pattern.

Note: Belt buckles and snap hooks come in varying widths. To adjust your crochet to fit the buckle or hook, use the row gauge to determine how many rows to crochet to fit your piece of hardware. For example, if you have a really great belt buckle that is 2" wide, multiply 6 (rows per inch) × 2 = 12 rows. Then work 12 rows of sc in desired stripe pattern.

Note: This will create a belt with approximately 4" of overlap. If you would like your belt to be longer or shorter, just adjust the length of the foundation chain.

Finishing

To add a belt buckle to one end, weave in ends on one end of belt. Fold over ½" of the end of the belt and use a whipstitch to hem it to the body of the belt. Thread hemmed edge around the belt buckle post, fold over the hemmed edge to WS of belt, sew folded edge to WS of belt. To wear, thread the fringed end through the buckle and tighten to fit.

GUITAR STRAP

Guitar straps usually run 44–54" long, but check with your local Joe Strummer or Joan Jett to find out their preference. Or you can measure an existing strap to find a comfortable length. Make a foundation ch of the desired length + 2" for hems. Or determine length of ch with the following formula:

(Desired length in inches + 2" for hems) × 4.5 sts (per inch) = number of ch sts in foundation ch.

Example: For a 47" strap: (47 + 2) × 4.5 = 220.5 (round up) = 221 ch to start.

With A, make a ch of desired length. Fasten off.

Work same as scarf, omitting fringe if desired.

Finishing

Weave in ends. Fold both ends to WS of strap and sew hems same as for belt. Attach to D rings or snap hooks same as for belt to attach the strap to a guitar.

About Chelsea I am an IT project manager for a major natural foods retailer and currently live just outside of Washington, D.C. My grandmother taught me to crochet when I was very young, considering it to be an important life skill. And while it didn't save lives, my uncles were never without warm winter scarves. As I grew older, frustration over the lack of good crochet patterns led me to learn to knit. However, I have never given up on crochet, and am very glad to be contributing to its revival. You can see more of my fibery exploits (and not a single TP cozy) on my online journal at www.thedevashands.blogspot.com.

Sweet Pea Shawl

Stylish, sophisticated, and simple. I set out to design an openwork shawl that was all these things. The shawl had to be wearable in the car while I was driving and at work while I was teaching, too. It also had to be stylish and dressy—made from a yarn that had some depth to it. Last, it needed to be worked up quickly, since I needed to wear it the next day! This of-the-moment Sweet Pea Shawl is fabulously feminine and exudes an airy charm. When tied at the front, it creates a graceful, flowing silhouette with the fringe cascading down the contours of the wearer. Gathered at the side, the shawl delivers a sprightly asymmetrical hemline of dancing shell designs.

Finished Size

58" wide × 35" deep, excluding fringe

Materials

Yarn

Classic Elite Yarns Flash (100% Mercerized Marled Cotton; 1.75 oz [50 g]/93 yd [85 m]): 6 skeins of #6189 Pink Tweed

Hook

Size I/9 (5.5 mm) crochet hook or size needed to obtain gauge

Notions

Yarn needle

7"-long piece of cardboard

Gauge

(Shell, sc) in pattern = 3";
4 rows in pattern = 3½"

Special Stitch

Shell: (Dtr, [ch 2, dtr] 4 times) in same st

SHAWL

Ch 202.

Row 1 (RS): Sc in second ch from hook, *ch 1, sk next 4 ch, shell in next ch, ch 1, sk next 4 ch, sc in next ch; rep from * across, turn—20 shells.

Row 2: Sl st in each st to center dtr of first shell (dec made), ch 1, sc in same st, *ch 3, sk next ch-2 space, dc in next ch-2 space, ch 3, sk next 2 ch-1 spaces, dc in next ch-2 space, ch 3, skip next ch-2 space, sc in next dtr; rep from * across to center dtr of last shell, turn, leaving rem sts unworked (dec made)—57 ch-3 loops.

4 Classic Elite Yarns Flash, medium (worsted) weight

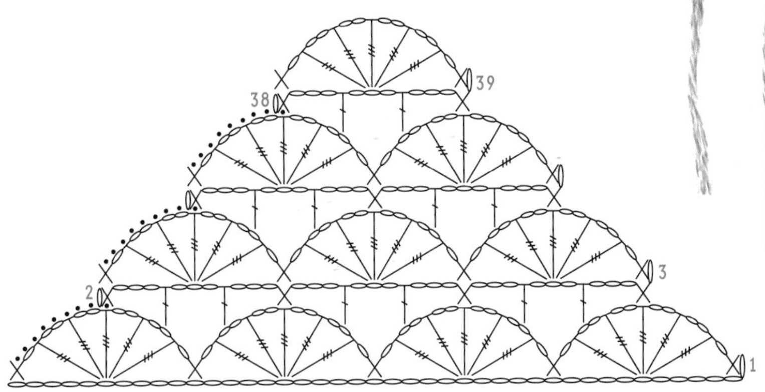

Reduced sample

Row 3: Ch 1, sc in first sc, *ch 1, sk next ch-3 space, shell in center ch of next ch-3 loop, ch 1, sk next ch-3 space, sc in next sc; rep from * across, turn—19 shells.

Rows 4–39: Rep rows 2–3 (18 times)—1 shell at end of row 39. Fasten off. Weave in ends.

Finishing

Wrap yarn around 7" piece of cardboard 164 times. Cut yarn at the bottom only, to create 14"-long strands. Using 4 strands for each fringe, knot one fringe in first sc on each end of all even-numbered rows. At the bottom tip of shawl, knot one fringe in center dtr of bottom shell.

About Amie My great-grandmother taught me to crochet when I was nine, and I've loved it ever since. After getting degrees in art education and graphic design, I wanted a creative outlet. So I started NexStitch (www.nexstitch.com), a stylish crochet pattern business featuring ponchos, shawls, scarves, handbags, and bikinis. Unique to NexStitch are free Tunisian crochet video tutorials, articles, and a crochet newsletter. My goal is to "hip" everyone to crochet! I currently live in Scotch Plains, New Jersey, with my wonderful fiancé, Larry.

Cold Shoulders

This easy-to-make 1940s-style capelet is done in fluffy mohair with double and triple crochet. Constructed in one piece, it has a collar and a tie closure with large pom-poms. I based this design on a wool capelet I saw in a vintage fashion magazine. My first "practice" version was made from a "frogged" mohair sweater I found at a thrift shop, while this one is made with a beautiful wine-colored mohair yarn. This Cold Shoulders capelet would make a great cover-up for a cool late-summer evening.

Finished Size

Directions are given for size Small/Medium (S/M). Changes for Large/Extra Large are in parentheses.

Neck edge: 19 (21½)"

Bottom edge: 54 (60)"

Length from neck to bottom edge: 12"

Materials

Yarn

Classic Elite La Gran (76.5% mohair/17.5% wool/6% nylon; 1.5 oz [42 g]/90 yd [82 m]): 3 skeins of #6553 Chianti

Hook

Size I/9 (5.5 mm) crochet hook or size needed to obtain gauge

Notions

Yarn needle

Pom-pom maker (see page 85)

Gauge

10 sts and 4 rows dc = 4"

1 shell in pattern = 3"

Special Stitches

Shell: (Tr, [ch 1, tr] 5 times) in same st

CAPELET

Ch 51 (57).

Row 1: Dc in fourth ch from hook, dc in each ch across, turn—48 (54) sts.

Row 2: Ch 3 (counts as first dc), dc in each st across, turn—48 (54) sts.

Row 3: Ch 3 (counts as first dc), 2 dc in next dc, *dc in next dc, 2 dc in next dc; rep from * across to last 0 (2) sts, dc in each of last 0 (2) sts, turn—72 (80) sts.

Row 4: Ch 3 (counts as first dc), 2 dc in next dc, *dc in next dc, 2 dc in next dc; rep from * across, turn—108 (120) sts.

Rows 5–6: Ch 3 (counts as first dc), dc in each st across, turn—108 (120) sts.

Row 7: Ch 3 (counts as first dc), dc in first dc (inc made), dc in each st across to last st, 2 dc in last st, turn—110 (122) sts.

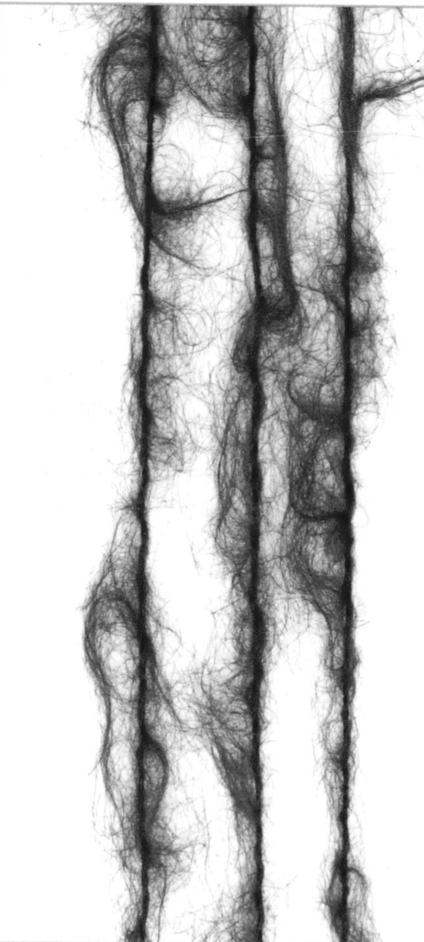

Classic Elite La Gran Mohair, medium (worsted) weight

Shell Pattern

Row 8: Ch 5 (counts as tr, ch 1), (tr, ch 1, tr) in first tr (half shell made), *ch 1, sk next 6 dc, shell between last skipped and next dc; rep from * across to last 7 sts, ch 1, sk next 6 sts, (tr, ch 1, tr, ch 1, tr) in last st (half shell made), turn—17 (19) shells + 2 half shells.

Rows 9–12: Ch 5 (counts as tr, ch 1), (tr, ch 1, tr) in first tr (half shell made), *ch 1, sk next 5 ch-1 spaces, shell in next ch-1 space (center ch-1 space of shell); rep from * across to last 5 ch-1 spaces, ch 1, skip next 5 ch-1 spaces, (tr, ch 1, tr, ch 1, tr) in last st (half shell made), turn—17 (19) shells + 2 half shells.

For longer capelet, rep row 9 for desired length.

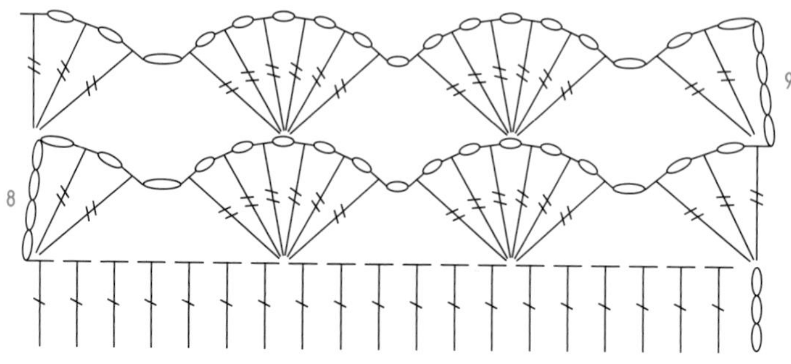

Reduced sample of shell pattern

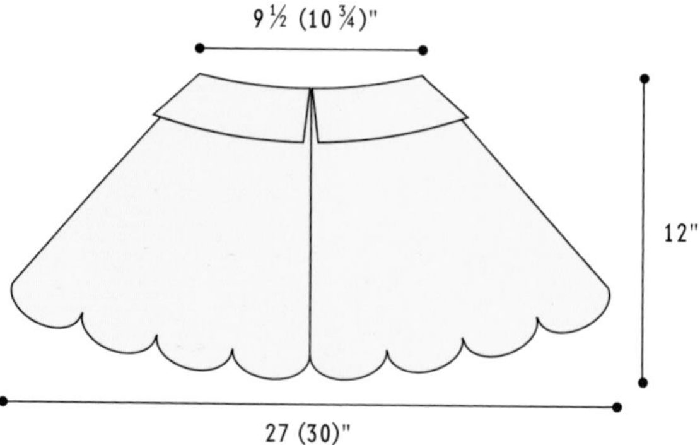

Collar

Row 1: With RS facing, working across opposite side of foundation ch, join yarn in first ch on neck edge, ch 3, dc in each ch across, turn—48 (54) sts.

Rows 2–3: Ch 3 (counts as first dc), dc in first dc (inc made), dc in each dc across to last st, 2 dc in last st, turn—52 (58) sts at end of last row.

Tie

Join yarn at base of collar on one side of neck, ch 48. Fasten off. Rep tie on other side of neck.

Finishing

Using pom-pom maker, make two 2½" pom-poms. Tie one pom-pom to end of each tie.

About Laurie I'm a 32-year-old artist and textile designer living in Madison, Wisconsin. I make hand-dyed and -printed fabrics and clothing under the label Darcy Sparrow. When I'm not elbow deep in dye, I usually have one of my crochet or knitting projects in hand. After procrastinating for many years, I finally taught myself to crochet four years ago from instructions in a tattered 1920s needle arts book I found at a garage sale. I enjoy making up my own designs for projects, often looking to vintage fashions for inspiration. A highlight of my week is getting together with my friends in the lively Madison Stitch 'n Bitch group. My current project is a giant tote bag crocheted from silk organza fabric scraps.

Dot Matthews

YeeHAW LAdY

Whether you're from the city or the country, this hat will set your inner cowgirl free. You'll love the sassy, free-spirited mood you acquire the moment you put it on. And don't forget that cowboy in your life—he'll want one, too, when he sees how much fun you're having wearing yours. The appealing decorative stitch on the sides and the ropelike trim around the brim will hold the interest of the intermediate hooker and add to your stitch library. This pattern might be a challenge for a beginner, but, hey, if you're adventurous and ready to expand your crochet knowledge, it will be a fun and rewarding project.

Finished Size

21" in circumference around base of brim

Materials

Yarn

Lion Brand Lion Cotton (100% cotton; 5 oz [140 g]/236 yd [212 m]): 2 balls of #112 Poppy Red

Hook

Size J/10 (6 mm) crochet hook or size needed to obtain gauge

Notions

Yarn needle

Stitch markers

2 yds of floral wire

Gauge

With 2 strands of yarn held tog as one, 14 sts and 14 rows sc = 4"

Special Stitches

Cluster: Yo, insert hook in st, yo, draw yarn through st (3 loops on hook), sk next st, yo, insert hook in next st, yo, draw yarn through st, yo, draw yarn through 5 loops on hook

Reverse hdc: Yo, insert hook in next st to the right, yo, draw yarn through st, yo, draw yarn through 3 loops on hook

HAT

Note: Entire hat is worked with 2 strands of yarn held tog as one.

With 2 strands of yarn held together as one, ch 8.

Rnd 1 (RS): Sc in fourth ch from hook, sc in each of next 3 ch, 3 sc in last ch; working across opposite side of foundation ch, sc in each of next 4 ch, 4 sc in next ch-3 space, sl st in next sc to join—15 sc.

Rnd 2: Ch 1 (counts as first pointed front sc), sc in each of next 3 sc, 2 sc in next sc, (sc, ch 2, sc) in next sc (front tip of hat), 2 sc in next sc, sc in each of next 4 sc, 2 sc in each of next 4 sc (rounded back of hat), sl st in next sc to join—22 sc.

4 *Lion Brand Lion Cotton, medium (worsted) weight*

About Dot Mom taught me the stitches and how to make a doily when I was 12, but I didn't learn to read a pattern until I was 19 and returned to crochet. My first project was a 6-foot-long tablecloth for my mother-in-law, which took about nine months to complete and used about five miles of thread. I'm retired from my local government job, and now enjoy crocheting for family—I have nine grandchildren—friends, and charity. I started creating my own patterns in April 2004, when I designed a ponytail hat for my granddaughters to wear with their long hair. You can visit my blog, Crochet By the Hook, at www.bythehook.blogdrive.com, or my pattern-only blog, Patterns by Dot, at www.patbythehook.blogdrive.com.

Rnd 3: Ch 1 (counts as first sc), sk first sc, sc in each of next 4 sc, 2 sc in next sc, sc in next sc, (sc, ch 2, sc) in next ch-2 space, sc in next sc, 2 sc in next sc, sc in each of next 5 sc, *2 sc in next sc, sc in next sc; rep from * 3 times, sl st in next sc to join—30 sc.

Rnd 4: Ch 1 (counts as first sc), sk first sc, sc in each of next 6 sc, 2 sc in next sc, sc in next sc, (sc, ch 2, sc) in next ch-2 space, sc in next sc, 2 sc in next sc, sc in each of next 7 sc, *2 sc in next sc, sc in each of next 2 sc; rep from * 3 times, sl st in next sc to join—38 sc.

Rnd 5: Ch 1 (counts as first sc), sk first sc, sc in each of next 8 sc, 2 sc in next sc, sc in next sc, (sc, ch 2, sc) in next ch-2 space, sc in next sc, 2 sc in next sc, sc in each of next 9 sc, *2 sc in next sc, sc in each of next 3 sc; rep from * 3 times, sl st in next sc to join—46 sc.

Rnd 6: Ch 1 (counts as first sc), sk first sc, sc in each of next 12 sc, (sc, ch 2, sc) in next ch-2 space, sc in each of next 13 sc, *2 sc in next sc, sc in each of next 4 sc; rep from * 3 times, sl st in next sc to join—52 sc.

Rnd 7: Ch 1 (counts as first sc), sk first sc, sc in each of next 13 sc, (sc, ch 2, sc) in next ch-2 space, sc in each of next 14 sc, *2 sc in next sc, sc in each of next 5 sc; rep from * 3 times, sl st in next sc to join—58 sc. Place a marker in each of last 4 increases, move marker up as work progresses.

Rnd 8: Ch 1 (counts as first sc), sk first sc, sc in back loop of each sc and ch around, sl st in next sc to join—60 sc.

Rnd 9: Ch 1 (counts as first sc), sk first sc, working in both loops of sts sc in each sc around, working 2 sc in each marked st (4 increases around back of hat), do not sl st in next sc to join—64 sc. Work in a spiral, marking beg of each rnd, moving marker up as work progresses.

Rnd 10: Sc in each sc around—64 sc.

Rnd 11: Sc in each sc around, working 2 sc in each of 4 marked sts around back of hat—68 sc.

Rnds 12–13: Rep rnds 10–11—72 sc at end of rnd 13.

Rnds 14–16: Rep rnd 10—72 sc. Sl st in next sc to join at end of Rnd 16.

Rnds 17–20: Ch 2, starting in first st, work a cluster across next 3 sts, ch 1, *beginning in same st as second leg of last cluster, work a cluster across next 3 sts, ch 1; rep from * around, sl st in second ch of turning ch to join—36 clusters.

Rnd 21: Ch 1, *sc in next cluster, sc in next ch-1 space; rep from * around, do not sl st in first sc to join—72 sc. Work in a spiral as before, marking beg of each rnd, moving marker up as work progresses.

Rnd 22: Working in front loops of sts, *sc of each of next 8 sc, 2 sc in next sc; rep from * around—80 sc.

Rnd 23: Working in both loops of sts, sc in each sc around—80 sc.

Rnd 24: *2 sc in next sc, sc in each of next 5 sc; rep from * 12 times, sc in each of last 2 sc—93 sc.

Rnd 25: Sc in each sc around—93 sc.

Rnd 26: *2 sc in next sc, sc in each of next 4 sc; rep from * 17 times, sc in each of last 3 sc—111 sc.

Rnd 27: Sc in each sc around—111 sc.

Rnd 28: *2 sc in next sc, sc in each of next 9 sc; rep from * 10 times, sc in last sc—122 sc.

Rnd 29: Sc in each sc around, sl st in next sc to join—121 sc.

Fold floral wire in half. Lay doubled wire over sts in last rnd.

Rnd 30: Ch 2 (counts as first reverse hdc), working over floral wire from left to right, reverse hdc in each sc around, sl st in second ch of turning ch to join—121 reverse hdc. Fasten off. Weave in ends. Weave in excess wire. Shape hat.

the pdq

This hat is worked in the back loop of each stitch, which gives it a cool stripy effect, while granny squares influence the patterned rows of clustered stitches. Vintage buttons give it two looks, since the earflaps can be worn fastened up or left hanging down for cozy warmth. This is a quick beginner's pattern and can be easily made in one devoted evening, as the whole thing's done with a combo of double crochet stitches. Any worsted weight yarn will work, but the low cost and color variety available in acrylic mean you can make a bright one for every outfit.

Finished Size

23" circumference

Materials

Yarn

Red Heart Classic (100% acrylic; 3.5 oz [100 g]/198 yd [181 m]): 1 skein each of #513 Parakeet (A), #645 Honey Gold (B), and #261 Maize (C) for striped hat; 1 skein of #12 Black for solid-color hat.

Hook

Size H/8 (5 mm) crochet hook or size needed to obtain gauge

Notions

Two ¾" round vintage buttons for each hat

Sewing needle

Matching sewing thread

Gauge

12 sts and 6 rows dc = 4"

Special Stitches

Shell: 3 dc in same st

HAT

Note: Body of hat is worked in back loops of sts throughout, creating a ridged effect. Ear flaps are worked in back loops of sts on RS rows and front loops of sts on WS rows to create a ridge on RS. Colors can be carried up loosely on WS to be picked up in later rnds. Ear flaps and edging are worked with A.

With A, ch 3 and join with sl st in first ch.

Rnd 1 (RS): Ch 3 (counts as first dc), work 10 dc in ring, sl st in third ch of turning ch to join—11 sts.

Rnd 2: Using B and working in back loops of sts, ch 3, dc in first st, 2 dc in each dc around, sl st in third ch of turning ch to join—22 sts.

Rnd 3: Using C and working in back loops of sts, ch 3, dc in first st, dc in next dc, *2 dc in next dc, dc in next dc; rep from * around, sl st in third ch of turning ch to join—33 sts.

 *Red Heart Classic, medium (worsted) weight*

Rnd 4: Using A and working in back loops of sts, ch 3, dc in first st, dc in each of next 2 dc, *2 dc in next dc, dc in each of next 2 dc; rep from * around, sl st in third ch of turning ch to join—44 sts.

Rnd 5: Using B and working in back loops of sts, ch 3, dc in first st, dc in each of next 3 dc, *2 dc in next dc, dc in each of next 3 dc; rep from * around, sl st in third ch of turning ch to join—55 sts.

Rnd 6: Using C and working in back loops of sts, ch 3, dc in first st, dc in each dc around, sl st in third ch of turning ch to join—56 sts.

Rnd 7: Using A and working in back loops of sts, ch 3, 2 dc in first st (first shell made), ch 2, sk next 3 sts, *shell in next dc, ch 2, sk next 3 sts; rep from * around, sl st in third ch of turning ch to join—14 shells.

Rnd 8: Using B and working in back loops of sts, ch 3, dc in each dc and in each ch around, sl st in third ch of turning ch to join—70 sts.

Rnd 9: Using C and working in back loops of sts, ch 3, dc in each dc around, sl st in third ch of turning ch to join—70 sts.

Rnd 10: Using A and working in back loops of sts, ch 3, 2 dc in first st (first shell made), ch 2 , sk next 4 sts, *shell in next dc, ch 2 , sk next 4 sts; rep from * around, sl st in third ch of turning ch to join—14 shells.

Rnds 11–12: Rep rnds 8–9—70 dc. Do not fasten off.

Use single-color yarn for a solid-colored hat.

First Ear Flap

Row 1 (RS): Using color A and working all rows with same color yarn, working in back loops of sts, ch 3, dc in each of next 14 dc, turn, leaving rem sts unworked—15 sts.

Row 2 (WS): Working in front loops of sts, ch 3, dc in each of next 13 dc, turn, leaving rem st unworked—14 sts.

Row 3 (RS): Working in back loops of sts, ch 3, dc in each of next 12 dc, turn, leaving rem st unworked—13 sts.

Row 4 (WS): Working in front loops of sts, ch 3, dc in each of next 11 dc, turn, leaving rem st unworked—12 sts. Fasten off.

Second Ear Flap

Row 1 (RS): With RS facing, sk next 20 sts to the left of last st made in row 1 of first ear flap. Using A and working in back loops, join yarn in next st, ch 3, dc in each of next 14 dc, turn, leaving rem sts unworked—15 sts.

Rows 2–4: Rep rows 2–4 of first ear flap. Do not fasten off.

Edging

With RS facing, using A, ch 1, sc evenly around entire edge of hat. Fasten off. Weave in ends.

Finishing

Fold ear flaps up to RS of hat. Sew buttons on hat to be aligned with center of rnd 4 of each ear flap. Use center space in Row 4 of ear flaps for buttonholes.

About Kittee I live and crochet a few blocks from the Mississippi River in New Orleans, Louisiana. I started knitting under the guidance of my mom and Grandma Millie when I was little and taught myself to crochet a couple of years ago. I cherish the hooks, needles, and vintage patterns my grandma gave me and hope one day to be as skilled as she was. In fact, among the few things I took when I evacuated my home was my grandma's set of needles and an old book of her patterns. When not working at a huge natural foods supermarket, you can find me sipping avocado bubble tea and successfully dodging hurricanes, termites, and stinging caterpillars. Although I'm not sure where I'll be living when this book comes out, I hope it will be back in New Orleans, where I can spend endless hours conquering my zone 9 garden and making everything I possibly can from scratch. Please visit my Web site, www.pakupaku.info, for extremely yummy vegan recipes and info you can't live without.

ANARCHY IRONY HAT

The thought of a crocheted anarchy sign made me giggle, and I thought it was a cool symbol from my past (think eighties and trying hard to catch the very last drop of what was left of seventies punk). Since everything is co-opted nowadays, I figured why not put some humor into it. What could be more ironic than a crocheted anarchy sign on a crocheted hat? I like it in red and black yarn because the colors match my jeans and favorite sweater, but you can use any color combo. This hat is great for beginners because it is done with repeated single crochet stitches going around and around, so all you have to do is count. The anarchy sign isn't complicated, either, because it's done in pieces.

Finished Size

22" in circumference, 9½" long

Materials

Yarn

Lion Brand Wool-Ease (80% Acrylic/ 20% Wool; 3 oz [85 g]/197 yd [180 m]): 1 ball of #102 Ranch Red (A) and 1 ball of #153 Black (B)

Hooks

Size J/10 (6 mm) crochet hook or size needed to obtain gauge

Size 0 (3.25 mm) crochet hook for making anarchy sign

Notions

Yarn needle

Gauge

16 sts and 16 rows sc = 4"

HAT

Starting at center top, with larger hook and A, leaving a 10" sewing length, ch 30 and without twisting ch, join with sl st in first ch.

Rnd 1 (RS): Ch 2, hdc in first ch, hdc in each ch around, sl st in first hdc to join—30 hdc.

Rnd 2: Ch 2, 2 hdc in each hdc around, sl st in first hdc to join—60 hdc.

Rnds 3–7: Ch 1, sc in each st around—60 sts.

Rnd 8: Ch 1, *2 sc in sc, sc in each of next 19 sc; rep from * around, sl st in first sc to join—63 sts.

Rnd 9: Ch 1, *2 sc in sc, sc in each of next 20 sc; rep from * around, sl st in first sc to join—66 sts.

Rnd 10: Ch 1, *2 sc in sc, sc in each of next 21 sc; rep from * around, sl st in first sc to join—69 sts.

Rnd 11: Ch 1, *2 sc in sc, sc in each of next 22 sc; rep from * around, sl st in first sc to join—72 sts.

4 *Lion Brand Wool-Ease, medium (worsted) weight*

About Tera It was my Abuelita (grandmother), who lives in Mexico, who taught me to crochet when I was five and to knit at seven, and I have been doing both ever since. She was taught by her great aunts when she was very young, and passed the same style on to me. It is cool to be part of such a long line of skilled craftswomen, and I see my work as both preserving and adding on to an important and distinct tradition. In 2001 I created www.abuelitaschango.com (Spanglish for Grandmother's Monkey) as a venue to sell the items I make under the label One Tough Monkey. It's a place to put all the items I crochet while watching TV and listening to old records, 45s and 78s. My designs are inspired by my collections of all things vintage, retro, and kitschy.

Rnds 13–41: Ch 1, sc in each sc around, sl st in first sc to join—72 sts. Fasten off.

Rnd 42: With RS facing, join B in any sc, ch 1, sc in each sc around, sl st in first sc to join—72 sts. Fasten off.

Finishing

Turn hat inside out. With yarn needle, weave sewing length through the sts in center ring at top of hat, gather together, and secure. Check to see if there are any holes or large spaces on top of hat. If there are, sew together and secure.

ANARCHY SIGN

Circle

With smaller hook and B, ch 40 and without twisting ch, join with sl st in first ch.

Rnd 1: Sl st in each ch around, sl st in first sl st to join—40 sl sts. Do not fasten off.

First Side of "A"

With smaller hook and B, ch 18.

Row 1: Sl st in second ch from hook, sl st in each ch across, turn—17 sl sts. Do not fasten off; continue with second side of "A."

Second Side of "A"

Rep first side of "A." Fasten off, leaving an 18" sewing length.

Bar of "A"

With smaller hook and B, ch 18.

Row 1: Sl st in second ch from hook, sl st in each ch across, turn—17 sl sts. Fasten off, leaving a 12" sewing length.

Use black yarn as color A and red yarn as B for this version.

Assembly

Arrange the circle and the sides of the "A" on front of hat as pictured and sew in place. Satin st at the top of the "A" to form the tip. Sew bar across center of the "A" as pictured. At this point you can also shape the sign with your sewing needle and yarn, but remember, Anarchy is not about order and perfectly formed shapes.

boy beanie

When I first started designing and selling my hand-crocheted hats at local markets in the Seattle area, I caught on quickly to the fact that many young men were interested in handmade goods, but they just didn't have very much to choose from. So, as long as I had a few "boy beanies" in stock, guys would stop at my booth to talk, sometimes even to tell me that they, too, love to crochet! This hat, which can be made in endless color combos, is one of my most popular designs, with a combination of stitches that adds an interesting texture to the stripe pattern. It's a stretchy, close-fitting, and comfortable hat in a style that's popular as casual street wear and with outdoor sports enthusiasts, boarders, skaters, and bikers. Made in 100% acrylic yarn for easy care, one size fits just about everyone, ages teen to adult.

Finished Size

20" circumference. Stretches to fit up to 24".

Materials

Yarn

Red Heart Super Saver (100% acrylic; 8 oz [226 g]/425 yd [389 m]): 1 skein each of #971 Camouflage (MC) and #354 Vibrant Orange (CC) for camouflage hat; 1 skein each of #400 Grey Heather (MC) and #312 Black (CC) for gray hat

Hook

Size I/9 (5.5 mm) crochet hook or size needed to obtain gauge

Notions

Yarn needle

Gauge

11 sts and 6 rows dc = 4"

HAT

With MC, ch 4 and join with sl st in first ch.

Rnd 1: Ch 3 (counts as first dc), 9 dc in ring, sl st in third ch of turning ch to join—10 sts.

Rnd 2: Ch 3, dc in first st, 2 dc in each dc around, sl st in third ch of turning ch to join—20 sts.

Rnd 3: Ch 3, 2 dc in next dc, *dc in next dc, 2 dc in next dc; rep from * around, sl st in third ch of turning ch to join—30 sts.

Rnd 4: Ch 3, dc in next dc, 2 dc in next dc, *dc in each of next 2 dc, 2 dc in next dc; rep from * around, sl st in third ch of turning ch to join—40 sts.

Rnd 5: Ch 3, dc in each of next 2 dc, 2 dc in next dc, *dc in each of next 3 dc, 2 dc in next dc; rep from * around, sl st in third ch of turning ch to join—50 sts.

Rnd 6: Ch 3, dc in each of next 8 dc, 2 dc in next dc, *dc in each of next 9 dc, 2 dc in next dc; rep from * around, sl st in third ch of turning ch to join—55 sts.

Rnds 7–9: Ch 3, dc in each dc around, sl st in third ch of turning ch to join—55 sts. Fasten off MC, join CC.

Rnd 10: With CC, ch 1, sc in each st around, sl st in first sc to join—55 sc. Fasten off CC, join MC.

Rnd 11: With MC, ch 3, dc in back loop only of each sc around, sl st in third ch of turning ch to join—55 sts. Fasten off MC, join CC.

Rnds 12–13: Rep rnds 10–11. Fasten off MC, join CC.

Rnd 14: Rep rnd 10. Fasten off CC, join MC.

Rnd 15: With MC, ch 1, sc in back loop only of each sc around, sl st in first sc to join—55 sc.

Rnd 16: Ch 1, sc in both loops of each sc around, sl st in first sc to join—55 sc. Fasten off. Weave in ends.

About Laura I love to crochet. I spend most of my days (and nights) crocheting, filling orders, making stock to take to local markets, and working out new design ideas. Even though it's my job, crochet is still my favorite hobby, too, and I combine my love of crocheting with sewing in making folk art rag dolls out of leftover materials. I also enjoy spending time online with some of my crafting pals at LiveJournal.com, snarking the fads and fashions and plotting for the crochet revolution. You can see my current line of hand-crocheted hats and accessories at Seattle's Fremont Sunday Market each week year-round or visit my Web site, www.croshaydesign.com, for more of my original crochet patterns.

4 *Red Heart Super Saver, medium (worsted) weight*

Black and gray hat shown underneath camouflage hat.

Nilda Mesa

Strut

Fun. Easy. Proud. Warm. That's what I want in a good wool hat, so that's what I set out to make. There's nothing like a fun hat to help you brave a gray day. All those feathered hats in fall fashion shows made me wonder how to make a hat with the same bold colors as peacock feathers but in wool. It had to be felted to make it more rigid and sculptural as well as warmer than a regular crocheted hat. I hit on this Noro colorway, combined it with a shell stitch, a lot of hot soapy water and agitation, and Strut was born. The shell stitch is easy and fast, and it creates a scalloped edge that lets the color variations bob in and out in each row. It also felts well into a slightly quilted effect. This hat takes only a few hours to crochet, and an hour or so to felt. It would make a great gift—if you didn't keep forgetting to give it away.

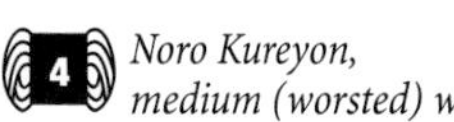
Noro Kureyon, medium (worsted) weight

HAT

Crown

Starting at center top of hat, ch 2.

Rnd 1: 6 sc in second ch from hook, sl st in first sc to join—6 sc.

Rnd 2: Ch 1, 2 sc in each sc around, sl st in first sc to join—12 sc.

Rnd 3: Ch 1, *sc in sc, 2 sc in next sc; rep from * around, sl st in first sc to join—18 sc.

Rnd 4: Ch 1, *sc in each of next 2 sc, 2 sc in next sc; rep from * around, sl st in first sc to join—24 sc.

Finished Size

Directions are given for size Small/Medium (S/M). Changes for Large/Extra Large (L/XL) are in parentheses.

After Felting

Crown diameter: 7" (8")

Circumference around base of brim: approximately 19½" (21)"

Materials

Yarn

Noro Kureyon (100% wool; 1.75 oz [50 g]/109 yd [100 m]): 4 skeins #40 Bright Blues/Purple/Green

Hook

Size J/10 (6 mm) crochet hook or size needed to obtain gauge

Notions

Yarn needle

Stitch markers (optional)

Gauge

Before felting: 12 sts and 13 rows sc = 4"; 2 small shells and 4 rnds in small shell pattern = 4". *After felting:* 14 sts and 16 rows sc = 4"; 2 small shells and 4 rnds in small shell pattern = 3".

Note: Gauge is not critical, as this will be felted, but it would be a good idea to felt and measure a swatch before starting the piece. Crochet the stitches loosely.

Special Stitches

Small shell: 5 dc in same st

Large shell: 7 dc in same st

Rnd 5: Ch 1, *sc in each of next 3 sc, 2 sc in next sc; rep from * around, sl st in first sc to join—30 sc.

Rnd 6: Ch 1, *sc in each of next 4 sc, 2 sc in next sc; rep from * around, sl st in first sc to join—36 sc.

Rnd 7: Ch 1, *sc in each of next 5 sc, 2 sc in next sc; rep from * around, sl st in first sc to join—42 sc.

Rnd 8: Ch 1, *sc in each of next 6 sc, 2 sc in next sc; rep from * around, sl st in first sc to join—48 sc.

Rnd 9: Ch 1, *sc in each of next 7 sc, 2 sc in next sc; rep from * around, sl st in first sc to join—54 sc.

Rnd 10: Ch 1, *sc in each of next 8 sc, 2 sc in next sc; rep from * around, sl st in first sc to join—60 sc.

Rnd 11: Ch 1, *sc in each of next 9 sc, 2 sc in next sc; rep from * around, sl st in first sc to join—66 sc.

Rnd 12: Ch 1, *sc in each of next 10 sc, 2 sc in next sc; rep from * around, sl st in first sc to join—72 sc.

Rnd 13: Ch 1, *sc in each of next 11 sc, 2 sc in next sc; rep from * around, sl st in first sc to join—78 sc.

Size Large/X-Large Only

Rnd 14: Ch 1, *sc in each of next 12 sc, 2 sc in next sc; rep from * around, sl st in first sc to join—84 sc

Note: Crown should measure approximately 8 (8½)" in diameter.

Sides

Rnd 1: Ch 1, sc in first sc, skip next 2 sc, *5 dc in next sc (small shell made), sk next 2 sc, sc in next sc, sk next 2 sc; rep from * around, sl st in first sc to join—13 (14) small shells.

Rnd 2: Ch 3 (counts as first dc), 2 dc in first sc (half shell made), *sk next 2 dc, sc in next dc, sk next 2 dc, 5 dc in next sc; rep from * around, ending with 2 dc in first sc already holding half shell (completes first small shell), sl st in third ch of turning ch to join—13 (14) small shells.

Rnd 3: Ch 1, sc in first st, skip next 2 dc, *5 dc in next sc, skip next 2 dc, sc in next dc, skip next 2 dc; rep from * around, sl st in first sc to join—13 (14) small shells.

Rnds 4–7: Rep rnds 2–3 twice.

Note: Hat should measure approximately 26 (28)" in circumference.

Brim

Rnd 8: Ch 3 (counts as first dc), 3 dc in first sc (half shell made), *sk next 2 dc, sc in next dc, sk next 2 dc, 7 dc in next sc, (large shell made); rep from * around, ending with 3 dc in first sc already holding half shell (completes first large shell), sl st in third ch of turning ch to join—13 (14) large shells.

Rnd 9: Ch 1, sc in first st, sk next 3 dc, *7 dc in next sc (large shell made), sk next 2 dc, sc in next dc, sk next 3 dc; rep from * around, sl st in first sc to join—13 (14) large shells.

Rnd 10: Ch 1, sc in first st, sk next 3 dc, *7 dc in next sc, sk next 3 dc, sc in next dc, sk next 3 dc; rep from * around, sl st in first sc to join—13 (14) large shells.

Rnds 11–14: Rep rnds 9–10 twice. Fasten off.

Note: Brim should measure approximately 32½ (35)" in circumference.

Felting

Place hat in zippered mesh bag or pillowcase. Run through 1 long heavy wash cycle in washing machine, using hot water and a few squirts of soap, such as Ivory liquid, *not* laundry detergent. Pull it out and check the measurements. You may need to run it through 1½ or 2 cycles. Check it every 5–10 minutes after the first cycle, so it doesn't shrink too much. When the size is right, pull the hat out and shape it gently to its proper dimensions, pulling on the brim gently if necessary to make its final flared shape. It will dry into the shape you give it. Let it dry upright over a coffee can, lightly wadded tissue paper, or other large tubular item.

About Nilda I was a crocheting fiend as a kid. My Spanish grandmother taught me to crochet and knit the summer I turned eight. She made the most beautiful crocheted lace, as my cousins in Spain still do. But I always made colorful useful things, like Barbie clothes, 8-foot-long ties for Father's Day, baby hats, seat covers, and purses. I love crochet's ability to hold a form, and how fast it is to work. As an adult, I crochet impractical things, like abstract wire sculptures to hang outdoors. But I return to my colorful practical crochet roots, as in Strut. My work has appeared in *Stitch 'n Bitch Nation, Knitty,* and *Interweave Knits Crochet,* as well as in KnitLits 2 and 3. I live with my husband, two daughters, and two cats in New York and France, where I'm codirector of MICA's artists' residency program, and keep a blog about my life and my knitting: Waltzing Knitilda (www.nildamesa.typepad.com/waltzing_knitilda).

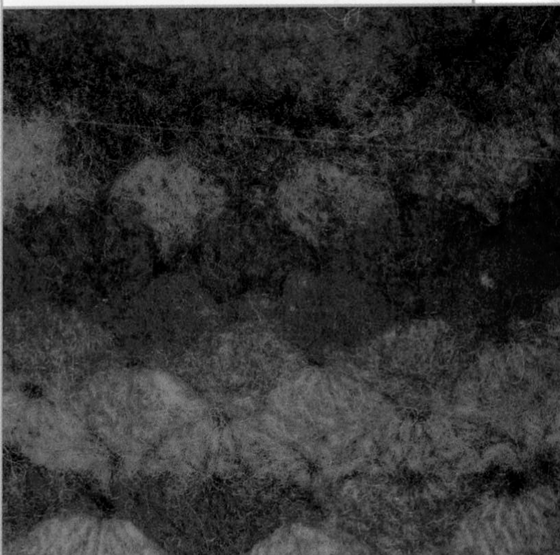

Emily Nelson

Spring in Winter

HAT AND SCARF SET

In South Carolina, winter gets very cold—for a couple of weeks. But for the rest of the season, it's often warm enough to wear short sleeves. That's why I decided to create an openwork accessory set—something that would block chilly breezes without being too hot. I try to keep my designs versatile enough to suit many moods, which is why this pattern includes a flower that can be placed anywhere on the hat or scarf. The suggested yarn is so silky, you'll forget it's wool as you wrap it around your neck in 75 degree weather! This airy hat and scarf set will get you through the warmer winters, and the movable flower will remind you that spring is just around the corner.

Finished Size

Scarf: 6" × 70"

Hat: 21" in circumference

Flower: 4" in diameter

Materials

Yarn

Karabella Aurora Bulky (100% merino wool; 1.75 oz [50 g]/54 yd [49 m]): 5 balls of #28 orange (MC) and 3 balls of #26 magenta (CC)

Hook

Size I/9 (5.5 mm) crochet hook or size needed to obtain gauge

Notions

Yarn needle

One 1½" button (shown with La Petite # 408)

Gauge

4 V-sts = 4" and

4 rows in V-st pattern = 4"

Special Stitches

V-stitch (V-st): (tr, ch 2, tr) in same st

SCARF

With MC, ch 25.

Row 1 (RS): Tr in seventh ch from hook (first V-st made), *sk next 2 ch, V-st in next ch; rep from * 4 times, skip next 2 ch, tr in last ch, turn—6 V-sts.

Rows 2-74: Ch 6, tr in first tr (first V-st made), *sk next ch-2 space, V-st in next tr; rep from * 4 times, sk next ch-2 space, tr in fourth ch of turning ch, turn—6 V-sts. Fasten off. Weave in ends.

Border

Rnd 1: With RS facing, join CC in top right-hand corner space, ch 1, **work 2 sc in space bet first 2 tr, *3 sc in next ch-2 space, sc bet next 2 tr; rep from * 4 times,

5 *Karabella Aurora Bulky, bulky weight*

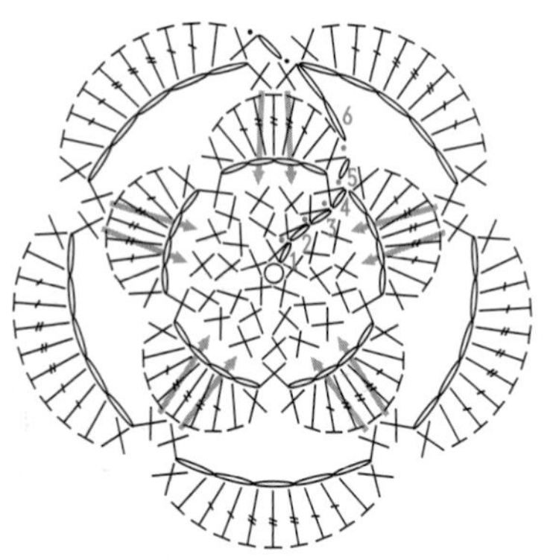

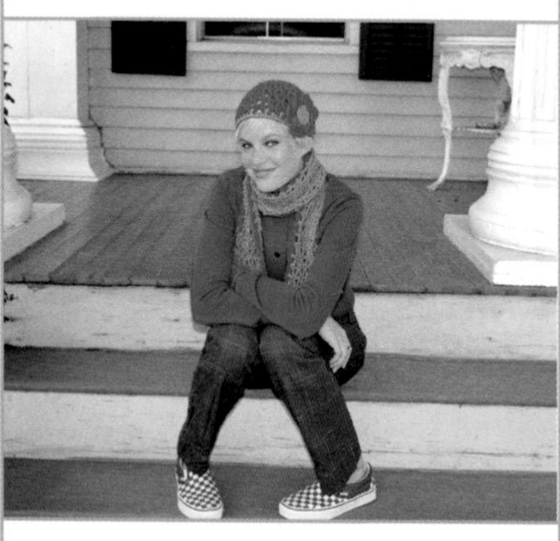

2 sc in corner space, working down long edge of scarf, work 4 sc in each row-end tr across to next corner; rep from ** once, sl st in first sc to join, turn.

Top Edging

Row 1 (RS): Ch 3, 3 dc in next sc, *sk next 2 sc, sc in each of next 2 sc, sk next 2 sc, 5 dc in next sc; rep from * once, sk next 2 sc, sc in next 2 sc, sk next 2 sc, 3 dc in next sc, ch 3, sl st in next sc. Fasten off.

Bottom Edging

Row 1 (RS): Join CC in bottom left-hand corner sc, 3 dc in next sc, *sk next 2 sc, sc in each of next 2 sc, sk next 2 sc, 5 dc in next sc; rep from * once, sk next 2 sc, sc in next 2 sc, sk next 2 sc, 3 dc in next sc, ch 3, sl st in next sc. Fasten off. Weave in ends.

HAT

With CC, ch 4 and join with sl st in first ch.

Rnd 1: Ch 6, tr in ring (counts as first V-st), work 5 V-st in ring, sl st in fourth ch of turning ch to join—6 V-sts.

Rnd 2: Ch 6 (counts as tr, ch 2), (2 tr, ch 2, tr) in first st, sk next tr, *(tr, ch 2, 2 tr, ch 2, tr) in next tr, skip next tr; rep from * around, sl st in fourth ch of turning ch to join—12 V-sts.

Rnd 3: Ch 6 (counts as tr, ch 2), (2 tr, ch 2, tr) in first st, sk next tr, V-st in next tr, sk next tr, *(tr, ch 2, 2 tr, ch 2, tr) in next tr, sk next tr, V-st in next tr, sk next tr; rep from * around, sl st in fourth ch of turning ch to join—18 V-sts.

Rnds 4-8: Ch 6, tr in first st (counts as first V-st), sk next tr, *V-st in next tr, sk next tr; rep from * around, sl st in fourth ch of turning ch to join—18 V-sts. Fasten off.

Rnd 9: With RS facing, join MC in any ch-2 space, ch 1, *3 sc in ch-2 space, sc bet next 2 tr; rep from * around, sl st in first sc to join—72 sc. Fasten off. Weave in ends.

Flower Petals

With CC, wrap yarn around finger to form a loop (see page 52).

Rnd 1: Ch 1, 5 sc in loop, sl st in first sc to join—5 sc. Pull on beg strand to tighten center loop.

Rnd 2: Ch 1, 2 sc in each sc around, sl st in first sc to join—10 sc.

Rnd 3: Ch 1, *2 sc in sc, sc in next sc; rep from * around, sl st in first sc to join—15 sc.

Rnd 4: Ch 1, *sc in sc, ch 4, sk next 2 sc; rep from * around, sl st in first sc to join—5 ch-4 loops.

Rnd 5: (front petals): Ch 1, (sc, hdc, dc, 3 tr, dc, hdc, sc) in each ch-4 loop around, sl st in first sc to join—5 petals.

Rnd 6: Ch 2, working in skipped sts in Rnd 3 and behind petals in Rnd 5, sl st to first skipped sc in Rnd 3, ch 1, *sc in next 2 sc, ch 5, sk next sc in Rnd 4; rep from * around, sl st in first sc to join—5 ch-5 loops.

Rnd 7: (back petals): Ch 1, (sc, hdc, 2 dc, 3 tr, 2 dc, hdc, sc) in each ch-5 loop around, sl st in first sc to join—5 petals. Fasten off. Weave in ends.

Flower Center

With MC, wrap yarn around finger to form a loop (see page 52).

Rnd 1: Ch 1, 6 sc in loop, sl st in first sc to join—6 sc.

Rnd 2: Ch 1, 2 sc in each sc around, sl st in first sc to join—12 sc.

Rnd 3: Ch 1, *2 sc in sc, sc in next sc; rep from * around, sl st in first sc to join—18 sc. Fasten off, leaving a sewing length.

Finishing

With yarn needle and MC sewing length, sew flower center to flower petals around outer edge of center. With beginning (CC) sewing length, sew the button to back of assembled flower. Be sure to leave space between the button and the flower if your button doesn't already have a shank. Attach flower to hat where desired by pushing button through any space in side of hat.

About Emily I live in South Carolina, where I am studying to be an early childhood educator. I taught myself to crochet in 2003 and have been unstoppable ever since. My innocent hobby has transformed into full-fledged addiction, and I love sharing the art of crochet with others. I teach crochet classes and workshops, and have contributed to almost every issue of *Crochet Me* since its beginning. I also offer free patterns at my Web site, Hook Me Up! Crochet, www.hookmeupcrochet.com.

Ileana Rodriguez

In Bloom and Fit to Be Tied

Finished Size

11" wide × 6" tall

Materials

Yarn

Cascade Yarns Cascade 220 (100% Peruvian Highland Wool; 3.5 oz [100 g]/220 yd [201 m]): 1 skein each of #9452 pale blue heather (A), #8412 pale yellow (B), and #7829 coral (C) for In Bloom (blue clutch); 1 skein of #8412 pale yellow (A) for Fit to Be Tied (yellow clutch)

Hook

Size G/6 (4 mm) crochet hook or size needed to obtain gauge

Notions

For both versions: Yarn needle, 10" × 12" cotton fabric for lining, sewing needle or sewing machine, matching sewing thread, sew-on snap, iron

For In Bloom: Pin back, flower loom, hot glue, and glue gun

For Fit to Be Tied: 2 yds [1.8 m] 3/8" yellow satin ribbon

Gauge

15 sts and 12 rows hdc = 4"

My closet is jam-packed with handbags in all shapes, sizes, and colors. My favorites are the handmade knit and crocheted bags that I've scored at vintage stores. In fact, this pattern was inspired by a crocheted bag that I found in a thrift shop. I was heartbroken when I lost the bag after having it for only a week, so I challenged myself to re-create one just like it. The pattern is perfect for folks who have a short attention span and prefer projects that provide almost instant gratification. The bag works up quickly, and the simple one-piece design easily lends itself to all sorts of interesting variations. If you have trouble finding a flower loom, try looking in a vintage shop or on eBay, or just crochet a flower as your decoration. You can also order premade flowers and kits from my Web site, www.indiaromeo.com.

IN BLOOM (FLOWERED VERSION)

First Handle

4 *Cascade Yarns Cascade 220, medium (worsted) weight*

Starting at top edge, with A, ch 45.

Row 1: Hdc in third ch from hook, hdc in each ch across, turn—43 hdc.

Rows 2–4: Ch 2, hdc in each hdc across, turn—43 hdc.

Row 5: Ch 2, hdc in each of next 15 hdc, ch 13, skip next 13 hdc, hdc in each of next 15 hdc, turn—30 hdc + ch-13 loop.

Row 6: Ch 2, hdc in each of next 15 hdc, hdc in each of next 13 ch, hdc in each of next 15 hdc, turn—43 hdc.

Body

Rows 7–33: rep row 2.

Second Handle

Row 34: Rep row 5.

Row 35: Rep row 6.

Rows 36–39: Rep row 2.
Fasten off, leaving a sewing length.

Finishing

Fold bag in half, RS tog. With yarn needle and A, sew side seams. Weave in ends. Turn right-side out. Block lightly.

Lining

With RS facing, fold the fabric in half by bringing the longer sides tog. With sewing needle or sewing machine, leaving a ½" seam allowance, sew side seams. Fold top back ½" and press flat. Fold top back another ½" and press flat to hide raw edge. Place lining inside bag and handstitch it in place, beginning below handles. Sew half of snap on front and other half on back, centered under handle opening.

Flower Pin

With B, using flower loom, wrap yarn 3 times around each set of outside pegs to make the bottom layer of petals. With C, wrap yarn 3 times around each set of middle pegs to make the next row of petals. With A, wrap yarn 3 times around each set of inside pegs to make the top row of petals. Thread yarn needle with a 36" length of B and draw it up from the behind the loom, going through the middle of one of the sets of petals. Cross yarn over the next set of petals and pass it through the opening between the petals on the next peg. Continue stitching around each set of petals, until each one has been stitched twice.

Glue pin back to the flower, and attach it to the bag.

FIT TO BE TIED (RIBBON VERSION)

First Handle

Starting at top edge, with A, ch 45.

Rows 1–6: Follow directions for In Bloom version—43 hdc.

Body

Row 7: Rep row 2.

Row 8 (eyelet row): Ch 2, hdc in next hdc, *ch 1, sk next hdc, hdc in next hdc; rep from * across, turn—43 sts (21 ch-1 spaces).

Row 9: Ch 2, hdc in each hdc and each ch-1 space across, turn—43 hdc.

Rows 10–30: Rep row 2.

Rows 31–32: Rep rows 8–9.

Row 33: Rep row 2.

Second Handle

Row 34: Rep row 5.

Row 35: Rep row 6.

Rows 36–39: Rep row 2. Fasten off, leaving a sewing length.

Finishing

Fold bag in half, RS tog. With yarn needle and A, sew side seams. Weave in ends. Turn right-side out. Block lightly. Starting and ending 2½" from left side of front, weave ribbon through the eyelets around bag, and tie in a bow. Trim ends on an angle.

Lining

Make and attach lining same as In Bloom version. Sew on snap.

About Ileana I started hooking at the tender age of eight, when my mother gave me some squeaky acrylic yarn and started me on my first afghan. Homework and piano lessons kept me from finishing it, but when I was packing for college, I discovered the half-completed project at the back of my closet. I sat down with the yarn and hook and was surprised by how quickly I remembered the pattern and stitches. I've been crocheting ever since, and I've successfully taught most of my friends how to be hookers, too. I design handbags, accessories, and all sorts of crafty goods that I sell at my online boutique, www.indiaromeo.com. I also am a cofounder and editor of Craft Revolution (www.craftrevolution.com), an online magazine that promotes independent designers and encourages shoppers to buy handmade goods.

Granny's No Square

One thing's for sure: Granny squares don't have to be so, well, grannyish. Case in point: all the cool-yet-quirky crochet work done by high-fashion designers these days. Although I'm ashamed to admit I'm such a label whore, when I started thinking about designing a granny square bag, I was inspired by the idea of trendy bohemian chic. So I channeled my inner fashionista and came up with something—I hope—that's modern and graphic with a bit of an edge (thank you, rivets), just like all the high-end stuff found on the runway, minus the thousand-dollar price tag. The best part? It was fun and easy to make.

BAG

Basic Motif

Make 2 each of Motifs 1, 2, 3 and 5; make 4 of Motif 4 following color sequence chart (see page 142) to identify first and second color.

With first color, ch 4 and join with sl st in first ch.

Rnd 1 (RS): Work 8 sc in ring, sl st in first sc to join—8 sc.

Rnd 2: Ch 1, 2 sc into each sc around, sl st in first sc to join—16 sc. Fasten off first color, join second color.

Rnd 3: With second color, ch 1, *sc in sc, 2 sc in next sc; rep from * around, sl st in first sc to join—24 sc.

Rnd 4: Ch 1, *sc in each of next 2 sc, 2 sc in next sc; rep from * around, sl st in first sc to join—32 sc. Fasten off second color, join first color.

Rnd 5: With first color, ch 1, *sc in each of next 3 sc, 2 sc in next sc; rep from * around, sl st in first sc to join—40 sc. Fasten off first color, join E.

Rnd 6: With E: ch 1, *3 sc in sc (corner made), sc in each of next 9 sc; rep from * around, sl st in first sc to join—48 sc; 4 corners. Place a marker in center sc of each corner, moving marker up as work progresses.

Finished Size

13½" wide at bottom × 10¾" tall excluding strap

Materials

Yarn

Berroco Cottontwist (70% mercerized cotton/30% rayon; 1.75 oz [50 g]/85 yd [78 m]): 1 hank each of #8357 Tile (pink) (A), #8343 Flame (orange) (B), #8366 Heath Pink (mauve) (C), and #8387 Soul (purple) (D). Berroco Suede (100% nylon; 1.75 oz [50 g]/120 yd [111 m]): 3 balls of #3727 Dale Evans (cream) (E) and 1 ball of #3717 Wild Bill Hickcock (brown) (F).

Hook

Size F/5 (3.75 mm) crochet hook or size needed to obtain gauge

Notions

Yarn needle

17 half-dome gold rivets (½")

2 gold O-rings (2") (available from www.mjtrim.com)

Gauge

Motif = 4½ × 4½"

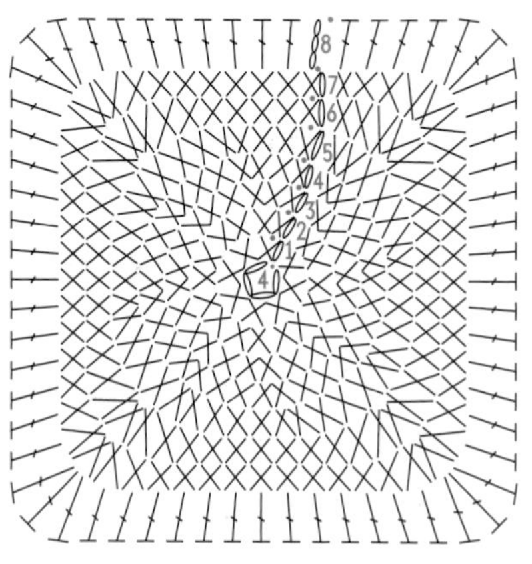

Basic motif

Strip			
Strip 2	Motif 1	Motif 2	Motif 3
Strip 1	Motif 4	Motif 5	Motif 4

Construction chart front & back

Motif	First Color	2nd Color
1	A	B
2	C	A
3	B	C
4	D	C
5	D	B

Color sequence chart

Rnd 7: Ch 1, sc in each sc around, working 3 sc in each marked corner sc, sl st in first sc to join—56 sc.

Rnd 8: Ch 3 (counts as first dc), dc in each sc around, working 3 dc in each marked corner sc, sl st in third ch of turning ch to join—64 sts. Fasten off.

Trim Rnd

With WS facing, join matching color around the post of any sc in Rnd 5, sl st around the post of each sc around, sl st in first sl st to join—40 sl sts. Fasten off.

Assemble Into Strips

Follow construction chart for placement. Join motifs together in 2 strips of 3 motifs for both front and back as follows: With RS of 2 motifs tog, working through double thickness, join F in one corner of motif, matching sts across one side, and sl st in each st across to next corner. Fasten off. Rep to join third motif in strip.

Strip Edgings

With RS of strip 1 facing, join D in top right-hand corner of strip, ch 1, sc evenly across 3 motifs to top left-hand corner st. Fasten off. Rep strip edging across bottom edge of strip 2. Rep strip edging across top and bottom edges of remaining strips 1 and 2 for back.

Assemble Front & Back

With RS of strip 1 and strip 2 of front tog, working through double thickness, join F in top right-hand corner of strips, matching sts across top, sl st in each st across to next corner. Fasten off. Join 2 strips for back in same manner. Join front to back across sides in same manner.

Bottom

Rnd 1: With RS of bag facing, join D in side seam on bottom edge of bag, ch 1, sc in each st around, sl st in first sc to join. Fasten off D, join F.

Rnds 2–4: With F, ch 1, sc in each sc around, sl st in first sc to join. Turn bag inside out. Flatten bag at side seams.

Row 5: With RS tog, matching sts across last rnd of bottom, working through double thickness, sl st in each st across. Fasten off. Turn bag right-side out.

Top Edging

Rnd 1: With RS of bag facing, join D in side seam on top edge of bag, ch 1, sc in each st around, sl st in first sc to join. Fasten off D, join F.

Rnds 2–3: With F, ch 1, sc in each sc around, sl st in first sc to join. Fasten off F, join D.

Rnd 4: With D, ch 1, sc in each sc around, sl st in first sc to join. Fasten off D, join E.

Rnd 5: With E, ch 1, *sc in each of next 4 sc, skip next sc; rep from * around, sc in each remaining sc, sl st in first sc to join.

Rnd 6: With E, ch 1, *sc in each of next 3 sc, skip next sc; rep from * around, sc in each remaining sc, sl st in first sc to join.

Rnd 7: Sl st in each sc around, sl st in first sl st to join. Fasten off.

Attach Rings

Mark center 6 sts on each side of top edge of bag.

Row 1: With RS facing, join 2 strands of E in first marked st to the right of side seam, ch 1, sc in same st, sc in each of next 5 sts, turn—6 sc.

Row 2: Place one gold O-ring over last row of sts, ch 1, working over ring, sc in each sc across—6 sc. Fasten off. In same manner, attach other O-ring on opposite side of bag.

Strap

Row 1: Join 2 strands E in one O-ring, ch 1, work 6 sc in O-ring, turn—6 sc.

Row 2: Ch 1, sc in each sc across, turn—6 sc.

Rep row 2 until strap measures 12" or desired length (keep in mind strap will stretch with use!).

Last row: Place top of other O-ring over last row of sts, ch 1, working over O-ring, sc in each sc across—6 sc. Fasten off.

Finishing

Attach one rivet to center of each motif. Attach 5 rivets, evenly spaced across center top of strap. Be careful not to damage rivets as you "nail" them to the bag. Weave in ends.

About Diana My great-grandmother Hallie taught me to crochet when I was a kid. These days I find myself picking up a hook when I feel like having fun; I love how flexible and improvisational crochet is. Crocheting makes me feel so totally crafty, which, to quote Martha, is a very good thing. In addition to teaching people how to make stuff, most days you'll find me working as founder–creative director of Make Workshop, a craft school on the Lower East Side of Manhattan (www.makeworkshop.com).

4 *Berroco Suede, medium (worsted) weight, and Berroco Cottontwist, medium (worsted) weight*

Orange You Glad and Fashion First Aid

Finished Size

Orange You Glad Bag: 7 × 7" excluding handle

Fashion First Aid Bag: 8 × 8" excluding handle

Materials

Yarn

Cascade Yarns Cascade 220 (100% Peruvian Highland Wool; 3.5 oz [100 g]/220 yd [201 m]): 1 skein each of #7828 Yellow (A), #7825 Orange (B), and #8893 Green (C) for Orange You Glad Bag; 2 skeins of #8414 Red (MC) and 1 skein of #8505 White (CC) for Fashion First Aid Bag

Hook

Size H/8 (5 mm) crochet hook or size needed to obtain gauge

Notions

Yarn needle

Large safety pins

Gauge

20 sts and 22 rows sc = 4"

Special Stitches

Surface Crochet: with yarn at back, insert hook and draw loop through. Insert hook into next stitch and draw loop through fabric and loop on hook.

I wanted to make a quick and simple handbag that would be easy to work up without having to follow a complicated pattern, so I came up with this little citrus bag, then made a second version with a red cross pattern. The pattern is quickly customizable and gives you a great chance to practice changing colors. This petite bag is perfect for carrying little essentials for a beauty emergency. Toss in a snack and you're good to go!

To change color: Work last sc of first color until 2 loops rem on hook, yo with second color, draw second color through 2 loops on hook, drop first color to WS to be picked up later. Background color can be carried loosely across, working over strand with other color, or attach a separate ball of yarn for each color section.

ORANGE YOU GLAD BAG

Front

With A, ch 36.

Row 1: Sc in second ch from hook, sc in each ch across, turn—35 sc.

Rows 2–35: Ch 1, sc in each ch across following chart for color changes, turn—35 sc. Do not fasten off.

4 *Cascade Yarns Cascade 220, medium (worsted) weight*

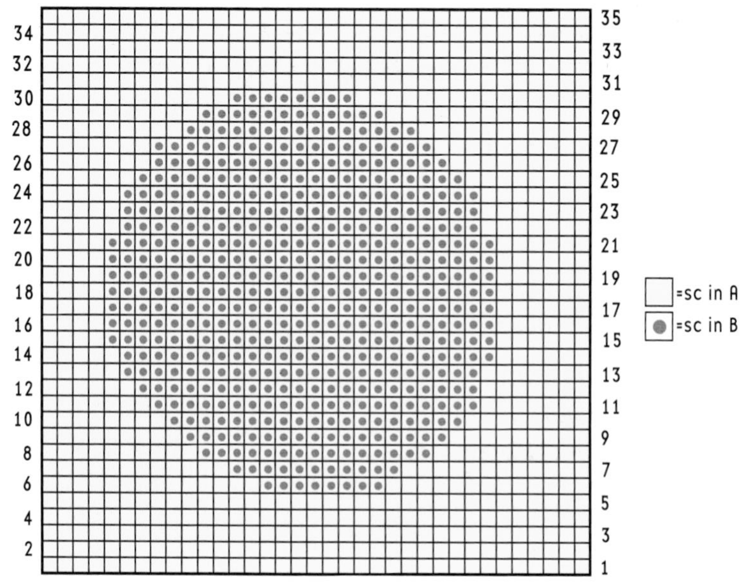

Bottom

Row 36: With A only, ch 1, sc in back loop only of each sc across, turn—35 sc.

Rows 37–43: With A only, ch 1, sc in both loops of each sc across, turn—35 sc.

Row 44: Rep row 36—35 sc. Do not fasten off.

Back

Rows 45–78: Rep row 37—35 sc. Fasten off.

Orange detail

With A, surface crochet around outside of orange and add detail to front as pictured.

Handle

With A, ch 9.

Row 1: Sc in second ch from hook, sc in each ch across, turn—8 sc.

Row 2: Ch 1, sc in each ch across, turn—8 sc.

Rows 3–154: Rep row 2, working in the following color sequence: 5 more rows A; *7 rows B; 7 rows C; 7 rows A; rep from * 7 times. Fasten off, leaving a sewing length.

Leaf A

With C, ch 12.

Row 1: Sc in second ch from hook, sc in each ch across to last ch, 3 sc in last ch; working across opposite side of foundation ch, sc in each of next 7 ch, turn—20 sc.

Row 2: Ch 1, working in front loops of sts, sc in of each of first 8 sc, 3 sc in next sc, sc in each of next 8 sc, turn—19 sc.

Row 3: Ch 1, working in front loops of sts, sc in of each of first 9 sc, 3 sc in next sc, sc in each of next 6 sc, turn—18 sc.

Row 4: Ch 1, working in front loops of sts, sc in of each of first 7 sc, 2 sc in next sc—9 sc. Fasten off, leaving a sewing length.

Leaf B

With C, ch 8.

Row 1: Sc in second ch from hook, sc in each ch across to last ch, 3 sc in last ch, working across opposite side of foundation ch, sc in each of next 5 ch, turn—15 sc.

Row 2: Ch 1, working in front loops of sts, sc in of each of first 6 sc, 3 sc in next sc, sc in each of next 5 sc, turn—14 sc.

Row 3: Ch 1, working in front loops of sts, sc in of each of first 6 sc, 2 sc in next sc—8 sc. Fasten off, leaving a sewing length.

Stem

With C, ch 5.

Row 1: Sc in second ch from hook, sc in each ch across—4 sc. Fasten off, leaving a sewing length.

Assembly

Weave in ends. Arrange leaves and stem on orange on front of bag and with yarn needle and sewing lengths, sew in place. With RS of bag and handle facing, and with ends of handle aligned with bottom of bag, pin long edges of handle to sides of bag. With yarn needle and A yarn, sew handle to sides and bottom of bag.

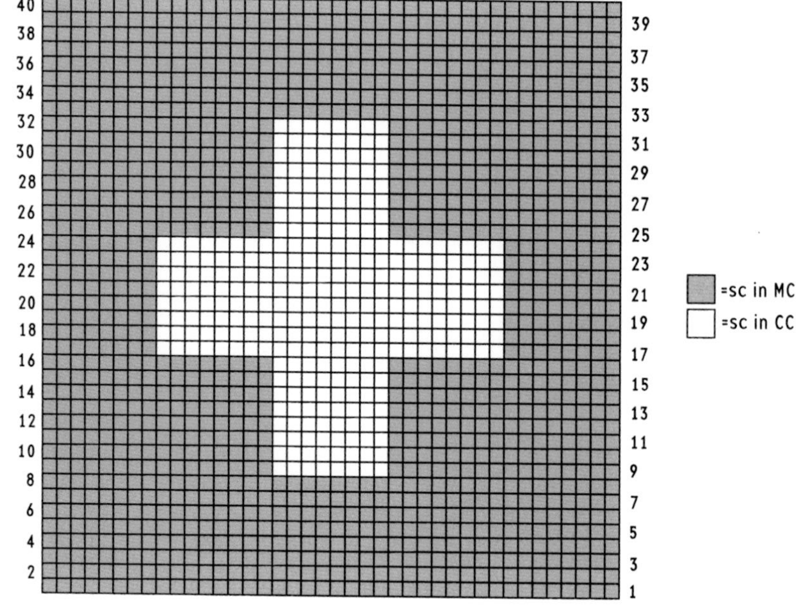

FASHION FIRST AID BAG

Front

With MC, ch 41.

Row 1: Sc in second ch from hook, sc in each ch across, turn—40 sc.

Rows 2–40: Ch 1, sc in each ch across following chart for color changes, turn—40 sc. Do not fasten off.

Bottom

Row 41: With MC only, ch 1, sc in back loop only of each sc across, turn—40 sc.

Rows 42–48: With MC only, ch 1, sc in both loops of each sc across, turn—40 sc.

Row 49: Rep row 41—40 sc. Do not fasten off.

Cascade Yarns Cascade 220, medium (worsted) weight

Back

Rows 50–88: Rep row 42—40 sc. Fasten off.

Handle

With MC, ch 141.

Row 1: Sc in second ch from hook, sc in each ch across, turn—140 sc.

Rows 2–8: Ch 1, sc in each ch across, turn—140 sc. Fasten off, leaving a sewing length.

Assembly

Weave in ends. With WS of bag and handle together and ends of handle aligned with bottom of bag, pin long edges of handle to sides of bag. With yarn needle and MC, sew handle to sides and bottom of bag.

About Sarah I vaguely recall learning to crochet as a kid in Alaska. The first thing I made was an orange ruffled bonnet for one of my dolls or maybe it was our cat. We were always dressing her up, much to her dismay. I entered it into the local fair and got a blue ribbon. I didn't crochet for the next ten years, until illness left me homebound for long stretches of time and I needed a way to occupy myself. Inspired by the amazing free-form creations I was seeing online, I picked up a crochet hook again and I started making hats, bags, and accessories. I even found a way to start selling a few online through my Web site, www.myheadphones.org, to earn some extra pocket money.

exchange bag

Every February, a dozen or so of my far-flung college friends and I send each other gifts in a mystery exchange—no one knows who's sending what to whom until the package arrives. There is only one rule: You have to make it yourself. The first year I'd just found nylon cord at the craft store and knew it would make a perfect little handbag. I was so happy with the result that it was hard to send the original version off. It was definitely worth it, though, when my own gift arrived—a personalized miniature of a favorite sculpture that spelled out my name in wire frame letters.

Of course, I immediately made myself an Exchange Bag. The nylon cord may take some getting used to as it's stiffer than your average yarn. But it's worth the extra effort—the finished bag is so sturdy that it's nearly indestructible. I've also discovered that it's unharmed by a trip through the washing machine, making this truly a handbag that can go with you anywhere—to work, to the beach, or out all night.

Note: To prevent the ends of the nylon cord from unraveling, dab the ends with glue or clear nail polish immediately after cutting.

2 *Hilos La Espiga No. 18, fine (sport) weight*

BAG

Ch 72 loosely and without twisting ch, sl st in first ch.

Rnd 1 (RS): Ch 1, sc in first ch, sc in each ch around, sl st in first sc to join, turn—72 sc.

Rnd 2 (WS): Ch 1, *sc in sc, sk next 2 sc, shell in next sc, sk next 2 sc; rep from * around, sl st in first sc to join, turn—12 shells.

Finished Size

8" wide × 7½" tall excluding strap

Materials

Yarn

Hilos La Espiga No. 18 nylon thread (100% nylon; 7 oz [200 g]/197 yd [180 m]): 2 tubes #8, Dark Pink.

Hook

Size F/5 (3.75 mm) crochet hook or size needed to obtain gauge

Notions

Metal tapestry needle

½-inch sew-on snap

Glue or clear nail polish

Sewing needle and matching sewing thread

Gauge

18 sts and 18 rows sc = 4"

Special Stitches

Shell: 7 dc in same st

Sc2tog: (Insert hook in next st, yo, draw yarn through st) twice, yo, draw yarn through 3 loops on hook

Dc2tog: (Yo, insert hook in next st, yo, draw yarn through st, yo, draw yarn through 2 loops on hook) twice, yo, draw yarn through 3 loops on hook

3-dc cluster: (Yo, insert hook in next st, yo, draw yarn through st, yo, draw yarn through 2 loops on hook) 3 times, yo, draw yarn through all 4 loops on hook

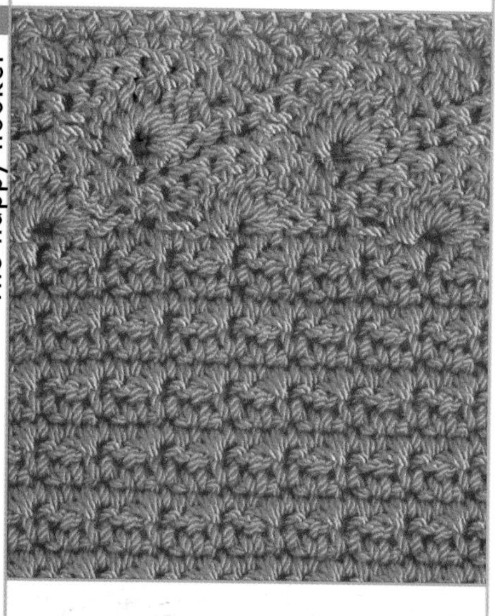

Rnd 3: Working in back loops of sts, ch 1, sc in back loop of each dc around, sl st in first sc to join, turn—96 sc.

Rnd 4: Ch 3, 6 dc in first sc (counts as first shell), *sk next 3 sc, sc in next sc, sk next 3 sc, shell in next sc; rep from * around to last 7 sts, sk next 2 sts, sc in next sc, sk next 3 sts, sl st in third ch of turning ch to join, turn—12 shells.

Rnd 5: Working in back loops of sts, ch 3, dc2tog in next 2 sts (counts as first cluster), hdc in next st, sc in next 3 sts, hdc in next st, *3-dc cluster in next 3 sts, hdc in next st, sc in each of next 3 sts, hdc in next st; rep from * around, sl st in third ch of turning ch to join, turn—72 sts.

Rnd 6: Ch 1, sc in first st, dc in next st, *sc in next st, dc in next st; rep from * around, sl st in first sc to join, turn—72 sts.

Rnd 7: Ch 1, sc in each st around, sl st in first sc to join, turn—72 sts.

Rnds 8–23: Rep rnds 6–7 8 times.

Rnd 24: Ch 3, 6 dc in first st (counts as first shell), *sk next 2 sts, sc in next st, sk next 2 sts, shell in next st; rep from * around, sl st in third ch of turning ch to join, turn—12 shells.

Rnd 25: Rep rnd 3—96 sc.

Rnd 26: Rep rnd 4—72 sts.

Rnd 27: Rep rnd 5. Turn. Do not fasten off.

Strap

Row 1 (WS): Ch 1, sc in each of next 7 sts, turn.

Row 2 (RS): Ch 1, sc2tog in next 2 sts, sc in each of next 3 sc, sc2tog in last 2 sts, turn—5 sts.

Row 3: Ch 1, sc in each sc across, turn—5 sc.

Rep rnd 3 90 times or until strap measures desired length.

Next row: Ch 1, 2 sc in first sc, sc in each of next 3 sc, 2 sc in last sc, turn—7 sc.

Last row: Ch 1, sc in each sc across, turn—7 sc. Do not fasten off.

Joining Row

With RS of strap and bag held tog and WS of bag facing, matching last row of strap to corresponding sts on opposite side of bag and working through double thickness, sl st in each st across. Fasten off. Weave in ends.

Base

Rnd 1: With RS of bag facing, working across opposite side of foundation ch, join yarn in first ch, ch 1, sc in each ch around, sl st in first sc to join—72 sc.

Rnd 2: Ch 1, sc in each of first 2 sc, sc2tog in next 2 sc, sc in each of next 26 sc, sc2tog in next 2 sc, sc in each of next 6 sc, sc2tog in next 2 sc, sc in each of next 26 sc, sc2tog in next 2 sc, sc in each of next 4 sc, sl st in first sc to join—68 sts.

Rnd 3: Ch 1, sc in first sc, sc2tog in next 2 sc, sc in each of next 26 sc, sc2tog in next 2 sc, sc in each of next 4 sc, sc2tog in next 2 sc, sc in each of next 26 sc, sc2tog in next 2 sc, sc in each of next 3 sc, sl st in first sc to join—64 sts. Fasten off, leaving a sewing length.

Finishing

With WS facing, sew bottom seam.

With RS facing, join yarn in first st on top edge of bag to the left of one strap, ch 1, sc in each st across top edge of bag, sc in each row-end st across side edge of strap, sl st in first sc to join. Fasten off. Rep edging around other edge of bag and strap.

Using sewing needle and thread, sew snap to the inside of the center top of the body.

About Jana After I moved to North Carolina in 1999 to start my Ph.D. in genetics, I found myself spending my little free time unwinding in front of the TV. Not wanting to waste a precious minute and needing something to occupy my hands, I decided to relearn how to crochet. It took a comical phone call home to Mom for help on how to hold the yarn, and I was off. A couple of years later a college friend sent me a particularly cool knitted gift, I suspect with the ulterior motive of convincing me to learn how to knit. It worked. I now spend my Monday nights either knitting or crocheting and always laughing along with the Chapel Hill Stitch 'n Bitch group.

fat-bottom bag

A girl can never have too many bags, especially if she can make them herself. I find myself particularly drawn to kitschy ones with flair and a bit of fun style. The trendy wide-bottomed handbags I've seen in fashion magazines inspired this bag. Its versatile design complements any occasion: In cotton, it's perfect for a casual shopping trip; in shimmering gold, it's great for a night on the town. Of course, the embellishments set the tone: Instead of adding a brooch or pin, you could decorate the bag with ribbon, 1-inch-wide tulle, or strips of fabric woven through the top or the body of the bag. Having two young kids, I need fast projects and this one is really quick to work up.

SPECIAL STITCHES

hhdc (herringbone half-double crochet): Yo, insert hook in next st, yo, draw yarn through st and first loop on hook, yo, draw through both loops on hook.

hhdc2tog (herringbone half-double crochet decrease): Yo, insert hook in next st, yo, draw yarn through st and first loop on hook, yo, insert hook in next st, yo, draw yarn through st and first loop on hook, yo, pull through all three loops on hook.

sc2tog (single crochet 2 together): Insert hook in next st, yo, draw yarn through st, insert hook in next st, yo, draw yarn through st, yo, draw through all three loops on hook.

GREEN BAG

With A, ch. 18.

Note: Ch 2 at beginning of each row counts as a st. Skip the first st of each row and work in the turning ch at the end of row.

Row 1: Hhdc in third ch from hook, hhdc in each of next 3 ch, 2 hhdc in next ch, hhdc in each of next 5 ch, 2 hhdc in next ch, hhdc in each of last 5 ch, turn—19 sts.

Finished Size

11" wide × 7" deep, excluding handles

Materials

Yarn

For Green Bag: Lion Brand Lion Cotton (100% Cotton; 5 oz [140 g]/236 yd [212 m]): 1 ball #181 Sage (A); small amount of contrasting color of choice (CC) for weaving

For Gold Bag: Crystal Palace Soiree (60% Metallic Polyester/40% Polyamide; 1.75 oz [50 g]/160 yd [146 m]): 2 skeins of #3620 Gold (B); and J & P Coats Metallic Knit-Cro-Sheen (86% cotton/ 14% metallic filament; 6 oz [17 g]/ 100 yd [91.5 m]): 2 balls of #90G Gold/ Gold (C)

Hook

Size I/9 (5.5 mm) crochet hook or size needed to obtain gauge

Notions

For Green Bag: one pair of 6" round cane rings for handles, silk flower detached from stem and attached to a pin

For Gold Bag: one pair of 5" acrylic rings for handles, vintage flower pin

For both bags: yarn needle

Gauge

For Green Bag, with A, 13 sts and 11 rows hhdc = 4"

For Gold Bag, with 1 strand each of B and C held tog as one, 14 st and 12 rows hhdc = 4"

About Julie My mother taught me crochet and macramé when I was a kid in the seventies. As knitting became all the rage, I found myself regularly converting knitting patterns I liked to crochet patterns. Eventually, I realized that what I really wanted to do was design and create my own contemporary crochet patterns. In 2004, I left my full-time job as a retail buyer to be a stay-at-home mom and to pursue my interests in crochet and design. I am a technical editor and regular contributor to *Crochet Me* magazine, and I showcase the designs I've created on my own SkaMama Designs Web site, www.skamama.com. I live and play in the Seattle area, where I cruise the many fabulous yarn shops and am hardly ever without a hook and yarn.

Row 2: Ch 2, hhdc in each of next 5 sts, 2 hhdc in next st, hhdc in each of next 5 sts, 2 hhdc in next st, hhdc in each of last 6 sts, turn—21 sts.

Row 3: Ch 2, hhdc in each of next 6 sts, 2 hhdc in next st (inc made), place a marker in second st of inc, hhdc in each of next 5 sts, 2 hhdc in next st (inc made), place a marker in first st of inc, hhdc in each of last 7 sts, turn—23 sts. Move markers up to corresponding st in next row as work progresses.

Rows 4–14: Ch 2, hhdc in each st across to marked st, 2 hhdc in next marked st, hhdc in each of next 5 sts, 2 hhdc in next marked st, hhdc in each remaining st across, turn—45 sts at end of Row 14.

Rows 15–38: Ch 2, hhdc in each st across, turn—45 sts.

Row 39: Ch 2, hhdc in next 17 sts, hhdc2tog in next 2 sts (dec made), hhdc in next 5 sts, hhdc2tog in next 2 sts (dec made), hhdc in each of last 18 sts, turn—43 sts. Place a marker in each hhdc2tog, move markers up to corresponding dec st in each row as work progresses.

Rows 40–51: Ch 2, hhdc in st across to one st before marker, hhdc2tog in next 2 sts, hhdc in next 5 sts, hhdc2tog in next 2 sts, hhdc in each rem st across, turn—19 sts at end of Row 51.

Row 52: Ch 2, hhdc in next 4 sts, hhdc2tog in next 2 sts, hhdc in next 5 sts, hhdc2tog in next 2 sts, hhdc in each of last 5 sts—17 sts. Fasten off. Weave in ends.

Handle Flap

Row 1: With RS of bag facing, working across row-end sts on one side edge, join A in first row-end st, ch 1, * sc2tog worked across 2 row-end sts; rep from * across, turn—26 sts.

Row 2: Ch 1, sc in first st, sc2tog in next 2 sts, sc in each sc across to last 3 sts, sc2tog over next 2 sts, sc in last st, turn—24 sts.

Rows 3–6: Ch 2, hhdc in each st across, turn—24 sts.

Row 7: Ch 1, sc in first hhdc, sc in each st across—24 sts. Fasten off, leaving a long sewing length.

Work handle flap on opposite side edge of bag.

Finishing

Wrap one handle flap around one cane ring; with sewing length, sew top edge of flap to row 3 of flap, just above the gathering rows. Rep for other handle. Cut four 12" strands of CC. Weave 2 strands of CC through the sts in row 2 of one flap, weaving over and then under every other st across. Rep on other flap. Weave in ends. Attach flower pin to front of bag.

GOLD BAG

With one strand each of B and C held tog as one, work same as Green Bag through row 14.

Row 15: Ch 2, hhdc in each of next 18 sts, 2 hhdc in next st, hhdc in next 5 sts, 2 hhdc in next st, hhdc in each of last 19 sts, turn—47 sts.

Rows 16–39: Ch 2, hhdc in each st across, turn—47 sts.

Row 40: Ch 2, hhdc in next 18 sts, hhdc2tog in next 2 sts, hhdc in next 5 sts, hhdc2tog in next 2 sts, hhdc in each of last 19 sts, turn—45 sts.

Rows 41–54: Rep rows 39–52 of Green Bag. Fasten off.

Handle Flap

Row 1: With RS of bag facing, working across row-end sts on one side edge, join B only in first row-end st, ch 1, * sc2tog worked across 2 row-end sts; rep from * across, turn—27 sts.

Row 2: Ch 1, sc in first st, sc2tog in next 2 sts, sc in each sc across to last 3 sts, sc2tog over next 2 sts, sc in last st, turn—25 sts.

Row 3–6: Ch 2, hhdc in each st across, turn—25 sts.

Row 7: Ch 1, sc in first hhdc, sc in each st across—25 sc. Fasten off, leaving a long sewing length.

Work handle flap on opposite side edge of bag.

Finishing

Finish same as Green Bag, using C to sew flaps over handles.

4 *Above, Lion Brand Lion Cotton, medium (worsted) weight; below, Crystal Palace Soiree, medium (worsted) weight and J & P Coats Metallic Knit-Cro-Sheen, #10, bedspread weight*

Keridiana Chez

Blissful

Made in mouthwatering linen, which softens with each wash and drapes beautifully, Blissful can carry you through the stickiest summer day with elegance. (Of course, you can substitute with any other summer-weight yarn.) Pair it with a slim white skirt for uptown flair, or with jeans for downtown funk. If you're a tad shy, wear it over a silky camisole and let the colors peek through the lace pattern. Besides providing vital aeration, the wave stitch is a delight for the crocheting hand: easy to remember and works up very fast. Instant gratification was never more gratifying.

SPECIAL STITCHES

sc2tog: (Insert hook in next st, yo, draw yarn through st) twice, yo, draw yarn through 3 loops on hook.

hdc2tog: (Yo, insert hook in next st, yo, draw yarn through st, yo, draw yarn through 2 loops on hook) twice, yo, draw yarn through 3 loops on hook.

dc2tog: (Yo, insert hook in next st, yo, draw yarn through st, yo, draw yarn through 2 loops on hook) twice, yo, draw yarn through 3 loops on hook.

dc3tog: (Yo, insert hook in next st, yo, draw yarn through st, yo, draw yarn through 2 loops on hook) 3 times, yo, draw yarn through 3 loops on hook.

2-tr bobble: *Yo twice, insert hook in st, yo, draw yarn through st, (yo, draw yarn through 2 loops on hook) twice; rep from * in same st, yo, draw yarn through 3 loops on hook.

2 *Louet Sales Euroflax Originals, fine (sport) weight*

Finished Size

Directions are given for size Small (S). Changes for Medium (M), Large (L), Extra Large (XL), and Extra Extra Large (XXL) are in parentheses.

Finished bust: 29 (33½, 38, 42½, 47)"

Length: 16½ (17, 17½, 18, 18½)" excluding ties

Materials

Yarn

Louet Sales Euroflax Originals (wet spun 100% linen; 3.5 oz [100 g]/270 yd [247 m]): 2 (3, 3, 4, 4) skeins of Berry Red

Hooks

Sizes G/6 (4 mm) and F/5 (3.75 mm) crochet hooks or sizes needed to obtain gauge

Notions

Yarn needle

Sewing needle

Matching sewing thread

Stitch markers

5 hook-and-eye closures

2 yds of ⅞" matching grosgrain ribbon

Gauge

With smaller hook, 17 sts and 16 rows sc = 4"

With larger hook, 19 sts = 4½"; 5 rows = 4" in wave pattern

HALTER

Skirt (wave pattern)

Starting at bottom edge, with larger hook ch 117 (136, 155, 174, 193).

Row 1 (RS): 5 dc in fourth ch from hook, (sk next ch, dc in next ch) 3 times, sk next ch, dc2tog worked across next 3 ch, (sk next ch, dc in next ch) 3 times, sk next ch, *6 dc in each of next 2 ch, (sk next ch, dc in next ch) 3 times, sk next ch, dc2tog worked across next 3 ch, (sk next ch, dc in next ch) 3 times, sk next ch; rep from * across to last st, 6 dc in last st, turn—6 (7, 8, 9, 10) waves made.

Row 2: Ch 3 (counts as first dc), 5 dc in first dc, (sk next dc, dc in next dc) 3 times, sk next dc, dc2tog worked across next 3 sts, (sk next dc, dc in next dc) 3 times, sk next dc, *6 dc in each of next 2 dc, (sk next dc, dc in next dc) 3 times, sk next dc, dc2tog worked across next 3 sts, (sk next dc, dc in next dc) 3 times, sk next dc; rep from * across to last st, 6 dc in last st, turn—6 (7, 8, 9, 10) waves made.

Rows 3–12 or for desired length: Rep row 2.

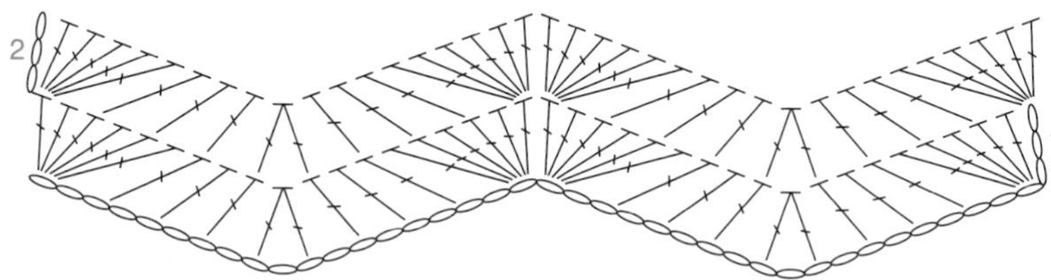

Reduced sample of wave pattern

Bodice

Row 1 (RS): Change to smaller hook, ch 1, sc in each dc across, turn—114 (133, 152, 171, 190) sc.

Row 2: Ch 1, sc in each sc across, turn—114 (133, 152, 171, 190) sc.

Row 3 (weaving row): Ch 4, tr in first st (counts as first bobble), 2-tr bobble in each sc across, turn—114 (133, 152, 171, 190) bobbles.

Row 4–7: Ch 1, sc in each st across, turn—114 (133, 152, 171, 190) hdc.

Row 8: Ch 2, hdc in each st across—114 (133, 152, 171, 190) hdc. Fasten off.

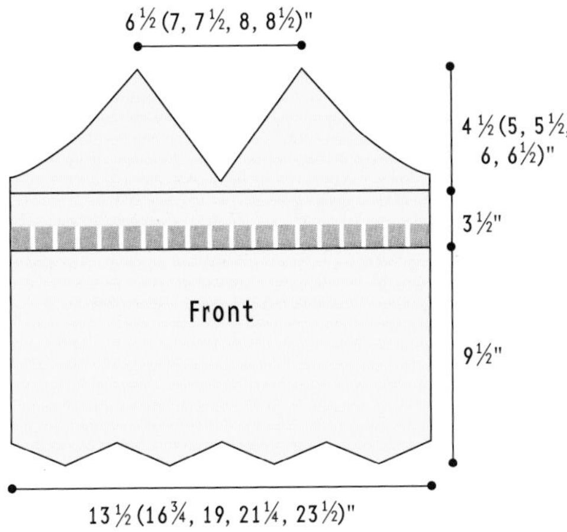

Begin Bib

Row 1 (RS): With RS facing, sk first 21 (26, 30, 35, 39) sts, join yarn in next hdc, ch 2, hdc in same st, hdc in each of next 71 (77, 87, 101, 111) hdc, turn, leaving remaining sts unworked—72 (78, 88, 102, 112) sts.

Row 2: Ch 2, (hdc2tog in next 2 sts) twice, hdc in each hdc across to last 4 sts, (hdc2tog in next 2 sts) twice, turn—68 (74, 84, 98, 108) sts.

Left Cup

Row 1: Ch 2, (hdc2tog in next 2 sts) twice, hdc in each of next 30 (35, 40, 45, 50) hdc, turn, leaving remaining sts unworked—32 (37, 42, 47, 52) sts.

Row 2: Ch 2, hdc2tog in next 2 hdc, hdc in each hdc across to last 4 sts, (hdc2tog in next 2 sts) twice, turn—29 (34, 39, 44, 49) sts.

Row 3: Ch 2, (hdc2tog in next 2 hdc) twice, hdc in each hdc across to last 2 sts, hdc2tog in last 2 sts, turn—26 (31, 36, 41, 46) sts.

Continue to work in rows of hdc, dec 1 hdc at neck edge and dec 2 hdc at armhole edge on each of next 2 (3, 4, 5, 6) rows, then dec 1 hdc at each end of next 8 (9, 10, 11, 12) rows—4 sts at end of row 10 (12, 14, 16, 18).

Last row: Ch 3 (counts as dc), dc3tog in last 3 sts. Do not fasten off.

Tie

Make a ch approximately 15 (15, 16, 16, 17)" long or desired length to tie at back of neck, hdc in third ch from hook, hdc in each ch across, sl st in top of last row of cup. Fasten off.

Right Cup

Row 1 (RS): With RS facing, join yarn in first st to the left of last st made in row 1 of left cup, ch 2, hdc in each of next 30 (35, 40, 45, 50) hdc, turn, leaving remaining sts unworked—32 (37, 42, 47, 52) sts.

Row 2: Ch 2, (hdc2tog in next 2 hdc) twice, hdc in each hdc across to last 2 sts, hdc2tog in last 2 sts, turn—29 (34, 39, 44, 49) sts.

Row 3: Ch 2, hdc2tog in next 2 hdc, hdc in each hdc across to last 4 sts, (hdc2tog in next 2 sts) twice, turn—26 (31, 36, 41, 46) sts.

Continue to work in rows of hdc, dec 1 hdc at neck edge and dec 2 hdc at armhole edge on each of next 2 (3, 4, 5, 6) rows, then dec 1 hdc at each end of next 8 (9, 10, 11, 12) rows—4 sts at end of row 10 (12, 14, 16, 18).

Last row: Ch 3 (counts as dc), dc3tog in last 3 sts. Do not fasten off.

About Keridiana Although both my grandmothers once wielded needles like weapons of mass creation, I learned to crochet from the woman I called Grandma Anita. After this sweetie introduced me to granny squares, I spent a summer whipping out throws for my friends. Six of these color-challenged creations and many pounds of acrylic unlove later, I forsook all needles for years. Then, the shawl craze of 2004 swept me back into crochet-mania, and I've since taught myself how to knit as well. Having also made the switch from practicing corporate law to pursuing a Ph.D. in English literature, my creative potential has mushroomed. Nowadays, I crochet and knit every minute I can spare from burying my nose in a book, my yarn bin exploding all over to the annoyance of my Pomeranian. You can find other fun and vintage-inspired patterns, as well as some unique handmade items, on my Web site at www.keridiana.com.

Tie

Work same as tie on left cup. Fasten off.

First Placket

Row 1 (RS): With RS facing, join yarn in first row-end st in last row of bodice at top left-hand corner of bodice, ch 1, work 35 sc evenly across to bottom left-hand corner of skirt, turn—35 sc.

Rows 2–5: Ch 1, sc in each sc across, turn—35 sc. Fasten off.

Second Placket

Row 1 (RS): With RS facing, join yarn in bottom left-hand corner st at bottom edge of skirt, ch 1, work 35 sc evenly across to last row-end st at top edge of bodice, turn—35 sc.

Rows 2–5: Ch 1, sc in each sc across, turn—35 sc. Fasten off.

Finishing

Weave in ends. Steam block lightly. Weave ribbon through sts in row 3 of bodice (weaving row). Starting and ending on WS, weave ribbon over 3 bobbles and under 1 bobble across. Leaving a ½" hem allowance on each end, cut excess ribbon and set aside. Fold ends down ½" and sew in place to edge of placket. Cut two 4" lengths of ribbon. (**Note:** If you want hooks and eyes to go all the way down placket, cut two lengths of ribbon equal to length of placket and use as many hooks and eyes as necessary.) With sewing needle and sewing thread, sew 5 hook-and-eye closures ¾" apart across at center 3" along edge of ribbons. Fold ¼" hem at each end of 4" ribbons and sew on WS to top 3½" of each placket. Store and wash with hooks and eyes clasped securely to avoid snagging.

DONAHUE

cupcake

I make a knitted version of this top for my line Fresh Baked Goods, so I thought a crocheted one would be cute. It turned out even better than I had pictured, and it makes the perfect little summer sweater. It's cool, flirty, and would be great with a cute skirt or jeans for a first date! It's made with an affordable cotton yarn and crochets up really quickly and easily. In fact, I made the back in just a few hours while watching the door at my husband's gig one night! This sweet and pretty top is simply delicious—just like a cupcake.

Finished Size

Finished bust: 31½ (36, 40½, 45, 49½)"

Back length: 22 (22, 23, 23½, 24½)"

Materials

Yarn

Nova Yarns Amazon DK Cotton (100% cotton; 1.75 oz [50 g]/115 yd [106 m]): 6 (6, 8, 8, 10) balls #6262 lavender

Hook

Size I/9 (5.5 mm) crochet hook or size needed to obtain gauge

Notions

Yarn needle

1 yd ¼" purple satin ribbon

Gauge

10½ sts and 10 rows hdc = 4"

Special Stitches

Hdc2tog: (Yo, insert hook in next st, yo, draw yarn through st) twice, yo, draw yarn through 5 sts on hook

3 *Nova Yarns Amazon DK Cotton, light (DK) weight*

TOP

Back

Ch 48 (54, 60, 66, 72).

Row 1: Hdc in third ch from hook, hdc in each ch across, turn—46 (52, 58, 64, 70) hdc.

Rows 2–7: Ch 2, hdc in each st across, turn—46 (52, 58, 64, 70) hdc.

Row 8: Ch 2, hdc2tog in next 2 sts, hdc in each st across to last 2 sts, hdc2tog in last 2 sts, turn—44 (50, 56, 62, 68) sts.

Row 9: Ch 2, hdc in each st across, turn—44 (50, 56, 62, 68) hdc.

Repeat rows 8 & 9 3 more times—38 (44, 50, 56, 62) sts at end of last row.

Work even on 38 (44, 50, 56, 62) hdc for 17 (17, 18, 19, 20) rows.

Next row: Ch 2, 2 hdc in next st, hdc in each st across to last st, 2 hdc in last st, turn—40 (46, 52, 58, 64) sts.

Next row: Ch 2, hdc in each st across, turn.

Next row: Ch 2, 2 hdc in next st, hdc in each st across to last st, 2 hdc in last st, turn—42 (48, 54, 60, 66) sts.

About Laura-Jean I've been making my line of knitwear, Fresh Baked Goods, in Toronto for over ten years. I have two retail stores where I sell my work and the work of 15 other cool Toronto designers. Check out the Web sites: www.freshbakedgoods.com and www.freshcollective.com. I have always used some crochet on my sweaters—to assemble the pieces, to make the button panel, or to add cute details around the edges. I love crocheting! It's so fast and relaxing. I can't stand doing nothing, so I always have something to work on if I'm just at home watching TV.

Shape Armhole

Next row: Sl st in each of first 3 st, ch 2, hdc in each hdc across to last 3 sts, turn, leaving remaining sts unworked—36 (42, 48, 54, 60) sts.

Hdc2tog at each end of next row and every other row 4 times (8 rows)—28 (34, 40, 46, 52) sts at end of last row.

Work even on 28 (34, 40, 46, 52) sts for 11 (11, 12, 12, 13) rows. Fasten off.

Front

Work same as back until front measures 14 rows less than finished back.

Shape Neck

Mark center 18 sts on last row for neck opening.

Row 1: Ch 2, maintaining dec pattern at armhole edge as established, work in hdc across to first marker, turn, leaving remaining sts unworked.

Row 2: Work even in hdc.

Row 3: Ch 2, maintaining dec pattern at armhole edge as established, work in hdc to last 2sts, hdc2tog, turn.

Rows 4–5: Repeat rows 2 & 3—3 (6, 9, 12, 15) sts.

Rows 6–14: Work even on 3 (6, 9, 12, 15) sts.

Shape Other Side of Neck

Row 1: With appropriate side facing, sk 18 sts to the left of last st made in first row of Shape Neck, join yarn in next st, ch 2, work in hdc across, maintaining dec pattern at armhole edge, turn.

Row 2: Work even in hdc.

Row 3: Ch 2, hdc2tog, hdc in each stitch across, maintaining dec pattern at armhole edge, turn.

Rows 4–5: Repeat rows 2 & 3—3 (6, 9, 12, 15) sts.

Rows 6–14: Work even on 3 (6, 9, 12, 15) sts.

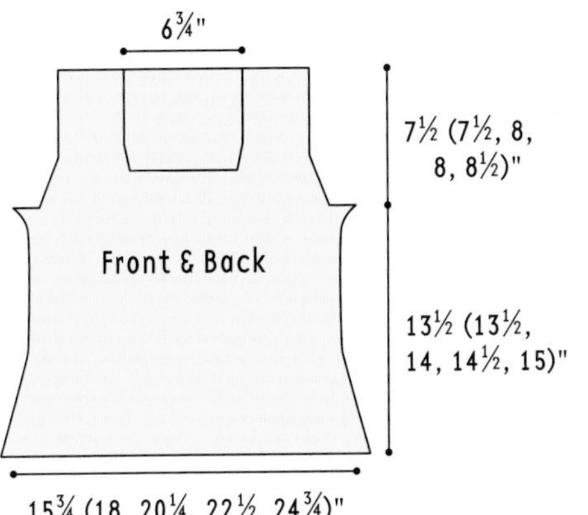

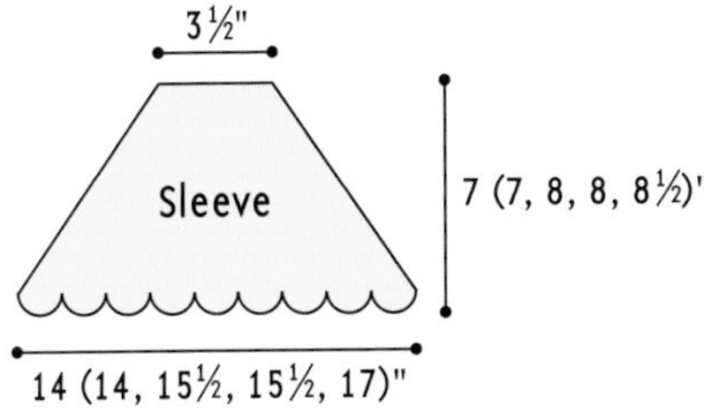

Sleeve (make 2)

Starting at top, ch 11.

Row 1: Hdc in second ch from hook, hdc in each ch across, turn—9 sts.

Row 2: Ch 2, 2 hdc in next st, hdc in each st across to last st, 2 hdc in last st, turn—11 sts.

Rep row 2 13 (13, 15, 15, 17) times—37 (37, 41, 41, 45) sts at end of last row.

Sleeve Edging

Row 1: Sk first 2 sts, 5 dc in next st (shell made), sk next st, sl st in next st, *sk next st, 5 dc in next st (shell made), sk next st, sl st in next st; rep from * across, turn—9 (9, 10, 10, 11) shells.

Row 2: Ch 5 (counts as first dc and ch-2 space), sk next 2 sts, sl st in next dc (center dc of shell), ch 2, sk next 2 sts, dc in next st; rep from * across, turn—18 (18, 20, 20, 22) ch-2 spaces.

Row 3: Ch 3 (counts as first dc), 2 dc in first space (half shell made), *sk next ch-2 space, sl st in next st, sk next ch-2 space, 5 dc in next dc; rep from * across, ending with 3 dc in third ch of turning ch (half shell made), turn—8 (8, 9, 9, 10) shells + 2 half shells.

Assembly

Sew front to back across shoulders. Sew side seams. Sew sleeve seam from bottom edge across first 1". Matching sleeve seam and side seam, sew sleeves into armholes, easing in fullness.

Neck Edging

Rnd 1: With RS facing, join yarn at left shoulder seam on neck edge, working evenly around, *sk ½", work 6 dc in next st (shell made), sk next ½", sl st in next st; rep from * as evenly as possible around, ending with sl st in left shoulder seam.

Bottom Edging

Rnd 1: With RS facing, join yarn at bottom edge of one side seam, working evenly around, *sk ½", work 6 dc in next st (shell made), sk next ½", sl st in next st; rep from * as evenly as possible around, ending with sl st in first side seam.

Finishing

Weave in ends. Starting and ending at center front of neck, weave ribbon in and out of the spaces of neck edging, about every ½". Tie in a bow. Trim ends on an angle. Wear and look cute and sexy!

Angela "La Vonne" Best

Short 'N Sweet

I have always liked having a little jacket to wear over a long dress, a low halter (that you may not be comfortable wearing by itself), or that too-skimpy tank, which is why I designed this lacy bolero. It can give that little touch of class to a plain strapless number while also hiding a multitude of sins. Or wear it more casually, to add some romance to a simple outfit of T-shirt and jeans. It's done here in a luxurious, silky cotton, but could just as easily be made in a glittery yarn for extra bling. Crocheted in one piece from the shoulders down, there is no seaming anywhere—the sleeves are worked right onto the piece, so when you're done, you're done! I designed it using the relief shell stitch, which is one of my favorite stitches. It combines elements of the shell stitch with crocheting around the posts of previous stitches, yielding a wonderful textured-yet-lacy look that can't be beat. And while it may seem complicated at first, I promise that, after a few repeats, you'll be able to make the stitch with barely a glance at the chart.

BOLERO

Bolero is worked in one piece without seams. Begin by working the back from shoulders to underarm. Then work fronts off of foundation ch at shoulders, joining fronts and back at underarm. Sleeves are worked in rnds, directly onto body in armhole openings.

Back

Starting at shoulder, ch 56 (74, 92, 110) sts.

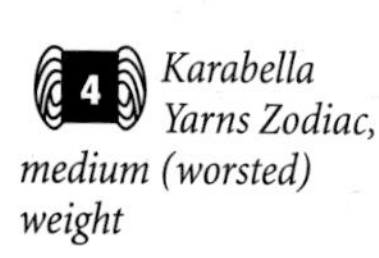

Karabella Yarns Zodiac, medium (worsted) weight

Foundation row (WS): Sc in second ch from hook, sc in each ch across, turn—55 (73, 91, 109) sc.

Finished Size

Directions are given for size Small (S). Changes for Medium (M), Large (L) and Extra Large (XL) are in parentheses.

Finished bust: 27 (32½, 45, 50½)"; sizes Medium and Extra Large have a 3½" gap in front

To fit up to approximate bust size: 27 (36, 45, 54)"

Materials

Yarn

Karabella Yarns Zodiac (100% mercerized cotton; 1.75 oz [50 g]/98 yd [90 m]): 5 (5, 6, 7) balls of #463 dark red

Hook

Size H/8 (5 mm) crochet hook or size needed to obtain gauge

Notions

Yarn needle

Gauge

16 sc = 4". One pattern rep = 4½". 8 rows in pattern = 4".

Special Stitches

V-stitch (V-st): (dc, ch 1, dc) in same st

Front post double crochet (FPdc): Yo, insert hook front to back, to front again around the post of st, yo, draw yarn through st, (yo, draw yarn through 2 loops on hook) twice

Back post double crochet (BPdc): Yo, insert hook back to front, to back again around the post of st, yo, draw yarn through st, (yo, draw yarn through 2 loops on hook) twice

designer wannabe tank top

Finished Size

Directions are given for adult size Small (S). Changes for Medium (M), Large (L), Extra Large (XL) and Extra Extra Large (XXL) are in parentheses.

Finished bust: 32 (36, 40, 44, 48)"

Finished length: 21 (22, 23, 24, 24½)"

Note: Fabric will be stretchy. Finished bust and length may vary up to 1".

Materials

Yarn

Schachenmayr Nomotta Catania (100% cotton; 1.75 oz [50 g]/137 yd [125 m]): 3 (4, 4, 5) skeins each of #157 marone (brown) (A), #146 plau (aqua) (B), and #205 apfel (green) (C)

Hooks

Sizes C/2 (2.75 mm) and E/4 (3.5 mm) crochet hooks or size needed to obtain gauge

Notions

Yarn needle

Matching colored sequins (optional)

Sewing needle and matching sewing thread to sew on sequins

Gauge

16 sts and 7 rows dc = 4"

After seeing the crochet boom in the recent collections on the catwalks of Milan, Paris, and New York, all I wanted was one of those designer tops. But I could only admire them, not afford them. So I opted for plan B and created my own. This tank is easy to make and is very adaptable, as crochet molds around the contours of your body. You can add personal touches such as hand-sewn sequins or beads. Most are available in craft and hobby stores and come in a rainbow of colors and finishes (clear, iridescent, matte, shiny, and metallic), so it's very easy to match them to the yarns you use in your project. Don't be afraid to experiment with yarn, gauge, colors, or shape of the garment. After all, you want your own designer-inspired "original," don't you?

TANK TOP

Note: Sweater is worked in stripes of one row each of 3 colors, turning at the end of each row. Work in the following color sequence: *1 row A, 1 row B, 1 row C; rep from * throughout. Colors can be carried loosely up the side to be picked up in later row.

Back

Starting at bottom edge, with larger hook and A, ch 66 (74, 82, 90, 98).

Row 1 (RS): Change to smaller hook, dc in fourth ch from the hook, dc in each ch across, turn—64 (72, 80, 88, 96) sts. Fasten off A or carry along edge, join B.

Row 2: With B, ch 3, sk first dc, dc in each ch across, ending with dc in third ch of turning ch, turn. Fasten off B or carry along edge, join C.

Maintaining color sequence as established, rep row 2 until 24 (25, 26, 27, 27) rows have been completed from beginning. Fasten off.

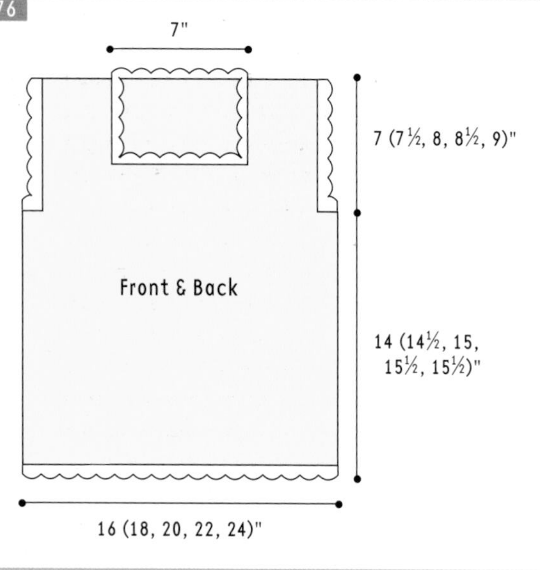

Shape Armhole

Next row: With appropriate side facing, sk first 5 (6, 7, 8, 10) dc, join next color in sequence in next dc, ch 3, sk first dc, dc in each dc across to last 5 (6, 7, 8, 10) sts, turn, leaving rem sts unworked—54 (60, 66, 72, 76) sts. Fasten off, join next color in sequence. Maintaining established color sequence, work even on 54 (60, 66, 72, 76) sts until 12 (13, 14, 15, 16) rows have been completed from beginning of armhole shaping. Fasten off.

Front

Work same as back until front measures 9 rows less than finished back.

Shape Neck

Next row: With appropriate side facing, join next color in sequence, ch 3, sk first dc, dc in each of next 11 (14, 17, 20, 22) dc, hdc in next dc, sc in each of next 28 dc, hdc in next dc, dc in each of last 12 (15, 18, 21, 23) sts, turn—54 (60, 66, 72, 76) sts.

First Front

Next row: With appropriate side facing, join next color in sequence, ch 3, sk first dc, dc in each of next 11 (14, 17, 20, 22) dc, turn, leaving remaining sts unworked—12 (15, 18, 21, 23) sts. Maintaining established color sequence, work even on 12 (15, 18, 21, 23) sts for 7 more rows. Fasten off.

Second Front

Next row: With appropriate side facing, sk 30 sts to the left of last st made in first row of first front, join next color in sequence in next dc, ch 3, dc in each of dc across, turn—12 (15, 18, 21, 23) sts.

Maintaining established color sequence, work even on 12 (15, 18, 21, 23) sts for 7 more rows. Fasten off.

Assembly

With WS facing, using yarn needle and matching colors, sew side seams.

Bottom Edging

Rnd 1: With RS facing, working across opposite side of foundation ch, join C in first ch on bottom edge of back, ch 1, sc in same st, ch 5, sk next 4 ch, *sc in next ch, ch 5, sk next 4 ch; rep from * as evenly as possible around, sl st in first sc to join.

Rnd 2: Ch 1, *sc in sc, (sc, hdc, 3 dc, hdc, sc) in next ch-5 loop; rep from * around, sl st in first sc to join. Fasten off C, join B.

Rnd 3: With B, ch 1, sc in each st around, sl st in first sc to join.

Neck Edging

Row 1 (RS): With RS facing, join B in left shoulder seam at neck edge, ch 1, sc evenly around neck opening, working 1 sc in each st across back neck edge and front neck edge, and 2 sc in each row-end st at sides of neck opening, working a multiple of 5 sts total, sl st in first sc to join.

Rnd 2: Ch 1, *sc in sc, ch 5, sk next 4 sc; rep from * around, sl st in first sc to join.

Rnd 3: Ch 1, *sc in sc, (sc, hdc, 3 dc, hdc, sc) in next ch-5 loop; rep from * around, sl st in first sc to join. Fasten off B, join C.

Rnd 4: With C, ch 1, sc in each st around, sl st in first sc to join.

Armhole Edging

On each armhole:

Row 1 (RS): With RS facing, join A in side seam on bottom of one armhole opening, ch 1, sc evenly around armhole opening, working a multiple of 5 sts total, sl st in first sc to join.

Rnds 2–4: Rep rnds 2–4 of neck edging, working 2 rnds A, 1 rnd B.

Finishing

Sequins or wooden beads can be sewn onto center of each scallop around bottom edging and neck edging as embellishments. Also, edging can be replaced by fringe, or can be finished off with a round of reverse sc.

About Ajda Ajda is Bosnian for Ida. Like my name, my love of crafts came from Bosnia. My mother taught me how to crochet when I was little. By age eight, I was making my own doll clothes and wishing to be a designer someday. In 1995, my family left war-torn Bosnia for a new life in the States, where in 1999 I received my B.F.A. in surface pattern and textile design from Syracuse University. Ever since, I've been working at what I know and love the most—designing. I hadn't been doing any crafts since my childhood. But when I tragically lost my mom to cancer, I turned back to crochet as a way of remembering her. Currently, I live in St. Louis with my boyfriend and 16-year-old cat, Dylan. I share my love of handicrafts with others through lessons and projects on my Web site, www.gotwool.com.

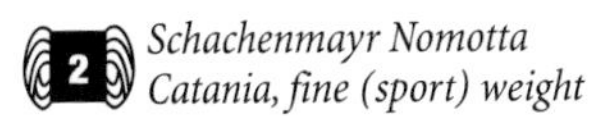

Schachenmayr Nomotta Catania, fine (sport) weight

Jen Neitzel and Kim State

Knot Ugly Shrug

Last year we found a sweater pattern in a crochet book from 1978 that was technically impressive—it was designed with only two pieces—and it got us wondering if it would be possible to make a sweater in just one piece. In the end, we wound up creating this shrug pattern, which starts with the back, works up to the sleeves, then one of the front sides. After you fasten off, complete the second sleeve and the other front side. The simple mesh pattern is fun to do, and the finished piece is loveable, wearable, and stylish. This shrug looks great over anything tight or strappy: tank tops, sundresses, slinky evening dresses, or just a simple (but tight) T-shirt. We have two versions of the shrug: one simple, for those who want a basic, fashionable crocheted sweater, and a deluxe version with ruffles on the neck and the ends of the sleeves.

SIMPLE SHRUG

Back

Starting at bottom edge, with larger hook, ch 46 (50, 54, 58, 62).

Row 1: Dc in sixth ch from hook (counts as first dc and ch-1 space), *ch 1, sk next ch, dc in next ch; rep from * across, turn—21 (23, 25, 27, 29) ch-1 spaces.

Rows 2–11: Ch 4 (counts first dc and ch-1 space), dc in next dc, *ch 1, sk next ch-1 space, dc in next dc; rep from * across, ending with dc in third ch of turning ch, turn—21 (23, 25, 27, 29) ch-1 spaces. At end of row 11, drop loop to be picked up later.

Shape Sleeves

Attach a separate strand of yarn to first st in row 11, ch 42 (42, 44, 46, 48) for sleeve. Fasten off.

Row 12: Pick up dropped loop at end of row 11, ch 45 (45, 47, 49, 51) for sleeve, dc in sixth ch from hook (counts as first dc and ch-1 space), *ch 1,

Finished Size

Directions are given for adult size Small (S). Changes for Medium (M), Large (L), Extra Large (XL), and Extra Extra Large (XXL) are in parentheses.

Finished bust: 32 (35, 38, 41, 44)"

Back length: 17 (17, 18, 19, 19½)"

Sleeve length: 16 (16½, 17, 17½)"

Sleeve length: 16 (16, 16½, 17, 17½)"

Materials

Yarn

Simple Shrug: Plymouth Suri Merino (55% suri alpaca/45% extra-fine merino wool; 1.75 oz [50 g]/109 yd [100 m]): 4 (4, 5, 6, 7) skeins #500 Black

Deluxe Shrug: Plymouth Baby Alpaca DK (100% suri alpaca; 1.75 oz [50 g]/ 125 yd [114 m]): 4 (4, 5, 6, 7) skeins #3425 pink

Hooks

Sizes K/10½ (6.5 mm) and L/11 (8 mm) crochet hooks or sizes needed to obtain gauge

Notions

Yarn needle

Gauge

10½ sts and 5 rows dc = 4"

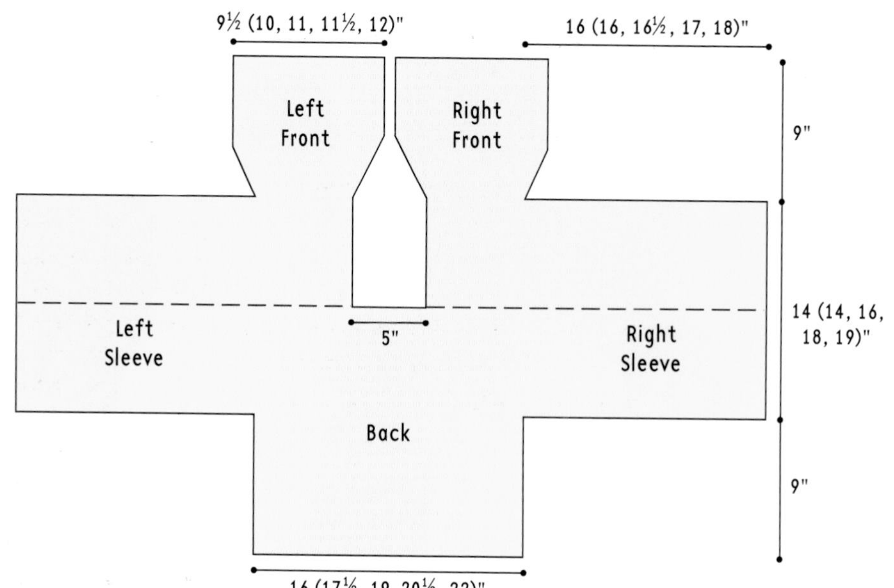

sk next ch, dc in next ch*; rep from * to * 18 (18, 19, 20, 21) times across first sleeve ch, **ch 1, sk next ch-1 space, dc in next dc; rep from ** across back, rep from * to * across second sleeve ch, turn—63 (65, 69, 73, 77) ch-1 spaces.

Work even in established pattern for 8 (8, 9, 10, 11) rows—63 (65, 69, 73, 77) ch-1 spaces.

Shape Neck

Next row: Ch 4 (counts as first dc and ch-1 space), sk next ch-1 space, dc in next dc, *ch 1, sk next ch-1 space, dc in next dc; rep from * 26 (27, 29, 31, 33) times, turn, leaving rem sts unworked—28 (29, 31, 33, 35) ch-1 spaces.

Work even in established pattern for 8 (8, 9, 10, 11) rows.

First Front

(If last row ends at center front edge)

Next row: Ch 4 (counts as first ch-1 space), dc in first dc (inc made), *ch 1, sk next ch-1 space, dc in next dc; rep from * 7 (8, 9, 10, 11) times, turn, leaving remaining sts unworked—8 (9, 10, 11, 12) ch-1 spaces.

Next row: Ch 4 (counts as dc, ch 1), dc in first dc, ch 1 (inc made), *ch 1, sk next ch-1 space, dc in next dc; rep from * across—9 (10, 11, 12, 13) ch-1 spaces.

Rep last row 3 times—12 (13, 14, 15, 16) ch-1 spaces.

Work even in established pattern for 6 rows—12 (13, 14, 15, 16) ch-1 spaces. Fasten off.

First Front

(If last row ends at side edge)

Fasten off at end of last row.

Next row: Sk first 21 (21, 22, 23, 24) ch-1 spaces, rejoin yarn in next dc, ch 4 (counts as first dc and ch-1 space), sk next ch-1 space, dc in next dc, *ch 1, sk next ch-1 space, dc in next dc; rep from * 4 (5, 6, 7, 8) times, ch 1, sk next ch-1 space, (dc, ch 1, dc) in next dc (inc made), turn, leaving rem sts unworked—8 (9, 10, 11, 12) ch-1 spaces.

Inc 1 space at beg of each of next 4 rows—12 (13, 14, 15, 16) ch-1 spaces.

Work even in established pattern for 6 rows—12 (13, 14, 15, 16) ch-1 spaces. Fasten off.

Shape Other Side of Neck

Next row: With RS facing, sk 7 ch-1 spaces to the left of last st made in first row of Shape Neck, join yarn in next dc, ch 4, (counts as first dc and ch-1 space), dc in next dc, *ch 1, sk next ch-1 space, dc in next dc; rep from * across, ending with dc in third ch of turning ch, turn—28 (29, 31, 33, 35) ch-1 spaces.

Work even in pattern for 8 (8, 9, 10, 11) rows.

Second Front

With appropriate side facing, work same as first front.

Assembly

With WS facing, using yarn needle and yarn, sew side and underarm seams.

Front Edging

Row 1: With RS facing, using smaller hook, join yarn in bottom right-hand corner of left front edge, ch 1, sc evenly across left front edge, around neck edge, and down right front edge to bottom left-hand corner, working 2 sc in each row-end dc and sc in each st across back neck edge, turn.

Rows 2–4: Ch 1, sc in each sc across, turn. Fasten off.

DELUXE SHRUG

Omit front edging and work ruffled front edging and ruffled sleeve edging as follows:

Ruffled Front Edging

Row 1: With RS facing, using smaller hook, join yarn in bottom right-hand corner of left front edge, ch 1, sc evenly across left front edge, around neck

About Jen and Kim Jen is a self-taught crocheter who, as a child, made everything possible with the chain stitch: belt, shoelace, jump rope. Over the years she taught herself more stitches. She really didn't like the patterns she found, though, so she started making her own. When Jen met Kim (aka the Yarn Goddess), Kim was stuck in afghan mode. Jen encouraged her to step outside the traditional crochet themes and try some hats and scarves, loosely based on afghan patterns. Jen is the owner of Knot Ugly Designs, www.knotugly.com, in Portland, Oregon. Kim has been co-designing with Jen since February 2004. Jen likes working out 3-dimensional mental images in yarn, while Kim enjoys counting things and loves to tweak a pattern. They are both mothers and yarn renegades.

Black Shrug, Plymouth Suri Merino, medium (worsted) weight

Pink Shrug, Plymouth Baby Alpaca DK, light (DK) weight

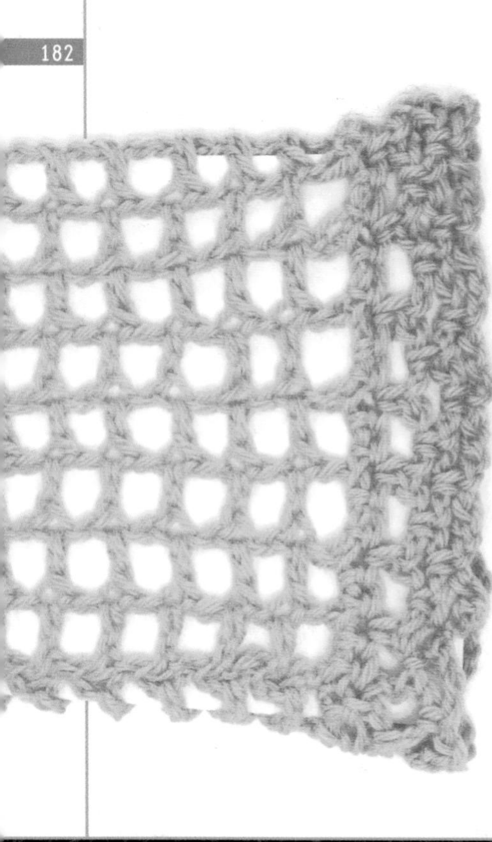

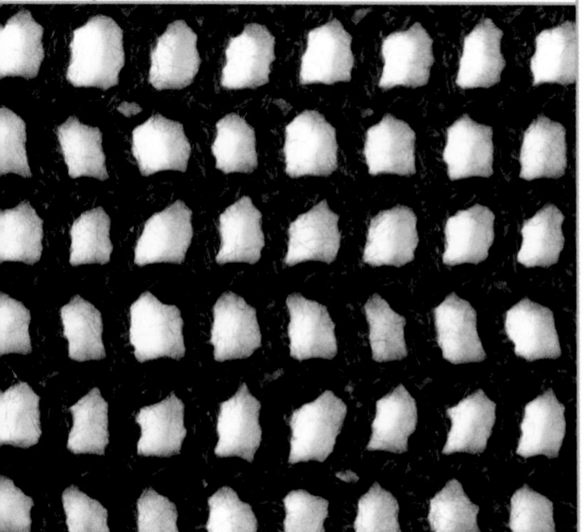

edge, and down right front edge to bottom left-hand corner, working 2 sc in each row-end dc and sc in each st across back neck edge, turn.

Row 2: Ch 1, sc in each sc across, turn.

Rows 3–4: Ch 1, 2 sc in each sc across, turn. Fasten off.

Ruffled Sleeve Edging

Rnd 1: With RS facing, join yarn in sleeve seam on cuff edge of one sleeve, ch 1, work 2 sc in each row-end dc around, sl st in first sc to join.

Rnd 2: Ch 1, sc in first sc, *ch 3, sk next sc, sc in next sc; rep from * around, ending with ch 1, hdc in first sc to join.

Rnd 3: Ch 1, sc in first ch-3 loop, ch 3, (sc, ch 3) in each ch-3 loop around, ending with ch 1, hdc in first sc to join.

Rnd 4: Ch 1, sc in first ch-3 loop, ch 3, (sc, ch 3) in each ch-3 loop around, sl st in first sc to join. Fasten off. Rep on cuff edge of other sleeve.

BOTH VERSIONS

Waistband and Ties

Row 1: With RS facing, join yarn at bottom left-hand corner of right front border, working across bottom edge of shrug, ch 1, sc in each row-end st of border, *2 sc in next ch-1 space, sc in next ch-1 space; rep from * across to border on left front, sc in each row-end st across border, ch 14 (for tie), turn.

Row 2: Sc in second ch from hook, sc in each of next 12 ch, sc in each sc across bottom edge, ch 14 (for tie), turn.

Row 3: Sc in second ch from hook, sc in each of next 12 ch, *sc in each of next 9 sc, sk next sc; rep from * across to last 13 sts, sc in each of last 13 sc, turn.

Row 4: Ch 1, sc in each of first 13 sc, *sc in each of next 8 sc, sk next sc; rep from * across to last 13 sts, sc in each of last 13 sc, turn.

Row 5: Ch 1, sc in each sc across to last 13 sts, turn, leaving remaining sts unworked.

Anna Kosturova

bikini in a bag

Finished Size

Directions are given for size Small (S). Changes for Medium (M), Large (L), Extra Large (XL), and Extra Extra Large (XXL) are in parentheses.

Bag: 4" diameter, 4" height

Bikini:

Bottom to fit (with ties): 32 (35, 38, 42, 45)" hips

Cups to fit: 32 (35, 38, 42, 45)" bust

Materials

Yarn

Brown Sheep Cotton Fine (80% cotton/ 20% wool; 1.75 oz [50 g]/222 yd [203 m]): 2 (3, 3, 3, 4) skeins of #CW520 Carribean Sea (A), 1 skein each of #CW810 Cherry Moon (B) and #CW360 Wild Sage (C)

Hook

Size B/1 (2.25 mm) crochet hook or size needed to obtain gauge

Notions

Yarn needle

Embroidery needle

½ yd lining fabric

Matching sewing thread

Sewing machine or needle

Stitch markers

Gauge

30 sts and 16 rows dc = 4"

The female body is the centerpiece of my work. As a swimsuit designer, my aim is to highlight it with a style that reflects each wearer's multidimensionality. This design is very girly, and it's just perfect for the beach and traveling. It packs neatly into the crocheted bag, so you'll always find the top and bottom in the same place, and you can also use the bag to carry keys, change, and cell phone to the beach. Wear this bikini when you're feeling preppy, or wear it as a mood changer. If you're feeling mean, it will make you feel sweet and innocent in a snap—almost like therapy.

SPECIAL STITCHES

5-dc shell: 5 dc in same st or space

6-dc shell: 6 dc in same st or space

7-dc shell: 7 dc in same st or space

BIKINI BOTTOM

Front

Starting at crotch, with A, ch 20.

Row 1 (RS): Dc in fourth ch from hook (beginning ch 3 counts as first dc), dc in each ch across, turn—18 sts.

Rows 2–10: Ch 3, dc in each st across, turn—18 sts.

Sizes Medium, Large, Extra Large, and Extra Extra Large Only

Rows 11–13 (11–16, 11–20, 11–24): Ch 3, 2 dc in each of next 2 sts, dc in each st across to last 3 sts, 2 dc in each of next 2 sts, dc in last st, turn—30 (42, 58, 74) sts at end of last row.

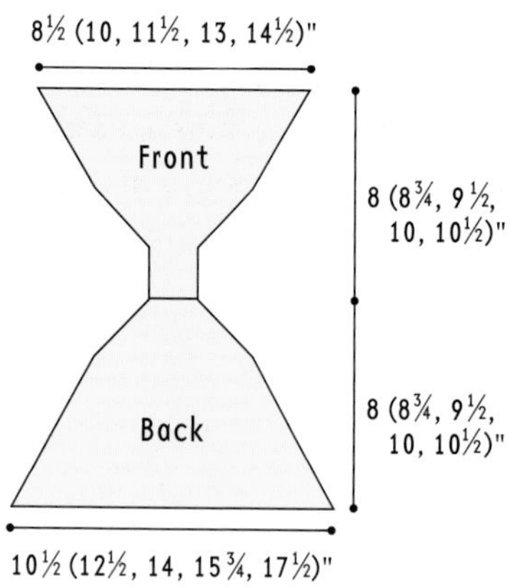

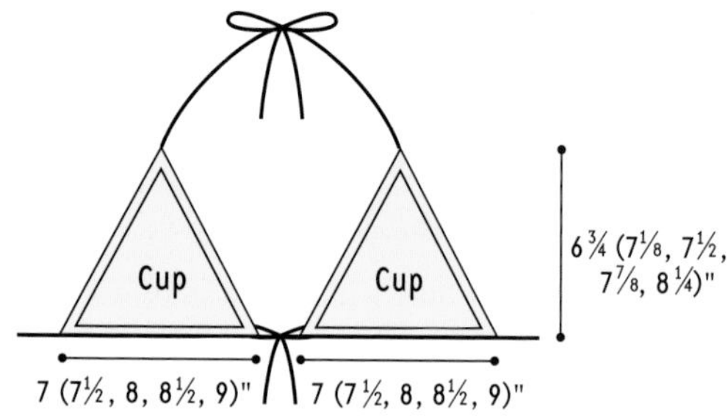

All Sizes

Rows 11–32 (14–35, 17–38, 21–40, 25–42): Ch 3, 2 dc in next dc, dc in each st across to last 2 sts, 2 dc in next st, dc in last st, turn—62 (74, 86, 98, 110) sts at end of last row. Fasten off.

Back

Row 1 (RS): Working across opposite side of foundation ch, join yarn in first ch, ch 3 (counts as first dc), dc in each ch across, turn—18 sts.

Sizes Medium, Large, Extra Large, and Extra Extra Large Only

Rows 2–4 (2–7, 2–11, 2–15): Ch 3, 2 dc in each of next 2 sts, dc in each st across to last 3 sts, 2 dc in each of next 2 sts, dc in last st, turn—30 (42, 58, 74) sts at end of last row.

All Sizes

Rows 2–33 (5–36, 8–39, 12–41, 16–43): Ch 3, 2 dc in next dc, dc in each st across to last 2 sts, 2 dc in next st, dc in last st, turn—82 (94, 106, 118, 130) sts at end of last row. Fasten off.

Border

Rnd 1 (RS): Join B in top right corner st on back, ch 1, 2 sc in corner st, sc evenly around entire piece, working 1 sc in each st across top edges, 3 sc in each row-end st across sides and 3 sc in each corner st, at end of rnd work 1 more sc in first corner st, sl st in first sc to join.

Rnd 2: Ch 6 (counts as dc, ch 3), dc in same corner sc, sk next 2 sts, ** *dc in next st, ch 2; rep from * across to next corner, (dc, ch 3, dc, ch 2) in corner sc; rep from ** around, omitting last corner, sl st in third ch of turning ch to join.

Rnd 3: Sl st in corner ch-3 space, ch 1, ***sc in corner space, ch a multiple of 3 sts measuring approximately 18" long (for tie), dc in fourth ch from hook, sk next 2 ch, *(sc, ch 3, dc) in next ch, sk next 2 ch; rep from * across ch, sc in same corner ch-3 space, 5-dc shell in next ch-2 space, **sc in next ch-2 space, 5-dc shell in next ch-2 space; rep from ** across to next corner space, rep from *** to *** around, sl st in first sc to join. Fasten off. Weave in ends.

Embroidery

With embroidery needle and B, embroider 3 lazy daisy

flowers (with 5 petals each) on front of bottom as pictured. Make a French knot in the center of each flower. With C, embroider 6 lazy daisy leaves (with 2 petals each) as pictured.

Lining

Cut lining same size and shape as front without border. Place right side of lining to wrong side of back. Sew along the foundation row using a straight stitch. Fold up so that WS of lining and WS of front are together. Sew along 3 remaining sides using a zigzag stitch.

TOP

Cup (make 2)

With A, ch 20.

Row 1: Dc in fourth ch from hook, dc in each ch across, turn—18 sts.

Row 2: Ch 3 (counts as first dc), dc in each st across, 7-dc shell in end ch-3 space; working across opposite side of foundation ch, dc in each ch across, turn—43 sts.

Rows 3–8: Ch 3 (counts as first dc), dc in each st across to center dc at top, 7-dc shell in center top dc, dc in each st across, turn—79 sts at end of row 8.

Rows 9–12 (9–13, 9–14, 9–15, 9–16): Ch 3 (counts as first dc), dc in each st across to center dc at top, with 5-dc shell in center top dc, dc in each st across, turn—95 (99, 103, 107, 111) sts at end of last row. Fasten off.

Border

Choose which side will be right side of cups before beginning border.

Rnd 1 (RS): With RS facing, join B in bottom right-hand corner st of one cup, ch 1, 2 sc in corner st, sc evenly around cup, working 1 sc in each st across each side edge of cup, 3 sc in each row-end st across bottom edge and 3 sc in each corner st, at end of rnd work 1 more sc in first corner st, sl st in first sc to join. **Note:** For a rounder cup, work fewer sts around edge.

Rnd 2: Ch 6 (counts as dc, ch 3), dc in same corner sc, sk next 2 sts, *** dc in next st, ch 2, sk next 2 sts; rep from * across to next corner, (dc, ch 3, dc) in corner sc; rep from ** around, omitting last corner, sl st in third ch of turning ch to join.

Rnd 3: Sl st in corner ch-3 space, ch 1, sc in corner ch-3 space, *5-dc shell in next ch-2 space, sc in next ch-2 space*; rep from * to * across to next corner space, sc in corner space, ch a multiple of 3 sts measuring approximately 18" long (for tie), dc in fourth ch from hook, sk next 2 ch, **(sc, ch 3, dc) in next ch, sk next 2 ch; rep from ** across ch, sc in same corner ch-3 space, 5-dc shell in next ch-2 space, rep from * to * around rem 2 sides, sl st in first sc to join. Fasten off. Weave in ends.

String

Ch a multiple of 3 sts equal to desired length to fit around chest and tie in a bow at back. (String pictured is 300 sts and approximately 5 feet long).

Row 1: Dc in fourth ch from hook, sk next 2 ch, *(sc, ch 3, dc) in next ch, sk next 2 ch; rep from * across. Fasten off.

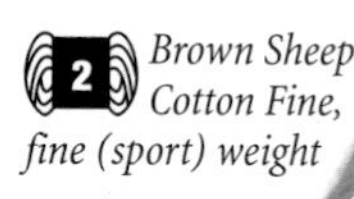
Brown Sheep Cotton Fine, fine (sport) weight

Weave in ends. Weave string over and then under each st across bottom edge of one cup, then the other cup, leaving equal lengths on each side of cups.

Embroidery

With embroidery needle and B, embroider 2 lazy daisy flowers (with 5 petals each) on left-hand side of right cup as pictured on page 187. Make a French knot in the center of each flower. With C, embroider 4 lazy daisy leaves (with 2 petals each) as pictured.

Lining *(make 2)*

Fold one cup in half along the increases. Lay this down on the fold of lining fabric. Cut out a triangle shape using the cup as a guide. Mark a line along the "extra" fabric at center from bottom edge to middle of cup. Sew a dart in the lining from the center point along the line. Attach the lining to the cup, wrong side to wrong side along 3 sides using a zigzag stitch. Rep for other cup.

BAG

Base

With A, ch 6 and join with sl st in first ch.

Rnd 1: 6 sc in ring, do not sl st to join—6 sc. Work in a spiral, marking beginning of each rnd, moving marker up as work progresses.

Rnd 2: 2 sc in each sc around—12 sc.

Rnd 3: *2 sc in next sc, sc in next sc; rep from * around—18 sc.

Rnd 4: *2 sc in next sc, sc in each of next 2 sc; rep from * around—24 sc.

Rnd 5: *2 sc in next sc, sc in each of next 3 sc; rep from * around—30 sc.

Rnd 6: *2 sc in next sc, sc in each of next 4 sc; rep from * around—36 sc.

Rnd 7: *2 sc in next sc, sc in each of next 5 sc; rep from * around—42 sc.

Rnd 8: *2 sc in next sc, sc in each of next 6 sc; rep from * around—48 sc.

Rnd 9: *2 sc in next sc, sc in each of next 7 sc; rep from * around—54 sc.

Rnd 10: 2 sc in next sc, hdc in next sc, dc in next sc, *2 dc in next sc, 1 dc in each of next 2 sc; rep from * around—72 sts.

Sides

Rnds 11–19: Dc in each st around—72 dc.

Rnds 20–21: *Dc in next dc, ch 1, sk next dc; rep from * around—36 ch-1 spaces.

Rnd 22: Dc in each st around—72 dc.

Rnd 23: *2 dc in next dc, dc in each of next 2 dc; rep from * around—96 sts. Do not fasten off.

Handle

Row 1: With yarn from base, hdc in next dc, sc in next dc, sl st in next dc, turn—3 sts.

Row 2: Ch 3 (counts as first dc), dc in each of next 2 sts, turn.

Rep row 2 until handle measures 12" from beginning.

Joining row: With RS of handle and bag facing, align last row of handle with corresponding 3 sts on opposite side of bag. Working through double thickness, sl st in each st across. Fasten off. Weave in ends.

DRAWSTRING

First End Heart

With A, ch 6 and join with sl st in first ch.

Rnd 1: Ch 3 (counts as first dc), 11 dc in ring, sl st in third ch of turning ch to join—12 sts.

Rnd 2: Ch 1, *sc in st, sk next dc, 6-dc shell in next dc; rep from * around—3 shells. Do not fasten off.

String

Make a ch approximately 33" long. Fasten off, leaving a 5-yd length to complete second end heart. Draw up a large loop through last ch so it won't unravel while weaving drawstring through top of bag.

Weaving

Designate one side as front of bag. Locate center space in rnd 21 on front of bag. Starting in space to the left of center front, weave drawstring through every other space around rnd 21, ending in space to right of center front.

Second End Heart

Pick up dropped loop at end of string.

Sl st in sixth ch from hook to form a loop.

Rnd 1: Ch 3 (counts as first dc), 11 dc in ring, sl st in third ch of turning ch to join—12 sts.

Rnd 2: Ch 1, *sc in st, sk next dc, 6-dc shell in next dc; rep from * around—3 shells. Fasten off.

Embroidery

With embroidery needle and B, embroider 3 lazy daisy flowers (with 5 petals each) on front of bag as pictured. Make a French knot in the center of each flower. With C, embroider 3 lazy daisy leaves (with 2 petals each) as pictured.

About Anna I've been designing for as long as I can remember, and I always feel the happiest when I am near water. I lost touch with these things for a few years when school numbed my soul. But then my survival reflex kicked in, and I could no longer ignore my affinity for art, fashion, and my need to live near the ocean, and I made them my life again. Designing my own line of swimwear, Anna Kosturova (www.annakosturova.com), is like a homecoming for me. I live on the coast of Vancouver, Canada, where the beach is my office and where my swimwear gets a road test. When I'm not working on my line, I like to go see bands, practice guitar, and surf.

Fay Lin

PREPPY SPRING JACKET

Finished Size

Finished bust: 32 (36, 40, 44, 48)"

Finished length: 19¼ (20, 20, 20¾, 20¾)"

Sleeve length: 10¾ (10¾, 10¾, 12, 12)"

Materials

Yarn

Cascade Yarns Cascade 220 Quattro (100% Peruvian highland wool; 3.5 oz [100 g]/220 yd [201 m]): 5 (6, 7, 8, 8) skeins of #9434 turquoise tweed

Hook

Size F/5 (3.75 mm) crochet hook or size needed to obtain gauge

Notions

Yarn needle

Seven ¾" buttons

Stitch markers or paper clips

Gauge

15½ sts = 4";
12 rows in pattern = 4½"

Special Stitches

Dc2tog: (Yo, insert hook in next st, yo, draw yarn through st, yo, draw yarn through 2 loops on hook) twice, yo, draw yarn through 3 loops on hook

Sc2tog: (Insert hook in next st, yo, draw yarn through st) twice, yo, draw yarn through 3 loops on hook

This preppy jacket capitalizes on crochet's great advantages: a textured tweedy surface, easy curve-flattering shaping, speedy production, and flexibility for alterations. Depending on the yarn, trim, and wearer, you can remake the prep into a girlie-girl or an indie rocker. The jacket is cropped to the waist with no ease, for a trim, Babe Paley fit. If you are substituting yarn, be sure to choose something with a twist or print variegated color to hide later changes in stitch direction.

JACKET

Note: All odd-numbered RS rows are sc. All even-numbered WS rows are dc. Increases, decreases, and short row shaping are done only on dc rows.

Back

Ch 57 (65, 73, 81, 89).

Row 1 (RS): Sc in second ch from hook, sc in each ch across, turn—56 (64, 72, 80, 88) sc.

Row 2: Ch 3 (counts as first dc), sk first sc, dc in each sc across, turn—56 (64, 72, 80, 88) sts.

Row 3: Ch 1, sc in each st across, turn—56 (64, 72, 80, 88) sc.

Rep rows 2–3 for pattern throughout. Work even in pattern until 13 rows have been completed from beginning.

Row 14 (inc row): Ch 3, dc in first sc (inc made), dc in each sc across to last sc, 2 dc in last sc (inc made), turn—58 (66, 74, 82, 90) sts.

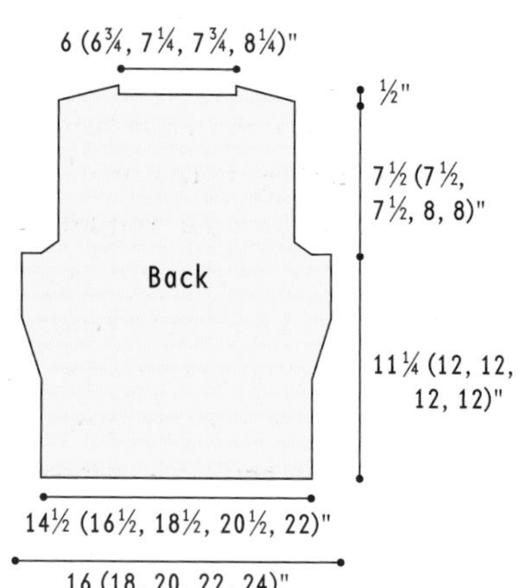

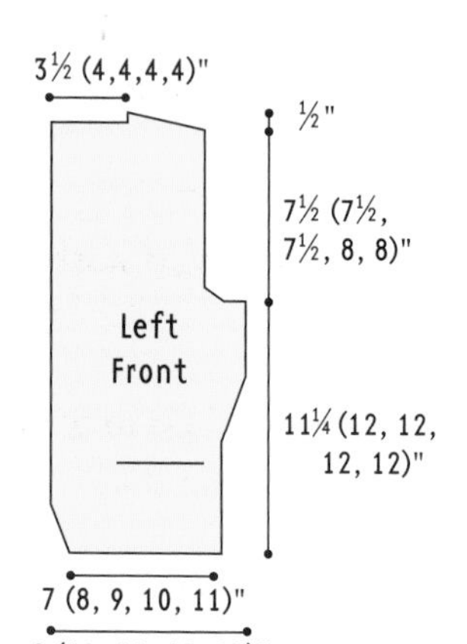

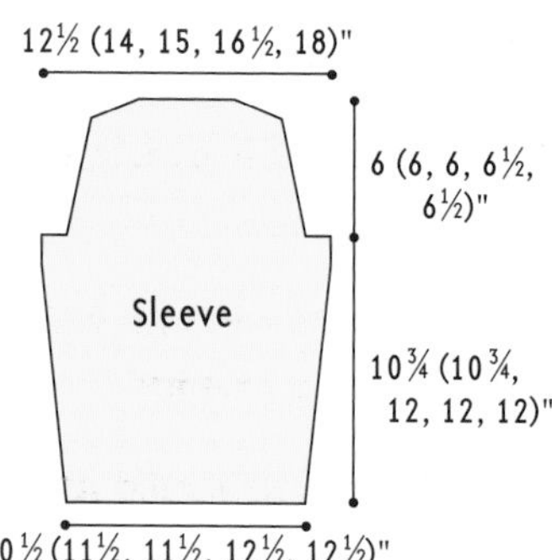

Work in established pattern, inc 1 dc at each end of every fourth row twice more (rows 18 and 22)—62 (70, 78, 86, 94) sts. Place a marker at each end of last inc row for matching seams later.

Work even on 62 (70, 78, 86, 94) sts until back measures 11¼ (12, 12, 12, 12)" from beginning, ending with a sc row. Place a marker at each end of last sc row.

Shape Armholes

Next row: Sl st in each of first 2 (3, 5, 5, 7) sts, ch 1, sc in each of next 1 (2, 2, 3, 3) sts, hdc in each of next 1 (2, 2, 3, 3) sts, dc in each st across to last 4 (7, 9, 11, 12) sts, hdc in each of next 1 (2, 2, 3, 3) sts, sc in each of next 1 (2, 2, 3, 3) sts, turn, leaving rem sts 2 (3, 5, 5, 7) unworked—58 (64, 68, 76, 80) sts excluding sl sts. Fasten off.

Next row: With WS facing, join yarn in first dc, ch 1, sc in each dc across, turn, leaving rem sts unworked—54 (56, 60, 64, 68) sc.

Work even in established pattern until armhole measures 7¼ (7¼, 7¼, 8, 8)" from beginning, ending with a sc row.

Shape Neck

Next row: Ch 3 (counts as first dc), dc in each of next 14 (14, 15, 16, 17) sts, hdc in next st, sc in each of next 22 (24, 26, 28, 30) sts, hdc in next st, dc in each of last 15 (15, 16, 17, 18) sts, turn—54 (56, 60, 64, 68) sts.

Next row: Ch 1, sc in each st across, turn—54 (56, 60, 64, 68) sts.

Shape First Shoulder

Next row: Sl st in each of first 3 (3, 4, 4, 4) sts, ch 1, sc in each of next 3 (3, 4, 4, 4) sts, hdc in each of next 3 (3, 4, 4, 4) sts, dc in each of next 6 (6, 4, 5, 6) sts—15 (15, 16, 17, 18) sts including sl sts. Fasten off.

Shape Second Shoulder

Next row: With same side facing, sk 24 (26, 28, 30, 32) sts to the left of last st made in first shoulder, join yarn in next st, ch 3, dc in each of next 5 (5, 3, 4, 5) sts, hdc in each of next 3 (3, 4, 4, 4) sts, sc in each of next 3 (3, 4, 4, 4) sts, sl st in each st across—15 (15, 16, 17, 18) sts including sl sts. Fasten off.

Remove armhole markers. Keep inc row markers to match sts when seaming sides.

Right Front

Ch 28 (32, 36, 40, 44).

Row 1 (RS): Sc in second ch from hook, sc in each ch across, turn—27 (31, 35, 39, 43) sc.

Row 2: Ch 3 (counts as first dc), dc in each sc across to last st, (2 dc, tr) in last sc, turn—29 (33, 37, 41, 45) sts.

Row 3: Ch 1, sc in each st across, turn—29 (33, 37, 41, 45) sts.

Row 4: Rep row 2—31 (35, 39, 43, 47) sts.

Row 5: Rep row 3—31 (35, 39, 43, 47) sts.

Row 6: Ch 3 (counts as first dc), dc in each sc across to last st, 2 dc in last sc, turn—32 (36, 40, 44, 48) sts.

Rows 7–10: Work even in established st pattern.

Row 11 (buttonhole row): Ch 1, sc in each of first 3 sts, ch 2, sk next 2 sts, sc in each st across, turn—30 (34, 38, 42, 45) sc + ch-2 space.

Row 12: Ch 3 (counts as first dc), dc in each sc and each ch across, turn—32 (36, 40, 44, 47) sts.

Row 13 (pocket opening): Ch 1, sc in each of first 10 sts, ch 16, sk next 16 sts (for pocket opening), sc in each st across, turn—32 (36, 40, 44, 47) sts counting each ch 1 as a st.

Row 14: Ch 3 (counts as first dc), dc in first st (inc made), dc in each sc and each ch across, turn—33 (37, 41, 45, 48) sts.

Work in established pattern, inc 1 dc at armhole edge every fourth row twice more (rows 18 and 22)—35 (39, 43, 47, 50) sts at end of shaping. Place a marker at end of last inc row for matching seams later. At the same time, work buttonhole row every 10 (12, 12, 12, 12) rows twice more—rows 21 and 31 (23 and 35, 23 and 35, 23 and 35, 23 and 35). At the same time, work short row shaping as follows:

SHORT ROW SHAPING

Short row shaping is done to form "darts" on front for a fitted look.

For B, C, and D Cup Sizing

Note: Short row shaping is worked on dc rows only. Work all sc rows even.

Row 24 (26, 26, 26, 26): Ch 1, sc in each of first 3 sts, hdc in next st, dc in each st across, turn.

Row 25 (27, 27, 27, 27): Ch 1, sc in each st across, turn.

Row 26 (28, 28, 28, 28): Ch 1, sc in each of first 5 sts, hdc in next st, dc in each st across, turn.

Row 27 (29, 29, 29, 29): Ch 1, sc in each st across, turn.

Row 28 (30, 30, 30, 30): Ch 1, sc in each of first 8 sts, hdc in next st, dc in each st across, turn.

Row 29 (31, 31, 31, 31): Ch 1, sc in each st across, turn.

4 *Cascade Yarns Cascade 220 Quattro, medium (worsted) weight*

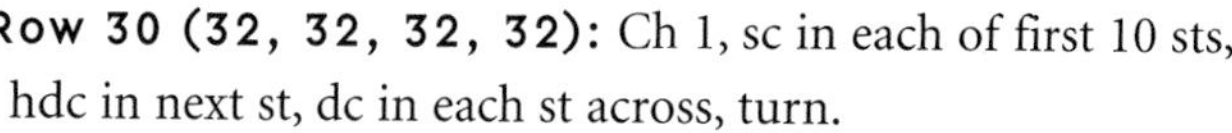

Row 30 (32, 32, 32, 32): Ch 1, sc in each of first 10 sts, hdc in next st, dc in each st across, turn.

For D Cup Sizing Only

Row 31 (33, 33, 33, 33): Ch 1, sc in each st across (working buttonhole for size S only), turn.

Row 32 (34, 34, 34, 34): Ch 1, sc in each of first 13 sts, hdc in next st, dc in each st across, turn.

Row 33 (35, 35, 35, 35): Ch 1, sc in each st across (working buttonhole for sizes M, L, XL, and XXL only), turn.

Row 34 (36, 36, 36, 36): Ch 1, sc in each of first 15 sts, hdc in next st, dc in each st across, turn.

Note: For B and C cups, front row count up to armhole will be 2 rows greater than back row count. For D cups, front row count will be 4 rows greater than back row count. Measurements along front edge will be longer than back, but vertical measurements at side seam will be the same. That is the beauty of short rows—they give your breasts some room in front.

All Cup Sizes

Work even on 35 (39, 43, 47, 50) sts until right front measures 11¼ (12, 12, 12, 12)" from beginning along side edge, ending with a sc row. Place a marker at end of last sc row.

Shape Armholes

Next row: Sl st in each of first 2 (3, 5, 5, 6) sts, ch 1, sc in each of next 1 (2, 2, 3, 3) sts, hdc in each of next 1 (2, 2, 3, 3) sts, dc in each st across, turn—33 (36, 38, 42, 44) sts excluding sl sts.

Next row: Ch 1, sc in each dc across, turn, leaving rem sts unworked—31 (32, 34, 36, 38) sc.

Work even in established pattern until armhole measures 5¼ (5¼, 5¼, 6, 6)" from beginning, ending with a sc row.

Shape Neck

Next row: Ch 3 (counts as first dc), dc in each of next 14 (14, 16, 18, 20) sts, dc2tog in next 2 sts, turn—16 (16, 18, 20, 22) sts. Place marker in last st of row.

Next row: Ch 1, sc in each st across, turn 16 (16, 18, 20, 22) sc.

Next row: Ch 3 (counts as first dc), dc in each sc across to last 2 sts, dc2tog in next 2 sts, turn—15 (15, 17, 19, 21) sts.

Next row: Ch 1, sc in each st across, turn—15 (15, 17, 19, 21) sc.

Rep last 2 rows 0 (0, 1, 2, 3) times—15 (15, 16, 17, 18) sts at end of last row. Fasten off. Remove armhole markers. Keep inc row markers to match seam with front side seams when seaming. Keep neck edge marker.

Left Front

For textured or variegated yarns, work same as right front, omitting buttonholes. Sew left front on with opposite side facing. For yarns with clear stitch definition, work same as right front, reversing shaping and omitting buttonholes.

Sleeve (make 2)

Ch 41 (45, 45, 49, 51).

Row 1: Sc in second ch from hook sc in each ch across, turn—40 (44, 44, 48, 50) sc.

Work in established pattern same as back, inc 1 dc at each end of row 10 (10, 6, 6, 4), then inc 1 dc at each end of every sixth row 3 (0, 0, 0, 0) times, then inc 1 dc at each end of every fourth row 0 (4, 6, 5, 4) times, then inc 1 dc at each end of every other row 0 (0, 0, 2, 5) times—48 (54, 58, 64, 70) sts at end of last row.

Work even on 48 (54, 58, 64, 70) sts until sleeve measures 10¾ (10¾, 12, 12, 12)" from beginning, ending with an sc row.

Shape Cap

Row 1 (WS): Sl st in each of first 2 (3, 5, 5, 6) sts, sc in next 1 (2, 2, 3, 3) sts, hdc in each of next 1 (2, 2, 3, 3) sts, dc in each st across to last 4 (7, 9, 11, 12) sts, hdc in each of next 1 (2, 2, 3, 3) sts, sc in next 1 (2, 2, 3, 3) sts, turn, leaving rem sts unworked—44 (48, 48, 54, 58) sts, excluding sl sts. Fasten off, leaving a long sewing length.

Row 2: With RS facing, join yarn in first dc, ch 1, sc in each dc across, turn, leaving rem sts unworked—40 (40, 40, 42, 46) sc.

Work in established pattern, dec 1 dc at each end of next row and every other row 3 (3, 3, 4, 5) times more—32 (32, 32, 32, 34) sts at end of last row.

Work even in established pattern until sleeve cap measures 4¾ (4¾, 4¾, 5¼, 5¼)" from beginning, ending with an sc row.

Next row: Ch 1, sc in each of first 2 sts, hdc in each of next 2 sts, dc in each st across to last 4 sts, hdc in next 2 sts, sc in last 2 sts, turn—32 (32, 32, 32, 34) sts.

Next row: Sl st in each of first 4 sts, ch 1, sc in each dc across, turn, leaving remaining sts unworked—24 (24, 24, 24, 26) sc.

Next row: Ch 1, sc in each of first 2 sts, hdc in each of next 2 sts, dc in each st across to last 4 sts, hdc in next 2 sts, sc in last 2 sts, turn—16 (16, 16, 16, 18) dc remain. Fasten off.

Assembly

Sew fronts to back across shoulders. Place a marker at center top of sleeve cap. Matching marker to shoulder seam, sew sleeve into armhole opening, easing in fullness. Sew sleeve seams. Matching markers on sides, loosely sew side seams.

Collar

Place markers at the left neck edge inside corner, right neck edge inside corner, shoulder seams, and center of back neck edge. Move markers up as work progresses.

Row 1: With RS facing, join yarn at marker at inside corner on right neck edge, ch 1, sc evenly across neck edge to marker at inside corner of left neck edge, turn.

Row 2: Ch 3 (counts as first dc), dc in first st (inc made), *dc in each st across to next shoulder marker, hdc in next marked st; rep from * once, dc in each st across to last st, 2 dc in last st, turn.

Row 3: Ch 1, sc in each sc across, turn.

Row 4: Ch 3 (counts as first dc), *dc in each st across to next marker, 2 dc in next marked st; rep from * twice, dc in each st across, turn.

Row 5: Ch 1, sc in each sc across, turn.

Row 6: Rep row 4.

Sew sides of collar to adjacent front neck edge from the neck edge corner marker to the bottom of collar row 4, leaving top rows free for notched collar.

Pocket Flap (make 2)

Starting at top edge, ch 17.

Row 1: Sc in second ch from hook sc in each ch across, turn—16 sc.

Row 2: Ch 2 (counts as first dc), dc in each sc across, turn—16 sts.

Row 3: Ch 1, sc in each of first 7 sts, ch 2, sk next 2 sts (for buttonhole), sc in each st across, turn—14 sc + ch-2 space.

Row 4: Ch 2 (counts as first dc), dc in each sc and ch across, turn—16 sts. Sew top edge of each pocket flap to outer loops of sts on top edge of pocket opening.

Pocket (make 2)

Starting at bottom edge, ch 17.

Row 1: Sc in second ch from hook sc in each ch across, turn—16 sc.

Work even in established st pattern same as back until 14 rows have been completed from beginning. Fasten off, leaving a sewing length.

Sew top of each pocket to inside loops on top edge of pocket opening. Sew bottom and sides of pocket to inside of front.

Sew 3 buttons to left front, opposite buttonholes. Sew 1 button to each pocket, opposite buttonholes on flaps. Sew 1 button centered on back of sleeve, 2" above cuff edge. Sew 1 button 1" above last button on each sleeve.

Cuff Edging

Rnd 1: With RS facing, working across opposite side of foundation ch, join yarn in first ch on cuff edge of sleeve, ch 1, sc in each ch around, sl st in first sc to join. Fasten off. Rep on other sleeve.

Jacket Edging

Rnd 1: With RS facing, join yarn at left side seam at bottom edge of jacket, ch 1, sc evenly around entire edge of jacket, working 3 sc in each outside corner and sc2tog at each inside corner of collar, working increases at bottom corners of fronts as needed to keep work flat, sl st in first sc to join. Fasten off.

Finishing

Weave in ends. Wet block to flatten edges and to set collar. Do not steam block or iron as it does odd things to crocheted fabric and gauge. Wear it to the polo fields looking effortlessly elegant.

About Fay I have nothing in common with Jessica Simpson, but I wanted her shawl. And so I learned to crochet. Now, as a cardiology fellow in New York, crocheting and knitting relax me, although I must save my wrists for the cath lab. Many thanks to my husband, Llewellyn, friends, and family for consuming my knit and crochet output, and to my dog, Fred, who suffers his baby blue hand-knit winter sweater with dignity.

Lynn Zykowski

joLLy roger

The Jolly Roger is an homage to my skate-punk days, when everything I owned was black and had a skull on it. The sweater's comfortable fit and tunic length make it suitable for men or women, and as you get the hang of juggling several skeins at once, it's fun to watch the design develop.

SWEATER

Note: To change color: Work last hdc of first color until 3 loops rem on hook, yo with second color, draw second color through 3 loops on hook, drop first color to WS to be picked up later. Do not carry colors; attach a separate ball of yarn for each color area.

Front

Foundation row: With MC, work in FSC for 53 (59, 65, 71, 77) sts.

Row 1 (RS): Ch 2, hdc in each sc across, turn—53 (59, 65, 71, 77) sts.

Rows 2–21: With A only, ch 2, hdc in each st across, turn—53 (59, 65, 71, 77) sts.

Rows 22–52: Ch 2, hdc in first 10 (13, 16, 19, 21) sts, place marker, follow chart for next 33 sts, place marker, hdc in rem 10 (13, 16, 19, 21) sts, turn—53 (59, 65, 71, 77) sts.

Shape Armholes

Row 53: Ch 2, hdc in each st across to last 4 sts, following Front Chart between markers, turn, leaving rem sts unworked—49 (55, 61, 67, 73) sts.

Row 54: Ch 2, hdc in each st across to last 4 sts, following Front Chart between markers, turn, leaving rem sts unworked—45 (51, 57, 63, 69) sts.

4 *Brown Sheep Lamb's Pride Superwash Worsted, medium (worsted) weight*

Finished Size

Finished bust: 33 (36, 40, 44, 47)"

Back length: 27 (27½, 27¾, 28, 28½)"

Sleeve length: 19 (19¾, 20½, 20½, 20½)"

Materials

Yarn

Brown Sheep Lamb's Pride Superwash Worsted (100% washable wool; 3.5 oz [100 g]/200 yd [183 m]): 6 (7, 7, 8, 9) skeins of #SW05 Onyx (MC), 1 skein of #SW11 White Frost (CC)

Hook

Size H/8 (5 mm) crochet hook or size needed to obtain gauge

Notions

Yarn needle

Stitch markers

Gauge

13 sts and 11 rows hdc = 4"

Special Stitches

Foundationless single crochet (FSC): Ch 2, sc in second ch from hook, *insert hook through 2 strands on left side of last sc, yo, draw yarn through st, yo, draw through 2 loops on hook; rep from * until foundation row is desired length

Hdc2tog: (Yo, insert hook in next st, yo, draw yarn through st) twice, yo, draw yarn through 5 loops on hook

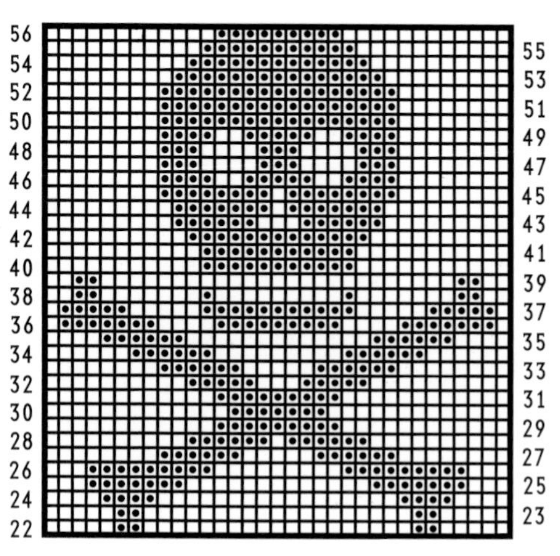

☐ = hdc in MC
◙ = hdc in CC

Rows 55–56: Ch 2, hdc in each st across, following Front Chart between markers, turn—45 (51, 57, 63, 69) sts.

Rows 57–62 (55–62, 55–62, 55–63, 55–64): With A only, work even on 45 (51, 57, 63, 69) hdc.

First Front

Row 63 (63, 63, 64, 65): With MC, ch 2, hdc in each of next 22 (25, 28, 31, 34) hdc, turn, leaving rem sts unworked—22 (25, 28, 31, 34) sts.

Row 64 (64, 64, 65, 66): Ch 2, hdc2tog in next 2 sts, hdc in each st across, turn—21 (24, 27, 30, 33) sts.

Row 65 (65, 65, 66, 67): Ch 2, hdc in each st across to last 2 sts, hdc2tog in last 2 sts, turn—20 (23, 26, 29, 32) sts.

Rows 66–74 (66–75, 66–76, 67–77, 68–78): Hdc2tog at neck edge on each of next 4 (5, 6, 6, 6) rows, then hdc2tog at neck edge every other row twice, then work 1 row even—14 (16, 18, 21, 24) sts at end of last row. Fasten off.

Second Front

Row 63 (63, 63, 64, 65): With appropriate side facing, sk 1 st to the left of last st made in first row of first front, join MC in next st, ch 2, hdc in each st across, turn—22 (25, 28, 31, 34) sts.

Row 64 (64, 64, 65, 66): Ch 2 , hdc in each st across to last 2 sts, hdc2tog in last 2 sts, turn—21 (24, 27, 30, 33) sts.

Row 65 (65, 65, 66, 67): Ch 2, hdc2tog in next 2 sts, hdc in each st across, turn—20 (23, 26, 29, 32) sts.

Rows 66–74 (66–75, 66–76, 67–77, 68–78): Hdc2tog at neck edge on each of next 4 (5, 6, 6, 6) rows, then hdc2tog at neck edge every other row twice, then work 1 row even—14 (16, 18, 21, 24) sts at end of last row. Fasten off.

Back

Foundation row: With MC, work in FSC for 53 (59, 65, 71, 77) sts.

Row 1 (RS): Ch 2, hdc in each sc across, turn—53 (59, 65, 71, 77) sts.

Rows 2–52: Ch 2, hdc in each st across, turn—53 (59, 65, 71, 77) sts.

Shape Armholes

Row 53: Ch 2, hdc in each st across to last 4 sts, turn, leaving remaining sts unworked—49 (55, 61, 67, 73) sts.

Row 54: Ch 2 , hdc in each st across to last 4 sts, turn leaving rem sts unworked—45 (51, 57, 63, 69) sts. Fasten off.

Work even in hdc on 45 (51, 57, 63, 69) sts until 74 (75, 76, 77, 78) rows have been completed from beginning. Fasten off.

Sleeve (make 2)

Foundation row: With MC, work in FSC for 30 (30, 32, 32, 34) sts.

Row 1 (RS): Ch 2, hdc in each sc across, turn—30 (30, 32, 32, 34) sts.

Rows 2–4: Ch 2, hdc in each st across, turn—30 (30, 32, 32, 34) sts.

Work 2 hdc in first and last st of next row and every fifth row thereafter 5 (5, 5, 0, 0) times, then work 2 hdc in first and last st of every fourth row 5 (7, 7, 13, 13) times—52 (56, 58, 60, 62) sts. Work even on 52 (56, 58, 60, 62) sts for 8 (0, 2, 3, 3) rows or until sleeve measures 1¼" more than desired length. Fasten off. Weave in ends.

Assembly

With yarn needle and A, sew front to back across shoulders, leaving center 17 (19, 21, 21, 21) sts free on back neck edge. Fold sleeve in half lengthwise and match fold to shoulder seam. Unfold sleeve and sew into armhole opening; sew top edges of sleeve to skipped sts at base of armhole. Rep for other sleeve. Sew side and underarm seams.

Neck Edging

Rnd 1: With RS facing, join A in left shoulder seam on neck edge, ch 1, sc evenly around neck opening, sl st in first sc to join.

Rnds 2–3: Ch 1, sc in each sc around, sl st in first sc to join. Fasten off. Weave in ends.

About Lynn My mother tried to teach me to crochet lace snowflakes for Christmas gifts. Twenty years later I picked up a crochet hook again and discovered that doilies were not my only option. Having departed ballroom dancing and grant writing in favor of looking after a turbo-charged toddler, occasionally I find time to complete a project. As I've watched so many young people applying fashion-forward style to the craft of crochet, I'm inspired to work with fun patterns that can elicit a smile while they pay homage to the skill of our foremothers.

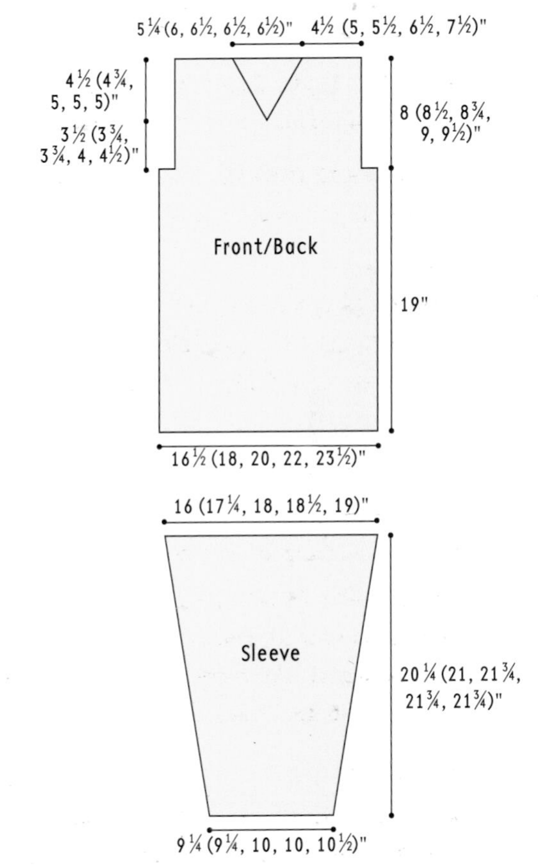

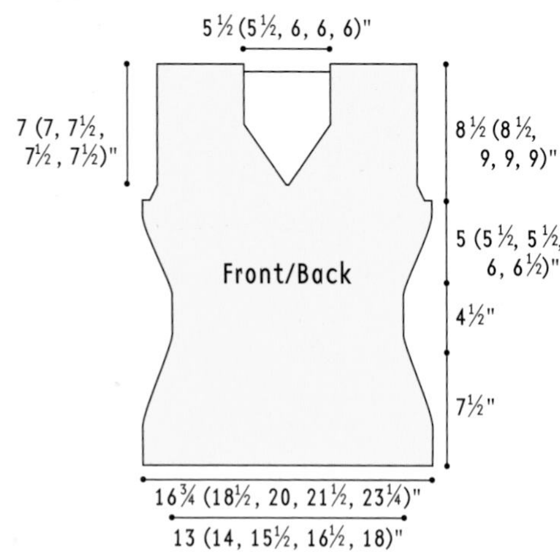

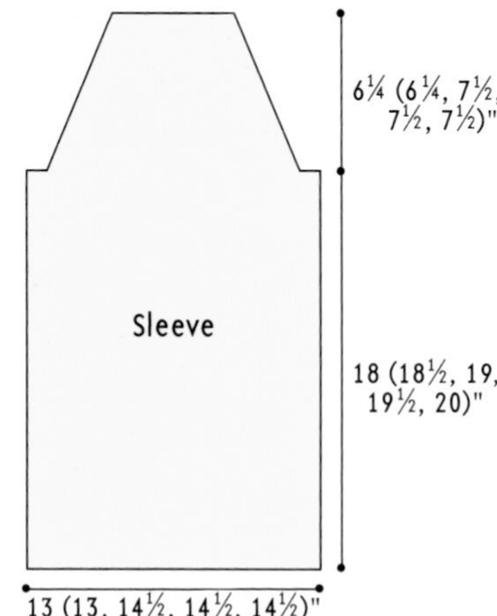

Body

Ch 84 (92, 100, 108, 116) and without twisting ch, sl st in first ch to join.

Rnd 1 (RS): Ch 3 (counts as first dc), sk first 2 ch, *V-st in next ch, sk next ch; rep from * around, dc in first ch already holding beginning ch-3 (completes first V-st), sl st in third ch of turning ch to join—42 (46, 50, 54, 58) V-sts.

Rnd 2: Ch 3 (counts as first dc), sk next dc, *V-st in space between 2 dc of V-st; rep from * around, ending with dc in space between last dc and beginning ch-3, sl st in third ch of turning ch to join—42 (46, 50, 54, 58) V-sts.

Rnds 3–13: Rep rnd 2.

Waist Shaping

Waist shaping will occur naturally without any decreasing.

Rnd 1: Ch 1, sc in first st, ch 1, *sc in space between 2 dc of next V-st, ch 1; rep from * around to last 2 dc, sk last 2 dc, sl st in first sc to join—42 (46, 50, 54, 58) ch-1 spaces.

Rnd 2: Ch 1, (sc, ch 1) in each ch-1 space around, sl st in first sc to join—42 (46, 50, 54, 58) ch-1 spaces.

Rnds 3–16: Rep rnd 2.

Upper Body

Rnd 1: Ch 3 (counts as first dc), V-st in each ch-1 space around, ending with dc in last ch-1 space (with beginning ch, counts as first V-st), sl st in third ch of turning ch to join—42 (46, 50, 54, 58) V-sts.

Rnd 2: Ch 3 (counts as first dc), sk next dc, V-st in each V-st around, ending with dc in space between last dc and beginning ch-3, sl st in third ch of turning ch to join—42 (46, 50, 54, 58) V-sts.

Rep rnd 2 until body measures 17 (17½, 17½, 18, 18½)" from beginning.

Divide for Front and Back

Work now progresses in rows. Place marker in space between beginning ch-3 and first dc for left side seam

(LSS). Sk next 21 (23, 25, 27, 29) V-sts, place marker between next 2 V-sts for right side seam (RSS). Place marker in center V-st on front (CF) and back (CB).

Front

Row 1 (RS): Sl st in each of next 2 dc, ch 3, V-st in each of next 19 (21, 23, 25, 27) V-sts, dc between 2 dc of next V-st, turn, leaving rem sts unworked—19 (21, 23, 25, 27) V-sts.

Row 2 (WS): Ch 3 (counts as first dc), dc2tog in next 2 V-sts (dec made), dc in same V-st as second leg of last dec, V-st in each V-st across to last 2 V-sts, dc in next V-st, dc2tog in same V-st and next V-st, dc in third ch of turning ch, turn—17 (19, 21, 23, 25) V-sts.

Shape Left Front

Row 3: Ch 3 (counts as first dc), V-st between next 2 sts, V-st in each of next 6 (7, 8, 9, 10) V-sts, dc2tog in next 2 V-sts, turn—7 (8, 9, 10, 11) V-sts.

Row 4: Ch 3 (counts as first dc), V-st in each V-st across, dc in third ch of turning ch, turn—7 (8, 9, 10, 11) V-sts.

Row 5: Ch 3 (counts as first dc), V-st in each V-st across to last V-st, work dc2tog in next V-st and third ch of turning ch, turn—6 (7, 8, 9, 10) V-sts.

Rows 6-7 (6-7, 6-9, 6-9, 6-9): Rep rows 4–5 1 (1, 2, 2, 2) times—5 (6, 6, 7, 8) V-sts.

Row 8 (8, 10, 10, 10): Rep row 4—5 (6, 6, 7, 8) V-sts.

Row 9 (9, 11, 11, 11): Ch 3 (counts as first dc), V-st in each V-st across, dc in third ch of turning ch, turn—5 (6, 6, 7, 8) V-sts.

Row 10 (10, 12, 12, 12): Ch 3 (counts as first dc), dc in space between turning ch and first dc (counts as first V-st),V-st in each V-st across, dc in third ch of turning ch, turn—5 (6, 6, 7, 8) V-sts.

Row 11 (11, 13, 13, 13): Ch 3 (counts as first dc), V-st in each V-st across to last dc, dc between last dc and turning ch, dc in third ch of turning ch (counts as last V-st), turn—5 (6, 6, 7, 8) V-sts.

Rep last 2 rows until 14 (14, 15, 15, 15) rows have been completed from beginning of front. Fasten off.

Shape Right Front

Row 3: With RS facing, join yarn in center front marked V-st (CF) (already holding last st of row 3 of left front), ch 3, dc in next V-st, V-st in each of next 7 (8, 9, 10, 11) V-sts, dc in third ch of turning ch, turn—7 (8, 9, 10, 11) V-sts.

Row 4: Ch 3 (counts as first dc), V-st in each V-st across, dc in third ch of turning ch, turn—7 (8, 9, 10, 11) V-sts.

Row 5: Ch 3 (counts as first dc), dc in next V-st, V-st in each V-st across, dc in third ch of turning ch, turn—6 (7, 8, 9, 10) V-sts.

Rows 6–7 (6–7, 6–9, 6–9, 6–9): Rep rows 4–5 1 (1, 2, 2, 2) times—5 (6, 6, 7, 8) V-sts.

Row 8 (8, 10, 10, 10): Rep row 4–5 (6, 6, 7, 8) V-sts.

Row 9 (9, 11, 11, 11): Ch 3 (counts as first dc), dc in next V-st (counts as first V-st), V-st in each V-st across, dc in third ch of turning ch, turn—5 (6, 6, 7, 8) V-sts.

Row 10 (10, 12, 12, 12): Ch 3 (counts as first dc), V-st in each V-st across to last V-st, dc between last dc and ch-3 turning ch, dc in third ch of turning ch (counts as last V-st), turn—5 (6, 6, 7, 8) V-sts.

Row 11 (11, 13, 13, 13): Ch 3 (counts as first dc), dc in space between turning ch and first dc (counts as first V-st), V-st in each V-st across, dc in third ch of turning ch, turn—5 (6, 6, 7, 8) V-sts.

Rep last 2 rows until 14 (14, 15, 15, 15) rows have been completed from beginning of front. Fasten off.

Back

Row 1 (RS): With RS facing, join yarn in first V-st to the left of last st made in row 1 of front (space to the left of RSS marker), ch 3 (counts as first dc), V-st in each of next 19 (21, 23, 25, 27) V-sts, dc between 2 dc of next V-st (space to the right of LSS marker), turn, leaving remaining sts unworked—19 (21, 23, 25, 27) V-sts.

Row 2 (WS): Ch 3 (counts as first dc), dc2tog in next 2 V-sts (dec made), dc in same V-st as second leg of last dec, V-st in each V-st across to last 2 V-sts, dc in next V-st, dc2tog in same V-st and next V-st, dc in third ch of turning ch, turn—17 (19, 21, 23, 25) V-sts.

Row 3: Ch 3 (counts as first dc), V-st in each V-st across, dc in third ch of turning ch, turn—17 (19, 21, 23, 25) V-sts.

Rep row 3 until 13 (13, 14, 14, 14) rows have been completed from beginning of back.

Shape First Shoulder

Row 14 (14, 15, 15, 15): Ch 3 (counts as first dc), V-st in each of next 5 (6, 6, 7, 8) V-sts—5 (6, 6, 7, 8) V-sts. Fasten off.

Shape Second Shoulder

Row 14 (14, 15, 15, 15): With appropriate side facing, sk 7 (7, 9, 9, 9) V-sts to the left of last st made in first shoulder, join yarn in next V-st, ch 3 (counts as first dc), dc in same V-st (counts as first V-st), V-st in each of next 4 (5, 5, 6, 7) V-sts—5 (6, 6, 7, 8) V-sts. Fasten off.

Sleeve (make 2)

Ch 44 (44, 48, 48, 48).

Row 1 (RS): Sc in second ch from hook, *ch 1, sk next ch, sc in next ch; rep from * across, turn—21 (21, 23, 23, 23) ch-1 spaces.

Row 2: Ch 1, sc in first sc, (ch 1, sc) in each ch-1 space across, sc in last sc, turn—20 (20, 22, 22, 22) ch-1 spaces.

Row 3: Ch 1, sc in first sc, ch 1, (sc, ch 1) in each ch-1 space across, sc in last sc, turn—21 (21, 23, 23, 23) ch-1 spaces.

Rep rows 2–3 until sleeve measures 18 (18½, 19, 19½, 20)" from beginning, ending with row 2 of pattern. Do not fasten off.

Shape Cap

Row 1: Sl st to first ch-1 space, ch 1, (sc, ch 1) in each ch-1 space across to last ch-1 space, sc in last ch-1 space, turn—18 (18, 20, 20, 20) ch-1 spaces.

Row 2: Ch 1, sc2tog in first 2 sts, ch 1, (sc, ch 1) in each ch-1 space across to last ch-1 space, sc2tog in last 2 sts, turn—17 (17, 19, 19, 19) ch-1 spaces.

Work even for 3 rows, then dec 1 sc at each end of next row and every other row thereafter until 9 ch-1 spaces rem, then work even for 1 row. Fasten off.

Assembly

With WS of front and back facing, sl st shoulder seams together. With WS facing, sl st sleeve seams. Turn sweater and sleeves RS out, set sleeve in armholes. With WS facing, sl st sleeves into armholes, easing in fullness.

Neck Edging

Note: Neck edging is worked across row-end sts on front neck edge. Work approximately 3 sc in each row-end dc, adjusting number of sts to keep work lying flat.

With RS facing, join yarn at left shoulder seam, ch 1, sc in same space, *work picot, work 3 sc evenly spaced across sts of neck edge*; rep from * to * across to one st before center front V, sc2tog in 2 sts at center front V, rep from * to * around, sl st in first sc to join.

About Cal Watching my grandmother crochet is a memory that so pervaded my childhood, I feel I internalized the motions before ever touching a hook. When I finally learned to crochet as an adult, I took to it immediately, relishing its free-form capabilities. As a clothing designer, I love incorporating crochet into my work because it is one of the few techniques that can't be imitated by a machine; it is the epitome of "handmade." Now that I also teach crochet, I am proud to be a part of reclaiming and revitalizing this domestic art that just a few years ago seemed endangered. I live and work in Brooklyn, New York, with my chihuahua, Gertie, who has even more crocheted sweaters than I do. I have a Web site at www.hodgepodgefarm.com.

Cuff Edging

With RS facing, join yarn in sleeve seam at one cuff edge, ch 1, sc in same space, *ch 4, sk next 3 sts, (sc, ch 4, sc, ch 4, sc) in next st; rep from * around, sl st in first sc to join.

Bottom Edging

Note: Rnd 1 of bottom edging requires a multiple of 12 sts.

Sizes Small and Extra Large Only

Rnd 1 (RS): Flatten sweater with front and back aligned; working across opposite side of foundation ch on lower edge, join yarn in ch at left side edge, ch 1, *(sc in ch, ch 5, sk next 4 ch) twice, (sc in next ch, ch 5) twice; rep from * around, sl st in first sc to join—28 (32) ch-5 loops.

Sizes Medium and Extra Extra Large Only

Rnd 1 (RS): Flatten sweater with front and back aligned; working across opposite side of foundation ch on lower edge, join yarn in ch at left side edge, ch 1, *(sc in ch, ch 5, sk next 4 ch) twice, (sc in next ch, ch 5) twice**, sc in next ch, ch 5, sk next 4 ch, sc in next ch, ch 5, sk next 3 ch; rep from * 3 times, rep from * to ** 0 (2) times, sl st in first sc to join—32 (40) ch-5 loops.

Size Large Only

Rnd 1 (RS): Flatten sweater with front and back aligned; working across opposite side of foundation ch on lower edge, join yarn in ch at left side edge, ch 1, *(sc in ch, ch 5, sk next 4 ch) twice, (sc in next ch, ch 5) twice, sc in next ch, ch 5, sk next 4 ch, sc in next ch, ch 5, sk next 5 ch; rep from * around, sl st in first sc to join—36 ch-5 loops.

All Sizes

Rnd 2: Sl st to center of first ch-5 loop, ch 1, (sc, ch 3) in each ch-5 loop around, sl st in first sc to join—28 (32, 32, 36, 40) ch-3 loops.

Rnd 3: Sl st in first ch-3 loop, ch 1, *(sc, ch 5, sc, ch 5, sc) in ch-3 loop, ch 5, sk next ch-3 loop, sc in next ch-3 loop, ch 5, sk next ch-3 loop; rep from * around, sl st in first sc to join—28 (32, 32, 36, 40) ch-5 loops. Fasten off. Weave in ends.

froufrou

It's often been said that crochet isn't suitable for creating clothing because crocheted items are stiff and heavy. This project shows that it doesn't have to be that way. By using "granite stitch" (also called "seed stitch") and a large hook, you can create a light and airy piece. Also, because of the large hook, FrouFrou won't take forever to finish. The ruffles and fitted form make this cardigan very feminine. Add a personal touch by choosing a closure you like: a shiny brooch, cool pin, heavy button, or romantic ribbon.

SWEATER

Note: Sweater is worked in one piece from bottom edge of back to armhole, adding sleeves to each side, then working up to and over shoulders, then separating for fronts and working down each front. Increases are worked into pattern, forming shawl collar. Lower back is flared. Side seams will form darts that show on front.

4 *Rowan Kid Classic, medium (worsted) weight*

Back

Ch 78 (86, 94, 102, 110) + 2 (counts as first ch-1 space).

Row 1 (RS): Sc in third ch from hook, *ch 1, sk next ch, sc in next ch; rep from * across, turn—40 (44, 48, 52, 56) ch-1 spaces.

Rows 2–4: Work even in GSP—40 (44, 48, 52, 56) ch-1 spaces.

Row 5: Ch 2, sc2tog in next 2 ch-1 space (dec made), work in GSP across to last 2 ch-1 spaces, sc2tog in last 2 ch-1 spaces (dec made), turn—38 (42, 46, 50, 54) ch-1 spaces.

Work in GSP, dec 1 ch-1 space at each end of every seventh row 5 times—28 (32, 36, 40, 44) ch-1 spaces.

Finished Size

Finished bust: 32 (36, 41, 46, 50)"

Back length: 26½ (27, 27½, 28, 28½)"

Sleeve length: 18½ (18½, 19, 19, 19½)"

Materials

Yarn

Rowan Kid Classic (70% lambswool/ 26% kid mohair/4% nylon; 1.75 oz [50 g]/151 yd [138 m]): 9 (9, 11, 12, 13) balls of #835 Royal

Hook

Size K/10½ (7 mm) crochet hook or size needed to obtain gauge

Notions

Yarn needle

Contrasting yarn or stitch markers

Brooch, pin, button, or ribbon for closure

Gauge

14 sts and 14 rows in granite st pattern = 4"

Special Stitches

Granite Stitch Pattern (GSP): Ch 2 (counts as first ch-1 space), sc in next ch-1 space, *ch 1, sk next sc, sc in next ch-1 space; rep from * across for pattern, turn

Sc2tog (dec 1 ch-1 space): (Insert hook in next ch-1 space, yo, draw yarn through st) twice, yo, draw yarn through 3 loops on hook

Work even in GSP for 21 rows—28 (32, 36, 40, 44) ch-1 spaces. Drop loop from hook to be picked up later.

Shape Sleeves

Attach a separate strand of yarn in first st of last row, ch 55 (55, 57, 57, 59). Fasten off strand.

Next row: Pick up dropped loop, ch 55 (55, 57, 57, 59), sc in third ch from hook, *ch 1, sk next ch, sc in next ch; rep from * across added ch, work in GSP across back, rep from * across added ch—82 (86, 92, 96, 102) ch-1 spaces. Work even in GSP for 28 (32, 35, 38, 42) rows—82 (86, 92, 96, 102) ch-1 spaces.

Shape Collar

Place a marker in center ch-1 space of last row.

Next row: Work in GSP across to marked st, (sc, ch 1, sc, ch 1) in marked st (inc made), work in GSP across, turn—83 (87, 93, 97, 103) ch-1 spaces.

Place a marker in 2 ch-1 spaces of inc.

Next row: Work in GSP across, working (sc, ch 1, sc, ch 1) in each marked st (2 inc made), turn—85 (89, 95, 99, 105) ch-1 spaces.

In each successive row, move left marker up and to the left 1 ch-1 space; move right marker up and to the right 1 ch-1 space.

Rep last row for 16 rows, inc 1 ch-1 space at each marker—117 (121, 127, 131, 137) ch-1 spaces at end of last row. Increases will form a V from center outward to form collar.

Work even in GSP for 3 rows. Fasten off.

First Front

Next row: With appropriate side facing, sk first 27 (27, 28, 28, 29) ch-1 spaces, join yarn in next ch-1 space, ch 2, sc in next ch-1 space, *ch 1, sk next sc, sc in next ch-1 space; rep from * 29 (31, 33, 35, 37) times, turn, leaving rem sts unworked—31 (33, 35, 37, 39) ch-1 spaces.

Next row: Ch 2 (dec made), sc in next ch-1 space, work in GSP across, turn—30 (32, 34, 36, 38) ch-1 spaces.

Size S Only

Next row: Work even in GSP across—30 ch-1 spaces.

Rep last 2 rows, dec 1 ch-1 space at neck edge every other row until 1 ch-1 space remains. Fasten off.

Sizes M, L, XL, and XXL Only

Next row: Work in GSP across to last 2 ch-1 spaces, sc2tog in last 2 ch-1 spaces (dec made)—31 (33, 35, 37) ch-1 spaces.

Rep last 2 rows, dec 1 ch-1 space at neck edge every row until 28 (26, 24, 22) ch-1 spaces rem.

Dec 1 ch-1 space at neck edge every other row until 1 ch-1 space remains. Fasten off.

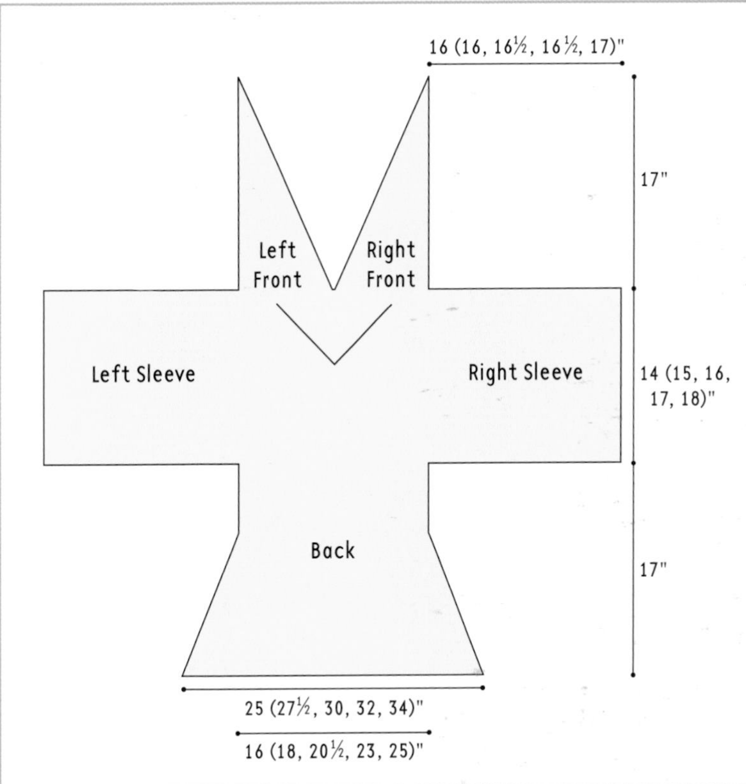

Second Front

Next row: With appropriate side facing, sk 1 ch-1 space to the left of last st made in first row of first front, join yarn in next ch-1 space, ch 1, sc in next ch-1 space, work in granite st across to last 27 (27, 28, 28, 29) ch-1 spaces, turn, leaving rem sts unworked—31 (33, 35, 37, 39) ch-1 spaces.

Dec 1 ch-1 space at neck edge on next row and every row thereafter until 30 (28, 26, 24, 22) ch-1 spaces remain. Then dec 1 ch-1 space at neck edge every other row until 1 ch-space remains. Fasten off.

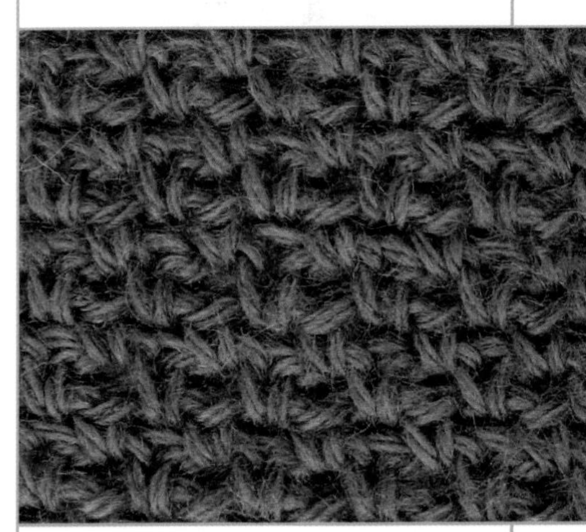

Right Side Trim

With RS facing, join yarn in first row-end st on armhole edge at bottom of right front, ch 1, sc in each of first 30 row-end sts. Fasten off.

Left Side Trim

With RS facing, join yarn in 30th row-end st on armhole edge of left front,

ch 1, sc in each row-end st across to bottom edge. Fasten off. Because seams will show on front, side trims will form "darts."

Assembly

Weave in ends. Sew side and underarm seams.

Cuffs

Rnd 1: With RS facing, join yarn in seam on cuff edge of one sleeve, ch 1, sc evenly around cuff edge.

Rnd 2: Ch 3, *draw up a ½" loop in next sc, sk next sc, draw up a ½" loop in next sc, yo, draw yarn through 3 loops on hook, ch 3; rep from * around, sl st in third ch of turning ch to join.

Rnds 3–6: Ch 3, draw up a ½" loop in first st, draw up a ½" loop in next ch-3 loop, yo, draw yarn through 3 loops on hook, ch 3, *draw up a ½" loop in same ch-3 loop as last st, draw up a ½" loop in next ch-3 loop, yo, draw yarn through 3 loops on hook, ch 3; rep from * around, sl st in third ch of turning ch to join. Fasten off. Weave in ends.

Rep cuff on other sleeve.

Sweater Border

Rnd 1: With RS facing, join yarn in one seam at bottom edge of sweater, ch 1, sc evenly around entire edge of sweater.

Rnds 2–6: Rep rnds 2–6 of cuff.

Fasten off. Weave in ends.

About Suzanne I live in Amsterdam, the Netherlands, where I'm studying for my major in social psychology at the University of Amsterdam. Last year I inherited some wool and hooks from my grandmother. My mother used those to teach me how to crochet, and I have been addicted ever since. I think crocheting is the ideal way to relax after a hard day's work. To challenge myself I try to incorporate new stitches or techniques in every project I make. Aside from writing my thesis and crocheting (which both take up a lot of time), I like to do a little Web site design, read, and work out. Despite my very tiny kitchen, I love to entertain my friends with a nice home-cooked meal. Some of my other projects can be found at www.crochetgallery.blogspot.com.

Jennifer Hansen

go for baroque

the pattern for this jacket was born from the fan motif spotted on a thrift-store bed jacket and the challenge to create something lacy that even a macho girl might wear. The jacket is designed to be form-fitting, worn over a simple dress, tank top, or halter. A key to the shaping is the ornate fan-pattern stitch motif, which provides flaring at the sleeves and waist without the need to increase or decrease. The style accentuates the waist with two luxurious silk ribbons, and the change in stitch direction at the lower rear creates a subtle bustlelike effect.

1 *Filatura di Crosa Brilla, super fine (fingering) weight*

Finished Size

Directions are given for size Small (S). Changes for Medium (M), Large (L), Extra Large (XL), and Extra Extra Large (XXL) are in parentheses.

Finished bust: 31 (35, 38¾, 42½, 46½)"

Back length: 27½ (27½, 28, 28, 28½)"

Sleeve length: approximately 23"

Materials

Yarn

Filatura di Crosa Brilla (58% Viscose/42% cotton; 1.75 oz [50 g]/120 yd [110 m]): 9 (9, 10, 11, 12) skeins #404 brown

Hook

Size D/3 (3.25 mm) crochet hook or size needed to obtain gauge

Notions

Yarn needle

3¼ (3½, 3¾, 4, 4) yds of Artemis Hanah Silk Ribbon 1¼" wide in complementary color (Eggplant Olive shown)

Gauge

2 pattern repeats = 3¾"; 6 rows in pattern = 3½". Note: Fabric is stretchy and gauge will vary throughout the jacket.

Special Stitches

Shell: 4 tr in same st or space

JACKET

Upper Waist Panel

Ch 121 (139, 157, 175, 193).

Row 1 (RS): Tr in fourth ch from hook (counts as first half shell), *ch 2, sk next 2 ch, sc in next ch, ch 3, sk next 2 ch, sc in next ch, ch 2, sk next 2 ch, shell in next ch; rep from * across, ending with 2 tr in last ch (half shell made), turn—12 (14, 16, 18, 20) full shells + 2 half shells.

Row 2: Ch 5 (counts as tr, ch 2), tr in next tr, *ch 3, sk next ch-2 space, sc in next ch-3 space, ch 3, sk next ch-2 space, (tr, ch 2) in each of next 3 tr, tr in next tr; rep from * 11 (13, 15, 17, 19) times, sk next ch-2 space, sc in next ch-3 space, ch 3, sk next ch-2 space, tr in next tr, ch 2, tr in third ch of turning ch, turn—12 (14, 16, 18, 20) full patterns + 2 half patterns.

Row 3: Ch 6 (counts as tr, ch 3), tr in next tr, *sk next 2 ch-3 spaces, (tr, ch 3) in each of next 3 tr, tr in next tr; rep from * 11 (13, 15, 17, 19) times, sk next 2 ch-3 spaces, tr in next tr, ch 3, tr in third ch of turning ch, turn—12 (14, 16, 18, 20) full patterns + 2 half patterns.

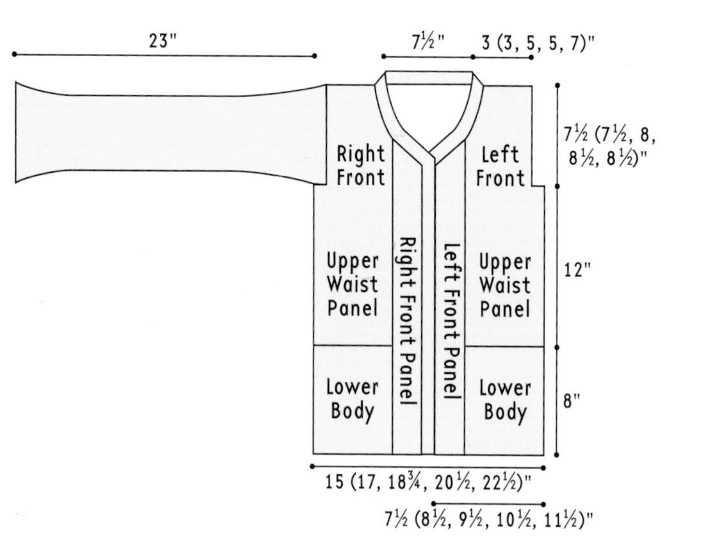

Row 4: Ch 3 (counts as first tr), tr in first tr (counts as first half shell), *ch 2, sc in next ch-3 space, ch 3, sc in next ch-3 space, ch 2, shell in next ch-3 space; rep from * across, ending with 2 tr in third ch of turning ch (half shell made), turn—12 (14, 16, 18, 20) full shells + 2 half shells.

Rows 5–16: Rep rows 2–4 4 times.

Rows 17–18: Rep rows 2–3.

DIVIDE FOR FRONTS AND BACK

Right Front

Row 19: Ch 3 (counts as first tr), tr in first tr (counts as first half shell), *ch 2, sc in next ch-3 space, ch 3, sc in next ch-3 space, ch 2, shell in next ch-3 space; rep from * 0 (0, 1, 1, 2) times, ch 2, sc in next ch-3 space, ch 3, sc in next ch-3 space, ch 2, 2 tr in third ch of turning ch (half shell made), turn, leaving rem sts unworked—1 (1, 2, 2, 3) full shells + 2 half shells.

Rows 20–22: Work even in established pattern.

Shape Neck

Row 23: Ch 3 (counts as first tr), tr in next tr, work in established pattern of row 2 across, turn.

Row 24: Work in established pattern of row 3 across to last 2 ch-3 spaces, sk next 2 ch-3 spaces, tr in next tr, tr in third ch of turning ch, turn.

Row 25: Ch 4, sk next ch-3 space, shell in the next ch-3 space, work in established pattern of row 4 across, turn.

Row 26: Work in established pattern of row 2 across to ch-4 turning ch, tr in fourth ch of turning ch, turn.

Row 27: Ch 3 (counts as first tr), work in established pattern of row 3 across, turn.

Note: In order to make armhole depth shorter for sizes Small and Medium, work next 3 rows in dc instead of tr. For sizes Large and Extra Large, work next 3 rows in tr. To make armhole deeper for size Extra Extra Large, work next 3 rows in dtr instead of tr.

Row 28: Work in established pattern of row 4 across to last ch-3 space, sc in next ch-3 space, turn, leaving rem sts unworked.

Row 29: Ch 3, work in established pattern of row 2 across, turn.

Row 30: Work in established pattern of row 3 across to last 3 tr, tr in next tr, sk next tr, tr in third ch of turning ch. Fasten off.

Back

Row 19 (RS): With RS facing, sk 2 (5, 2, 5, 2) ch-3 spaces to the left of last st made in row 19 of right front, join yarn in next ch-3 space, ch 3, tr in first ch-3 space (counts as first half shell), *ch 2, sc in next ch-3 space, ch 3, sc in next ch-3 space, ch 2, shell in next ch-3 space; rep from * 5 (5, 7, 7, 9) times, ch 2, sc in next ch-3 space, ch 3, sc in next ch-3 space, ch 2, 2 tr in next ch-3 space (half shell made), turn, leaving rem sts unworked—6 (6, 8, 8, 10) full shells + 2 half shells.

Rows 20–27: Work even in established pattern of upper waist panel. Fasten off.

Sizes Small and Medium Only

Rows 28–30: Work even in established pattern of upper waist panel, substituting dc's for tr's in pattern. Fasten off.

Sizes Large and Extra Large Only

Rows 28–30: Work even in established pattern of upper waist panel. Fasten off.

Sizes Extra Extra Large Only

Rows 28–30: Work even in established pattern of upper waist panel, substituting dtr's for tr's in pattern. Fasten off.

Left Front

Row 19 (WS): Join yarn in third ch of turning ch at beginning of row 18, ch 3 (counts as first tr), tr in first st (counts as half shell), *ch 2, sc in next ch-3 space, ch 3, sc in next ch-3 space, ch 2, shell in next ch-3 space; rep from * 0 (0, 1, 1, 2) times, ch 2, sc in next ch-3 space, ch 3, sc in next ch-3 space, ch 2, 2 tr in third ch of turning ch (half shell made), turn, leaving rem sts unworked—1 (1, 2, 2, 3) full shells + 2 half shells.

Rows 20–30: Rep rows 20–30 of right front.

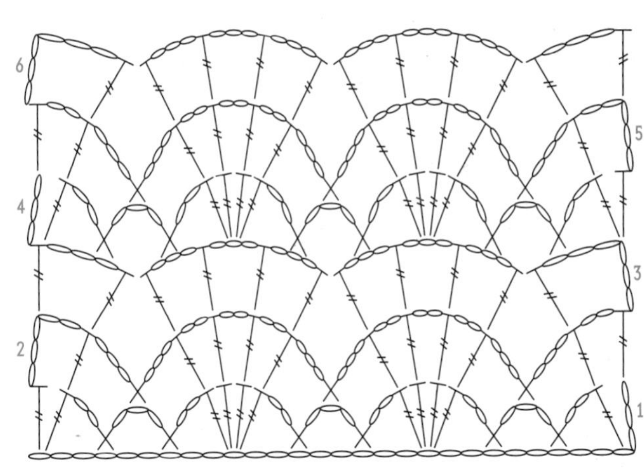

Reduced sample of pattern

Lower Body

Row 1: With RS facing, working across opposite side of foundation ch, join yarn in first ch, ch 3, tr in same ch (counts as first half shell), *ch 2, sc in next ch-2 space, ch 3, sc in next ch-2 space, ch 2, shell in next ch-2 space; rep from * across to last 3 ch-2 space, ch 2, sc in next ch-2 space,

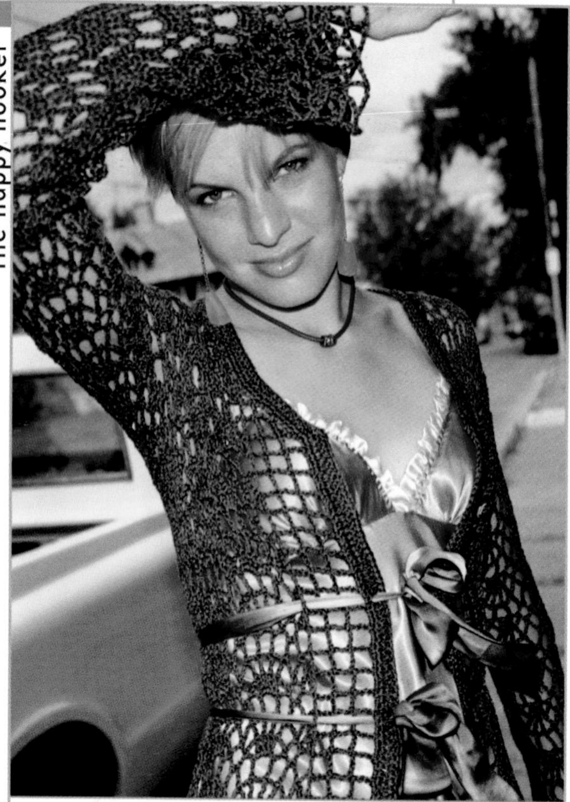

ch 3, sc in next ch-2 space, ch 2, sk next ch-2 space, 2 tr in last ch (half shell made), turn—12 (14, 16, 18, 20) full shells + 2 half shells.

Rows 2–12: Work even in established pattern of upper waist panel. Fasten off.

Assembly

Sew fronts to back across shoulders.

First Sleeve

Sleeves are crocheted in rnds, working in row-end sts and ch-3 spaces around armholes. There should be 26 (29, 26, 29, 26) spaces around each armhole. First rnd is a transitional rnd of (tr, ch 3) spaces. Rnd 1 of each size is worked differently to establish correct number of spaces to begin pattern for the rest of sleeve.

Size Small Only

Rnd 1: With RS facing, join yarn in any space at bottom of underarm of one armhole opening, ch 6 (counts as tr, ch 3), working in row-end tr and ch-3 spaces around armhole, *tr in each of next 2 spaces (dec made), ch 3, tr in next space, ch 3; rep from * 7 times, tr in next space, ch 3, sl st in third ch of turning ch to join—18 ch-3 spaces.

Size Medium Only

Rnd 1: With RS facing, join yarn in any space at bottom of underarm of one armhole opening, ch 6 (counts as tr, ch 3), working in row-end tr and ch-3 spaces around armhole, *tr in each of next 2 spaces (dec made), ch 3, tr in next space, ch 3, tr in each of next 2 spaces, ch 3, (tr, ch 3) in each of next 2 spaces; rep from * 3 times, sl st in third ch of turning ch to join—21 ch-3 spaces.

Size Large Only

Rnd 1: With RS facing, join yarn in any space at bottom of underarm of one armhole opening, ch 6 (counts as tr, ch 3), working in row-end tr and ch-3 spaces around armhole, *tr in each of next 2 spaces (dec made), (tr, ch 3) in each of next 4 spaces; rep from * 3 times, tr in next space, ch 3, sl st in third ch of turning ch to join—24 ch-3 spaces.

Size Extra Large Only

Rnd 1: With RS facing, join yarn in any space at bottom of underarm of one armhole opening, ch 6 (counts as tr, ch 3), working in row-end tr and ch-3 spaces around armhole, *tr in each of next 2 spaces (dec made), (tr, ch 3) in each of next 4 spaces; rep from * 3 times, tr in each of next 2 spaces (dec made), ch 3, (tr, ch 3) in each of next 2 spaces, sl st in third ch of turning ch to join—24 ch-3 spaces.

Size Extra Extra Large Only

Rnd 1: With RS facing, join yarn in any space at bottom of underarm of one armhole opening, ch 6 (counts as tr, ch 3), working in row-end tr and ch-3 spaces around armhole, tr in first space (inc made), ch 3, (tr, ch 3) in each space around, sl st in third ch of turning ch to join—27 ch-3 spaces.

All Sizes

Rnd 2: Sl st in first ch-3 space, ch 3 (counts as first tr), 2 tr in first ch-2 space, *ch 3, sc in next ch-3 space, ch 3, sc in next ch-3 space, ch 2, shell in next ch-3 space; rep from * around, ending with tr in first ch-3 space to complete first shell, sl st in third ch of turning ch to join—6 (7, 8, 8, 9) shells.

Rnd 3: Ch 5 (counts as tr, ch 2), tr in next tr, ch 2, tr in next tr, ch 3, sk next ch-2 space, sc in next ch-3 space, ch 3, sk next ch-2 space, (tr, ch 2) in each of next 3 tr, tr in next tr; rep from * around to last 3 spaces, ch 3, sk next ch-2 space, sc in next ch-3 space, ch 3, tr in next tr, ch 2, sl st in third ch of turning ch to join—6 (7, 8, 8, 9) patterns.

Rnd 4: Ch 6 (counts as tr, ch 3), tr in next tr, ch 3, tr in next tr, sk next 2 ch-3 spaces, *(tr, ch 3) in each of next 3 tr, tr in next tr; rep from * around to last 2 ch-3 spaces, sk next 2 ch-3 spaces, tr in next tr, ch 3, sl st in third ch of turning ch to join—6 (7, 8, 8, 9) patterns.

Rnd 5: Sl st in first ch-3 space, ch 3 (counts as first tr), 2 tr in first ch-3 space, *ch 3, sc in next ch-3 space, ch 3, sc in next ch-3 space, ch 2, shell in next ch-3 space; rep from * around, ending with tr in first ch-3 space to complete first shell, sl st in third ch of turning ch to join—6 (7, 8, 8, 9) shells.

Rnds 6–35: Rep rnds 3–5 (10 times).

Rnds 36–37: Rep rnds 3–4. Fasten off.

Note: For shorter or longer sleeves, work in established pattern for desired length, ending with rnd 4 of sleeve pattern.

Rep sleeve in other armhole opening.

Right Front Panel

Row 1 (RS): Join yarn at bottom right-hand corner of right front edge, ch 6 (counts as tr, ch 3), sk first row-end st, (tr, ch 3) in base of each of next 32 row-end sts, tr in base of next row-end st, dtr in base of next row-end st, turn. **Note:** Ch-3 spaces may be a little too wide if worked across entire row. Work ch-2 spaces instead of ch-3 spaces periodically as needed to keep row 1 lying flat.

Row 2: Ch 4 (counts as first dtr), tr in next tr, (ch 3, tr) in each tr across, ending with ch 3, tr in third ch of turning ch, turn.

Row 3: Ch 6 (counts as tr, ch 3), (tr, ch 3) in each tr across to 2 ch-3 space, tr in next tr, dtr in fourth ch of turning ch, turn. Fasten off.

Left Front Panel

Row 1 (WS): Join yarn at bottom left-hand corner of left front edge, ch 6 (counts as tr, ch 3), sk first row-end st, (tr, ch 3) in base of each of next 32 row-end sts, tr in base of

About Jennifer My friends and family think I'm cheap, and even though they are right, that isn't the only reason I'm a thrift-store shopper. Despite their surreal toilet paper cozies, plasticky granny afghans, and dainty doilies, thrift stores are a crocheter's paradise for those who ignore bad first impressions. Although my professional background is in architecture and engineering, I am now working in knit and crochet design full-time. My designs have been featured in various online and in-print books and magazines, but I mostly publish my designs for Stitch Diva Studios. My focus at Stitch Diva Studios is to create designs for knit and crochet that are easy to make and stylish, sexy, and feminine to wear. Stitch Diva Studios patterns can be purchased by immediate download online at www.stitchdiva.com or at yarn stores nationwide. A special thanks to Chie O'Briant for working up this sample.

next row-end st, dtr in base of next row-end st, turn. **Note:** Ch-3 spaces may be a little too wide if worked across entire row. Work ch-2 spaces instead of ch-3 spaces periodically as needed to keep row 1 lying flat.

Rows 2–3: Rep rows 2–3 of right front panel. Fasten off.

Sweater Border

Row 1 (WS): Join yarn at bottom right-hand corner of right front panel, ch 1, working 3 or 4 sc in each space, sc evenly across right front, back neck edge, and down left front edge to bottom left-hand corner, turn.

Row 2: Ch 3 (counts as first tr), tr in each sc around, working 4 tr in corner sc at beginning of neck shaping on both sides, turn.

Row 3: Ch 1, sc in each tr around, working 3 sc in corner tr at beginning of neck shaping on both sides, turn. Fasten off.

Finishing

Weave in ends. Block to desired measurements. When blocking, pay particular attention to flare of sleeves, as careful blocking will enhance the natural flare. Cut two 56 (60, 64, 68, 72)" lengths of ribbon. Place one ribbon through the sts of row 6 above foundation ch. Place second ribbon through the sts of rnd 13. Weave ribbon through front panel sts to hold in place.

Heather Dixon

Violet Beauregard

I find inspiration for my designs in many places; a large purple shawl found in a rummage sale was the starting point for this skirt. I'm confident in saying that it's very easy to complete, since it's only the third crochet project I have ever tackled! The drawstring waist offers the option to wear it as low as you'd like—showing off either your hips or your legs. The length can easily be altered—try it on after each scallop round until you're happy with the length. I'd like to thank my friend from Stitch 'n Bitch NYC, Jessamyn, for coming up with such a great name for this project.

Finished Size

Directions are given for adult size Small (S). Changes for Medium (M), Large (L), Extra Large (XL), and Extra Extra Large (XXL) are in parentheses.

Finished waist: 28 (32, 36, 40, 44)"

Finished hips: 36 (40, 44, 48, 52)"

Length: 19 (20, 20, 21, 21)"

Materials

Yarn

Tahki Cotton Classic (100% Mercerized Cotton; 1.75 oz [50 g]/ 108 yd [100 m]); 7 (7, 8, 9, 10) skeins of #3924 violet (A), 2 (2, 3, 3, 3) skeins each of #3914 orchid (B) and #3912 magenta (C)

Hook

Size F/5 (3.75 mm) crochet hook or size needed to obtain gauge

Notions

Yarn needle

Gauge

18 sts and 11 rows in dc = 4"

SKIRT

With A, ch 126 (144, 162, 180, 198) and without twisting ch, join with sl st in first ch.

Rnd 1 (RS): Ch 3 (counts as first dc), dc in each ch around, sl st in third ch of turning ch to join—126 (144, 162, 180, 198) sts.

Rnd 2 (eyelet rnd): Ch 3 (counts as first dc), dc in each of next 3 (1, 4, 2, 5) dc, ch 2, sk next 2 dc, *dc in each of next 3 dc, ch 2, sk next 2 dc; rep from * around, sl st in third ch of turning ch to join—25 (29, 32, 36, 39) ch-2 spaces.

Rnd 3: Ch 3, dc in each of next 3 (1, 4, 2, 5) dc, 2 dc in next ch-2 space, *dc in each of next 3 dc, 2 dc in next ch-2 space; rep from * around, sl st in third ch of turning ch to join—126 (144, 162, 180, 198) sts.

Rnd 4 (inc rnd): Ch 3 (counts as first dc), 2 dc in first st, dc in each of next 61 (70, 79, 88, 97) dc, 2 dc in next dc, place a marker (move marker up as work progresses), 2 dc in next dc, dc in each of next 61 (70, 79, 88, 97) dc, 2 dc in last dc, sl st in third ch of turning ch to join—130 (148, 166, 184, 202) sts.

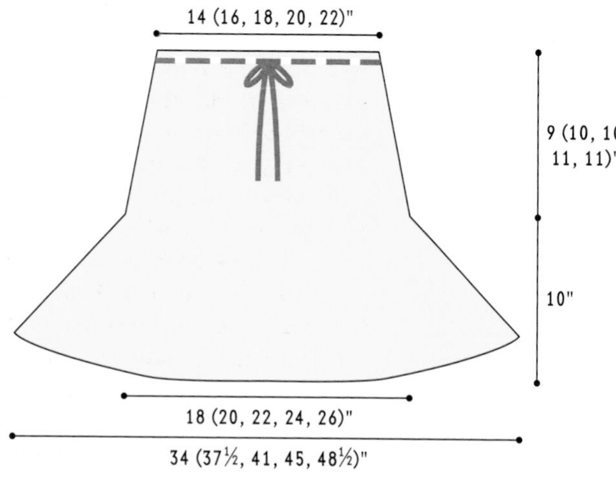

Rnd 5: Ch 3 (counts as first dc), dc in each dc around, sl st in third ch of turning ch to join—130 (148, 166, 184, 202) sts.

Rnd 6 (inc rnd): Ch 3 (counts as first dc), 2 dc in first st, dc in each dc across to 1 dc before marker, 2 dc in each of next 2 dc, dc in each dc across to last dc, 2 dc in last dc, sl st in third ch of turning ch to join—134 (152, 170, 188, 206) sts.

Rnds 7–16: Rep rnds 5–6 (5 times)—154 (172, 190, 208, 226) sts.

Rnds 17–18: Rep rnd 5—154 (172, 190, 208, 226) sts.

Rnd 19: Rep rnd 6—158 (176, 194, 212, 230) sts.

Rnds 20–22: Rep rnds 17–19—162 (180, 198, 216, 234) sts at end of rnd 22. Work even on 162 (180, 198, 216, 234) until skirt measures 9 (10, 10, 11, 11)" from beg or 10" less than desired length.

4 *Tahki Cotton Classic, medium (worsted) weight*

Scalloped Border

Rnd 1: Ch 5 (counts as dc, ch 2), sk next 2 sts, (3 dc, ch 2, 3 dc) in next st (shell made), ch 2, sk next 2 sts, *dc in next st, ch 2, sk next 2 sts, (3 dc, ch 2, 3 dc) in next st, ch 2, sk next 2 sts; rep from * around, sl st in third ch of turning ch to join—27 (30, 33, 36, 39) shells. Fasten off A, join B.

Rnd 2: With B, ch 5 (counts as dc, ch 2), sk next ch-2 space, (3 dc, ch 2, 3 dc) in next ch-2 space, ch 2, sk next ch-2 space, *dc in next dc, ch 2, sk next ch-2 space, (3 dc, ch 2, 3 dc) in next ch-2 space, ch 2, sk next ch-2 space; rep from * around, sl st in third ch of turning ch to join—27 (30, 33, 36, 39) shells.

Rnds 3–4: With B, rep rnd 2—27 (30, 33, 36, 39) shells. Fasten off B, join C.

Rnds 5–6: With C, ch 5 (counts as dc, ch 2), sk next ch-2 space, (4 dc, ch 3, 4 dc) in next shell space (shell made), ch 2, sk next ch-2 space, *dc in next dc, ch 2, sk next ch-2 space, (4 dc, ch 3, 4 dc) in next shell space, ch 2, sk next ch-2 space; rep from * around, sl st in third ch of turning ch to join—27 (30, 33, 36, 39) shells. Fasten off C, join A.

Rnd 7: With A, rep rnd 5—27 (30, 33, 36, 39) shells.

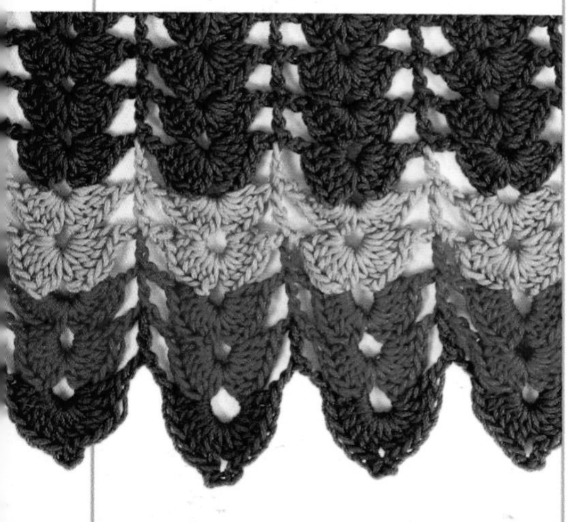

Rnds 8–10: Ch 5 (counts as dc, ch 2), sk next ch-2 space, (5 dc, ch 4, 5 dc) in next shell space (shell made), ch 2, sk next ch-2 space, *dc in next dc, ch 2, sk next ch-2 space, (5 dc, ch 4, 5 dc) in next shell space, ch 2, sk next ch-2 space; rep from * around, sl st in third ch of turning ch to join—27 (30, 33, 36, 39) shells. Fasten off A, join B.

Rnd 11: With B, rep rnd 8—27 (30, 33, 36, 39) shells.

Rnd 12: Ch 5 (counts as dc, ch 2), sk next ch-2 space, (6 dc, ch 4, 6 dc) in next shell space (shell made), ch 2, sk next ch-2 space, *dc in next dc, ch 2, sk next ch-2 space, (6 dc, ch 4, 6 dc) in next shell space, ch 2, sk next ch-2 space; rep from * around, sl st in third ch of turning ch to join—27 (30, 33, 36, 39) shells. Fasten off B, join C.

Rnds 13-14: With C, rep rnd 12—27 (30, 33, 36, 39) shells. Fasten off C, join A.

Rnd 15: With A, rep rnd 12—27 (30, 33, 36, 39) shells. Fasten off A.

Drawstring

With A, ch 200 (218, 236, 254, 272), sc in second ch from hook, sc in each ch across. Fasten off. Starting and ending at center front, weave drawstring through the spaces in rnd 2.

First Violet

With B, leaving a sewing length, ch 2.

Rnd 1 (RS): Work 5 sc in second ch from hook, sl st in first sc to join—5 sc. Fasten off B.

Rnd 2 (RS): Join A in any sc, ch 3, (tr, ch 3, sl st) in same sc, (sl st, ch 3, tr, ch 3, sl st) in each sc around, sl st in first sl st to join—5 petals. Fasten off.

Second Violet

Work same as first violet, using C for rnd 1 and A for rnd 2.

Finishing

Sew one flower to each end of drawstring. Weave in ends.

About Heather After knitting (with a couple of tea breaks here and there) for over three decades, I thought it was high time I tried my hand at crochet. My grandmother was a whiz with the old crochet hook, and I remember her whipping up granny squares at a fearsome pace. When she passed away last year at the grand old age of 92, it was I who inherited some of her old hooks (along with her gritty determination and her eye for a nice-looking young chap). With the help of instructions found on a Web site, my first attempt at a granny square was a little lop-sided, but by the second one I'd gotten the hang of it and was well on the way to making my grandmother proud. I'm a transplant from near Nottingham, England, and have been living and working in New York City for the past six years. My days are spent designing the sweater line Relais Knitware, and I also design my own line of accessories, which can be seen on my Web site, www.armyofknitters.com.

Laila Korn

One-Night Glam

Finished Size

Bracelet: 7½" long

Necklace: 18" long

Materials

Yarn

Dead Soft sterling silver wire (26 gauge; 15 yd [14 m]): 1 spool makes both bracelet and necklace.

Hook

Size K/10½ (6.5 mm) crochet hook or size needed to obtain gauge

Notions

For bracelet: 1 sterling magnetic clasp; six each of the following beads: 6 mm faceted bicone Erinite crystals, 8 mm faceted round Emerald crystals, 6 mm faceted bicone Chrysolite crystals, 8 mm faceted bicone Olivine crystals, 6 mm faceted round Peridot crystals

For necklace: 15 mm sterling double-push clasp; one 1½" sterling silver head pin (24 gauge); one tiny granulated sterling silver bead cap; lobster clasp; 5" length of 3 mm sterling silver curb chain; five each of the following beads: 6 mm faceted bicone Erinite crystals, 8 mm faceted round Emerald crystals, 6 mm faceted bicone Chrysolite crystals, 6 mm faceted round Peridot crystals, six 8 mm faceted bicone Olivine crystals

Round-nose jewelry pliers; wire clippers

All materials from artbeads.com

Gauge

9 sts = 4"

When I first started my jewelry line, I wanted to make bangle bracelets and a choker that would not only fit anyone (including my own plus-size figure) but look good on them, too. I knew that crocheted pieces have a lot of stretch, so I decided to incorporate a little hooking with semiprecious materials. The result: Classy and adjustable jewelry that anyone can wear. And the simple single crochet makes the beads really stand out. I use a combination of semiprecious stones, pearls, and crystals, but they also look great using just one type of bead.

SPECIAL STITCHES

Beaded ch: Draw bead up close to hook, yo, draw yarn through loop on hook

Beaded sc: Insert hook in next st, yo, draw yarn through st, draw bead up close to hook, yo, draw yarn through 2 loops on hook

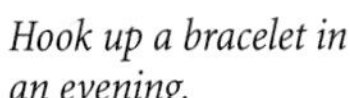

Hook up a bracelet in an evening.

BRACELET

String all beads onto wire in desired order.

Form a slipknot, leaving a 3" tail, *draw up a bead close to hook, yo, draw yarn through loop on hook (beaded ch made); rep from * 13 times—14 beaded ch.

About Laila These crocheted necklaces came out of two childhood passions: learning how to crochet blankets with my grandma and making jewelry. But I never believed I could do anything with them. Then five years ago, when I couldn't find the jewelry I wanted for my wedding, I decided to make all my bridal party's jewelry. It was so wildly popular that I began creating it and selling it at a local boutique. My grandmother was so excited about my new blooming career, and I really wanted to do something to honor her, so I began playing with crochet using sterling silver wire, crystals, faceted semiprecious stones, and pearls. Now I sell my jewelry line, Stylish Girl by Laila, through my Web site (www.stylishgirl.com), at art fairs near my home in Chicago, and to boutiques around the country.

Row 1: Draw up 2 beads close to hook, yo, draw yarn through loop on hook (turning ch made), insert hook in second ch from hook, yo, draw yarn through st, draw up a bead close to hook, yo, draw yarn through 2 loops on hook (beaded sc made), work 1 beaded sc in each ch across, ch 1—14 beaded sc. Fasten off, leaving a 3" tail. Pull on tail to tighten last st.

Finishing

There will be 2 tails at one end. Wrap one tail around the other a few times and then clip it off. Thread one half of the magnetic clasp onto the remaining tail. Stitch it into place as you would a button. Use the remaining scrap of wire to stitch the other half of the magnetic clasp onto the other end of the bracelet, threading it through the top of the 15th ch st.

NECKLACE

String 25 of the 26 beads onto wire in desired order.

Form a slipknot, leaving a 3" tail, *draw up a bead close to hook, yo, draw yarn through loop on hook (beaded ch made); rep from * 24 times, ch 1—25 beaded ch made. Fasten off, leaving a 3" tail. Pull on tail to tighten last st.

Finishing

Thread one tail onto the length of silver chain. Sew it in place as you would a button. Place the last bead and then the bead cap onto the head pin and use the round-nose pliers to form a loop at the top of the head pin. Thread the loop of the head pin onto the free end of the silver chain, then use the pliers to close the loop. Stitch the lobster clasp to the other tail of the crocheted necklace.

ruffled corset belt

The idea for this corset-inspired belt came while I was thinking about a few different clothing items from the history of fashion: the knotted fiber fertility skirts worn by the Paleolithic women of ancient Europe; the Victorian corset and other devices of the era that accentuated the female midsection; and the low-waisted, earthy fashions of the 1970s. All three are about the beauty of the belly, and they inspired me to want to make a fun and frilly ruffled belt that accentuates that positive, pretty part of the female form. This belt has a lot going for it: It's got an easy pattern stitch of crossed double crochets that give it a little texture and visual interest; it both conceals and compliments your backside; and its long ties dance along your leg as you walk. I wear mine tied on one hip, over super-tight jeans or a denim skirt, with a tight, high-necked sexy sweater on top.

Finished Size

Directions are given for size Small. Changes for Medium, Large, and Extra Large are in parentheses.

Finished waist: 30 (34, 38, 42)" after lacing

Length: 6"

Materials

Yarn

Brown Sheep Lamb's Pride Worsted (85% wool/15% mohair; 4 oz [113 g]/190 yd [174 m]); 1 skein of #M175 Bronze Patina

Hook

Size H/8 (5.5 mm) crochet hook or size needed to obtain gauge

Notions

Yarn needle

Gauge

13 sts and 9 rows in crossed dc pattern = 4"

Special Stitches

Crossed dc: Sk next st, dc in next st, dc in skipped st

Picot: Ch 3, sl st in third ch from hook

BELT

Starting at top edge, ch 90 (104, 128, 142).

Row 1 (WS): Sc in second ch from hook, sc in each ch across, turn—89 (103, 127, 141) sc.

Shannon Murphree

Fluffy Bunny Slippers

This project was inspired by those bunny slippers in cartoons. I wanted a pair of my own cartoon bunnies to schlep around in, and when I couldn't find any patterns for grown-ups, I created my own! These guys are really easy because they're made in several pieces, sewn together, then "fulled" to make them feel like real bunnies. The pattern is straightforward and good practice for crocheting in the round. You can give these hip hoppers button eyes or embroider your own.

Finished Size

4¼" wide × 9½" long

Materials

Yarn

For pink version: Brown Sheep Lamb's Pride Worsted (85% wool/15% mohair; 4 oz [113 g]/190 yd [174 m]): 2 skeins of #M34 Victorian Pink (A). Classic Elite La Gran Mohair (76.5% mohair/17.5% wool/6% nylon; 1.5 oz [42 g]/90 yd [82 m]): 2 skeins of #6519 Cameo Pink (B)

For gray version: Brown Sheep Lamb's Pride Worsted (85% wool/15% mohair; 4 oz [113 g]/190 yd [174 m]): 2 skeins of #M03 Grey Heather (A). Classic Elite La Gran Mohair (76.5% mohair/17.5% wool/6% nylon; 1.5 oz [42 g]/90 yd [82 m]): 2 skeins of #6575 Pebble (B)

Hook

Size H/8 (5.5 mm) crochet hook or size needed to obtain gauge

Notions

Yarn needle

Pink embroidery floss

Tapestry needle

4 buttons (for eyes)

Sewing needle

Matching sewing thread

Gauge

With yarns A and B held tog, 14 sts and 16 rows = 4"

SPECIAL STITCHES

hdc2tog: (Yo, insert hook in next st, yo, draw yarn through st) twice, yo, draw yarn through 5 loops on hook.

SLIPPER (MAKE 2)

Upper Sole (make 2)

With one strand each of A and B held tog as one, ch 23.

Rnd 1: Sc in second ch from hook, sc in each of next 20 ch; 3 sc in last ch, working across opposite side of foundation ch, sc in remaining loop of each of next 20 ch, 2 sc in next ch already holding 1 sc, sl st to first sc to join—46 sc.

Rnd 2: Ch 1, sc in first sc, 2 sc in next sc, sc in each of next 18 sc, (2 sc in next sc, sc in next sc) 3 times, sc in each of next 17 sc, 2 sc in next sc, sc in next sc, 2 sc in last sc, sl st to first sc to join—52 sc.

Brown Sheep Lamb's Pride Worsted, medium (worsted) weight, and Classic Elite La Gran Mohair, medium (worsted) weight

Rnd 3: Ch 1, sc in first sc, 2 sc in next sc, *sc in each of next 19 sc, (2 sc in next sc, sc in next 2 sc) 3 times, sc in each of next 17 sc, 2 sc in next sc, sc in next 2 sc, 2 sc in next sc, sc in last sc, sl st in first sc to join—58 sc.

Rnd 4: Ch 1, sc in first sc, 2 sc in next sc, *sc in each of next 20 sc, (2 sc in next sc, sc in next 3 sc) 3 times, sc in each of next 17 sc, 2 sc in next sc, sc in next 2 sc, 2 sc in next sc, sc in last 2 sc, sl st in first sc to join—64 sc.

Rnd 5: Ch 1, sc in first sc, 2 sc in next sc, *sc in each of next 21 sc, (2 sc in next sc, sc in next 4 sc) 3 times, sc in each of next 17 sc, 2 sc in next sc, sc in next 2 sc, 2 sc in next sc, sc in last 3 sc, sl st in first sc to join—70 sc.

Rnd 6: Ch 1, sc in first sc, 2 sc in next sc, *sc in each of next 22 sc, (2 sc in next sc, sc in next 5 sc) 3 times, sc in each of next 17 sc, 2 sc in next sc, sc in next 2 sc, 2 sc in next sc, sc in last 4 sc, sl st in first sc to join—76 sc.

Rnd 7: Ch 1, sc in first sc, 2 sc in next sc, *sc in each of next 23 sc, (2 sc in next sc, sc in next 6 sc) 3 times, sc in each of next 17 sc, 2 sc in next sc, sc in next 2 sc, 2 sc in next sc, sc in last 5 sc, sl st in first sc to join—82 sc. Fasten off. Weave in ends.

Bottom Sole (make 2)

With 2 strands of A held tog as one, ch 24.

Rnd 1: Dc in fourth ch from hook, dc in each of next 19 ch, 3 dc in last ch; working across opposite side of foundation ch, dc in remaining loop of each of next 20 ch, 2 dc in next ch, sl st to second ch of turning ch to join—46 sts.

Rnd 2: Ch 3 (counts as first dc), 2 dc in next dc, dc in each of next 18 dc, (2 dc in next dc, dc in next dc) 3 times, dc in each of next 17 dc, 2 dc in next dc, dc in next dc, 2 dc in last dc, sl st to third ch of turning ch to join—52 sts.

Rnd 3: Ch 3, dc in first dc, 2 dc in next dc, *dc in each of next 19 dc, (2 dc in next dc, dc in next 2 dc) 3 times, dc in each of next 17 dc, 2 dc in next dc, dc in next 2 dc, 2 dc in next dc, dc in last dc, sl st to third ch of turning ch to join—58 sts.

Rnd 4: Ch 3, dc in next 2 dc, 2 dc in next dc, *dc in each of next 20 dc, (2 dc in next dc, dc in next 3 dc) 3 times, dc in each of next 17 dc, 2 dc in next dc, dc in next 3 dc, 2 dc in next dc, dc in last 2 dc, sl st to third ch of turning ch to join—64 sts. Fasten off. Weave in ends.

Slipper Top (make 2)

With one strand each of A and B held tog as one, ch 12.

Row 1: Sc in second ch from hook, sc in each of next 9 ch, 3 sc in last ch, working across opposite side of foundation ch, sc in remaining loop of each of next 10 ch, turn—23 sc.

Row 2: Ch 1, sc in each of first 9 sc (2 sc in next sc, sc in next sc) 3 times, sc in each of last 8 sc, turn—26 sc.

Row 3: Ch 1, sc in each of first 9 sc (2 sc in next sc, sc in each of next 2 sc) 3 times, sc in each of last 8 sc, turn—29 sc.

Row 4: Ch 1, sc in each of first 9 sc (2 sc in next sc, sc in each of next 3 sc) 3 times, sc in each of last 8 sc, turn—32 sc.

Row 5: Ch 1, sc in each of first 9 sc (2 sc in next sc, sc in each of next 4 sc) 3 times, sc in each of last 8 sc, turn—35 sc.

Row 6: Ch 1, sc in each of first 9 sc (2 sc in next sc, sc in each of next 5 sc) 3 times, sc in each of last 8 sc, turn—38 sc.

Row 7: Ch 1, sc in each of first 9 sc (2 sc in next sc, sc in each of next 6 sc) 3 times, sc in each of last 8 sc, turn—41 sc.

Row 8: Ch 1, sc in each of first 9 sc (2 sc in next sc, sc in each of next 7 sc) 3 times, sc in each of last 8 sc, turn—44 sc. Fasten off. Weave in ends.

Ear (make 4)

With one strand each of A and B held tog as one, ch 10.

Row 1 (RS): Hdc in third ch from hook, hdc in each ch across, turn—8 hdc.

Rows 2–5: Ch 2, hdc in each hdc across, turn—8 hdc.

Row 6: Ch 2, (hdc2tog in next 2 sts) 3 times, hdc in last 2 sts, turn—5 sts.

Row 7: Ch 2, (hdc2tog in next 2 sts) twice, hdc in last st, turn—3 sts.

Row 8: Ch 2, hdc2tog in next 2 sts, turn—2 sts. Fasten off.

Ear Edging

Note: Edging will gather outer edge of ear and make it cup.

Row 1: With RS of ear facing, join one strand of A at bottom right-hand corner of ear, ch 1, sc evenly across side

edge to point, sc evenly across other side edge to bottom left-hand corner st, fold ear in half lengthwise, sc in sc at bottom right-hand corner to keep ear folded. Fasten off. Weave in ends.

Assembly

For each slipper: with RS of slipper top facing WS of upper sole, using yarn needle and A, sew rounded end of slipper top to one end of upper sole. Turn slipper right side out.

Slipper Edging

Rnd 1: With RS of slipper facing, join 1 strand each of A and B in any st on opening of slipper, ch 2, *hdc in next 3 sts, hdc2tog in next 2 sts; rep from * around, sl st in second ch of turning ch to join.

Rnd 2: Ch 1, *sc in each of next 3 sts, sc2tog in next 2 sts; rep from * around, sl st in first sc to join.

Rnd 3: Ch 1, sc in each sc around, sl st in first sc to join. Fasten off. Weave in ends.

Finishing

For each slipper: With WS of lower sole and upper sole facing, using A, sew lower sole to upper sole. Sew bottom (folded end) of ears to slipper top, 2½" from end of toe, with "inside" of ear facing toe. When both slippers are assembled, either toss them in the washing machine and dryer or scrub them by hand, alternating hot and cold water, with bar soap. This allows the mohair to become fluffy. Don't worry, they won't get any smaller. Allow to dry. With sewing needle and thread, sew 2 button eyes to each slipper. With embroidery needle and floss, satin st a triangle nose centered in front of eyes. Add a small pom-pom for a tail if desired.

About Shannon I am majoring in English education at Fredonia State University of New York, and preparing to undermine the education system from within as soon as I get my teaching certificate. I learned to crochet at 20, and by 21 was turning out quirky toys and crocheted clichés by the wagonload. To me, fiber is just like clay—you nudge the yarn where you want it to go, and you can reproduce any flight of the imagination with it. I keep track of my creative projects on my blog, Lucky Wings, www.catwings.blogspot.com.

pinups

BIRDIE AND FLOWER PINS

Plant one of these cute pins on your lapel, bag, jacket, scarf—wherever! I designed them at the end of an extra-long winter in an attempt to migrate to a warmer state of mind. Pins and brooches are a fun way to play with color combinations, yarn textures, and free-form stitches without a huge time or material commitment. It's like swatching, only better! Choose color combinations that will pull even your funkiest outfits together, and you'll be ready to hit the streets. Once you've made a few, you can even try collaging them with extra fabric, buttons, pom-poms, and more.

Finished Size

Birdie: $4\frac{1}{4}$" wide × $2\frac{1}{2}$" tall

Flowers: 4" in diameter

Materials

Yarn

Birdie: Brown Sheep Lamb's Pride Bulky (85% Wool/15% Mohair; 4 oz [113 g]/ 125 yd [114 m]): 1 ball of M78 Aztec Turquoise, M162 Mulberry, or M36 Lotus Pink (A). Lion Brand Moonlight Mohair (57% Acrylic, 28% Mohair, 9% cotton, 6% metallic polyester; 1.75 oz [50 g]/ 82 yd [75 m]): 1 ball of #210 Painted Desert (B)

6-Petal Flower: Lion Brand Moonlight Mohair (57% Acrylic, 28% Mohair, 9% cotton, 6% metallic polyester; 1.75 oz [50 g]/82 yd [75 m]): 1 ball of #210 Painted Desert (A). Brown Sheep Lamb's Pride Bulky (85% Wool/15% Mohair; 4 oz [113 g]/125 yd [114 m]): 1 ball each of M65 Sapphire (B) and M78 Aztec Turquoise (C)

Ferris Wheel Flower: Lion Brand Moonlight Mohair (57% Acrylic, 28% Mohair, 9% cotton, 6% metallic polyester; 1.75 oz [50 g]/82 yd [75 m]): 1 ball of #210 Painted Desert (A). Brown Sheep Lamb's Pride Bulky (85% Wool/15% Mohair; 4 oz [113 g]/125 yd [114 m]): 1 ball each of M78 Aztec Turquoise (B), M36 Lotus Pink (C), and M65 Sapphire (D)

(continued on next page)

BIRDIE

Body

Starting at center back, with A, wrap yarn around finger to form a loop (see page 52).

Rnd 1 (WS): Ch 2, 5 dc in loop, turn—5 dc. Tighten center loop by pulling on end.

Rnd 2: Ch 2, 2 dc in back loop of each of next 4 dc, 2 dc in second ch of turning ch, turn—10 dc. Do not fasten off.

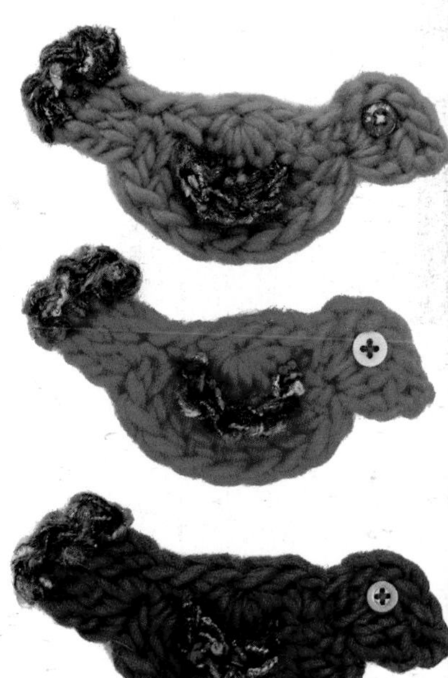

Head

Row 3: Ch 2, 3 dc into first dc, turn—3 dc.

Row 4 (RS): Ch 1, sl st in each of next 3 dc of head, work 9 sl sts evenly spaced across back edge of bird to base of corner st at end of row 2 of body, do not turn—12 sl sts.

Hook

Size J/10 (6 mm) crochet hook or size needed to obtain gauge

Notions

For Birdie only: One ⅜" button for eye

For all: Yarn needle

Sewing needle

Matching sewing thread

Pin back for each pin

Gauge

Birdie: 3 sts = 1" (2.5 cm). Gauge is not critical on this project.

Both Flowers: Rnd 1 = 1" in diameter. 3 sts = 1". Gauge is not critical on this project.

Note: To begin the pins, make a center loop as follows: Leaving a long end, wrap yarn twice around finger to form a loop. Work first row or rnd of sts in this loop. Use end to pull the center taut when done with first rnd of sts. This is also known as a "magic ring."

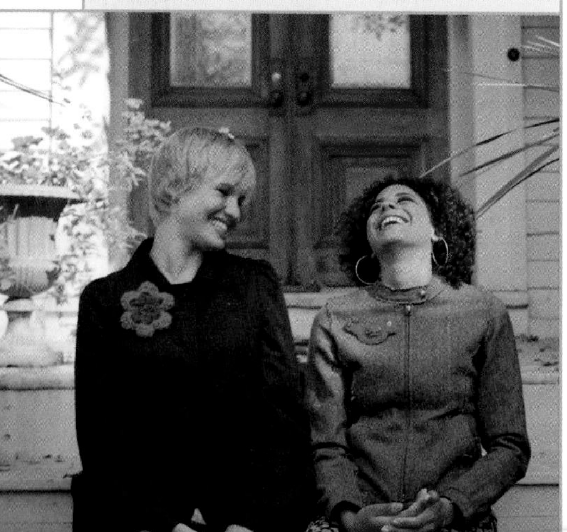

Tail

Row 5 (RS): Ch 2, work 3 dc in same row-end st. Fasten off.

Tail Feathers

With RS facing, join B in first st in row 5 of tail, ch 1, (dc, sl st) in first dc, (dc, sl st) in each of next 2 dc. Fasten off.

Wing

With RS of bird facing and row 2 of body on top, join B in rem front loop of second dc in row 1, dc in same dc, dc in rem front loop of each of next 2 dc, sl st in next dc. Fasten off.

Finishing

Weave in ends. With sewing needle and thread, sew button to top of head for eye. Sew on a pin back for a wearable brooch.

6-PETAL FLOWER

Starting at center, with A, wrap yarn around finger to form a loop (see page 52).

Rnd 1 (RS): Ch 1, 12 sc in loop, sl st in first sc to join—12 sc. Fasten off.

Rnd 2 (RS): Join B in first sc, *(hdc, 2 dc, hdc) in next sc, sl st in next sc; rep from * around, ending with sl st in first sc of last rnd to join—6 petals. Fasten off.

Rnd 3 (WS): Working in sts of rnd 1, join C around post of first sc in rnd 1, ch 1, *sc in around post of sc, ch 4, skip next sc; rep from * around, sl st in first sc to join—6 ch-4 loops.

Rnd 4: Ch 1, * (sc, hdc, dc, 3 tr, dc, hdc) in next ch-4 loop, sl st in next sc; rep from * around—6 petals. Fasten off.

Finishing

Weave in ends. Sew on a pin back for a wearable brooch.

FERRIS WHEEL FLOWER

Starting at center, with A, wrap yarn around finger to form a loop (see page 52).

Rnd 1 (RS): Ch 1, 8 sc in loop, sl st in first sc to join—8 sc. Fasten off.

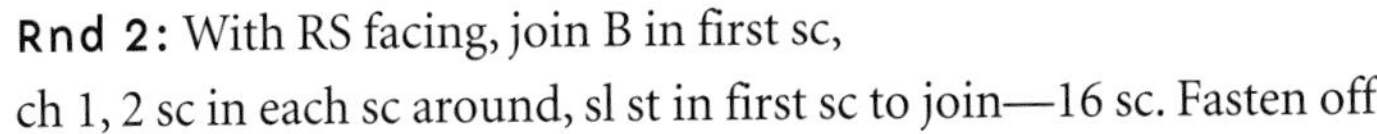

Rnd 2: With RS facing, join B in first sc, ch 1, 2 sc in each sc around, sl st in first sc to join—16 sc. Fasten off.

Rnd 3: With RS facing, join C in first sc, ch 1, *(hdc, dc, hdc) in next sc, sl st in next sc; rep from * around, ending with sl st in first sc of last rnd to join—8 petals. Fasten off.

Rnd 4: With RS facing, join D in any sc in rnd 2 holding a sl st, working over sl sts in rnd 3, ch 3, sk petal in rnd 3, sl st in next sc in rnd 2; rep from * around—8 ch-3 loops.

Rnd 5: With D, ch 1, (sc, 3 dc) in each ch-3 loop around, sl st in first sc to join—8 petals. The petals in rnd 5 should fall behind the petals in rnd 3. Press them back with your fingers if they came forward while you were working.

Finishing

Weave in ends. Sew on a pin back for wearable brooch.

About Linda My grandma taught me to crochet when I was small, and I picked it up again upon moving to New York (thanks to some helpful tips from a woman sitting next to me on a bus going to Nashua, NH). Once started, I crocheted obsessively—hooking up a slew of scarves and hats to supplement my previously Texan wardrobe. When that turned excessive, I opened up shop at my Web site, www.lindamade.com. I'm lucky enough to be an editor for a crafting magazine, which means I usually have glitter on my face regardless of whether it's Saturday night or not. I also hoard yarn at my desk, in my living room, even under the couch. When I'm not making something, I can be found reading, taking pictures, or riding the train to Coney Island.

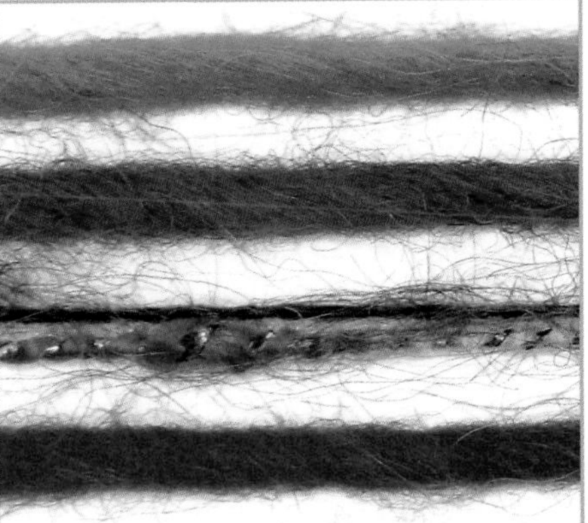

Brown Sheep Lamb's Pride Bulky, bulky weight

Lion Brand Moonlight Mohair, medium (worsted) weight

LadyLike Lace Gloves

My father bought me my first vinyl album, Cyndi Lauper's *She's So Unusual,* for my ninth birthday. Fast-forward to my eBay purchase of a "learn to crochet" magazine published in 1946 by Clark's J&P Coats, back when ladies not only wore gloves but also matched them to their hat and handbag. I've taken the side-to-side construction, ribbing, and lace from a vintage pattern in that magazine and updated it by modifying the lace, taking off the fingers, and adding shaping in the wrist. The ribbing makes the gloves stretchy and warm, and the lace is a nod to Cyndi.

SPECIAL STITCHES

2-dc cluster across 4 sts: Yo, insert hook in same st as last dc worked, yo, draw yarn through st, yo, draw yarn through 2 loops on hook, sk next 2 sc, yo, insert hook in next st, yo, draw yarn through st, yo, draw yarn through 2 loops on hook, yo, draw yarn through 3 loops on hook

2-dc cluster across 3 sts: Yo, insert hook in same st as last dc worked, yo, draw yarn through st, yo, draw yarn through 2 loops on hook, sk next sc, yo, insert hook in next st, yo, draw yarn through st, yo, draw yarn through 2 loops on hook, yo, draw yarn through 3 loops on hook

sc2tog: (Insert hook in next designated st, yo, draw yarn through st) twice, yo, draw yarn through 3 loops on hook

hdc2tog: (Yo, insert hook in next designated st, yo, draw yarn through st) twice, yo, draw yarn through 5 loops on hook

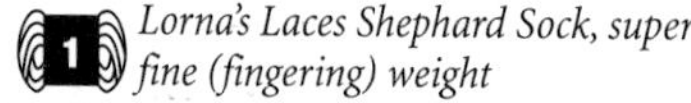
Lorna's Laces Shephard Sock, super fine (fingering) weight

Finished Size

Women's size Medium

Wrist: 5½" in circumference

Hand: 6" in circumference

Length: 7"

Thumb: 2" in circumference

Materials

Yarn

Lorna's Laces Shepherd Sock (75% superwash wool/25% nylon; 1.75 oz [50 g]/215 yd [197 m]): 1 skein of Charcoal

Hook

Size F/5 (3.75 mm) crochet hook or size needed to obtain gauge

Notions

Yarn needle

Coilless safety pins

Gauge

28 sts = 4"; 12 rows in cluster lace pattern on back = 2"; 8 rows (unstretched) in palm pattern = 2"

GLOVE (MAKE 2)

Back

Ch 51.

Row 1: Sc in second ch from hook, sc in back loop of each of next 22 ch, turn, leaving rem sts unworked—23 sc.

Row 2: Ch 1, sc in back loop of each sc across, turn—23 sc.

Row 3: Ch 1, sc in back loop of each of first 21 sc, 2 sc in back loop of next sc, sc2tog, working first sc in back loop of next sc, and second sc in first free ch on foundation ch (3 rows below), sc in each ch across, turn—50 sts.

Begin Cluster Lace Pattern

Next 4 rows establish cluster lace pattern.

Row 4 (cluster lace row): Ch 3 (counts as first dc), sk first 2 sc, dc in next sc (counts as first cluster), *ch 2, work 2-dc cluster across 4 sts (see special stitches); rep from * across to last 2 sts, ch 2, work 2-dc cluster across 3 sts (see special stitches), turn—17 clusters.

Row 5: Ch 1, *sc in next cluster, 2 sc in next ch-2 space; rep from * across to last 2 sts, sc in next dc, sc in third ch of turning ch, turn—50 sc.

Rows 6–7: Ch 1, sc in back loop of each sc across, turn—50 sc.

Rows 8–19: Rep rows 4–7 (3 times).

Row 20: Ch 1, sc in back loop of each st, turn—50 sc.

Row 21: Ch 1, sc in back loop of each of first 13 sc, turn, leaving rem sts unworked—13 sc. Do not fasten off.

Thumb

Row 22: Ch 10, sc in second ch from hook, sc in each of next 8 ch, working in rem sts in row 19, sc in back loop of each sc across, turn—46 sc.

Rows 23–25: Ch 1, sc in back loop of each sc across, turn—46 sc.

Row 26: Ch 1, sc in back loop of each of first 25 sc, turn, leaving rem sts unworked—25 sc.

Row 27: Ch 1, sc in back loop of each sc across, turn—25 sc.

Row 28: Ch 1, sc in back loop of each of first 23 sc, 2 sc in next sc, sc2tog, working first sc in back loop of next sc and second sc in back loop of first free sc 3 rows below (row 24); working in rem sts in row 24, sc in back loop of each sc across, turn—46 sc.

Row 29: Ch 3 (counts as first dc), sk first 2 dc, dc in next sc (counts as first cluster), *ch 2, work 2-dc cluster across 4 sts; rep from * across to last st, dc in last sc, turn—15 clusters.

Row 30: Ch 1, sc in first dc, *sc in next cluster, 2 sc in next ch-2 space; rep from * across to last 2 sts, sc in next dc, 2 sc in third ch of turning ch, turn—46 sc.

Row 31: Ch 1, sc in back loop of each sc across, turn—46 sc.

Row 32: Ch 1, sc in each of first 25 sc, turn, leaving rem sts unworked—25 sc.

Row 33: Ch 1, sc in back loop of each sc across, turn—25 sc.

Row 34: Ch 1, sc in back loop of each of first 23 sc, 2 sc in next sc, sc2tog, working first sc in back loop of next sc and second sc in back loop of first free sc 3 rows below (row 30), working in rem sts in row 30, sc in back loop of each sc across, turn—46 sc.

Row 35: Ch 1, sc in back loop of each sc across, turn—46 sc.

Row 36: Ch 1, sc in back loop of each of first 9 sc, turn, leaving rem sts unworked—9 sc. Do not fasten off.

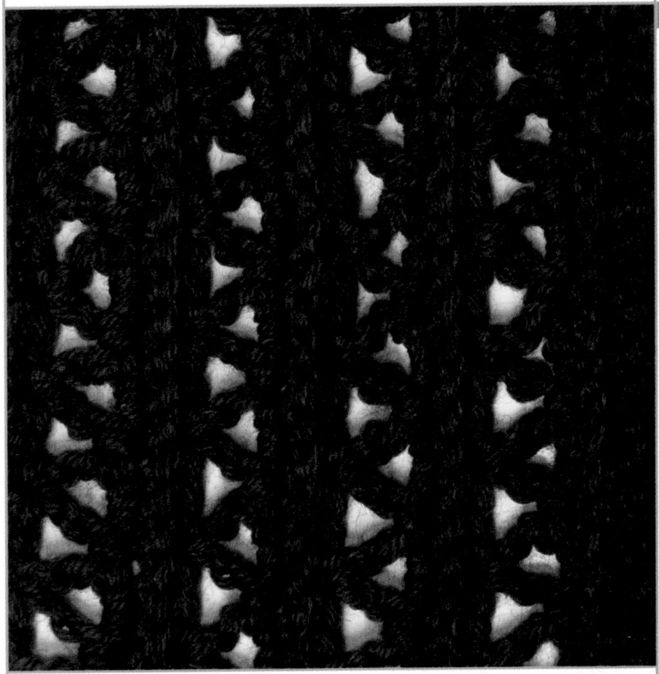

Palm

Row 37: Ch 14, sc in second ch from hook, sc in each of next 12 ch, working in rem sts in row 35, sc in back loop of next sc, turn—14 sc.

Row 38: Ch 1, sc in each sc across, turn—14 sc.

Row 39: Ch 1, sc in each of first 12 sc, 2 sc in next sc, sc2tog, working first sc in back loop of next sc and second sc back loop of first free sc 3 rows below (row 35), working in rem sts in row 34, sc in back loop of each sc across, turn—50 sc.

Row 40: Ch 1, sc in back loop of each sc across, turn—50 sc.

Row 41: Ch 1, sc in back loop of each of next 36 sc—50 sts.

Row 42: Ch 1, hdc in back loop of each st across—50 hdc.

Row 43: Ch 1, hdc in back loop of each of first 30 hdc, turn, leaving rem sts unworked—30 hdc.

Row 44: Ch 1, hdc in back loop of each hdc across, turn—30 hdc.

Row 45: Ch 1, hdc in back loop of each of first 29 hdc, 2 hdc in next hdc, hdc2tog, working first hdc in next row-end st and second hdc in back loop of first free hdc 3 rows below (row 42), working in rem sts in row 42, hdc in back loop of each hdc across, turn—50 sts.

Row 46: Ch 1, hdc in back loop of each st across—50 hdc.

Row 47–50: Rep rows 43–46

Row 51: Ch 1, hdc in back loop of each of first 20 hdc, turn, leaving rem sts unworked—20 hdc.

Row 52: Ch 1, hdc in back loop of each hdc across, turn—20 hdc.

Row 53: Ch 1, hdc in back loop of each of first 18 hdc, 2 hdc in next hdc, hdc2tog, working first hdc in next row-end st and second hdc in back loop of first free hdc 3 rows below (row 50), working in rem sts in row 50, hdc in back loop of each hdc across, turn—50 sts.

Row 54: Ch 1, sc in back loop of each st across—50 sc. Fasten off.

Finishing (for each glove)

For left glove, row 1 is considered a RS row; for right glove, row 1 is considered a WS row. Fold each glove in half, with WS facing. Pin together across side seam. With back facing up, make sure thumb is on left side of one glove and right side of the other glove. Pin seams together.

Edgings and Joining Seams

Edgings and joining seams are worked in one row from folded edge of wrist to top edge of thumb. Do not work edgings across top and bottom edge of palm side of gloves.

Bottom Edging

Flatten one glove with seam on one side, join yarn on wrist edge of glove in first row-end sc on folded side of glove to work across bottom edge of back side, ch 1, sc evenly across bottom edge of back, working 1 sc in each row-end sc and 3 sc in each row-end dc to last row-end sc on back. Do not fasten off.

Side Seam

Matching sts across last row and foundation ch, working through double thickness, sl st in each st across to top edge of glove. Do not fasten off.

Top Edging

Sc evenly across top edge of back, working 1 sc in each row-end sc and 3 sc in each row-end dc to last row-end sc on back. Do not fasten off.

Inner Seam

Matching sts in row 20 and foundation ch of row 36 (on palm side of glove), working through double thickness, sl st in each st across to base of thumb, matching sts in row 36 and foundation ch of row 21 (on palm side of thumb), working through double thickness, sl st in each st across to top edge of thumb. Do not fasten off.

Thumb Edging

Sc evenly around top edge of thumb, working 1 sc in each row-end sc and 3 sc in each row-end dc to thumb seam, sl st in first sc of thumb edging to join. Fasten off.

Turn gloves right side out to wear.

About MK I learned to crochet before I learned to write my name. As a young girl, I crocheted many an avant-garde asymmetrical garment for my dolls, but I didn't really get going with the craft until I wanted something to fill the time on my bus commute. Crocheting on the city bus was a great conversation starter, mostly with people telling me how they know someone who crocheted or how they wished they had learned. Why wish when you can do, I say. I carry spare crochet hooks and yarn, so it's easy to get newbies started making a chain and then playing with it. My students have gone out into the world, with their hooks in hand, and have been seen crocheting on public transport, at the beach, and in coffee shops. I blog about my crafting at mkcarroll.typepad.com and can be found at meetings of the Honolulu Stitch 'n Bitch or prowling local used bookstores, looking for vintage needlecraft books.

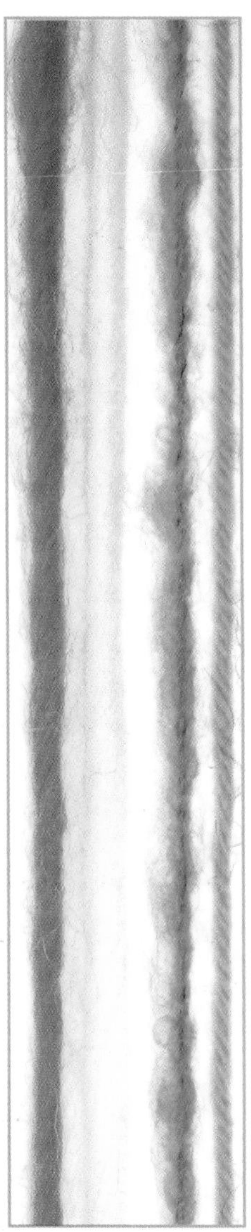

5 *From left: Garnstudio Eskimo, bulky weight (red and white)*

6 *Garnstudio Highlander, super bulky weight*

3 *Garnstudio Karisma Superwash, light (DK) weight*

Rnds 5–6: Sl st in each st around—30 sts.

Rnd 7: Sl st in each st around, working 5 inc evenly spaced around—35 sts.

Rnds 8–16: Sl st in each st around—35 sts.

Rnd 17: Sl st in each st around, dec 2 sl sts evenly spaced around—33 sts. Fasten off C, join B.

Rnds 18–20: With B, sl st in each st around—33 sts.

Rnd 21: Sl st in each st around, dec 2 sl sts evenly spaced around—31 sts.

Rnd 22: Sl st in each st around—31 sts.

Rnd 23: Sl st in each st around, working 2 dec evenly spaced around—29 sts.

Rnds 24–25: Sl st in each st around—29 sts.

Rnds 26–27: Sl st in each st around, working 2 dec evenly spaced around—25 sl sts at end of last rnd.

Stuff body and continue stuffing as work progresses.

Rnd 28: Sl st in each st around—25 sts.

Rnd 29: *Sl st in each of next 2 sts, slst2tog in next 2 sts; rep from * around to last st, sl st in last st—19 sts. Fasten off, leaving a sewing length.

Head

Starting at tip of nose, with A and smaller hook, ch 3 and join with sl st in first ch.

Rnd 1: 1 sl st in same ch, 2 sl st in each of next 2 ch, do not join—6 sl sts. Work in a spiral. Place marker in first st of each rnd, moving marker up as work progresses.

Rnd 2: *2 sl sts in next st, sl st in next st; rep from * around—9 sts.

Rnds 3–4: *2 sl sts in next st, sl st in each of next 2 sts; rep from * around—16 sts at end of last rnd.

Rnd 5: Sl st in each st around—16 sl sts.

Rnd 6: *2 sl sts in next st, sl st in each of next 3 sts; rep from * around—20 sts.

Rnd 7: *2 sl sts in next st, sl st in each of next 9 sts; rep from * around—22 sts.

Rnds 8–9: Sl st in each st around, inc 3 sl sts evenly spaced around—28 sts at end of last rnd.

Rnds 10–12: Sl st in each st around—28 sts.

Rnd 13: *2 sl sts in next st, sl st in next st; rep from * around—42 sts.

Rnd 14: Sl st in each st around—42 sts.

Rnd 15: *2 sl sts in next st, sl st in each of next 5 sts; rep from * around—48 sts.

Rnd 16: Sl st in each st around—48 sts.

Rnd 17: *2 sl sts in next st, sl st in each of next 15 sts; rep from * around—51 sts.

Rnd 18: *2 sl sts in next st, sl st in each of next 16 sts; rep from * around—54 sts.

Rnd 19: *2 sl sts in next st, sl st in each of next 17 sts; rep from * around—57 sts.

Rnd 20: Sl st in each st around, inc 9 sl sts evenly spaced around—66 sts.

Rnds 21–24: Sl st in each st around—66 sts. Fasten off A, join B.

Rnd 25: With smaller hook and B, *sl st in each of next 4 sts, slst2tog in next 2 sts; rep from * around—55 sts. Change to larger hook.

Rnd 26: *Sl st in each of next 3 sts, slst2tog in next 2 sts; rep from * around—44 sts. Attach eyes to front of head above nose, as pictured.

Rnds 27–31: Sl st in each st around—44 sts.

Rnd 32: Sl st in each st around, dec 6 sl sts evenly spaced around—38 sts. Stuff head and continue stuffing as work progresses.

Rnds 33–37: *Sl st in next st, slst2tog in next 2 sts; rep from * around—6 sl sts at end of last rnd. Fasten off, leaving a sewing length. With yarn needle, weave sewing length through the sts of last rnd, draw tight, and secure.

Ear (make 2)

With smaller hook and A, ch 3 and sl st in first ch to join.

Rnd 1: 1 sl st in same ch, 2 sl st in each of next 2 ch, do not join—6 sl sts. Work in a spiral. Place marker in first st of each rnd, moving marker up as work progresses.

Rnd 2: 2 sl sts in each st around—12 sts.

Rnd 3: *2 sl sts in next st, sl st in each of next 5 sts; rep from * around—14 sts.

Rnd 4: Sl st in each st around—14 sts.

Rnd 5: *2 sl sts in next st, sl st in next st; rep from * around—21 sts.

Rnd 6: Sl st in each st around—21 sts. Fasten off A, join B.

Rnd 7: With B, sl st in each st around—21 sl sts. Fasten off, leaving a sewing length.

Arm (make 2)

With smaller hook and A, ch 3 and sl st in first ch to join.

Rnd 1: 1 sl st in same ch, 2 sl st in each of next 2 ch, do not join—6 sl sts. Work in a spiral. Place marker in first st of each rnd, moving marker up as work progresses.

Rnd 2: 2 sl sts in each st around—12 sts.

Rnd 3: *2 sl sts in next st, sl st in each of next 5 sts; rep from * around—14 sts.

Rnd 4: Sl st in each st around—14 sts.

Rnd 5: *2 sl sts in next st, sl st in next st; rep from * around—21 sts.

Rnd 6: Sl st in each st around—21 sl sts. Fasten off A, join B.

Rnd 7: With B, sl st in each st around—21 sts.

Change to larger hook.

Rnd 8: *Sl st in next st, slst2tog in next 2 sts; rep from * around—14 sts.

Rnds 9–11: Sl st in each st around—14 sts.

Rnd 12: *Sl st in each of next 5 sts, slst2tog in next 2 sts; rep from * around—12 sts.

Rnds 13–16: Sl st in each st around—12 sl sts. Fasten off.

Leg (make 2)

Work same as arm through rnd 13. Fasten off B, join C.

Rnds 14–16: With C, sl st in each st around—12 sl sts. Fasten off.

Assembly

With yarn needle and sewing length, sew top of body to bottom of head. Sew ears to top of head as pictured. Sew arms to upper sides of body as pictured. Sew legs to bottom front of body as pictured. Satin st nose as pictured, using D.

BUNNY

Note: Bunny is worked in spiral rnds throughout. To change color, complete last st of first color with next color. Drop first color to WS and fasten off. **Work in *back loops* of slip stitches throughout.**

Body

Work same as bear body, using colors for bunny.

Head

Starting at tip of nose, with A and smaller hook, ch 3 and join with sl st in first ch.

Rnd 1: 1 sl st in same ch, 2 sl st in each of next 2 ch, do not join—6 sl sts. Work in a spiral. Place marker in first st of each rnd, moving marker up as work progresses.

Rnd 2: *2 sl sts in next st, sl st in next st; rep from * around—9 sts.

Rnd 3: *2 sl sts in next st, sl st in each of next 2 sts; rep from * around—16 sts.

Rnd 4: Sl st in each st around, inc 6 sl sts evenly spaced around—22 sts.

Rnd 5: Sl st in each st around, inc 4 sl sts evenly spaced around—26 sts.

Rnds 6–7: Sl st in each st around, inc 6 sl sts evenly spaced around—38 sts at end of last rnd.

Rnd 8: Sl st in each st around, inc 2 sl sts evenly spaced around—40 sts.

Rnd 9: Sl st in each st around—40 sts.

Rnds 10–15: Sl st in each st around, inc 4 sl sts evenly spaced around—64 sts at end of last rnd.

Rnd 16: Sl st in each st around, inc 2 sl sts evenly spaced around—66 sts.

Rnds 17–18: Sl st in each st around—66 sl sts. Fasten off A, join B.

Rnd 18: With B, *sl st in each of next 4 sts, slst2tog in next 2 sts; rep from * around—55 sts.

Change to larger hook.

Rnd 19: *Sl st in each of next 3 sts, slst2tog in next 2 sts; rep from * around—44 sl sts. Attach eyes to front of head above muzzle as pictured.

Rnds 20–24: Sl st in each st around—44 sts.

Rnd 25: Sl st in each st around, dec 6 sl sts evenly spaced around—38 sts. Stuff head and continue stuffing as work progresses.

Rnds 26–30: *Sl st in next st, slst2tog in next 2 sts; rep from * around—6 sl sts at end of last rnd. Fasten off, leaving a sewing length. With yarn needle, weave sewing length through the sts of last rnd, draw tight, and secure.

Ear (make 2)

With larger hook and B, ch 3 and sl st in first ch to join.

Rnd 1: 1 sl st in same ch, 2 sl st in each of next 2 ch, do not join—6 sl sts. Work in a spiral. Place marker in first st of each rnd, moving marker up as work progresses.

Rnd 2: 2 sl sts in each st around—12 sts.

Rnds 3–14: Sl st in each sl st around—12 sl sts. Fasten off.

About Camilla I have a Master of Fine Arts degree and live in Sweden, where I make my living as a graphic designer and as an illustrator. I also paint and have had some exhibitions. In January I started my blog, where I put pictures of my dog, my paintings, and things I do (www.camillaengman.com). Through this blog, I've "met" so many wonderful and creative people! I like to crochet because it is easy to carry wherever I go, and it takes up so little space—just some yarn and a little hook. You can sit in a public place and crochet, and you create a private sphere for yourself.

Arm (make 2)

With smaller hook and A, ch 3 and sl st in first ch to join.

Rnd 1: 1 sl st in same ch, 2 sl st in each of next 2 ch, do not join—6 sl sts. Work in a spiral. Place marker in first st of each rnd, moving marker up as work progresses.

Rnd 2: 2 sl sts in each st around—12 sts.

Rnd 3: *2 sl sts in next st, sl st in each of next 5 sts; rep from * around—14 sts.

Rnd 4: Sl st in each st around—14 sts.

Rnd 5: *2 sl sts in next st, sl st in next st; rep from * around—21 sts.

Rnd 6: Sl st in each st around—21 sl sts. Fasten off A, join B.

Rnd 7: With B, sl st in each st around—21 sts.

Change to larger hook.

Rnd 8: *Sl st in next st, slst2tog in next 2 sts; rep from * around—14 sts.

Rnds 9–11: Sl st in each st around—14 sts.

Rnd 12: *Sl st in each of next 5 sts, slst2tog in next 2 sts; rep from * around—12 sts.

Rnds 13–16: Sl st in each st around—12 sl sts. Fasten off.

Leg (make 2)

Work same as arm through rnd 13. Fasten off B, join C.

Rnds 14–16: With C, sl st in each st around—12 sl sts. Fasten off.

Assembly

With yarn needle and sewing length, sew top of body to bottom of head. Sew ears to top of head as pictured. Sew arms to upper sides of body as pictured. Sew legs to bottom front of body as pictured. Using D, satin st nose, backstitch mouth on Bunny using E as pictured.

Kacy Fallon

Skullholders

Finished Size

$9\frac{1}{2}$" wide × 8" tall

Materials

Yarn

Lion Brand Lion Cotton (100% cotton; 5 oz [140 g]/236 yd [212 m]): 1 ball each of #153 Black and #112 Poppy Red; or 1 ball each of #157 Sunflower and #108 Morning Glory

Hook

Size H/8 (5 mm) crochet hook or size needed to obtain gauge

Notions

Yarn needle

Gauge

15 sts and 16 rows sc = 4"

Two years ago, my friend Bryan asked me to make him an afghan with a skull design on it, so I had him draw a skull and then I graphed it out. In an effort to test the pattern on a smaller scale, the skullholder was born. I've used the same pattern on hats, used old macramé cord to make a mat with a skull on it, and made patches using thinner thread. Unfortunately, I have yet to make the actual afghan—mainly because it was contingent on his getting me the yarn, and he has yet to do that. At any rate, these make great housewarming gifts for people with hip kitchens, and they're really quick to make once you get the hang of switching colors.

PATTERN NOTES

Colors: From each pair of choices, choose one color for MC and the other color for CC. Switch MC and CC for second pot holder.

To change color: Work last sc of first color until 2 loops rem on hook, yo with second color, draw second color through 2 loops on hook, drop first color to WS and carry across, working over unused color to be picked up later in row.

POT HOLDER

Front/Back (make 2)

With MC, ch 35.

Row 1: Sc in second ch from hook, sc in each ch across, turn—34 sc.

Rows 2–30: Ch 1, sc in each sc across following chart for color changes, turn—34 sc. Fasten off.

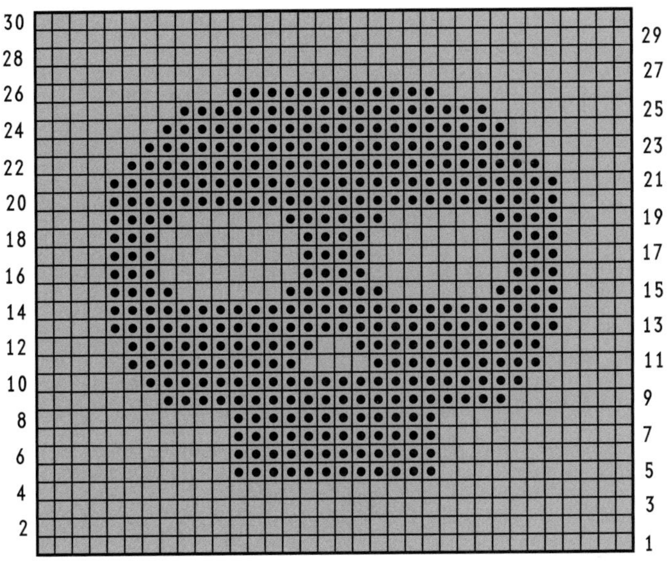

= sc in MC
● = sc in CC

About Kacy I learned how to crochet from my mother when I was around eight years old. My first project was a pair of slippers constructed from granny squares in a horrendous shade of orange acrylic yarn. In my teens I attempted to make baby blankets in a ripple stitch that I would never complete and that would eventually be sent to the local thrift store. In my midtwenties I picked up crochet again, and have since managed to hammer out a few simple scarves, hats, several afghans, and even mittens. I live in Chicago and work at a fine organization that provides residential and vocational services to individuals with developmental disabilities. And yes, boys, I am single.

Finishing

With WS of front and back facing, align top edges.

Edging

With RS of front facing, working through double thickness, join CC in top left-hand corner st, matching sts all around, ch 1, 2 sc in corner st, *sc in each st across to next corner, 3 sc in next corner st; rep from * around, ending with sc in first corner already holding 2 sc, ch 6 for hanging loop, sl st in next sc, work 6 sc in ch-6 loop just made, sl st in first sc to join. Fasten off. Weave in ends.

4 *Lion Brand Lion Cotton, medium (worsted) weight*

Faith Landsman

doris daymat

I love hardware stores, and a crafty girl can get into a lot of fun trouble there. This super-easy project was inspired by a trip to the hardware store to buy a new doormat. When the store didn't have any mats I liked, I thought, "I can make one myself!" and I bought all the supplies I needed right there in the shop. The Doris Daymat is rugged, it's cheap, and if you get bored with the pattern or you learn a new flower pattern, you can always take the flowers off and rearrange them or add more.

Note: Twine is slippery. Dot the knots with super glue or nail polish to keep them knotted.

Finished Size

28" wide × 18" deep

Materials

Yarn

Bevis Rope Medium-Duty Jute Twine (100% jute; 200 feet), 6 balls of green (MC); Mason Line Twine #18 (100% nylon; 225 feet), 1 ball each of pink (C1), gold (C2), and white (C3)

Hooks

Sizes G/6 (4 mm), J/10 (6.5 mm), and N/15 (10 mm) crochet hooks or sizes needed to obtain gauge

Notions

Clear nail polish or super glue

Yarn needle

Gauge

Mat, with hook N/15 and MC: 7 st and 7 rows in pattern = 4"

Small rose, with hook G/6 and Mason Line: 3" in diameter

Large rose, with hook J/10 and Mason Line: 3¾" in diameter

Small dahlia, with hook J/10 and Mason Line: 3¾" in diameter

Large dahlia, with hook N/15 and Mason Line: 5½" in diameter

MAT

With hook N/15 and MC, ch 45.

Row 1: Sc in second ch from hook, dc in next ch, *sc in next ch, dc in next ch; rep from * across, turn—44 sts.

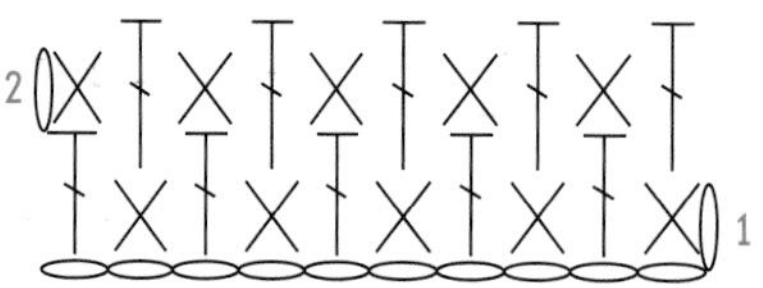

Reduced sample of mat pattern

Rows 2–26: Ch 1, sc in first dc, dc in next sc, *sc in next dc, dc in next sc; rep from * across, turn. Do not fasten off.

Edging

Working across top edge of mat, ch 1, **2 sc in corner st, 3 dc in next st, *sc (tightly) in next st, 3 dc in next st; rep from * across to next corner; rep from ** around, sl st in first sc to join. Fasten off. Weave in ends.

Small Rose

(make 3 using your choice of 2 colors of C1, C2, or C3 for each rose)

With hook G/6 and first color, ch 6 and join with sl st in first ch.

Rnd 1 (RS): Ch 1, work 15 sc in ring, sl st in first sc to join—15 sc. Fasten off.

Rnd 2 (RS): Join second color in any sc in rnd 1, ch 1, *sc in sc, ch 3, sk 2 sc; rep from * around, sl st in first sc of rnd 1—5 ch-3 loops.

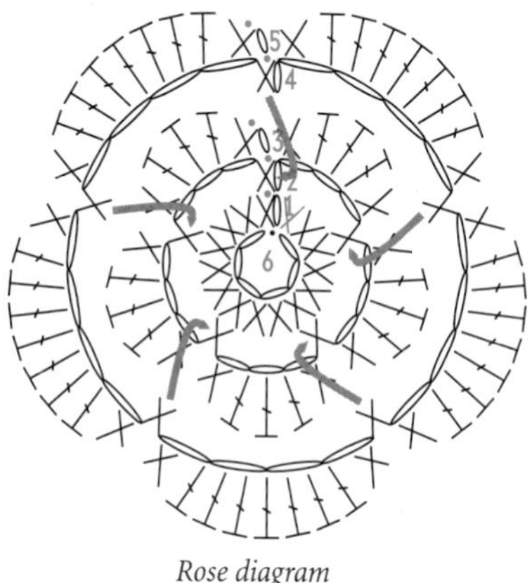

Rose diagram

Rnd 3: Ch 1, (sc, 3 dc, sc) in each ch-3 loop around, sl st in first sc to join—5 petals.

Rnd 4: Ch 1, working in front of petals in rnd 3, sc around post of corresponding sc in rnd 2, ch 4, sk next petal in rnd 3, sc around post of next sc in rnd 2; rep from * around—5 ch-4 loops.

Rnd 5: Ch 1, (sc, 7 dc, sc) in each ch-4 loop around, sl st in first sc to join. Fasten off, leaving a sewing length.

Large Rose

(make 3 using your choice of 2 colors of C1, C2, or C3 for each rose)

With J/10 hook, work same as small rose.

Small Dahlia

(make 2 using your choice of 2 colors of C1, C2, or C3 for each dahlia)

With J/10 hook and first color, ch 5 and join with sl st in first ch.

Rnd 1 (RS): Ch 3 (counts as first dc), work 16 dc in ring—17 sts. Fasten off.

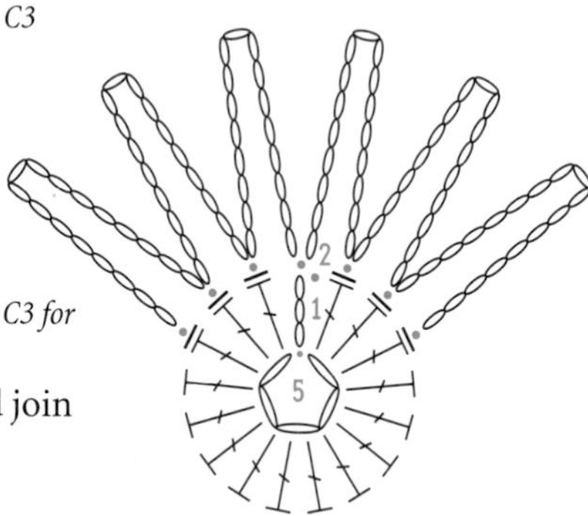

Dahlia diagram rnds 1–2 (rnd 2 worked in front loops)

Rnd 2 (RS): Join second color in first dc, *ch 17, sl st in front loop of next dc; rep from * around, ending with sl st in first dc of rnd 1—17 ch-17 loops.

Rnd 3: Working in remaining loops of sts in rnd 1 and behind loops in rnd 2, *ch 17, sl st in back loop of next dc; rep from * around, ending with sl st in first dc of rnd 1—17 ch-17 loops. Fasten off, leaving a sewing length.

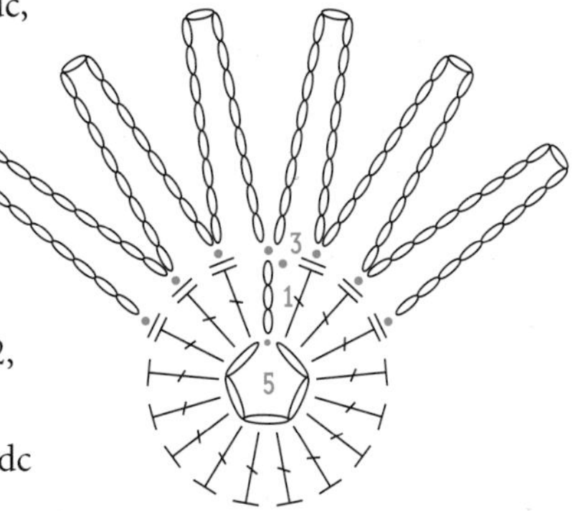

Dahlia diagram rnds 1 and 3 (rnd 3 worked in back loops)

Large Dahlia
(make 1 using your choice of 2 colors of C1, C2, or C3)

With N/15 hook, work same as small dahlia.

Finishing
With yarn needle and sewing lengths, sew large dahlia to center of mat, sew small dahlias to 2 opposite corners. Sew roses with WS facing up where desired. When tying ends, use nail polish or super glue to secure.

About Faith I am a third-generation native Angeleña and a rabbinical school dropout. I am also a crochet fiend and insist that you become one, too. My grandmother's lessons in making granny squares when I was ten have progressed to the point that I now teach crochet at Knit Café and A Mano Yarn Center in Los Angeles. I am also one of the moderators of Stitch 'n Bitch L.A. One of these days I will be a successful milliner. In a very strange alterna-life, my gay husband and I own Metro Limousine in Los Angeles.

cozy pod creatures

Finished Size

Approximately 3¼" wide × 4½" tall (fits a 20 gb iPod)

Materials

Yarn

Brown Sheep Cotton Fleece (80% Cotton/ 20% Merino Wool; 3.5 oz [100 g]/215 yd [197 m]):

For Bear: 1 skein #CW-220 Provincial Rose (MC), small amount of #CW-100 Cotton Ball (CC)

For Monkey: 1 skein #CW-770 Wisteria (MC), small amount of #CW-870 Mint Condition (CC)

For Kitty: 1 skein #CW-310 Wild Orange (MC), small amount of #CW-520 (CC) Caribbean Sea

Hook

Size F/5 (3.75 mm) crochet hook or size needed to obtain gauge

Notions

3/16" hole punch, available in the scrapbook section of most craft stores *(Note: A standard ½" hole punch will not work for this project)*

2½" × 4" scrap of 16-gauge vinyl for each creature, available in the home decorating section of most fabric stores *(Note: A thinner gauge vinyl can be used, but it will pucker more when you crochet around it)*

1 pair of ½" wiggly eyes for each creature; black embroidery floss, and needle; yarn needle, 5" scrap of yellow rickrack (for the Bear's collar), hot glue and glue gun, stitch marker

Gauge

21 sts and 24 rows sc = 4"

Tired of having your iPod go commando? Well, here's the perfect solution. These cozies are form-fitting and easy-access (you don't have to "undress" your iPod to get to the controls), and they can be made in an evening. Whether you choose the bear, the monkey, or the kitty, these cozies are basically the same pattern, which is densely crocheted in a cotton-blend worsted-weight yarn. At the center of it all is a heavy-gauge vinyl window with holes punched around it. You build your first row of single crochet stitches on these holes. The pattern might be a little tricky for beginners, but once you gain a little experience under your hooking belt, you will be happily on your way to a Cozy Pod Creature of your own!

SPECIAL STITCHES

Surface crochet sl st: Make a slipknot and hold it on back side of vinyl, insert hook from front to back in hole in vinyl, draw yarn loop through hole, *insert hook into next hole, yo, draw yarn through hole and loop on hook (sl st made); rep from * in each hole around vinyl, slip st in first hole to complete rnd.

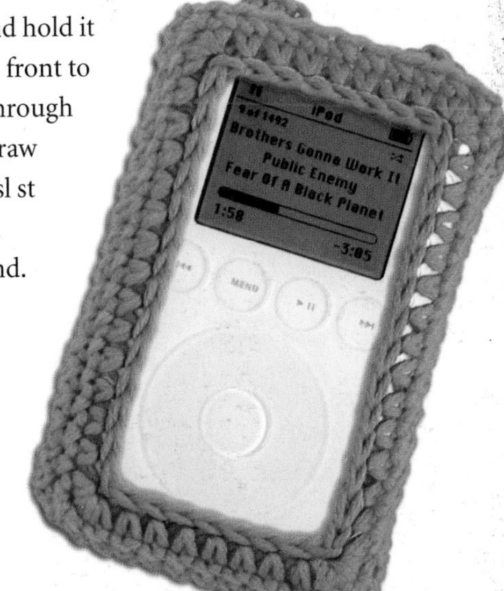

BEAR

Prepare Vinyl Window

Follow template to punch 44 holes ¼" from the edges of vinyl. Punch one hole at each corner, 13 holes evenly

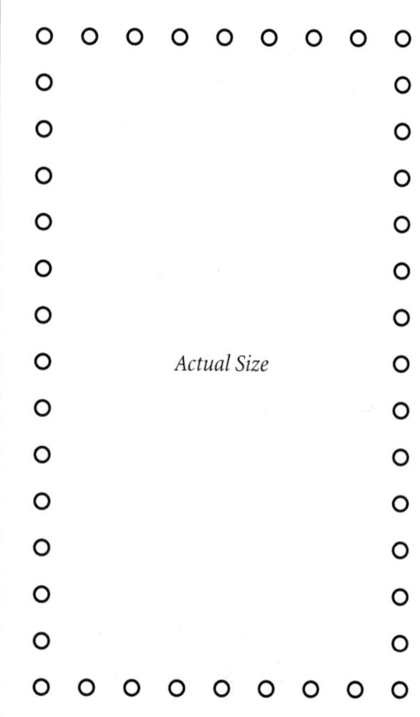

Vinyl template

spaced across each long edge, and 7 holes evenly spaced across each short edge. With scissors, round off the corners slightly.

Back Vinyl Border

Work in a spiral, marking beg of each rnd and moving marker up as work progresses.

Rnd 1 (RS): Join MC in top left-hand corner hole of vinyl piece, ch 1, *3 sc in corner hole, sc in each hole across to next corner; rep from * around, do not sl st to join—52 sc.

Rnd 2 (RS): Sc in next sc, *3 sc in next sc (corner), sc in each sc across to next corner st; rep from * 3 times to next marker—60 sc. Work now progresses in rows. Remove marker.

Row 3 (RS): Sc in first 21 sc, ending with sc in bottom left-hand corner sc, turn, leaving rem sts unworked—21 sc.

Row 4 (WS): Ch 1, sc in each of first 49 sc, ending with sc in bottom right-hand corner sc, turn—49 c.

Row 5 (RS): Ch 1, sc in each of first 31 sc, ending with sc in top left-hand corner sc, turn, leaving rem sts unworked—31 sc.

Begin Front

Row 1 (WS): Ch 1, sc in each of first 13 sc, ending with sc in top right-hand corner sc, turn, leaving rem sts unworked—13 sc.

Rows 2–10: Ch 1, sc in each sc across, turn—13 sc.

Begin Pocket Lining

Row 1 (WS): Ch 1, sc in first loop only of each sc across, turn—13 sc.

Rows 2–12: Ch 1, working in both loops of sts, sc in each sc across, turn—13 sc. Fasten off.

Pocket Front

Row 1 (WS): Join MC in rem loop of first sc in row 10 of front, ch 1, sc in rem loop of each sc across, turn—13 sc.

Rows 2–12: Ch 1, sc in each sc across, turn—13 sc. Fasten off.

First Ear

With RS facing, sk first 2 sc in row 12 of pocket front, join CC in next sc, (sc, 2 dc) in same sc, (2 dc, sc) in next sc. Fasten off.

Second Ear

With RS facing, sk next 5 sc in row 12 of pocket front, join CC in next sc, (sc, 2 dc) in same sc, (2 dc, sc) in next sc. Fasten off.

Top Edging

Row 1: With RS of pocket front facing, join MC in first sc in row 12 of pocket front, ch 1, sc in each of first 2 sc, sc in each of next 2 sts of first ear, 2 sc in each of next 2 ear sts, sc in each of the last 2 sts of first ear, sc in each of next 5 sts in row 12 of pocket front, sc in each of next 2 sts of second ear, 2 sc in each of next 2 ear sts, sc in each of the last 2 sts of second ear, sc in each of last 2 sc in row 12 of pocket front. Fasten off.

Window Trim

With RS of back facing, join CC in any corner hole on vinyl window, work in surface crochet sl st in each hole around window, sl st in first hole to join. Fasten off.

Embroidery

With 2 strands of black embroidery floss and embroidery needle, satin st nose and back st mouth and nose divider as pictured.

Assembly

Fold body in half with WS facing. With yarn needle and MC, matching sts, sew side of body together, incorporating sides of pocket. Weave in ends.

Finishing

Starting and ending at edge of window trim on back, glue piece of yellow rickrack across front of bear, approximately 1¾" above bottom edge. Trim ends. Glue 2 wiggly eyes to pocket front as pictured.

MONKEY

Work same as Bear through pocket front except do not fasten off at end of row 12.

Pocket Front (continued)

Row 13: Ch 1, sc in each sc across. Fasten off.

Window Trim

Work window trim same as bear.

Right Ear

Row 1: With RS facing, starting at top left-hand corner of pocket front, sk first 3 row-end sts, join MC in next

About Cynthia I live in the Washington, D.C., area, where I spend my working hours clearing photo and text rights for a nonprofit publisher and my free time lost in thoughts of rhubarb, Japanese craft books, junk shop finds, and knitting a cozy for my car. Craftiness runs in my family: My mother, the consummate craftsperson and teacher, taught me how to crochet, knit, sew, quilt, and how to bake darn good pie! My first venture into crochet pattern design was at age seven when I created a duck-shape cover for a bar of soap, complete with googly eyes. I've grown up since then, but I still put googly eyes on everything and often post the pictorial evidence on www.supermitten.com.

row-end st, ch 1, sc in same st, sc in each of next 5 row-end sts, turn—6 sc.

Row 2: Ch 1, sc in each sc across, turn—6 sc.

Row 3: Do not ch 1. Sc in first sc, hdc in next sc, 2 dc in each of next 2 sc, hdc in next sc, sc in last sc, sl st in next row-end st. Fasten off.

Left Ear

Row 1: With RS facing, starting at right-hand side edge of pocket front, join MC in 9th row-end st from top edge, ch 1, sc in same st, sc in each of next 5 row-end sts, turn—6 sc.

Rows 2–3: Rep rows 2–3 of right ear. Fasten off.

Muzzle

Do not sl st to join; work in a spiral.

With CC, ch 9.

Row 1: Sc in second ch from hook, sc in each of next 6 ch, 3 sc in last ch, working across opposite side of foundation ch, sc in each of next 6 ch, 3 sc in last ch—19 sc.

Row 2: 2 sc in next sc, sc in each of next 6 sc, 2 sc in next sc, 3 sc in next sc, 2 sc in next sc, sc in each of next 6 sc, 2 sc in next sc, 3 sc in next sc, sc in next sc, sl st in next sc to join—27 sc. Fasten off, leaving a sewing length.

With yarn needle and sewing length, sew muzzle to pocket front approximately 1" below top edge.

Embroidery

With 2 strands of black embroidery floss and embroidery needle, straight st 2 lines for nose and back st mouth as pictured.

Assembly

Fold body in half with WS facing. With yarn needle and MC, matching sts, sew side of body together, incorporating sides of pocket. Weave in ends.

Finishing

Glue 2 wiggly eyes to pocket front as pictured.

KITTY

Work same as bear through pocket front except do not fasten off at end of row 12.

Pocket Front (continued)

Row 13: Ch 1, sc in each of first 2 sc, *(sc, hdc) in next sc, (dc, tr, dc) in next sc, (hdc, sc) in next sc*, sc in each of next 3 sc; rep from * to * once, sc in each of last 2 sc. Fasten off.

Window Trim

Work window trim same as bear.

Flower

With CC, ch 2.

Rnd 1: 6 sc in second ch from hook, sl st in first sc to join—6 sc.

Rnd 2: Ch 4, sl st in first sc, (sl st, ch 4, sl st) in each ch around, sl st in first sc in rnd 1 to join. Fasten off, leaving a sewing length. Sew flower to lower left side of pocket front.

Embroidery

With 2 strands of black embroidery floss and embroidery needle, satin st nose, back st mouth, and straight st 3 whiskers on each side of face as pictured.

Assembly

Fold body in half with WS facing. With yarn needle and MC, matching sts, sew side of body together, incorporating sides of pocket. Weave in ends.

Finishing

Glue 2 wiggly eyes to pocket front as pictured.

4 *Brown Sheep Cotton Fleece, medium (worsted) weight*

color-bar blanket

My fondness for crochet developed in girlhood while visiting my Sicilian great-grandmother Nanny Tuccitto, who worked tirelessly on vibrant multicolored granny squares. Years later, when I became interested in the tradition of needlecraft being passed down from generation to generation and learning by doing, I made a special trip to see my grandmother Nana Mazza, Nanny's daughter, so she could teach me how to make the granny squares. I was so excited to finally get it right that I made hundreds of monochromatic squares. The pattern for this blanket came about because I have been working on a video project where each frame is made of stitches. The color bar pattern is basic to broadcast TV and video production as a way to calibrate the colors properly. Since I had so many of the colored granny squares, the idea of making a color-bar blanket seemed like a good one.

Finished Size

63" wide × 45" deep

Materials

Yarn

Lion Brand Wool-Ease (20% wool/80% acrylic; 3 oz [85 g]/197 yd [180 m]): 1 skein each of #176 Spring Green (A), #158 Buttercup (B), #102 Ranch Red (C), #116 Delft (D), #137 Fuchsia (E), #117 Colonial Blue (F), #152 Oxford Grey (G), #111 Navy (H), #100 White (I), and #153 Black (J)

Hook

Size I/9 (5.5 mm) crochet hook or size needed to obtain gauge

Notions

Yarn needle

Gauge

Rnd 1 of square = 2" in diameter

Square = 4½ × 4½"

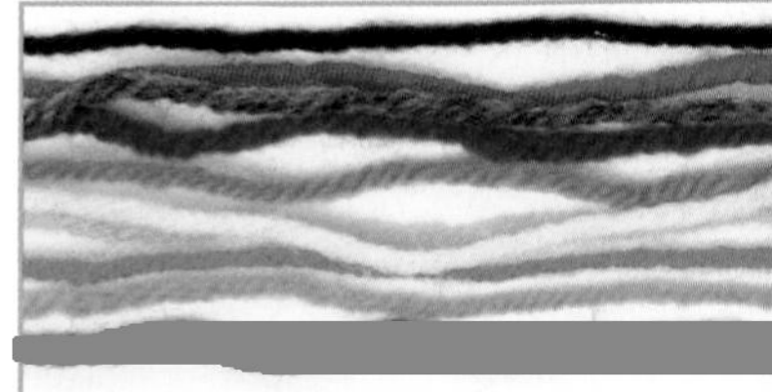

4 *Lion Brand Wool-Ease, medium (worsted) weight*

AFGHAN

Make 14 squares each with A, B, C, D, E, and F; 9 each with G and H; 21 with I; and 17 with J.

Square

Ch 6 and join with sl st in first ch.

Rnd 1 (RS): Ch 3 (counts as first dc), 2 dc in ring, ch 1, (3 dc, ch 1) 3 times in ring, sl st in third ch of turning ch to join—4 corner ch-1 spaces.

Rnd 2: Sl st to next corner ch-1 space, ch 3, (2 dc, ch 2, 3 dc) in first corner ch-1 space, ch 1, (3 dc, ch 2, 3 dc, ch 1) in each ch-2 space around, sl st in third ch of turning ch to join—4 corner ch-2 spaces.

About Cat I consider myself a "craftivist"—a crochet hobbyist who mixes crafting with antisweatshop activism. This combination inspired my Web site, www.microRevolt.org, which hosts knitPro, a free Web application that translates digital images into needlecraft grid patterns.

Rnd 3: Sl st to next corner ch-1 space, ch 3, (2 dc, ch 2, 3 dc) in first corner ch-1 space, ch 1, 3 dc in next ch-1 space, ch 1, *(3 dc, ch 2, 3 dc, ch 1) in next ch-2 space, ch 1, 3 dc in next ch-1 space, ch 1; rep from * around, sl st in third ch of turning ch to join—4 corner ch-2 spaces. Fasten off, leaving long sewing length. Weave in ends.

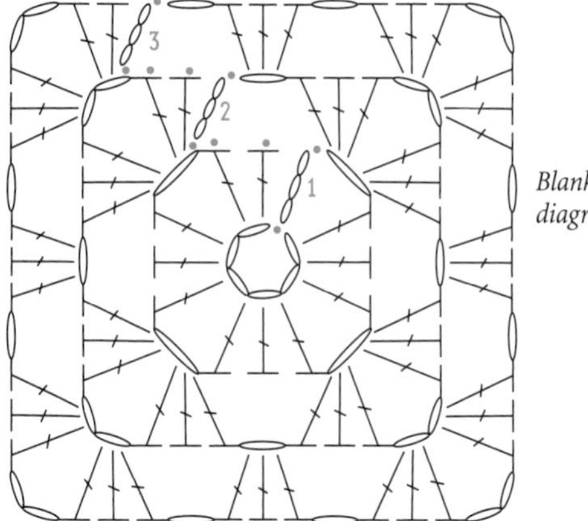

Blanket square diagram

Assembly

With WS of squares facing, working through back loops of sts, sew squares tog following construction chart for placement.

I	I	B	B	D	D	A	A	E	E	C	C	F	F
I	I	B	B	D	D	A	A	E	E	C	C	F	F
I	I	B	B	D	D	A	A	E	E	C	C	F	F
I	I	B	B	D	D	A	A	E	E	C	C	F	F
I	I	B	B	D	D	A	A	E	E	C	C	F	F
I	I	B	B	D	D	A	A	E	E	C	C	F	F
J	J	F	F	C	C	E	E	A	A	D	D	B	B
G	G	G	I	I	I	H	H	H	J	J	J	J	J
G	G	G	I	I	I	H	H	H	J	J	J	J	J
G	G	G	I	I	I	H	H	H	J	J	J	J	J

Construction chart

Carmen Watkins

Li'L MONKEY

BABY HAT AND MATCHING AFGHAN

Influenced by toys from my childhood, I developed a love of sock monkeys over the years and began creating them for my little niece and nephews. When my hands turned to crocheting, it was only natural that I'd want to make something that resembled a sock monkey. Once I had it figured out, I started putting this li'l sock monkey face on everything from hats, ponchos, and scarves to bags, sweaters, jeans, and T-shirts—and now onto this baby hat and afghan set. It's so easy to do—if you know a few basic crochet stitches and can make granny squares, you can crochet this! Made in "gender-neutral" colors of red, natural, and sock monkey tan, the hat can be finished off with a straight edging for a masculine look or with a scalloped edging for a softer, more feminine feel. And an added bonus for all the busy mommies—the yarns are 100% acrylic, so just wash 'n go. Everybody could use a sock monkey in their life—especially your li'l one!

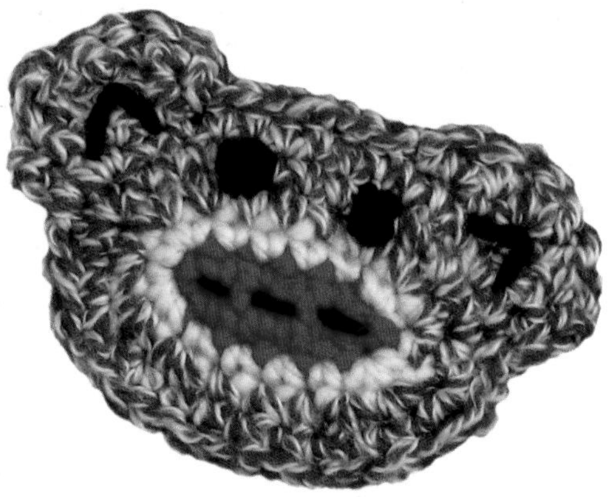

SOCK MONKEY FACE

Make 1 for each hat and 2 for afghan and set aside.

Mouth

With H/8 hook and A, ch 7.

Rnd 1: 2 sc in second ch from hook, sc in each of next 4 ch, 3 sc in last ch; working across opposite side of foundation ch, sc in each of next 5 ch, sl st in first sc to join—14 sc. Fasten off A, join B in first sc.

Finished Size

Hat: Size 6–12 months; 16" in circumference

Afghan: 27" × 27"

Materials

Yarn

Bernat Softee Chunky (100% acrylic; 3.5 oz [100 g]/164 yd [150 m]): 2 skeins of #39705 Berry Red (A); 1 skein each of #39008 Natural (B) and #39040 Black (C). Bernat Denim Style (70% acrylic/30% soft cotton; 3.5 oz [100 g]/196 yd [179 m]): 2 skeins of #03012 Rodeo Tan (D)

Hooks

Sizes H/8 (5 mm), K/10½ (6.5 mm), and N/13 (9 mm) crochet hooks or size needed to obtain gauge

Notions

Yarn needle

Gauge

First rnd of hat = 1½" in diameter; 8 sts = 4". First rnd of afghan square = 2" in diameter; square = 6¼" × 6¼"

Special Stitches

Sc2tog: (Insert hook in next st, yo, draw yarn through st) twice, yo, draw yarn through 3 loops on hook

Bobble: (Yo, insert hook in next space, yo, draw yarn through space, yo, draw yarn through 2 loops on hook) 3 times in same space, yo, draw yarn through 4 loops on hook

Above: Hat A
Below: Hat B

5 *Bernat Softee Chunky, bulky weight*

Rnd 2: With B, ch 1, 2 sc in each of first 2 sc, sc in each of next 4 sc, 2 sc in each of next 3 sc, sc in each of next 4 sc, 2 sc in last sc, sl st in first sc to join—20 sc. Fasten off B, join D in second sc.

Rnd 3: With D, ch 1, 2 sc in each of first 2 sc, sc in each of next 7 sc, 2 sc in each of next 3 sc, sc in each of next 7 sc, 2 sc in last sc, sl st in first sc to join—26 sc.

Rnd 4: Sl st in next sc, ch 1, 2 sc in first sc, sc in each of next 10 sc, 2 sc in each of next 3 sc, sc in each of next 10 sc, 2 sc in last sc, sl st in first sc to join—32 sc. Work now progresses in rows.

Row 5: Ch 1, 2 sc in each of first 2 sc, sc in each of next 10 sc, 2 sc in each of next 2 sc, turn, leaving rem sts unworked—18 sc. Do not fasten off.

First Ear

Row 6 (WS): Ch 1, sk first st, sc in each of next 5 sc, turn, leaving rem sts unworked—5 sc.

Row 7: Ch 1, sk first st, sc in each of next 4 sc, turn—4 sc.

Row 8: Ch 1, sk first st, sc2tog in next 2 sts, 2 sc in next sc; working across side of ear, sc in next row-end st, sl st in next st in row 5. Fasten off.

Second Ear

Row 6 (RS): Join D in first sc in row 5, ch 1, sk first st, sc in each of next 5 sc, turn, leaving rem sts unworked—5 sc.

Row 7: Ch 1, sk first st, sc in each of next 4 sc, turn—4 sc.

Row 8: Ch 1, sk first st, sc2tog in next 2 sts, 2 sc in next sc, working across side of ear, sc in next row-end st, sl st in next st in row 5. Fasten off, leaving long sewing length.

Embroidery

With yarn needle and C, work 3 straight sts across center of mouth, work an inverted V on center of each ear, and with 2 strands of C, work 1 French knot for each eye as pictured.

Hat A (with straight edge)

With K/10½ hook and A, ch 4 and join with sl st in first ch.

Rnd 1: Ch 3 (counts as first dc), work 11 dc in ring, sl st in third ch of turning ch to join—12 sts.

Rnd 2: Ch 3, 2 dc in each of next 2 dc, *dc in next dc, 2 dc in each of next 2 dc; rep from * around, sl st in third ch of turning ch to join—20 sts.

Rnd 3: Ch 3, *2 dc in each of next 2 dc, dc in next dc; rep from * around to last st, 2 dc in last dc, sl st in third ch of turning ch to join—33 sts.

Rnds 4–7: Ch 3, dc in each dc around, sl st in third ch of turning ch to join—33 sts. Fasten off A, join B.

Rnd 8: With B, ch 2 (counts as first hdc), hdc in each dc around, sl st in second ch of turning ch to join—33 sts. Fasten off B, join D.

Rnd 9: With D, ch 2 (counts as first hdc), hdc in each dc around, sl st in second ch of turning ch to join—33 sts. Fasten off. Weave in ends.

Hat B (with scalloped edge)

Work same as hat A through rnd 8.

Rnd 9 (RS): Join D in any hdc, ch 1, sc in first hdc, sk next hdc, 6 dc in next hdc (shell made), sk next hdc; rep from * around, sl st in first sc to join—8 shells. Fasten off. Weave in ends.

Finishing

With yarn needle and sewing length of D, sew one Sock Monkey face on each hat. Weave in ends.

AFGHAN

Square A (solid color; make 2)

With N/13 hook and D, ch 5 and join with sl st in first ch.

Rnd 1: Ch 3 (counts as first dc), 2 dc in ring, ch 2 (3 dc, ch 2) 3 times in ring, sl st in third ch of turning ch to join—4 corner ch-2 spaces.

Afghan square diagram

Rnd 2: Sl st to first ch-2 space, ch 3, (2 dc, ch 2, 3 dc) in same ch-2 space, ch 1, sk next dc, bobble in next dc, ch 1, *(3 dc, ch 2, 3 dc) in next ch-2 space, ch 1, sk next dc, bobble in next dc, ch 1; rep from * around, sl st in third ch of turning ch to join—4 corner ch-2 spaces.

Rnd 3: Sl st to first ch-2 space, ch 3, (2 dc, ch 2, 3 dc) in same ch-2 space, ch 1, (bobble, ch 1) in each of next 2 ch-1 spaces, *(3 dc, ch 2, 3 dc) in next ch-2 space, ch 1, (bobble, ch 1) in each of next 2 ch-1 spaces; rep from * around, sl st in third ch of turning ch to join—4 corner ch-2 spaces.

Rnd 4: Ch 2 (counts as first hdc), hdc in each st and space around, working 3 hdc in each corner ch-2 space, sl st in second ch of turning ch to join—56 sts. Fasten off.

Note: Squares B through G are worked with more than one color. Join each new color in corner st or space to begin next rnd. Fasten off colors when no longer needed.

Square B (make 3)

Work same as square A in the following color sequence: Center ring and rnds 1–3 with A; rnd 4 with D.

Square C (make 2)

Work same as square A in the following color sequence: Center ring and rnds 1–3 with B; rnd 4 with D.

Square D (make 3)

Work same as square A in the following color sequence: Center ring and rnd 1 with D; rnd 2 with A; rnd 3 with B; rnd 4 with D.

D	B	D	F
A	G	B	C
G	E	G	A
B	C	F	D

Construction diagram

Square E (make 1)

Work same as square A in the following color sequence: Center ring and rnd 1 with D; rnd 2 with B; rnd 3 with A; rnd 4 with D.

Square F (make 2)

Work same as square A in the following color sequence: Center ring and rnd 1 with B; rnd 2 with D; rnd 3 with A; rnd 4 with D.

Square G (make 3)

Work same as square A in the following color sequence: Center ring and rnd 1 with A; rnd 2 with D; rnd 3 with B; rnd 4 with D.

Assembly

With yarn needle and D, with RS of squares facing, sew squares tog following construction diagram for placement. Sew 4 squares tog in each strip, then sew strips tog.

Border

Rnd 1: With RS of afghan facing, join D in any corner st, ch 2 (counts as first hdc), 2 hdc in same corner st, hdc in each st around, working 3 hdc in each corner st, sl st in second ch of first ch to join. Fasten off D, join B.

Rnd 2: With B, ch 2, hdc in each st around, working 3 hdc in each corner st, sl st in second ch of turning ch to join. Fasten off B, join A.

Rnd 3: Ch 1, *sc in each of next 2 sc, (sc, ch 5, sl st in third ch from hook, ch 2, sc) in next sc; rep from * around, sl st in first sc to join. Fasten off. Weave in ends.

Finishing

With yarn needle and sewing length of D, sew 1 sock monkey face to each square B on an angle as shown on construction diagram.

About Carmen One evening last year, while cruising eBay auctions, I stumbled upon a crocheted cloche. After bidding on it and others like it, I decided it might be cheaper to learn to crochet than to keep buying all these amazing hats. I printed a crochet cloche pattern from the Internet, took it into my local craft store, and said, "I want to make this." I took one crochet class and I've had a hook and yarn close by ever since. I live in Frisco, Texas, where I'm a senior inventory analyst for a major retailer. In my spare time, I sell crocheted boutique-style children's clothing on eBay to support my expensive yarn addiction. My crochet items—and sock monkeys, of course—can be found at www.ccsockmonkeys.com.

Seija Set

BABY HAT AND STROLLER BLANKET

Finished Size

Hat: size 6 months, 16" in circumference

Blanket: 23½" × 24"

Materials

Yarn

Bernat Big Value Worsted Weight Yarn (100% acrylic; 6 oz [170 g]/335 yd [306 m]): 1 skein each of # 864 Brown (A), #856 Natural (B), and #434 Light Old Rose (C)

Hook

Size G/6 (4 mm) crochet hook or size needed to obtain gauge

Notions

Yarn needle

Gauge

Hat: first 2 rnds = 2½" in diameter

Blanket: 13 sts and 8 rows dc = 4"

When I couldn't find a hat pattern that I liked for my new granddaughter, I made my own. This project is quick and versatile and can be made with pastels, primary colors, or a single color for a different look each time. The hat is snug and covers the ears; the matching stroller blanket is just the right size so it doesn't touch the wheels or drag along the street. It was my daughter's idea to put the hole in the blanket for the seat belt, to keep both baby and blanket safe inside the stroller.

HAT

4 *Bernat Big Value, medium (worsted) weight*

With A, ch 6 and join with sl st in first ch.

Rnd 1 (RS): Ch 3 (counts as first dc), dc in same st, 2 dc in each ch around, sl st in third ch of turning ch to join—12 sts.

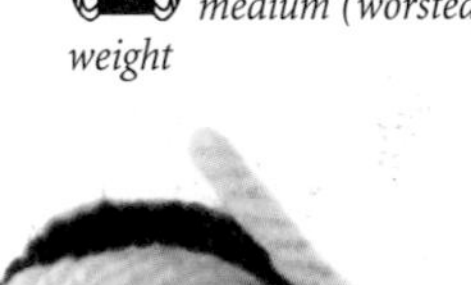

Rnd 2: Ch 3, dc in same st, 2 dc in each dc around, sl st in third ch of turning ch to join—24 sts.

Rnd 3: Ch 3, dc in same st, dc in next dc, *2 dc in next dc, dc in next dc; rep from * around, sl st in third ch of turning ch to join—36 sts. Fasten off A, join B.

Rnd 4: Ch 3, dc in same st, dc in next 2 dc, *2 dc in next dc, dc in next 2 dc; rep from * around, sl st in third ch of turning ch to join—48 sts.

Rnd 5: Ch 3, dc in each dc around, sl st in third ch of turning ch to join—48 sts. Fasten off B, join C.

Rnds 6–11: Rep rnd 5, working in the following color sequence: 2 rnds C; 2 rnds A; 2 rnds B.

First Ear Flap

Row 1 (RS): Sl st in each of next 5 dc, ch 3 (counts as first dc), sk next dc, dc in each of next 8 dc, sk next dc, dc in next st, turn leaving rem sts unworked—10 sts.

Rows 2–4: Ch 3, sk next dc, dc in each dc across to last 2 sts, sk next dc, dc in third ch of turning ch, turn—4 sts at end of row 4.

Row 5: Ch 3, sk next 2 dc, dc in third ch of turning ch. Fasten off.

Second Ear Flap

Row 1 (RS): With RS facing, sk first 15 st to the left of last st made in row 1 of first ear flap, join B in next dc, ch 3 (counts as first dc), sk next dc, dc in each of next 8 dc, sk next dc, dc in next st, turn leaving rem sts unworked—10 sts.

Rows 2–5: Rep rows 2–5 of first ear flap. Fasten off. Weave in ends.

Edging

With RS facing, join C at bottom of one ear flap, ch 1, sc evenly around entire edge of hat, sl st in first sc to join. Fasten off.

Braid

Cut six 24" lengths of each color. Using 3 strands of each color for each braid, fold bundle in half, pull folded end through hole in row 5 of one ear flap, draw ends of bundle through folded end. Divide fringe into 3 equal sections of different yarn colors, braid strands tog. Tie end in an overhand knot. Trim ends even.

Rep on other ear flap.

BLANKET

With A, ch 76.

Row 1: Dc in fourth ch from hook, dc in each ch across, turn—74 sts.

Row 2: Ch 3 (counts as first dc), dc in each dc across, turn—74 sts. Fasten off A, join B.

Rows 3–28: Rep row 2, working in the following color sequence: *2 rows B; 2 rows C; 2 rows A*; rep from * to * throughout, ending with a B row. Fasten off.

Seat Belt Hole (optional)

With RS facing, sk first 32 dc, join C in next dc, ch 8, sk next 8 dc, sl st in next dc. Fasten off.

Row 29: With RS facing, join C in first dc in row 28, ch 3, dc in each dc and each ch across, turn—74 dc.

Row 30–44: Rep row 2, maintaining color sequence as established, ending with 2 rows A. Fasten off. Weave in ends.

Border

Rnd 1: With RS facing, join C in top left-hand corner st, ch 1, 2 sc in each row-end dc across side edge, 3 sc in corner st, sc in each ch across bottom edge, 3 sc in corner st, 2 sc in each row-end dc up side edge, 3 sc in corner, sc in each dc across top edge, 2 sc in corner st, sl st in first sc to join.

Rnd 2: Ch 1, sc in each sc along side edge; working across bottom edge, **ch 4, sk next sc, dc in next sc, *ch 1, sk next sc, dc in next sc; rep from * across to corner sc, 2 sc in side of last dc made to turn corner**, sc in each sc up side edge; rep from ** to ** across top edge, sl st in first sc to join.

Rnd 3: Ch 1, sc in each st around, working 3 sc in each corner st, sl st in first sc to join. Fasten off. Weave in ends.

Braid (make 2)

Cut twelve 48" lengths of each color. Using 6 strands of each color for each braid, tie one end in an overhand knot. Divide into 3 equal sections of different yarn colors, braid strands tog; when braided section measures same as blanket width, tie braid end in an overhand knot. Trim ends even. Weave braid through spaces in rnd 2 of border on each end of blanket.

About Bev I have been crocheting for 35 years, since I was 15. One of my first projects was a minidress I crocheted for myself (hey, it was the seventies). Later, I crocheted for my home, for my children, and now, for my granddaughter. Basically, anything that can be covered in fabric, I will crochet for—I've even made doilies for the headrests of my car! I live in British Columbia, Canada, with my husband, my son, and our cat, Zubby. (Zubby likes to "help" me with my crocheting projects). I've worked in retail for over 30 years—my first job included crocheting displays for the yarn department—but now I'm on the marketing side of the retail industry. I fit in extra crocheting time by crocheting during my commute.

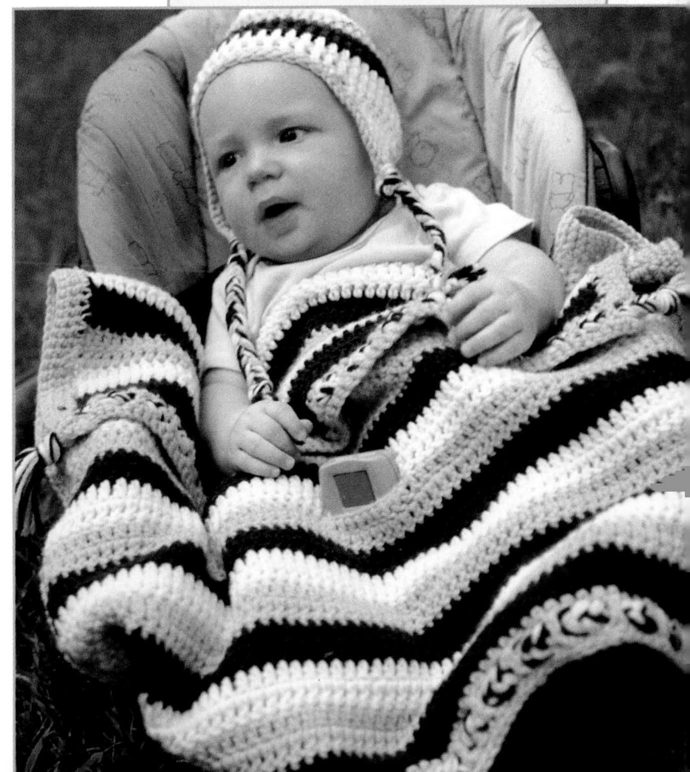

resource guide

YARNS

Aurora Yarns
P.O Box 3068
Moss Beach, CA 94038
650-728-2730

Bernat
320 Livingstone Avenue South
Listowel, ON
Canada
N4W 3H3
www.bernat.com
800-265-2864

Berroco
P.O. Box 367
14 Elmdale Road
Uxbridge, MA 01569-0367
www.berroco.com

Brown Sheep Company
100662 County Road 16
Mitchell, NE 69357
www.brownsheep.com

Cascade Yarns
1224 Andover Park East
Tukwila, WA 98188
www.cascadeyarns.com
206-574-0440

Classic Elite Yarns
122 Western Avenue
Lowell, MA 01851
www.classiceliteyarns.com

Coats & Clark
Attn: Consumer Services
P.O. Box 12229
Greenville, SC 29612
www.coatsandclark.com
800-648-1479

Crystal Palace
160 23rd Street
Richmond, CA 94804
www.crystalpalaceyarns.com
510-237-9988

Filatura di Crosa
Distributed by Tahki • Stacy Charles, Inc.
www.tahkistacycharles.com

Garnstudio
Distributed by Aurora Yarns

Hilos Omega
Callejón San Antonio Abad #23
Col. Transito
C.P. 06820
Mexico D.F.
www.hilosomega.com.mx

J & P Coats
Distributed by Coats & Clark
www.coatsandclark.com

Karabella Yarns
1201 Broadway
New York, NY 10001
www.karabellayarns.com
800-550-0898

KFI
P.O. Box 336
315 Bayview Avenue
Amityville, NY 11701
www.knittingfever.com
516-546-3600

Lion Brand Yarn
135 Kero Road
Corlstadt, NJ 07072
www.lionbrand.com
800-258-YARN

Lorna's Laces
4229 North Honore Street
Chicago, IL 60613
www.lornaslaces.net
773-935-3803

Louet Sales
808 Comerce Park Drive
Ogdensburg, NY 13669
www.louet.com

Noro
Distributed by KFI
www.knittingfever.com

Nova Yarn
155 Martin Ross, Unit 3
Toronto, ON
Canada
M352L9
www.novayarn.com
416-736-6111

Patons
320 Livingston Avenue South
Listowel, ON
Canada
N4W 3H3
www.patonsyarns.com

Plymouth Yarn
P.O. Box 28
Bristol, PA 19007
www.plymouthyarn.com
215-788-0459

Red Heart
Distributed by Coats & Clark
www.coatsandclark.com

Rowan Yarns
Distributed by Westminster Fibers
www.knitrowan.com

Schachenmayr Nomotta
Distributed by Westminster Fibers

Tahki • Stacy Charles, Inc.
70-30 80th Street
Building 36
Ridgewood, NY 11385
www.tahkistacycharles.com
800-338-YARN

Westminster Fibers
4 Townsend West, Unit 8
Nashua, NH 03063
603-886-5041

NOTIONS

Artbeads
11901 137th Avenue Ct. KPN
Unit 100
Gig Harbor, WA 98329
www.artbeads.com
866-715-BEAD (2323)

Artemis (Hannah silk ribbon)
5155 Myrtle Avenue
Ureka, CA 95503
Artemisinc.com
888-233-5187

M & J Trimming
1008 6th Avenue
New York, New York 10018
www.mjtrim.com
1-800-9-MJTRIM

credits

CONTRIBUTERS

Illustrations: Adrienne Yan
Fashion Photography: John Dolan
Spot Photography: Tod Seelie
Patterns & Schematics: Karen Manthey
Styling: Jenni Lee
Hair & Makeup: Bryan Lynde/ R.J. Bennett
Go for Baroque: © 2006 by Jennifer Hansen

PHOTO CREDITS

page 6: Library of Congress • *page 7:* AP Wide World Photos

FASHION CREDITS

page ii: boots, Irene Albright; shirt, earrings, and bracelet, Urban Outfitters; jacket, Screaming Mimi's; rings and necklace, Alex Woo

page vii: pants (male), H&M; sweater, jacket (male), and pants (female), Triple 5 Soul; jacket (female), Henry Duarte; jewelry, Urban Outfitters

pages 97 & 99: dress and hat, Urban Outfitters; jacket, Moschino; jewelry, H&M

page 100: jacket,Triple 5 Soul; skirt, Moschino; earrings, Urban Outfitters

pages 102 & 105: pants, Miss Sixty; top, Ashley Tyler; jacket, Triple 5 Soul; earrings, Urban Outfitters

pages 107 & 108: top, Daryl K; skirts, R. Taylor; earrings, H&M; ring, Stephen Dweck

pages 111 & 113: skirt, Ashley Tyler; top, Moschino; jewelry, H&M

pages 114 & 117: shorts, Bloomingdales; tank, Urban Outfitters; shirt, Screaming Mimi's; necklace, Heather Rubin; ring and bracelet, Stephen Dweck

pages 119 & 121: shirt and sweater, Urban Outfitters; pants, Triple 5 Soul; vest, Miss Sixty

page 122: pants (male), H&M; sweater, jacket (male) and pants (female), Triple 5 Soul; jacket (female), Henry Duarte; jewelry, Urban Outfitters

pages 125 &126: jacket and shirt, Urban Outfitters

pages 129 & 130: coat and dress, Moschino; jewelry, Stephen Dweck; sunglasses, Paul Smith *pages 132 & 134:* shoes, Urban Outfitters; pants, Miss Sixty; jacket, Triple 5 Soul; bracelets, Stephen Dweck

pages 136, 137 & 138: dresses, Screaming Mimi's; rings, Noir; shoes (left), Moschino

pages 141 & 143: top, earrings, and bracelet, Urban Outfitters; skirt, Bloomingdales; necklace, Stephen Dweck

pages 144, 146, 147 & 148: dress, Screaming Mimi's; boots (left) and denim skirt, Miss Sixty; boots (right), John Fluevogs; bracelet, Urban Outfitters; earrings (left), H&M; earrings (right), Stephen Dweck

pages 151 & 153: pants, Triple 5 Soul; shirt, Urban Outfitters; jacket, Ashley Tyler

page 155: skirt and top (right), Screaming Mimi's; necklace (right) and bracelet (right & left), Stephen Dweck; shoes (right), Moschino; top (left) and necklace, Urban Outfitters

pages 159, 160 & 163: shoes, skirt, and earrings, Urban Outfitters

page 164: skirt, Screaming Mimi's

pages 169 & 172: top and necklace, Urban Outfitters; bracelet and ring, Stephen Dweck

pages 178 & 182: top (left), Triple 5 Soul; pants (left), Miss Sixty; shoes, pants (right), top (right), and earrings (right), Urban Outfitters; earrings, H&M

pages 184 & 189: jewelry, Urban Outfitters; shoes, Irene Albright

pages 190, 193 & 196: necklace, Urban Outfitters; ring, Stephen Dweck; skirt and bracelets, Screaming Mimi's

page 199: pants, Trash & Vaudeville

pages 202, 205 & 209: legging, Darryl K; necklace, Urban Outfitters

pages 211 & 214: top and skirt, Moschino

pages 217, 220 & 223: pants, Boxfresh; top, Urban Outfitters; choker, Heather Rubin; earrings, Stephen Dweck

pages 225 & 227: boots, Irene Albright; shirt, earrings, and bracelet, Urban Outfitters; jacket, Screaming Mimi's; rings and necklace, Alex Woo

page 228: dress, Daryl K

pages 235 & 238: nighty, Screaming Mimi's

pages 240 & 242: jacket (left) and earrings (right), H&M; earrings (left), Stephen Dweck; jacket (right), Triple 5 Soul

pages 245 & 248: all items, Screaming Mimi's

pages 257 & 258: top, Urban Outfitters; skirt and apron, Screaming Mimi's; earrings, Stephen Dweck

pages 264, 267 & 268: dresses, Screaming Mimi's

pages 270 & 273: slip, Screaming Mimi's

index

A

b

c

d

f

g

H

i

j–k

L

U-V-W

Y-Z